AI and the Future of Law Enforcement:

Redefining Community Trust and Problem-Solving

Reza Gharoie Ahangar
Lewis University, USA

Stephen Sherwin
Lewis University, USA

IGI Global
Scientific Publishing
Publishing Tomorrow's Research Today

Published in the United States of America by
IGI Global Scientific Publishing
701 East Chocolate Avenue
Hershey, PA, 17033, USA
Tel: 717-533-8845
Fax: 717-533-7115
Website: https://www.igi-global.com E-mail: cust@igi-global.com

Library of Congress Cataloging-in-Publication Data

Names: Ahangar, Reza Gharoie editor | Sherwin, Stephen (Stephen L.) editor
Title: AI and the future of law enforcement : redefining community trust and problem-solving / edited by Reza Gharoie Ahangar, Stephen Sherwin.
Description: Hershey, PA : IGI Global Scientific Publishing, 2025. | Includes bibliographical references and index. | Summary: "This book explores how using AI in policing can redefine community trust and improve problem-solving while addressing the challenges and controversies surrounding its implementation"-- Provided by publisher.
Identifiers: LCCN 2025007595 (print) | LCCN 2025007596 (ebook) | ISBN 9798369379790 hardcover | ISBN 9798369379806 paperback | ISBN 9798369379813 ebook
Subjects: LCSH: Law enforcement--Technological innovations--United States | Law enforcement--United States--Data processing | Artificial intelligence--Social aspects--United States
Classification: LCC HV8141 .A3 2025 (print) | LCC HV8141 (ebook) | DDC 363.20285--dc23/eng/20250512
LC record available at https://lccn.loc.gov/2025007595
LC ebook record available at https://lccn.loc.gov/2025007596

British Cataloguing in Publication Data
A Cataloguing in Publication record for this book is available from the British Library.

Table of Contents

Preface

INTRODUCTION: THE IMPORTANCE OF THIS BOOK TO COLLEGE STUDENTS, ACADEMICIANS, RESEARCHERS, LAW ENFORCEMENT AGENCIES, AND GOVERNMENT AGENCIES

Overview-The book, "AI and the Future of Law Enforcement: Redefining Community Trust and Problem-Solving," delves into the intersection of artificial intelligence (AI) and law enforcement. It explores how using AI in policing can redefine community trust and improve problem-solving while addressing the challenges and controversies surrounding its implementation. The book provides a comprehensive examination of the impact of the COVID-19 pandemic on law enforcement, the role of proper training in building community trust, the power dynamics within law enforcement, the potential of higher education to transform thinking, the role of social media in shaping public perception, and the challenges and responsibilities of ethically implementing AI in law enforcement. The book aims to provide a balanced and thought-provoking perspective on the potential benefits and concerns of using AI in law enforcement.

Impact on the Research Community- This book is not just a comprehensive overview of AI and its applications in law enforcement, it is a catalyst for further research and discussions. By considering multiple perspectives and addressing key issues, it provides a solid foundation for ongoing research in the fields of criminal justice, sociology, technology, and ethics. Its potential sparks new ideas and insights into the ethical and responsible implementation of AI in the criminal justice system is immense. This book is a valuable resource for researchers and academics, offering a platform for intellectual exchange and advancement in the field.

Intended Audience-The book is intended for a wide range of readers, including policymakers, law enforcement professionals, academics, students, and anyone interested in the intersection of AI and law enforcement. It will provide valuable insights and information for those involved in shaping policies and practices related to law enforcement and technology and those interested in understanding how AI can potentially redefine community trust and problem-solving in policing. The book interests the public as it addresses relevant and timely issues surrounding law enforcement and AI.

ORGANIZATION OF THE BOOK

This book is organized into 10 chapters, and a brief description of each chapter is as follows:

Chapter 1: Introduction- Policing, Public Trust, AI and the Promise of Reform

Law enforcement has historically faced scrutiny regarding its application of power and authority. Misconduct by a minority of officers has tainted the public's perception, creating a generalized fear, anger, and mistrust of police officers. The resulting stigma affects even those officers who perform their duties with compassion and responsibility. This damaged relationship has prompted public demand for reforms, such as better training, stringent regulations, and technological advancements, including artificial intelligence (AI). The COVID-19 pandemic strained these relationships further, as law enforcement had to enforce controversial health mandates that exacerbated public resentment. Officer vaccination requirements added to this internal and external tension. Events like the George Floyd incident intensified global distrust in law enforcement, sparking social unrest and renewed calls for defunding police departments. Many police officers left the profession, creating staffing shortages and lowering hiring standards, which further compromised trust. The chapter emphasizes the need for humanistic police work, supported by technological innovation and higher education, to rebuild trust and ensure effective law enforcement.

Chapter 2: The Dual Impact of the Pandemic and Reform Movements on Law Enforcement

Chapter two delves into three areas: the pandemic's effect on law enforcement, misconceptions about defunding, and the critical need for community trust. Real-world examples illustrate how police officers navigate unpredictable situations requiring lawful, unbiased decisions. The chapter addresses public scrutiny following high-profile incidents and explores the societal impact of calls to defund the police. It highlights concerns over police militarization and the rising mental health crisis linked to drug use, particularly marijuana. The chapter stresses the importance of community trust and the use of humanistic policing methods, emphasizing leadership at all levels to rebuild these strained relationships. Police resilience during the pandemic demonstrated the existential need for law enforcement, while also underscoring the necessity of transparency, communication, and empathy.

Chapter 3: Humanistic Training and Community Engagement for Modern Policing

Chapter three is organized into three sections focusing on training, a humanistic theory developed by the author, and the criticism faced by law enforcement. Police training must be continuous and comprehensive, equipping officers with both technical and humanistic skills to handle complex situations. This chapter introduces the theory of Conterminous Spheres of Dependency, which emphasizes empathy and respect in police interactions. Special attention is given to Crisis Intervention Teams (CIT), which require officers to possess humanistic values for effective handling of mental health crises. Another theory, Fear, Anger, Hate, analyzes societal negativity toward police and underscores the psychological roots of these emotions. Effective training fosters self-awareness, critical thinking, and the ability to address public concerns, reinforcing officers' commitment to their protective role.

Chapter 4: The Evolving Role of Police Leadership and Organizational Culture

This chapter discusses three issues linked to law enforcement and society, all centered on the concept of "no." Police authority often requires the firm but respectful use of this word to maintain lawful order without provoking rebellion. The chapter builds on the Conterminous Spheres of Dependency theory, emphasizing that how police say "no" can preserve dignity and defuse conflicts. Real-life examples highlight the importance of communication and discretion. The chapter also stresses society's role in supporting solutions rather than deepening divisions. Positive police-community relationships depend on recruiting officers with strong moral values and fostering mutual respect. Personal anecdotes illustrate the human side of police work, underscoring the need for society to recognize the complexities and challenges officers face.

Chapter 5: Education and Expertise in Law Enforcement: Developing Skilled Officers

Chapter five explores the critical role of higher education in police reform. Early police reformers like August Vollmer championed the integration of humanities-based curricula to foster empathy, ethics, and professionalism. The author introduces a reverse developmental theory inspired by Vygotsky's zone of proximal development, advocating for the "unlearning" of biased perspectives. Collaboration between officers with and without liberal arts education promotes empathy and social awareness. This transformative learning process prepares officers to address modern societal challenges, such as racial bias and mental health crises. Liberal arts education equips officers with essential communication and critical thinking skills, fostering accountability and ethical behavior. The chapter calls for prioritizing the recruitment of candidates with higher education and developing community programs to strengthen trust and cooperation.

Chapter 6: Crisis Management and De-Escalation Tactics

Chapter six examines the powerful influence of social media on public perception of law enforcement. The George Floyd incident exemplifies how quickly viral content can shape opinions and provoke strong emotional responses. Social media's ability to amplify both positive and negative narratives impacts trust and respect for police officers. While social media can enhance transparency and community engagement, it also presents risks of misinformation and manipulation. The chapter discusses how police departments can use social media to share information, highlight positive interactions, and foster engagement. However, ethical challenges persist, including the spread of false narratives that can undermine police legitimacy. Addressing these challenges requires responsible social media use to maintain trust and accountability.

Chapter 7: Integrating AI into Restorative Justice and Conflict Resolution

Chapter seven highlights the transformative potential of AI in enhancing law enforcement operations. AI technologies, including facial recognition and predictive policing, improve efficiency and accuracy in investigations. However, the chapter also addresses concerns about bias, transparency, and accountability. Machine learning algorithms can inadvertently reinforce societal inequalities if trained on biased data. The opaque nature of AI decision-making complicates oversight, necessitating ethical guidelines and fairness-aware algorithms. Collaborative efforts between law enforcement, researchers, and communities are essential to develop responsible AI applications. The chapter underscores the need for a balanced approach that leverages AI's benefits while safeguarding civil rights and promoting public trust.

Chapter 8: AI and Community Partnerships for Enhanced Public Safety

Chapter eight builds on the discussion of AI, emphasizing the ethical challenges of integrating advanced technologies like 5G and robotics into law enforcement. Issues such as privacy, accountability, and bias require careful consideration. The chapter introduces a sociotechnical framework to address these concerns, highlighting the importance of transparency, community dialogue, and fairness. AI's potential to exacerbate existing biases underscores the need for diverse and reliable data sources. Ethical pitfalls include misapplication of AI solutions and oversimplification of complex social concepts. Cross-disciplinary collaboration and regulatory oversight are necessary to ensure that AI serves justice equitably while maintaining public trust.

Chapter 9: Ethical and Professional Challenges of AI Integration in Policing

Chapter nine explores the operational and ethical aspects of AI adoption in law enforcement. Technologies such as video analytics, drones, and predictive algorithms enhance crime prevention and investigation but also raise privacy and accountability concerns. The chapter discusses various fairness metrics and the need for nuanced approaches to mitigate bias. Transparency initiatives, such as community-driven oversight and responsible research models, are vital to maintaining trust. Privacy protection frameworks like differential privacy and GDPR offer strategies for managing sensitive data responsibly. Achieving accountability requires a shift toward shared moral responsibility, where all stakeholders contribute to ethical AI use. The chapter emphasizes collaborative policymaking and public engagement to balance innovation with civil rights protection.

Chapter 10: Conclusion: AI and the Future of Policing and Public Trust

The final chapter underscores the importance of police reform through mutual understanding and collaboration. The authors advocate for recognizing both the complexities of police work and society's valid concerns. Rebuilding trust requires a commitment to empathy, dialogue, and shared solutions. Key recommendations include requiring liberal arts education for police recruits, demilitarizing police departments, and establishing Crisis Intervention Teams. Social media teams can enhance communication and transparency. Police academy training should emphasize humanistic values, while AI tools can support ethical policing practices. Successful reform depends on strong leadership and a willingness to implement these strategies, ensuring that law enforcement remains effective and trusted by the communities it serves.

Reza Gharoie Ahangar
Lewis University, USA

Stephen Louis Sherwin
Lewis University, USA

Acknowledgment

Dr. Stephen L. Sherwin

Thank you to my brothers and sisters in Blue and to my family for loving me.

Dr. Reza Gharoie Ahangar

Thank you to all my family for their constant support in all aspects of work and life.

Chapter 1
Introduction:
Policing, Public Trust, AI, and the Promise of Reform

ABSTRACT

Law enforcement has long been a focal point of contention and concern with leaders and citizens frequently challenging whether the power and authority granted to law enforcement professionals has been humanistically practiced. Throughout history, the performance of members of law enforcement has been scrutinized by public officials, the media, and the public to ensure that fair and equal justice is applied to all citizens. Unfortunately, there have been historical incidents that have illuminated manifest issues of law enforcement personnel abusing their power and authority while simultaneously espousing corruption. These instances have been self-inflicted wounds that tarnished the reputation of the loyally competent law enforcement professionals. Most law enforcement professionals are dedicated, compassionate, and responsible public servants who take great pride in their duty to serve and protect society.

INTRODUCTION

This general belief of police officers among members of society inhibits objective discernment to distinguish between the good and the bad police officers especially when engaged in controversial conduct. Thus, the police officers uniform stimulates a collective stigma of all officers as they are seen as one entity, one group, and one threat. Unfortunately, the actions of a few "bad apples" have tainted the profession, leading citizens to lose trust in and respect for all law enforcement officers. This contamination has prompted federal oversight, Supreme Court rulings, and intense public pressure endorsing the need for comprehensive reforms within police depart-

DOI: 10.4018/979-8-3693-7979-0.ch001

ments and agencies. These reforms have led to progressive training, revised rules and regulations, more rigorous vetting processes, and the integration of advanced technologies, including artificial intelligence and social media tools. However, the COVID-19 pandemic further exacerbated the decline in public trust, compounding the challenges law enforcement faces in rebuilding relationships with the community.

During the pandemic, law enforcement professionals were tasked with enforcing a range of COVID-19 restrictions, including limitations on public gatherings, such as in places of worship, businesses, schools, and outdoor venues. The inherent contradiction in these mandates exasperated and already tense and fragile relationship between police officers and the public. On one hand, the public viewed the enforcement of these mandates as an infringement on their rights, leading to increased criticism, blame, and challenges to police authority. On the other hand, officers found themselves caught in a difficult position, striving to empathize with the public while also enforcing measures that they may not have agreed with. This caused significant stress not only between law enforcement and the public but also between police management and officers themselves.

A particularly contentious issue arose with the requirement for police officers to be vaccinated. Officers who refused to comply faced the threat of disciplinary action, including potential job loss. This situation mirrored the challenges faced by the wider population, as no one was exempt from the mandates imposed to control the spread of the virus. The conflict between public health measures, individual freedoms, and the role of law enforcement in enforcing these mandates further strained the already fragile trust between police and the communities they serve.

The George Floyd incident was a pivotal incendiary event that ignited widespread social unrest, leading to protests. Dubbed the "Summer of Love," this period caused irreparable divisions in society, significantly eroding trust and respect for law enforcement officers, both in the U.S. and globally. The protests, fueled by intense social and political divides, brought to light deep moral and ethical issues, especially regarding the role of government officials in responding to the destruction and violence that unfolded. These opposing views exacerbated tensions, causing immense harm to communities, citizens, and law enforcement alike. Furthermore, the incident spurred harsh criticism of police officers and fueled calls for drastic measures such as defunding or abolishing police departments further polarizing public opinion on the role and function of law enforcement in society.

BACKGROUND

Before the COVID-19 pandemic, the relationship between citizens and law enforcement was already tenuous, despite the support many citizens expressed for police officers. However, this support quickly deteriorated, further strained by political leaders calling for the defunding and even the abolition of police forces. These challenges led to a significant loss of police personnel, with many police officers quitting or retiring, creating additional pressure on police departments to maintain adequate staffing levels and continue providing safety and protection to their communities.

This crisis in personnel also triggered a troubling trend: a reduction in the qualifications required to become a police officer. The lowering of educational standards, particularly the lack of a bachelor's degree, especially one grounded in liberal arts, contradicts the level of knowledge, skills, and humanistic values necessary for law enforcement professionals to conduct the sociological, psychological, and technological complexities they face in the 21st century. The damage to the image of police officers has further stifled the recruitment process, leaving many vacancies unfilled. Political leaders' reluctance to hire sufficient police personnel has compounded the problem, leaving police departments scrambling to recruit candidates.

Another consequence of this situation is the compromise in the vetting process for police candidates, raising concerns about whether officers without a liberal arts education possess the humanistic qualities and critical thinking skills necessary for productive, non-violent encounters with the public. This situation calls into question whether the decision to lower educational requirements truly benefits the profession and public safety or undermines the quality of law enforcement and its ability to foster trust and respect within the community.

In addition, new technologies, particularly artificial intelligence (AI), are transforming various sectors, including law enforcement. As defined in the U.S. Code, AI encompasses machine-based systems that can make predictions, recommendations, or decisions influencing real or virtual environments using human-defined objectives. While the widespread adoption of AI in law enforcement is still evolving, its potential to enhance capabilities and increase efficiency is significant (Rigano, 2019).

AI applications in law enforcement span a broad spectrum, from automated license plate readers and facial recognition technologies to predictive policing models and natural language processing for public communication. For instance, AI-enhanced computer-aided dispatch (CAD) systems can optimize resource allocation by analyzing historical data and making predictive recommendations (Redden et al., 2020). Similarly, AI-powered facial recognition tools are being employed to combat human trafficking by scanning online advertisements (Rigano, 2019).

The integration of AI into law enforcement practices also extends to areas such as gunshot detection, DNA analysis, and video redaction. AI algorithms can potentially improve the accuracy and speed of DNA mixture interpretation, a critical aspect of forensic science (Rigano, 2019). Additionally, AI-driven video redaction tools are becoming increasingly important as body-worn cameras proliferate, helping to protect privacy while maintaining transparency (Redden et al., 2020).

However, the adoption of AI in law enforcement is not without challenges and ethical considerations. Concerns have been raised about potential biases in AI systems, particularly when trained on datasets that may contain inherent prejudices (Finklea, 2023). There are also questions about whether over-reliance on AI technology might lead officers to disregard contradictory evidence.

Recognizing these challenges, the U.S. government has taken steps to address the responsible development and use of AI in law enforcement. Executive Order 14110, issued on October 30, 2023, outlines a comprehensive approach to governing AI development and use, with specific directives for federal law enforcement (Finklea, 2023). These include assessing how AI can enhance law enforcement efficiency while protecting civil liberties, developing best practices for responsible AI use, and improving training for law enforcement professionals in AI-related areas.

As AI continues to evolve and integrate into law enforcement practices, ongoing research, policy development, and ethical considerations will be crucial to ensure its effective and responsible use. This introduction sets the stage for a deeper exploration of AI applications in law enforcement, their potential benefits, associated challenges, and the evolving regulatory landscape.

The purpose of this book is to examine both past and present techniques, methods, and skills employed by police officers, with the goal of advancing solutions that can restore respect and trust between law enforcement and society. By reflecting on real-world events and situations experienced by the authors, the book offers a balanced perspective, shedding light on both the positive and negative aspects of police officers' interactions with the public. It also presents exceptional ideas and strategies to ensure the continued relevance and sustainability of law enforcement throughout the 21st century.

As society evolves, so too must police work. However, certain fundamental values, such as a humanistic approach to community interactions, must be preserved. To foster lasting trust and respect between police officers and citizens, it is essential for police departments to continually strive to improve relationships with the communities they serve. Social media, artificial intelligence, and higher education, especially when grounded in a liberal arts curriculum, are crucial tools for advancing the skills and methods needed to develop police officers' commitment to serving and protecting all citizens effectively.

The authors emphasize both basic and advanced skills, integrated with emerging technologies such as artificial intelligence (AI), as essential to ensuring the police reform demanded by citizens. These advancements are key to addressing the concerns that fuel calls for defunding and abolishing police forces. Police officers remain an indispensable part of the criminal justice system, not only conducting investigations, arresting criminals, collecting evidence for legal proceedings, and testifying in court, but also serving as the first line of defense for their communities.

CONCLUSION

The visibility of police officers in communities serves more than just crime prevention; their role is crucial in maintaining public safety and acting as advocates for victims, giving them a voice in the pursuit of justice. Without the presence of police departments and dedicated police officers, criminals and their enterprises would operate with impunity. However, the integration of artificial intelligence provides police officers with sophisticated systems that enhance their ability to lawfully prevent crime, protect citizens, and improve their overall effectiveness. The goal is to rebuild and increase the trust and respect that citizens have for their police officers, ensuring that law enforcement continues to serve the public with integrity and competence.

REFERENCES

Adler, P., Falk, C., Friedler, S. A., ... (2016) Auditing black-box models by obscuring features. arXiv:1602.07043 [cs, stat]. Available at: http://arxiv.org/abs/1602.07043 (accessed 5 March 2016).

Agrawal, R., & Srikant, R. (2000). Privacy-preserving data mining. ACM Sigmod Record. ACM., Available at https://dl.acm.org/citation.cfm?id=335438, Retrieved August 20, 2015, from.

Arendt, H. (1971). *Eichmann in Jerusalem: A Report on the Banality of Evil.* Viking Press.

Barocas, S. (2014) Data mining and the discourse on discrimination. Available at: https://dataethics.github.io/proceedings/DataMiningandtheDiscourseOnDiscrimination.pdf (accessed 20 December 2015).

Burrell, J. (2016). How the machine 'thinks:' Understanding opacity in machine learning AI algorithms. *Big Data & Society*, 3(1), 1–12. DOI: 10.1177/2053951715622512

Burrell, J. (2016). How the machine 'thinks:' Understanding opacity in machine learning AI algorithms. *Big Data & Society*, 3(1), 1–12. DOI: 10.1177/2053951715622512

Calders, T., & Verwer, S. (2010). Three naive Bayes approaches for discrimination-free classification. *Data Mining and Knowledge Discovery*, 21(2), 277–292. DOI: 10.1007/s10618-010-0190-x

Davis, M., Kumiega, A., & Van Vliet, B. (2013). Ethics, finance, and automation: A preliminary survey of problems in high frequency trading. *Science and Engineering Ethics*, 19(3), 851–874. DOI: 10.1007/s11948-012-9412-5 PMID: 23138232

Diakopoulos, N. (2015). AI algorithmic accountability: Journalistic investigation of computational power structures. *Digital Journalism (Abingdon, England)*, 3(3), 398–415. DOI: 10.1080/21670811.2014.976411

Eleveld, M. (2003). *The Spoken Word Revolution: (slam, hip hop & the poetry of a new generation).* Sourcebooks, Inc.

European Commission. (2012) Regulation of the European Parliament and of the Council on the Protection of Individuals with regard to the processing of personal data and on the free movement of such data (General Data Protection Regulation). Brussels: European Commission. Available at: https://ec.europa.eu/justice/data-protection/document/review2012/com_2012_11_en.pdf (accessed 2 April 2013).

Fisher, R., & Ury, W. (1981). *Getting to Yes, Negotiating Agreement Without Giving In*. Penguin Books.

Floridi, L., Fresco, N., & Primiero, G. (2014). On malfunctioning software. *Synthese*, 192(4), 1199–1220. DOI: 10.1007/s11229-014-0610-3

Fule, P., & Roddick, J. F. (2004). Detecting privacy and ethical sensitivity in data mining results. In Proceedings of the 27th Australasian conference on computer science–Volume 26 (pp. 159–166). Australian Computer Society, Inc., Available at https://dl.acm.org/citation.cfm?id=979942, Retrieved August 24, 2015, from.

Hajian, S., Monreale, A., Pedreschi, D., ... (2012). Injecting discrimination and privacy awareness into pattern discovery. In Data mining workshops (ICDMW), 2012 IEEE 12th international conference on (pp. 360–369). IEEE., Available at https://ieeexplore.ieee.org/xpls/abs_all.jsp?arnumber=6406463, Retrieved November 3, 2015, from. DOI: 10.1109/ICDMW.2012.51

Kim, B., Patel, K., & Rostamizadeh, A.. (2015). *Scalable and interpretable data representation for high-dimensional, complex data*. AAAI. DOI: 10.1609/aaai.v29i1.9474

Lou, Y., Caruana, R., & Gehrke, J.. (2013) Accurate intelligible models with pairwise interactions. In: *Proceedings of the 19th ACM SIGKDD international conference on knowledge discovery and data mining*. Chicago, USA, ACM, pp. 623–631. DOI: 10.1145/2487575.2487579

Mittelstadt, B. D., & Floridi, L. (2016). The ethics of big data: Current and foreseeable issues in biomedical contexts. *Science and Engineering Ethics*, 22(2), 303–341. DOI: 10.1007/s11948-015-9652-2 PMID: 26002496

Orseau, L., & Armstrong, S. (2016) Safely interruptible agents. Available at: http://intelligence.org/files/Interruptibility.pdf (accessed 12 September 2016).

Pasquale, F. (2015). *The Black Box Society: The Secret AI algorithms that Control Money and Information*. Harvard University Press. DOI: 10.4159/harvard.9780674736061

Romei, A., & Ruggieri, S. (2014). A multidisciplinary survey on discrimination analysis. *The Knowledge Engineering Review*, 29(5), 582–638. DOI: 10.1017/S0269888913000039

Sandvig, C., Hamilton, K., Karahalios, K., ... (2014) Auditing AI algorithms: Research methods for detecting discrimination on internet platforms. Data and Discrimination: Converting Critical Concerns into Productive Inquiry. Available at: http://social.cs.uiuc.edu/papers/pdfs/ICA2014 Sandvig.pdf (accessed 13 February 2016).

Simon, J. (2015). Distributed epistemic responsibility in a hyper-connected era. In L. Floridi (Ed.), The Onlife Manifesto (pp. 145–159). Springer International Publishing., Available at https://link.springer.com/chapter/10.1007/978-3-319-04093-6_17, Retrieved June 17, 2016, from.

Taylor, L., Floridi, L., & van der Sloot, B. (Eds.). (2017). *Group Privacy: New Challenges of Data Technologies* (1st ed.). Springer. DOI: 10.1007/978-3-319-46608-8

Tufekci, Z. (2015). AI algorithmic harms beyond Facebook and Google: Emergent challenges of computational agency. *Journal on Telecommunications & High Technology Law*, 13, 203.

Tutt, A. (2016) An FDA for AI algorithms. SSRN Scholarly Paper. Rochester, NY: Social Science Research Network. Available at: https://papers.ssrn.com/abstract=2747994 DOI: 10.2139/ssrn.2747994

Van Wel, L., & Royakkers, L. (2004). Ethical issues in web data mining. *Ethics and Information Technology*, 6(2), 129–140. DOI: 10.1023/B:ETIN.0000047476.05912.3d

Vellido, A., Martín-Guerrero, J. D., & Lisboa, P. J. (2012) Making machine learning models interpretable. In: ESANN 2012 proceedings, Bruges, Belgium, pp. 163–172.

Zarsky, T. (2016). The trouble with AI algorithmic decisions: An analytic road map to examine efficiency and fairness in automated and opaque decision making. *Science, Technology & Human Values*, 41(1), 118–132. DOI: 10.1177/0162243915605575

Chapter 2
The Dual Impact of the Pandemic and Reform Movements on Law Enforcement

ABSTRACT

Chapter two explores key issues affecting law enforcement, divided into three sections. The first section examines how the COVID-19 pandemic has impacted sustainability, purpose, and ongoing need for policer officers. The second section addresses the misconceptions surrounding the calls to defund law enforcement, providing clarity on why such beliefs are not grounded in the reality of police officers' role. The third section focuses on how the pandemic has emphasized the critical need for trust between police officers and the communities they serve.

INTRODUCTION

The chapter goes beyond theoretical discussions by incorporating real-world examples from Sherwin's personal experiences working within communities, responding to calls for service, and interacting with citizens. These anecdotes help illustrate the themes discussed in the chapter, including the unpredictable nature of police work. No two days are the same for a police officer. Each work shift is filled with spontaneous situations that demand immediate attention and responses from a police officer. Police/citizen encounters frequently result in arrests that sometimes require the lawful use of force. Nonetheless, these situations must always be predicated on lawful decisions and methods depleted of bias. Police officers are expected to always exercise prudent judgment. No matter what type of police/citizen encounter,

DOI: 10.4018/979-8-3693-7979-0.ch002

or the manifest issues that occur during those situations, all police officers' actions must be grounded in a humanistic approach to policing.

Unfortunately, there are instances when police/citizen encounters result in public scrutiny. Those encounters stimulate citizens, politicians, and the media to question the lawfulness and appropriateness of police officers' methods. These situations further underscore the ongoing need for clear communication, transparency, and trust between police departments and citizens to bridge the gap between police officers and the communities they serve.

Chapter two tackles several critical discussions surrounding the defunding of law enforcement, addressing community concerns such as the militarization of police officers and the societal impact of that imagery. Chapter two highlights the growing mental health crisis in society that is predicated on the abuse of illicit drug use. And with the legalization of marijuana the mental health of our youths is in peril as the regular use of marijuana impairs natural cognitive maturation. The early onset use of marijuana is scrutinized for its detrimental impact on young people's brain development, which ultimately affects their ability to learn and become contributing members of society. The section is dedicated to examining this phenomenon by emphasizing how young people are the foundation of a sustainable future with a focus on society's responsibility to suppress tolerating anything that supplants the cognitive maturation and mental health of children.

Chapter two also explores the use of force paradigm, explaining its lawful application through real-life examples from my own experiences. These examples are meant to clarify the legal parameters under which lawful force is used by demonstrating how lawful force can be appropriately applied in a range of situations. A significant portion of chapter two is dedicated to discussing the Black Lives Matter (BLM) movement, including its mission, identity, and the purpose behind its activism. Considering this, Sherwin provide a unique perspective on the George Floyd incident, comparing it to his own professional experiences in similar situations, while drawing upon insights from law enforcement colleagues.

A core concern expressed in this chapter is the need for community trust. Without trust, the relationship between police officers and the community is reduced to an "us vs. them" mentality, which erodes the very fabric of effective policing. Trust requires more than just effort; it requires mindful and responsible leadership at every level. It is not only the responsibility of supervisors but also of individual officers to foster trust through their actions and conduct. The COVID-19 pandemic further highlighted this need for trust, particularly as police officers were tasked with enforcing radical mandates and policies that were often met with resistance by members of society. During this time, many officers lost public trust and respect, but the pandemic also illuminated the undeniable need for police officers to utilize humanistic methods while interacting with citizens in communities they serve and protect.

Chapter two provides a comprehensive review that highlights police officers' roles of enforcing the various illiberal proclamations for social control proscribed by politicians during the COVID-19 pandemic. Police officers' resilience, dedication, and concern for maintaining order and ensuring community safety became a major media and social focus for criticism as to their methods and failures. Nonetheless, the COVID-19 pandemic ultimately, without design, illuminated the existential threat of not having police officers serving and protecting society. The pandemic also reminded police departments of the essential need for having police officers who are models of humanistic qualities that imbues respect, trust, and integrity in their interactions and service with members of the communities they serve and protect.

SECTION-1: POLICING IN CRISIS: NAVIGATING THE PANDEMIC'S PRESSURE ON RESOURCES AND MORALE

Sustainability

The COVID-19 pandemic brought significant frustration, polarization, physical, and emotional harm to societies worldwide. Law enforcement officers, along with other first responders and medical professionals, were thrust into a variety of manifold situations that placed their lives in peril. Police officers were mandated to continue working without exception, leading to increased strain between them and the executive branch of the government. Police officers who refused to be vaccinated faced various forms of retribution for their personal decisions ranging from suspensions to persistent admonishments and threats of dismissal. Despite this, they continued to work, exposing themselves to COVID-19. Ironically, as both political and healthcare leaders assured everyone that the vaccinations were the magic bullet for preventing being infected with the Corona virus, the virus was not deterred. People were infected regardless of their vaccination status. This only exacerbated the stress that police officers were experiencing as both vaccinated and unvaccinated personnel contracted the virus which ultimately required the infected officers to be placed on medical leaves of absence. This caused a widespread shortage of police officers' availability to work which subsequently resulted in diminished police services. Citizens who required the services of police officers or paramedics were placed on a wait list as emergency 911 calls were prioritized. This frequently postponed emergency response resulted in hours or days of delayed service. Additionally, police stations were utilized as homeless shelters during the pandemic. This ultimately compromised employing official mandates for distancing people to prevent the spread of the virus. Thus, police stations became incubators for Corona virus, exposing police officers and citizens to increased environmental hazards and overcrowded, unsanitary conditions.

The widespread stress resulting from the COVID-19 pandemic mandates, rules, regulations, prohibitions, and the projected fear of spreading the Corona virus led to national frustration, anxiety, and depression. Nix, Ivanov, and Pickett (2021) observed that "the virus has caused significant societal disruptions to those not infected" (p. 546), as people were forced to stay home and refrain from gathering socially, including faith-based events. The constant fear of Corona virus infection fueled disputes among family and friends, with individuals becoming aggressive and hostile toward anyone not wearing a face mask in public spaces. Children, students, and young adults were confined to online learning, further stressing parents, especially those who worked. The role of police officers as enforcers of COVID-19 mandates placed them at the center of an emerging "perfect storm" during the so-called "Summer of Love," where societal pressure acted as a release valve for accumulated frustration. The pandemic's societal strain, combined with government-imposed mandates, created deep-seated distrust, anger, and rebellion. This antagonism was amplified by the executive branches of federal, state, and local governments, whose policies were enforced by police officers. Unfortunately, these enforcement actions undermined trust between police officers and citizens, destabilizing relationships and increasing polarization.

A crucial, frequently overlooked sociological factor is that police officers live within the same communities they serve and protect. This reality compounded the tension between officers and their families, friends, and neighbors, as they began to perceive police officers as enforcers of the political COVID-19 restrictions, rules, and mandates imposed on society. Unfortunately, the fact that police officers were also compelled to follow orders, despite their own personal reservations, did not resonate with many, further fueling animosity toward them. Relationships with friends, family members, and neighbors became strained as the positionality of the Corona virus polarized society. The lack of social interaction only intensified these feelings. The Corona vaccine's failure to provide sufficient immunity, coupled with government mandates and police enforcement, had devastating consequences. One significant impact was the existential threat officers felt regarding their domestic lives, as they risked transmitting the virus to their families. Additionally, there was a sharp reduction in the number of healthy, on-duty personnel available to protect the public. Both factors eroded the already declining confidence in public service leadership. This had a devastating effect on the morale among police officers which was projected unto society. The low morale and plummeting trust were not the only psychological strain sustained by police officers. Officers were often required to work longer hours, frequently without days off, as furloughs were either canceled or shortened. Many police officers worked solo shifts to reduce exposure and spreading of the Corona virus. This tactic inadvertently placed police officers at greater risk of harm as crime rates surged. These issues, combined with the growing stress, contributed to an increase in PTSD among police officers and society further amplified the strain on relationships between both. Heightened sentiments about the COVID-19 pandemic among police officers and citizens made interactions more volatile, with reactions often driven by emotion rather than thoughtful responses.

The pandemic caused another morale issue among police officers. The overwhelming and often unjustified contempt, hostility, and criticism expressed by citizen groups, politicians, and media platforms. These issues engendered introspection as many police officers reflected on their personal well-being and integrity. While criticism of police officers is not new, the intensity of the vitriol and the widespread calls to defund the police compounded with the decline in public respect and trust took a heavy toll on police officers' sense of self-esteem and integrity. As a result, "COVID-19 experienced a substantial increase in resignations and retirements" (Nam, Wolfe, and Nix, 2024, p. 126). Nam et al. (2024) report that "Americans' confidence in the police just hit its lowest point in at least 27 years and has especially diminished among African Americans" (p. 126). This loss of trust coincided with a notable rise in crime, galvanizing police departments to explore sustainable solutions for rebuilding legitimacy, integrity, respect, and trust within their communities. This issue is particularly concerning for future generations, especially within African American communities. African American youth are disproportionately exposed to violence, necessitating frequent police presence and interactions. These children repeatedly witness family members and friends involved in confrontational encounters with police, which, unfortunately, too often result in the use of force. The negative impact of these experiences is exacerbated by the fact that many African American children are "taught early on to be distrustful of the police and to anticipate being treated unfairly due to the color of their skin" (Whitaker and Snell, 2016; Maroney and Zuckerman, 2018, cited by Nam et al., 2024, p. 127). Fagan and Tyler (2005) emphasize that "children develop an orientation toward law and legal authorities early in life, and this early orientation shapes both adolescent and adult-law-related behavior" (cited by Nam et al., 2024, p. 128). The repeated portrayal of police bias against African Americans, whether true, false, or part of a larger movement to defund or abolish the police, is not the central issue. For the African American community, it is a "real" issue of concern and contention, one that law enforcement must take seriously to ensure sustainability. Police departments need to be held accountable for the actions of their police officers. Police departments must develop long-term solutions to regain the public's trust and respect. It is alarming and unacceptable that a segment of American citizens feels disconnected from their identity as "Americans." Wolfe and McLean (2021) recently suggested that some African

Americans may not feel "American" in the same way their White counterparts do, due to "adverse direct and vicarious legal socialization experiences" (Nam et al., 2024, p. 129). When citizens do not feel fully "American," they are less likely to believe in the legitimacy of the law and its representatives. Conversely, when they do feel connected to their identity as Americans, they are more inclined to trust and respect law enforcement and its legitimacy.

This is an issue of critical importance that demands immediate attention and sustainable solutions. People want law and order, they demand it. However, they also expect the police to carry out their duties with humanity and fairness. Americans are a forgiving society, but they require accountability, equal justice, and impartiality from law enforcement. Citizens expect police officers to "arrest lawbreakers and solve crimes" (Nam et al., 2024, p. 129), but they want these actions to be carried out in a humane, respectful, and lawfully just manner. For law enforcement to maintain its legitimacy, police officers must dedicate themselves to these principles, demonstrating that they can perform their duties without prejudice while simultaneously ensuring respect for all. This commitment must go beyond mere words meant to appease the public; it must be genuinely reflected in the officers' actions. People need to feel that the police genuinely care about them, that they are an integral part of the community, and that they take pride in serving it. Citizens do not want police officers who are merely going through the motions; they want officers who project confidence, authenticity, and dedication to both their profession and the people they serve. Tyler (1990) and Sunshine and Tyler (2003) support this view, emphasizing that police need to adhere to four fundamental principles during interactions with the public: respect, neutrality, trustworthiness, and giving citizens a voice (cited by Nam et al., 2024, p. 130).

Nam et al. (2024) argue that police officers must prioritize "procedural fairness" in their interactions with the public. I never believed in overwhelming people with multiple charges. I preferred to keep things straightforward, factual, and to the point, a practice that was also appreciated by the courts. I also never experienced a negative personal encounter, after all, how could it be personal when those individuals didn't know me? Even those I arrested didn't harbor ill will toward me during future encounters. In my experience, people in the community know who you are. Word gets around, and they are aware of whether you are fair. They also know if you are committed to procedural fairness, showing respect, neutrality, trustworthiness, and truth in your actions. I view these four values as central to treating people with dignity, grounded in ethical and moral principles, and delivered with humility and kindness. Tyler and Lind (1992) suggest that "when people feel they've been treated fairly by police, even if the outcome isn't in their favor—they are more likely to respect and trust the officers" (cited by Nam et al., 2024). Often, citizens would even thank me afterward. Here is an example.

Domestic Disturbance (As told by Sherwin)

I was assigned to work the day watch in a one-person patrol car. It was a beautiful summer morning, and I welcomed the opportunity to work alone while my partner had the day off. This allowed me time to think. The morning was quiet, with minimal radio traffic. I was patrolling the neighborhood, keeping an eye out for daytime burglars, when the dispatcher assigned me to a domestic disturbance call.

Coincidentally, the address was just two houses from the corner where I had stopped to take the call. Talk about being in the right place at the right time! I acknowledged the call with the dispatcher, informed him of my location, and noted that I would wait for backup. While sitting in my squad car, I positioned the vehicle so that I had a clear and unobstructed view of the house the call came from. About two minutes later, a woman in a bathrobe quickly ran out of the house toward the curb. I immediately exited my vehicle and approached her. She identified herself as the caller and explained that she and her husband had been arguing when he threatened to shoot her. When I asked if her husband owned a gun, she confirmed that he did. After ensuring she was unharmed, I told her we would wait until other officers arrived to assist. But they did not arrive quickly enough. What happened next unfolded very rapidly.

A man suddenly appeared on the front porch, standing in the doorway of the woman's house, holding a gun at his side. The woman screamed, "That's my husband! Don't shoot him!" The man kept the gun in his right hand, pointed downward. I drew my gun and ordered him to drop his weapon, but he refused. The woman continued screaming, "Don't shoot—don't shoot!" As he started to lift his gun, I quickly ran up to the porch. By then, he had raised the gun to a level position. I grabbed his gun hand and slammed it against the door frame, causing his weapon to drop. However, there was a complication. I still had my gun in my hand. The man seized my weapon, attempting to twist it out of my grip. We grappled for control of the gun, wrestling our way into the foyer of the house. Still, no backup had arrived. At that moment, another serious safety threat emerged.

While engaged in a wrestling match with the man, suddenly, two German Shepherds attacked me, biting and growling as they latched onto my back side, the place I use for sitting. The man still held tight to my gun hand, and we ended up on the floor, with the dogs seeming to think I was their next meal. Meanwhile, he twisted my gun toward my stomach, trying to pull the trigger. I found myself in a desperate struggle on three fronts: stopping the man, fending off the dogs, and praying for help. Thankfully, the first answer was to my prayer, the cavalry arrived, in the form of one officer. Armed with a broom, he managed to shoo the dogs away, herding them to the rear porch. With the dogs out of the way, I could finally focus fully on disarming the man. I overpowered him, secured my gun, and managed to cuff him just as more backup arrived.

Both the man and I were taken to the hospital. I received stitches in my gluteus maximus, while the man was treated and then released into police custody. I charged him with Aggravated Assault. He had a valid Firearm Owner's Identification (FOID) card. During the bench trial, the judge found him guilty. Prior to sentencing, the judge asked if I wanted monetary restitution for the damage to my uniform trousers, but I declined. They were an old pair of pants. The man was sentenced to supervision, which, in Cook County, was a significant outcome.

Epilogue

A few months later, while, once again, working the day watch, I was called to the police station to see the desk sergeant. Immediately, I wondered if I'd done something wrong as I made my way to the police station. When I arrived, I noticed a man standing near the front desk in deep conversation with the desk sergeant. At first glance I didn't recognize him however, as I walked toward the two interlocutors, the man turned to face me. His eyes sparkled, his face lit up, and a broad smile stretched across his face. I suddenly recognized him as the man from the front porch of the house with the two hungry German Shepherds. He extended his hand with a heartfelt "thank you," then pulled me into a bear hug and apologized. He explained that he had "gone a little crazy" that day; his wife had threatened divorce, but after the incident, she changed her mind. I congratulated him, thanked him for sharing, and wished them well. They stayed together happily, I believe. Domestic situations can certainly tug at the heartstrings.

"Procedurally fair treatment from the police communicates to citizens that they are valued members of society" (Nam et al., 2024, p. 132). Everyone wants to be heard and should not be dismissed, devalued, or disrespected for who they are, where they live, or what they believe. Their voice matters as it reflects their deeply held beliefs and experiences and thus should matter to police officers as well. A police officer should not take criticism personally; instead, they should approach it professionally, taking responsibility for their actions and decisions. There is no quick fix or assertive approach that will change people's minds, but actions do. When citizens observe police officers or interact with them, those moments are opportunities for officers to plant a seed of humanity. If nurtured consistently during police-citizen encounters, this humanistic approach can gradually transform negative perceptions citizens may hold of police officers to genuine respect and trust. An old saying captures this approach well: treat each person as you would your own grandmother. There is a time for authority, but never for oppression, and personal values should never be imposed on others. Sherwin once learned a humbling lesson that underscored this perspective. While interviewing a man during an investigation, Sherwin told him that he understood his concerns. He immediately replied, "No, you don't. You've got to be where I'm at to hear where I'm coming from." His words were profoundly true. This lesson reminded Sherwin of the importance of listening and understanding another person's position. Another crucial element of sustainability in policing is recognizing the needs of African American children.

School Absentees (As told by Sherwin)

I was working on the day watch by myself. During rollcall, the watch commander emphasized the importance of ensuring that youths attended school, encouraging us to address truancy and complete School Absentee cards for any students found wandering the streets during school hours. While patrolling near Parker High School on Chicago's south side around 10 a.m. on a school day, I noticed four young African American teenage boys walking together. I stopped them and asked why they weren't in class. Their answers took me by surprise. They said it didn't matter because of who they were and where they lived; they believed no one would accept them or give them a chance to succeed. I was saddened, not only by their lack of self-esteem but by the reality that these healthy, capable youths didn't see a future for themselves. For nearly an hour, I spoke with them, highlighting the value of education and encouraging them to believe in their potential. Instead of filling out absentee cards, I let them go with an admonishment while telling them to go to school. I watched as they headed back toward the school, and then I drove off, not giving it much further thought.

Epilogue

A year later, while on the same beat, a young man suddenly jumped in front of my squad car. Alarmed, I hit the brakes. The young man rushed to the driver's side of my door window and shouted, "I've been looking for you!" I was stunned. He went on to explain that he was one of the four boys I had spoken to about staying in school. He proudly shared his academic career goals and told me that he and his friends had successfully graduated from high school and were enrolled in a junior college. He thanked me for the talk we had the previous year, saying it had changed his and his friends' lives. This experience reminded me of how powerful our words, actions, and examples can have a greater impact on others than we often realize. The messages young people hear daily shape their lives in lasting ways.

What children hear about police officers leaves a lasting impression on them. Like sponges, children absorb what they see and hear, especially from influential figures like parents, relatives, community members and leaders, and media. Young and impressionable, they often lack the experience to judge whether this information is accurate or fair. When significant people in their lives, such as family or other impactful community members, warn them about police officers, children are especially vulnerable to accepting these views without questioning. Unfortunately, this learned socialization is often based on negative or troubling police-citizen encounters that these groups have either witnessed or experienced. This process is exemplified in "The Talk" that African American families often have with their children, focusing on "teaching African American children how to handle encounters with the police to avoid being harmed" (Jamieson, 2014; Malone and Gonzalez, 2019, 2020, cited by Nam et al., 2024, p. 132). "The Talk" reflects a troubling reality in police intervention methods during interactions with citizens.

All children, regardless of race or background, deserve to grow up in a world where they feel safe and can trust that police officers are there to protect, not harm, them. We need our youth to mature into responsible citizens who respect law enforcement professionals. Growth and progress come from embracing new ideas and beliefs, and police departments are no exception, they too, must evolve to ensure long-term sustainability. It's crucial that we create an environment in which young people learn to respect and trust police officers, rather than fear or resent them. Police departments have a societal responsibility to foster this trust through positive humanistic modeling among our youth.

Negative police-citizen encounters have become pervasive issues. Although they are not the daily norm for police departments across the United States, these incidents gain significant attention when they do occur. Even one instance is too many. Therefore, police departments must take accountability and proactive work to transform their image, rebuild public trust, and earn respect to ensure their sustainability. It is essential for the public to recognize that most police officers are committed to upholding public safety and solving crimes with integrity. While it is regrettable that some police officers act dishonorably, good officers are as appalled by these actions as the public is. They bear the burden of a tarnished image, facing disparaging remarks and criticisms, yet they, too, seek justice and a renewed sense of respect and trust from the community. Defunding or abolishing the police is not the solution. The solution lies within the commitment of everyone, both police officers and citizens, to work together toward the changes needed to sustain the protection, safety, and welfare that society expects from its police force.

Purpose

Nix et al. (2021) argue that police faced three major challenges during the COVID-19 pandemic. The first was the risk of officers contracting COVID-19, which led to a sharp reduction in the available workforce and necessitated "cutting back on self-initiated activities and enforcement of low-level crimes" (p. 546). The second issue involved the need to reduce jail populations. Officers were directed to avoid making arrests for misdemeanors, opting instead to issue citations, as administrators of jails were refusing to accept prisoners. Consequently, the decision to arrest was largely left to the officers' discretion. The third concern noted by Nix et al. (2021) was that "police were directed to enforce social distancing ordinances … [including] stay-at-home orders … [and] prohibitions against large gatherings" (p. 547). These challenges sparked diverse viewpoints and debates about both the government-imposed mandates and whether officers were fulfilling their core mission of crime prevention and public safety. This division, spanning citizens, families, and politicians, has fueled an ongoing debate about the legitimacy of these actions. Ultimately, the COVID-19 pandemic brought a renewed focus on the fundamental purpose of policing.

Nix et al. (2021) presented a complex social dilemma: how to enforce policing during a pandemic without compromising public safety or crime prevention. Criminal justice leaders largely agreed that the "Watchman" style of policing was the most effective approach to maintaining a sustainable balance between public safety and crime intervention, while still upholding justice and individual rights. The Watchman approach emphasizes "order maintenance, increased officer discretion, and enforcement flexibility" (Nix et al., 2021, p. 548). However, a key drawback of this style is the potential to heighten concerns about "police discrimination" and to strain police-community relations (Nix et al., 2021). Despite stay-at-home mandates, criminal activity did not cease; in fact, it increased, placing police officers in the spotlight as they faced heightened criticism and strain. Much of this criticism stemmed from enforcing social distancing and other COVID-19 mandates ordered by government officials. Allegations of racial discrimination and numerous lawsuits were filed against police officers, "challenging the constitutionality of stay-at-home orders" (Nix et al., 2021, p. 560). Nevertheless, most of the public, even amidst the pandemic, held the view "that the police should always be 'out there' on watch and on call" (Nix et al., 2021, p. 560) to protect them from criminal threats and harm.

The purpose of policing lost its objectivity in areas of crime prevention, public safety, and community service, as police officers were tasked with enforcing what many perceived as draconian mandates aimed at COVID-19 prevention. Police were directed to enforce mask-wearing and prohibit gatherings in public spaces, such as parks and recreational facilities, as well as restrict citizens from exercising their First Amendment right to worship in places of faith. In Chicago and numerous other communities, officers were instructed to enforce the closures of worship spaces, schools, and libraries. This led to widespread frustration among citizens, who often redirected their anger toward police officers who were merely enforcing government orders. This tension became especially visible during the so-called "Summer of Love," when many major U.S. cities experienced large-scale protests expressing discontent with the criminal justice system, especially law enforcement. These demonstrations escalated into riots, firebombing, property destruction, looting, shootings, physical violence, and numerous other serious crimes, reflecting the depth of public unrest.

Whether these events were part of a conspiracy, organized efforts, or spontaneous actions is a topic beyond the scope of this discussion. However, it is undeniable that the "Summer of Love" marked a watershed moment in questioning the role and purpose of policing. This period sparked numerous debates, congressional hearings, and community testimonials that fueled calls to defund the police. This movement deepened societal polarization as citizens, politicians, and law enforcement officials took sides, firmly entrenching their positions. In doing so, the original intent and standards of policing, as articulated in the writings and treatises of historical philosophers, became increasingly diluted.

Need for Law Enforcement

Locke (1980) argued that society requires individuals "having authority from the community" (p. 46) to enforce laws that protect citizens from harm, as mandated by society. Similarly, Mill (1974) advised political leaders that "It is one of the undisputed functions of government to take precautions against crime" (p. 165) to prevent, investigate, and bring to justice those who violate the laws, rules, and norms of the social contract. Kant's (1993) ethical framework further underscores the importance of holding wrongdoers accountable as a categorical imperative, advocating that police officers uphold respect for the law, as the law "is the incentive which can give an action moral worth" (p. 44). These philosophical perspectives illustrate a pursuit of justice that, unfortunately, is not always fairly applied by those in power, leading to public confusion about the purpose of certain laws and mandates. While society may tacitly accept the social contract, this acceptance is not always wholehearted.

People need to feel justice, not just hear about it. They need to experience real justice, not merely a perception of inequity. Justice must be realized as equal and fair, ensuring not only protection from physical or emotional harm but also safeguarding dignity, respect, and trust. Unfortunately, "African Americans viewed [sic] the police as less fair, less effective" (Nam et al., 2024, p. 150). Society needs equal justice, and it demands it to thrive free from oppression, violence, and prejudice. The core purpose of law enforcement is to ensure that justice is truly equal for all.

Legislators draw on the theories, ideas, and recommendations of philosophers like Locke, Mill, and Kant, using them as foundational templates for laws that grant police officers legitimacy. This legitimacy is crucial for police officers to lawfully uphold the constitutionally protected rights of every citizen, ensuring equal justice for all. Yet, these rights are now under intense scrutiny. The COVID-19 pandemic has heightened social divides among politicians, the judiciary, community leaders, and advocates, sparking heated debates over the validity and interpretation of the Constitution. Some argue from a strict constructionist stance, advocating a narrow, literal interpretation of legal texts, while others take a liberal constructionist view, suggesting the Constitution should be interpreted more flexibly, with an emphasis on intent and inferred meaning. Ironically, these debates often center on the rights and protections of lawbreakers rather than the rights of victims or potential victims, the law-abiding citizens.

As this debate continues among those with influence, it often stigmatizes rather than offers thoughtful solutions for the welfare and safety of society. But what about those without a platform? What about the community members who live in affected areas of crime and violence, the people who do not commit crimes yet are frequently victimized? Do they have a say about what's best for them, or are their needs overshadowed by those outside their community seeking to impose their own values? The "moral entrepreneurs" of society often view these communities through an opaque lens clouded by biases, focusing more on imposing their own values and agendas than on genuinely understanding or addressing the community's actual needs.

Kant (1993) argues that it is the moral duty of society's leaders, and those who enforce the laws enacted by Congress, to ensure equal justice for all citizens. Police officers carry the profound obligation, or as Kant would call it, duty, not only to enforce the laws but also to protect and safeguard those who have been victimized. Police officers bring stability to the communities they serve, as they are often the first responders when citizens call for help. Without their presence, enforcing laws and maintaining order, communities would descend into chaos. The COVID-19 pandemic underscored the need for sustainable police enforcement as violent protests erupted in many cities, resulting in widespread destruction. Buildings were burned, people were seriously injured, and some lost their lives. Many businesses closed permanently, even after order was restored, due to the lasting and devasting impacts of the lawlessness that erupted.

Amidst these challenges, police officers were further hindered by the implementation of misguided restorative justice practices. Restorative justice traditionally aims to hold offenders accountable for harm they've caused, but political leaders misappropriated the concept to gain social favor rather than prioritizing the safety of business owners and law-abiding citizens. This misuse of restorative justice fostered a damaging narrative that painted all officers as untrustworthy and abusive, undermining community respect for law enforcement. Consequently, the authority of police officers was dramatically reduced, stifling their ability to effectively serve and protect. In the name of social justice reforms, these initiatives ultimately compromised the rights of law-abiding citizens and victims, while enabling offenders to avoid accountability.

During the COVID-19 pandemic, emboldened offenders exploited this relaxed enforcement to openly shoplift, often resorting to violence or threats against employees who attempted to stop them. In cases where citizens or store employees defended themselves, they were sometimes arrested and charged with a crime, while the perpetrators faced no prosecution. A notable example occurred in New York city in July 2022, when Jose Alba fatally defended himself during an attempted armed robbery but faced severe legal consequences despite acting in self-defense. (NBC New York, 2022).

Today, the limitations placed on police discretion further complicate their role. For instance, police officers may be restricted from engaging in a foot chase without supervisor authorization, which may not be immediately available. In states like Illinois, officers are even prevented from removing trespassers from private property without specific protocols. (Bilyk, 2022). My street experience as a police officer was that senior citizens in areas like Chicago often feel the need to arm themselves for protection while others feel compelled to stay indoors to avoid potential harm. In inner-city communities, some children sleep under their beds for safety from stray bullets fired in gang-related violence. The most vulnerable members of society need the protection and humanistic authority of police to ensure their safety and uphold their constitutional rights for equal justice.

In some jurisdictions, such as Cook County, Illinois, individuals arrested for serious offenses are frequently released on their own recognizance, only to reoffend or fail to appear in court. Additionally, in certain areas, 911 calls for property crimes and other non-violent incidents are no longer responded to by police, with citizens directed to report these issues through non-emergency lines instead.

Before the COVID-19 pandemic, citizens were accustomed to flagging down a police car or calling 911 to have an officer assist or provide advice to them. Even those who had reservations about law enforcement appreciated the ability to call the police when needed. Sherwin has responded to countless calls from individuals who simply wanted to talk to an officer, seeking guidance or a listening ear. These interactions provided a valuable opportunity for building mutual respect and trust between citizens and police. Many people are lonely, isolated, vulnerable, or fearful, and the presence of a police officer often provides them with comfort. People need and want the police in their communities.

Those who claim to speak on behalf of an entire community with anti-police sentiments often represent only their own views. The truth is that most citizens not only want police presence in their neighborhoods, but they also demand it. They understand that police are often the only reliable safeguard for their community's safety and welfare. They want to sleep soundly at night, confident that they can rest without fear. Police officers provide that peace of mind. While no one is perfect, most police officers are committed to being professional, courteous, and trustworthy.

They, too, strive for justice and equality; they have children in the same schools, shop in the same stores, and pray in the same places of worship as the people they serve. They, too, want the freedom to pursue justice and happiness. Every community needs dedicated law enforcement to protect, serve, and uphold justice.

The COVID-19 pandemic offered an opportunity for those opposed to law enforcement to focus on police responses and enforcement actions, rather than on the underlying issues requiring police intervention. Critics used pandemic-era police responses to spread vitriol, stigmatizing police officers as oppressors. This stigma shifted the public image of police from protectors of good to agents of harm, eroding trust and respect for police officers. Sadly, it often seems easier for people to respond with hatred, punishment, or disrespect rather than empathy. Being at the center of social conflict is not new for police officers. They have historically been the subject of debate regarding social acceptance and their role as enforcers of laws. Police officers are often treated like a tool, kept in reserve until needed. Yet the COVID-19 pandemic has underscored that this "tool" must remain accessible and ready to always serve the community.

SECTION-2: THE DEFUND DEBATE: SEPARATING FACT FROM FICTION IN CALLS FOR REFORM

"Defunding the police" has become a rallying cry among critics of law enforcement, mobilizing people to advocate for reducing or dismantling police departments. However, the concept of restructuring or reducing police authority is not new. In the late 1800s, Sir Robert Peel reorganized the Metropolitan Police in London, replacing an ineffective and disreputable group of law enforcers after a strong outcry from citizens and political leaders over their incompetence and unlawful behavior. Similarly, in the "Old West" of the United States, townspeople called for law enforcement to rid their communities of miscreants who endangered their lives and disrupted the peace of their community. Yet, once law and order were restored, citizens often demanded that formal law enforcement leave, preferring a local sheriff, one who enforced laws but remained under the influence of the community. Even Wyatt Earp was eventually asked to step down after securing order in the towns he served in.

In 1988, Sherwin recalls recall Chicago Mayor Richard M. Daley proposing to lay off police officers of all ranks and replace them with security guards to reform the department. There are countless instances, both in the United States and globally, where police departments and law enforcement agencies have undergone transformation and restructuring due to corruption, brutality, racism, and other social injustices. A major transformation of the Chicago Police Department took place in 1960 after the notoriously egregious "Summerdale Scandal" that exposed the corruption of many patrol officers and supervisors throughout the police department as confederates involved a criminal enterprise. Mayor Richard J. Daley hired O. W. Wilson to take the position of Superintendent of Police. Wilson made considerable changes to the structure of the police department from reestablishing police districts, installing the latest technology in the communications center, to changing the historically black color of the police vehicles to blue and white. (Benzkofer, 2018).

Like any culture, traditional values in organizations can become habitual, making them difficult to change. Many of us have worked in places where suggestions for improvement were met with responses like "that's not how we do things here" or "we've never done it that way," followed by a reminder to stick with the established mode of operation. Breaking old habits sometimes requires radical steps, such as replacing non-compliant individuals, reorganizing responsibilities, adjusting budgets, introducing new training, and bringing in new leadership with the freedom to make impactful decisions.

Sherwin led units where he "reinvented the wheel." Many of the veteran members were thrilled and relieved by the changes, realizing the need for an update in their work environment. They eagerly contributed to developing and implementing new methods. This renovation instilled a new pride in themselves which lifted their morale and self-esteem subsequently galvanizing their spirit to serve and protect the community. They also took pride in their image, personal integrity, and the reputation of their unit of assignment. The change empowered them, uniting the team to not only fulfill their duties to the community but also to support and motivate each other. A new culture emerged that embraced and employed a humanistic value that aligned with contemporary social needs and acceptance. But change is temporary; we must continue to learn, adapt, and improve, pushing beyond the status quo to achieve lasting progress.

It is time to examine some of the current arguments for de-funding the police, which stem from various high-profile police-citizen encounters. Key issues include militarization, mental health response, and the tragic case of George Floyd, all of which warrant a closer examination of the underlying facts and context.

Militarization

The COVID-19 pandemic intensified the underlying distrust and dislike of police officers. During the "Summer of Love," citizens across the nation took to the streets which gave rise to police departments response to the unprecedented numbers of rebellious protestors. Many of these protesters were dressed in black clothing and wearing masks to hide their identity. This group of protesters aligned themselves with the enigmatic anti-fascist movement known as Antifa, an organization originally formed to counter right-wing extremism. Antifa members allied with other radical leftist groups, aiming to challenge conservative social views, which led police departments to adopt a defensive posture. The outcomes were marked by acts of extreme violence, including riots, looting, shootings, arson, and the destruction of government buildings. Police departments were thrust into a difficult position, tasked with protecting themselves, citizens, government property, and businesses while also safeguarding the First Amendment rights of all citizens, including members of Antifa and associated groups—a daunting responsibility.

The manifest tension generated by the protests extended to business owners who sought to defend their property from looters. One high-profile incident reported globally involved Kyle Rittenhouse, a seventeen-year-old who traveled to Kenosha, Wisconsin, to help a family member protect their business. While assisting community members in removing graffiti, Rittenhouse heard gunshots. As he went to investigate, he was chased and assaulted, ultimately firing his weapon in self-defense, injuring two people and fatally wounding a third (Reynolds, 2020-21).

Throughout Sherwin's thirty-eight years with the Chicago Police Department, he worked during numerous events, including protests, riots, and disasters, where citizens, firefighters, paramedics, and fellow police officers were often seriously and sometimes fatally injured. Entire neighborhoods were besieged, burned, and looted. These circumstances inflamed public feelings and placed tremendous strain on citizens, businesses, National Guard personnel, and first responders as they worked together in developing extensive strategies and resources to mitigate the situation. The intelligence and preparation process undertaken by law enforcement is a formidable task.

Sherwin graduated from the police academy in February 1968, and from his first week on patrol, he was thrust into challenging situations. Sherwin's initiation included protecting crime scenes and managing traffic control. On February 7, 1968, an enormous explosion took place at the Mickelberry Food Factory on 49th and Halsted, a facility that produced sausages and other meat products (Fox News Chicago, 2018). It was a typical cold winter day in Chicago, and as the "new kid," Sherwin stood post alone all day. The explosion was catastrophic, caused by a fuel truck mistakenly dumping over a thousand gallons of fuel into the basement of the factory, where it eventually ignited upon contact with one of the factory boilers. The blast leveled the factory, damaged, and destroyed nearby homes and vehicles. Tragically, "Four firefighters and five employees were killed…[and]… 77 people were injured" (Fox News Chicago, 2018).

In April 1968, Sherwin's first annual furlough was canceled following the assassination of Dr. Martin Luther King Jr. that inflamed the African American community who took to the streets and rioted in protest. During the ensuing riots, Sherwin was assigned to patrol the Englewood neighborhood alongside a platoon of Army infantry soldiers who had recently returned from Vietnam. This was a surreal experience for Sherwin, as he had served two tours in Vietnam with the Marine Corps in the infantry. It felt unsettling for Sherwin to be patrolling the streets of Chicago in military vehicles, alongside soldiers, in an American neighborhood. It reminded Sherwin of a Third-World country, a sentiment shared by many of the residents in those communities.

Sherwin also patrolled Chicago's West Side during the King riots, where the devastation in both Englewood and the West Side was profound, unforgivable, and enduring. None of the businesses that were completely burned and gutted by fire ever reopened; they, along with the jobs they provided, were lost forever. The empty lots left behind remain as scars, symbols of a community that never fully recovered.

The year 1968 was marked by chaos, protests, and the emergence of newly organized gangs fighting for territory. It was also the year of the Democratic National Convention (DNC), where Sherwin was one of many police officers assigned to protect the delegates and the city of Chicago. Thousands of leftist youths affiliated with protest groups, including the National Mobilization Committee to End the War in Vietnam ("the Mobe"), the Youth International Party ("Yippies"), Students for a Democratic Society (SDS), and the Black Panther Party, gathered to stage large-scale demonstrations (The Editors of Britannica, 2024).

During the convention at the Chicago Amphitheater, which was located at 43rd and Halsted Streets, some protesters attempted to breach the convention center. This same group advanced their protests at the Hilton Hotel, DNC's host hotel located at Balbo and Michigan Avenue. Meanwhile, other protesters engaged in "harassment tactics, e.g., throwing rocks and bottles and using obscene language" (The Editors of Britannica, 2024) in Grant Park. In a heightened attempt to disrupt the convention, the SDS organized a final, drastic move to have their message heard. Marching with locked arms, and in violation of their permit, proceeded to march in lockstep in the middle of Michigan Avenue. The SDS blocked the entire street with their impassioned single-minded confederates as they marched south toward the Hilton Hotel. At Balbo, Chicago police formed a line across Michigan Avenue to prevent their advance. Sherwin was in that line.

A confrontation erupted when the police command staff ordered the protesters to stop. Instead of complying, the demonstrators launched an assault, hurling bricks, bottles, and bags containing human feces and nails coated with urine (The Editors of Britannica, 2024). The SDS protesters focused on causing harm, defying lawful orders, injuring police officers, and tearing stars and nametags from police uniforms. A CBS mobile broadcast unit captured the incident on a live telecast, turning the episode into a dramatic scene as if on a movie set: "lights, action, camera!" There are many versions of this story, some contradicting Sherwin's, nonetheless, Sherwin was there.

Sherwin's involvement in these historical events gave me a unique perspective on both sides of the debate regarding police militarization. While Sherwin is personally not in favor of using military equipment or vehicles in community policing, he understands the rationale behind law enforcement's decision to adopt these methods and tactics for certain situations. Sherwin also empathizes with citizens' concerns, as these experiences underscored an unfortunate decline in mutual respect between police officers and the public, creating a deep divide that has eroded trust and respect.

This deterioration has fostered opposition fueled by emotional responses, hindering the collaborative, humane approach needed for true justice. Emotions can trigger a "fight or flight" response, undermining rational decision-making and pushing people, groups, and organizations into rigid stances that conflict with shared social values. These historical events served as both the precursor and catalyst to the militarization of police departments. Today, we see police equipped with camouflaged uniforms, heavily armed, and operating armored vehicles through residential streets. The sight of officers in military-style uniforms and vehicles projects an image of oppression, rather than protection.

It is unfortunate that police departments have felt the need to militarize in response to certain critical threats. However, using such tactics as routine patrol or crowd control measures can seem excessive and oppressive, an approach that contradicts the core mission of "Serving and Protecting."

There is an increasing polarization between police officers and the communities they serve, fueled by profound emotions of fear, anger, and resentment, which erode mutual trust and respect. Both police departments and citizens often adopt harsh, retributive stances, where force is too frequently met with force rather than a humanitarian approach, leading the oppressed to risk becoming oppressors (Freire, 1970). This dynamic has prompted an alarming response from police departments across the nation, as they adopt military-grade weapons and uniforms to control crime and manage citizen protests.

Police departments now deploy armored vehicles, along with police officers dressed in camouflaged uniforms, flak vests, and gas masks, armed with military weapons. These responses are used in a range of situations, from domestic disturbances to public protests. While officer safety is crucial, so too is the safety and well-being of citizens; thus, the choice of such militarized methods raises concerns. The sight of an armored vehicle patrolling a neighborhood or confronting citizen protests creates lasting, harsh images that evoke fear, anger, and resentment among citizens. The result is often a cycle of rebellion and retribution. Citizens take to the streets in protest, while police officers, feeling empowered by military-grade equipment, may seek retribution.

The visual impact of military equipment introduces a sense of power that can disrupt relationships between the police and the public. This power imagery not only instills fear among citizens but can also foster a sense of superiority among officers, deepening the divide between them and citizens.

Imagery

Imagery activates our sensory neurons, triggering immediate reactions that shape both extrinsic and intrinsic values. People are constantly exposed to a steady flow of images twenty-four hours a day through various media platforms. These projected images become concerning especially when police officers appear in military-style uniforms and wielding high-powered weapons while riding in military vehicles during interactions with the public. This type of imagery has a significant impact on attitudes and behaviors of officers and citizens. Kisielius and Roedder (1983) suggest that "if imagery elicits different associations to the focal object at the behavior phase than those available at the attitude phase, attitude-behavior consistency should be negatively affected" (p. 73). Phillips (2017) further explores this issue, discussing the complex public perception of militarized police responses during civil protests, emphasizing the potent influence of imagery on public trust and officer-citizen relations.

Phillips (2017) argues that militarized police responses may incite civil disobedience rather than suppress it. Citizens become highly critical of the militarization of police during these events, viewing it as "…an aggressive approach to dealing with protests" (p. 2). Phillips' (2017) study highlights how imagery related to appearance impacts public perception, noting that "Appearances can matter…when…officers dress in battle or camouflage uniforms or use armored vehicles, they demonstrate a military mind-set" (p. 3). Zimbardo (2007) reinforces this view, suggesting that such imagery conveys a strong sense of power and authority that can make citizens feel oppressed. A prominent example of this occurred in Ferguson, Missouri following the police shooting of Michael Brown. The law enforcement responders arrived wearing military styled apparel and armed with military styled weaponry. Projecting an image of overwhelming force can unintentionally produce behaviors and attitudes that contradict its intended goals. All imagery evokes both conscious and subconscious reactions that shape responses. The Editors (2014) highlight the powerful imagery associated with the Ferguson, Missouri Police Department's response to protesters in the wake of Michael Brown's death, noting a concerning "... image of police officers wearing camouflage and holding military-style weapons as they confront protesters" (p. 5). This portrayal reflects a troubling trend toward nationwide police militarization, funded by taxpayers. The critical question, then, is: what are the behavioral and attitudinal ramifications of such a trend?

The Editors (2014) present compelling arguments against the militarization of police departments, with perhaps the most impactful centered on how militarized imagery influences citizens' perception of police officers. They suggest that the appearance of military uniforms, camouflage, assault weapons, and armored vehicles, evokes a sense of fear and a combat-ready mindset, diverging from the principle of "Serving and Protecting." The Editors (2014), along with Phillips (2017), Kisielius & Roedder (1983), and Zimbardo (2007), argue that such imagery fosters attitudes and behaviors in police officers that are counter to humanistic values. Instead of promoting peace, trust, and collaboration with citizens to build positive relationships, officers risk becoming seen as oppressors. While there are situations where police officers require protective equipment, it should not be used in incidents where the goal is to calm anxious and emotionally charged citizens who deserve fairness and respect, not to be treated as adversaries.

Indoctrinated by the powerful influence of imagery, people often judge others quickly based on appearance alone. In law enforcement, using imagery to make rapid assessments can sometimes be beneficial, but it can also lead to fatal mistakes. Police officers, who rarely have the luxury of extended time to discern whether someone is acting with malice or integrity, must rely on more than just visual cues when determining a person's trustworthiness. The most effective tool at an officer's immediate disposal is their communication skills. However, opportunities for positive interactions with citizens are compromised when officers wear camouflaged uniforms, carry high-caliber weapons, and patrol in military vehicles. Such an image provokes rather than pacifies, thus hindering constructive dialogue and instead instilling fear, anger, and resentment.

Right from the beginning, I always strived to capture everything I saw as completely as possible. Norman Rockwell

Figure 1. Stock photo militarized police – Norman Rockwell (https://www.bing)

Imagery carries multiple dimensions, meanings, and interpretations. The two Norman Rockwell paintings depicted above are contrasting images that illustrate a police officer interacting with a youth in a diner. The first is a classic Norman Rockwell painting, created for the now-defunct *Saturday Evening Post* and published on September 20, 1958. It shows a police officer speaking with a young person who appears to be running away from home, leaving the perspective, theory, and outcome of the encounter open to the viewer's interpretation. Even so, Rockwell's painting conveys an overarching sense of warmth and friendliness. His deliberate style portrays a society that is friendly and caring, perhaps a romanticized view but one that imparts a message of goodness and hope. Munson (2000) notes that Rockwell's "characters…display…endearing qualities" (p. 65), filled with virtues that evoke peace, hope, and goodwill in those who view his work. Kisielius & Roedder (1983) suggest that stimulating imagery significantly impacts learning and perception, as reflected in the reactions of the subjects depicted in the second image.

The superimposed post-social content rendition of Rockwell's original painting introduces several epistemological inferences. This updated portrayal evokes a range of challenging, even traumatic, images, some readily apparent, while others depend on the viewer's interpretation. Although the basic theme aligns with Rockwell's original, the police officer's uniform and demeanor in the new image starkly contrast with the original's warmth and empathy. This shift is reflected in the body language of the youth and cook, who display apprehension rather than trust. The juxtaposition of the two images highlights a striking shift in perceived attitudes toward the community and its citizens. The once-friendly officer now appears as a figure of intimidation, a conqueror or oppressor. This second image powerfully conveys the emotional trauma felt by citizens as they encounter police officers patrolling in military gear, armed with assault weapons, and driving armored vehicles through their neighborhoods.

We've seen how militarized gear can sometimes give people a feeling like there's an occupying force, as opposed to a force that's part of the community that's protecting them and serving them. It can alienate and intimidate local residents and send the wrong message. Barack Obama

Figure 2. Stock images of police uniform transition (https://www.bing)

Serve and Protect

Figure 3. Stock photo militarized police – SWAT (https://www.bing)

Tanks A Lot!

Figure 4. Stock photo militarized police – SWAT (https://www.bing)

We Are Here For You

Figure 5. Stock photo militarized police – SWAT (https://www.bing)

Public Service

Figure 6. Stock photo militarized police – homeland security (https://www.bing)

Did You Call the Police?

Figure 7. Stock photo militarized police – SWAT (https://www.bing)

May I Be of Service

Figure 8. Stock photo militarized police – SWAT (https://www.bing)

Making Streets Safe

Figure 9. Stock photo militarized police – SWAT (https://www.bing)

Yes, Stay Calm – We Are Here to Help

Figure 10. Stock photo militarized police – SWAT (https://www.bing)

Mental Health Encounters

Flash Gordon (As told by Sherwin)

It was a summer day, and I was working day watch. My partner had the day off, so I was working alone. I enjoyed the occasional solo shift; after working with the same person for years, a break could be refreshing, giving me time to think and focus. Working with an unfamiliar partner can sometimes be challenging. I'm not your typical police officer; I don't drink coffee or smoke. My parents were coffee drinkers, and while I enjoy the aroma of coffee brewing, I never acquired a taste for it. In the Marine Corps, I had a buddy who prided himself on his coffee-making skills, claiming to be a true coffee aficionado. But even then, coffee never appealed to me.

The morning began as a warm, cloudy, and quiet day. A lull in police calls reflected the absence of citizens on the streets, the late-night crowd hadn't yet woken up. It was unusually calm for our police district, though it was still only 10:30 a.m. While driving along 63rd Street, just west of Morgan Street, the dispatcher assigned me to a disturbance involving a customer at a bar. I acknowledged the call with a 10-99, and the dispatcher reminded me to call if I needed backup. I decided to check it out myself first before calling for help. No need to get excited just yet.

I approached the address given by the dispatcher and, out of habit, parked a couple of doors away for safety. When I walked into the establishment, I found myself in the package goods area, separated from the lounge by a door that only opened when someone was buzzed in. While waiting for someone to greet me, I kept myself busy by inspecting the licenses displayed on the wall, checking their expiration dates. As I did this, I overheard a loud male voice coming from the lounge. The voice was shouting profanities, some words were new to me, casting insults about people's genetic heritage, intelligence, and daring anyone to challenge his "observations."

After a few moments, a large, middle-aged man appeared behind the counter. I asked if he was the one who had called the police. He introduced himself as the owner, confirming that he had 911 for help. When I inquired about the problem, he gave me a look that clearly conveyed, "Are you kidding me?" I asked what he wanted me to do. In a half-growling, half-frustrated tone, he urged me to remove the troublemaker from his establishment. I then asked if he was willing to sign a complaint, and he agreed. The owner stepped into the lounge and opened the door that separated it from the package goods area to allow me entry.

The lounge was dimly lit. As I scanned the room, I noticed two women sitting together at a table in the center of the room, while two men sat separately at tables along the wall near the bar. Standing at the bar was a towering man, dressed impeccably in an expensive suit, with a tall, half-filled stein of beer placed atop the bar in front of him. He was loud, cursing, and complaining, his remarks aimed at no one in particular. He was visibly agitated, directing his anger toward the inanimate objects around him rather than speaking to the patrons.

As I approached, I couldn't help but notice his hands, they were the size of baseball mitts. His broad shoulders, bulging biceps, and no-neck stance made him look even more imposing, easily standing over six feet tall. As I got closer, he suddenly turned, looked down at me, and growled, "What the 'f' do you want?" In that instant, the dispatcher's final words echoed in my mind: "Call if you need backup." This guy looked like he could pick me up with one hand and toss me around like a ragdoll. I took a deep breath and greeted him, "Hi, what's your name?" He replied, "Flash Gordon, why?"

I looked directly into his eyes and said, "Flash, you're being a bad boy!" Hi eyes widened and his lips pouted and then he responded, "What do you mean, bad? I'm not doing anything wrong! I'm just drinking a beer!" I explained that he was scaring people and pointed to the ladies at the table, telling him that his loud words were making them uncomfortable. Flash's expression softened with remorse. Looking down, he muttered, "I don't want to scare anybody." I explained to him, intentionally or not, that's exactly what he was doing.

Then I asked, "When was the last time you took your medicine?" A puzzled look crossed his face. "You know about that?" he asked. "Of course," I replied. "I'm the police, I know everything." Flash admitted he hadn't been to the mental health clinic in over a month and was out of his medication. I offered him a deal: I'd help him get to the clinic if he apologized to everyone in the bar, especially the ladies and the owner. Flash's face brightened, and he broke into a grin, revealing a perfect set of pearly white teeth. "You'd do that for me?" he asked. I nodded, "Yes, finish your beer, and we'll get out of here."

Flash looked around, apologized to everyone, gave a heartfelt apology to the two ladies, finished his beer with a hearty gulp, slammed the stein on the bar, draped his massive arm over my shoulder, and said, "OKAY!"

We were heading toward the entrance when the cavalry suddenly burst into the lounge. The owner had apparently called for backup. About ten officers, clubs and guns at the ready, stormed in, prepared for action. Strangely, I hadn't felt nervous until that moment. I quickly reassured them that everything was under control and asked the champions of crime to step outside and wait. The officers complied and exited the lounge. Flash and I followed.

Outside, the officers stood at the ready, with a patrol wagon parked by the entrance. One of the police officers opened the rear door of the patrol wagon, and with a wave and a playful bow, I said to Flash, "Sir, your chariot awaits you!" Without a second thought, Flash ran to the wagon, stepped up onto the foot rail, causing the vehicle to dip under his weight, and climbed inside. Just as the officer was closing the door, it swung back open! Flash leapt out, ran to where I was standing, grabbed my shoulders, planted a big kiss on my cheek, told me he loved me, and then cheerfully ran back into the wagon without another word. My fellow officers shook their heads, chuckling, and with playful sarcasm chimed in that they "loved" me too. Quite the bunch!

Epilogue

I later learned that Flash was 6'9", weighed 300 pounds, and had "prison muscles." A couple of weeks after that memorable encounter, just before our shift switched to the midnight watch, the desk sergeant called me into the station. When I arrived at the front desk, there was Flash, leaning casually on the front desk and chatting with the sergeant, dressed in yet another expensive suit. As I approached, he turned to me with a huge smile and extended his hand, which was overflowing with candy bars. He wanted me to take them as a token of his gratitude. He was feeling better. I don't eat candy, either, so I left the candy bars for the desk crew to enjoy.

Police officers have traditionally been dispatched to calls involving individuals experiencing mental health crises. The two most dangerous types of service calls for police officers to be assigned to are domestic violence and mental health crises, in that order. In my experience, both types of calls frequently involve drugs, whether alcohol, prescription, or illicit, which can intensify the underlying emotions of those consuming the drugs. Sherwin has been bitten, beaten, stabbed, and even shot at while responding to domestic violence and mental health calls. When officers are assigned to these situations, they have little idea of what to expect upon arrival. This is unlike calls for incidents like burglary, robbery, or shootings, where there is an inherent expectation of violence, allowing officers to mentally prepare. In contrast, domestic and mental health calls can vary widely, from minor family disputes to life-threatening acts of violence, suicide attempts, or a senior citizen needing support.

For example, Sherwin responded to a call from an elderly woman who reported to 911 that extraterrestrials were secretly watching and listening to her from her kitchen exhaust vent. When Sherwin arrived around 2 a.m., she greeted me at the door, visibly frightened. She explained her concern about "visitors from another planet" using her vent to spy on her. She had called the police many times, only to be told she should see a psychiatrist, which left her feeling frustrated and stigmatized. Taking her hand, Sherwin walked with her to the kitchen and aimed his flashlight at the vent. After a few seconds of Sherwin's light focusing on the vent, he informed the dowager that the intruders had been "evaporated". She smiled, thanked Sherwin, and gave him a hug. There were no more midnight calls from her after that. She didn't need intervention, she needed attention, respect, and a moment of reassurance.

Nonetheless, both types of calls carry the constant risk of sudden violence. Sherwin has responded to countless domestic and mental health situations and believes they often overlap, with domestic violence frequently involving mental health issues, creating a high risk of escalating violence. Unfortunately, these calls have become increasingly common for police officers. Sherwin argues that two major social factors contribute to this growing crisis: drug use and the lack of equitable access to mental health care.

Drugs

Across the nation, legislators have increasingly viewed the legalization of marijuana to bolster state finances, allowing regulated production and sale under state oversight. This shift has sparked debates and research, particularly concerning the dangers posed to adolescent mental health by recreational marijuana use, as opposed to its medicinal application. The new cannabis legislation has largely minimized concerns about the potential harm marijuana use can inflict on the brain, especially in adolescents. A primary issue is the significantly higher levels of tetrahydrocannabinol (THC) in state-licensed marijuana compared to the cannabis sold at illegal street markets. According to a post by Royal Queen Seeds (2024), "the potency of cannabis has increased exceptionally (over 300%) over the last 40–50 years." This dramatic increase raises concerns about cannabis's impact on mental health and its potential as a gateway to more potent drugs. Legalization has inadvertently promoted a perspective that downplays marijuana's potentially harmful effects on adolescent brain development.

Dhein (2020) cautions that "Cannabis use in adolescence, in particular, in the case of heavy users, is known to be related to impaired cognitive functioning, low educational attainment, and educational problems leading to socio-economic consequences" (p. 613). The regular use of cannabis among young people may interfere with normal brain development, potentially impacting their ability to lead successful lives. This, in turn, increases the risk of dysfunctional behavior and frequent encounters with law enforcement. Given these serious social concerns, one must ask: Is the legalization of cannabis jeopardizing the future success of adolescents?

According to Battistella et al. (2014), there are clear links between cannabis use and the deterioration of brain function. They state that "long-term cannabis use is associated with brain morphology alterations in regions linked to memory and executive and affective processing" (p. 2041). Battistella and colleagues argue that regular cannabis use causes significant changes to the brain's gray matter, thereby compromising high-level cognitive functions.

Figure 11. Marijuana's effects on the brain (Stringer, 2023)

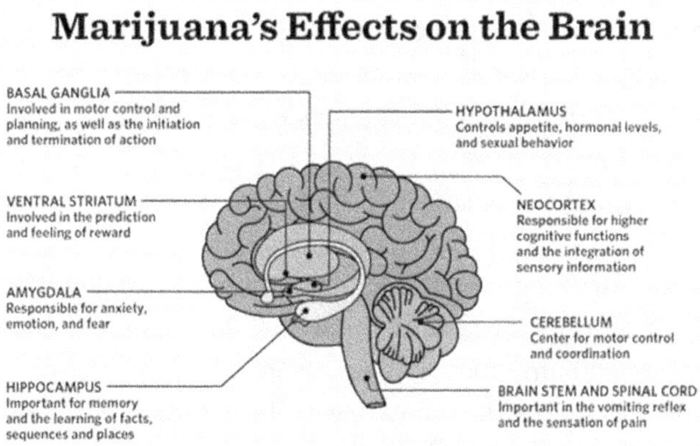

Burggren et al. (2019) highlight the effects of long-term cannabis use on the hippocampus, arguing that "changes in hippocampal structure due to heavy cannabis use, starting in adolescence, persist well into adulthood" (p. 4). They further contend that prolonged cannabis use "alters brain function…in networks that support working memory, attention, and cognitive control processing" (p. 6). Similarly, Georgieva, Benkova, Vlaeva, Karamalakova, Miteva, Abrashev, and Nikolova (2022) warn that the prolonged use of illicit drugs can lead to irreversible structural changes in the brain, which "can result in impulsive, antisocial, aggressive, and criminal behavior"

(p. 2). Heradstvelt, Skogen, Hetland, and Hysing (2017) add that "mental health problems are demonstrated as influential factors in relation to both adolescent alcohol and illicit drug use" (p. 2).

Dhein (2020) expresses concern over the growing number of adolescents aged 15 to 18 who use cannabis daily, noting that "early onset of cannabis use is associated with neuropsychological deficits" (p. 610), which may contribute to the rising number of patients with schizophrenia. Another worry is that adolescent cannabis use may impair natural development and maturation. Dhein (2020) cautions that "chronic cannabis use in adolescence may result in psycho-emotional deficits and may arrest the personality in a puberty-like state" (p. 614). Burggren, Shirazi, Ginder, and London (2019) warn that early cannabis use fosters an unhealthy dependence, which could "interfere with educational and vocational training, leading to long-term consequences in adulthood" (p. 4). This raises the question: why proceed with the legalization of cannabis when evidence challenges its medical safety, particularly for adolescent users?

While there are medicinal uses for cannabis, these are typically overseen by a physician. Here, we are discussing the future of society, our youth. Are we equipping them with the prudent and moral guidance needed to become successful adults, or are we setting them up for failure? Dhein (2020) argues that "early use of cannabis is associated with lower income and lower work commitment in early adulthood" (p. 613), which may compromise young adults' potential to become responsible, contributing members of society thus increasing their risk of engaging in criminal behavior and using other illicit drugs. Agrawal, Lynskey, Madden, Bucholz, and Heath (2019) further contend that cannabis use often serves as "a precursor to initiation of other illicit drug use" (p. 94). The progression to other drugs can exacerbate mental health issues, leading to increased interactions between citizens and law enforcement.

Butler, Zakimi, and Greer (2022) caution that "International illicit drug markets are expanding and becoming more dangerous in spite of global drug prohibitions" (p. 2). Researchers warn that the rising rate of illicit drug use is driving an increase in mental health calls for service, placing an even greater strain on law enforcement and healthcare facilities already facing overwhelming demand.

Illicit drug use has been linked to the alarming rise in suicide rates. Rossow and Lauritzen (1999) and Darke and Ross (2000) "found high rates of self-reported suicide attempts among problematic opioid users" (Degenhardt et al., 2024, p. 1124). People may take their own lives for a variety of reasons, including financial loss, domestic issues, job loss, homelessness, or the death of a loved one. However, there is a growing concern that illicit drug abuse significantly contributes to suicide deaths. Suicide remains a critical social and mental health issue, with rising numbers and decreasing access to services, often resulting in police involvement as a last resort.

Darke and Ross (1997) suggest that "many individuals suffer from psychiatric disorders linked to illicit drug use, with substances contributing to mental health issues such as depression and anxiety" (Degenhardt, Hall, Warner-Smith, and Lynskey, 2024, p. 1125). Agrawal et al. (2019) present critical evidence that illicit drug use correlates with an increased risk of "depression, anxiety disorders, anti-social personality disorders, and alcohol or nicotine dependence" (p. 95). Mellsop, Rapsell, and Holmes (2019) argue that factors associated with illicit drug use are contributing to the rise in schizophrenia and similar mental health conditions. They note that substances like "methamphetamine and stronger forms of cannabis" can cause "a psychotic disorder which mimics schizophrenia" (p. 1), with the potency of these drugs worsening mental health outcomes.

According to the Mayo Clinic (2024), "Schizophrenia is a serious mental health condition that affects how people think, feel, and behave. It may result in a mix of hallucinations, delusions, and disorganized thinking and behavior. Hallucinations involve seeing things or hearing voices that aren't observed by others. Delusions involve firm beliefs about things that are not true. People with schizophrenia can seem to lose touch with reality, which can make daily living very hard." The increasing prevalence of illicit drug use is driving a rise in mental health crises across society, posing serious challenges.

Illicit drug use also has a profound impact on crime rates. Robberies, burglaries, and thieves are commonly committed by drug addicts trying to finance their habit. However, I have investigated many heinous crimes where perpetrators have even killed family members to obtain money for drugs. This poses a danger for police officers, especially when encountering someone desperate for a drug like heroin. The most dangerous action an officer can take is to try to stop an addict in the process of injecting heroin. In that moment, they will do anything, even resort to violence, to complete their injection. It's often safer to allow them to "shoot up," wait for them to go into their "nod," and then take them to the hospital for medical care. Similarly, if someone is experiencing withdrawal symptoms, they should be taken to the hospital immediately.

Individuals under the influence of phencyclidine (PCP), methamphetamine, or cocaine can become aggressive and difficult to control. Illicit drugs can lead to "structural changes in the brain… resulting in impulsive, antisocial, aggressive, and criminal behavior" (Georgieva et al., 2022, p. 2). Committing a crime while under the influence of drugs puts citizens, police officers, and the person using drugs at great risk, as confusion and aggression often require officers to use force to apprehend them.

When someone is committing a crime, officers take the necessary action to arrest them. However, in cases where an individual is experiencing a mental health crisis, "the police are often the only resource available to intervene during these crisis incidents" (David, 2023, p. 135). The limitations on mental health intervention place officers in a challenging position, restricting their discretion due to the lack of accessible mental health services and the closure of state-run treatment facilities.

Social Equity

Research indicates that inequities in access to mental health care are a global issue with multiple contributing factors. One factor is that "unmet need for care is positively associated with socioeconomic marginalization" (Hyshka, Anderson, and Wild, 2017, p. 295). Another factor involves "motivational or attitudinal barriers" (Hyshka et al., 2017, p. 296), where individuals may lack the desire or motivation to seek proper care. When feeling unwell, many attempt to self-manage their issues without seeking medical attention or guidance. Additionally, there is a systemic barrier to cost and accessibility. Many individuals with mental health disorders lack the financial resources or access to appropriate care, leading them to self-medicate with illicit drugs or over-the-counter medications, which can be harmful and may worsen their symptoms.

Willis, Comartin, Victor, Kern, and Kubiak (2021) highlight a troubling reality of mental health crises, the delay in receiving treatment. A person who is experiencing a mental health episode receives the medical help they need usually only after a crisis has escalated. This delay is exacerbated by the lack of affordable "or accessible proper treatment" (p. 118), ultimately shifting the responsibility to law enforcement when they are called to respond. This situation supports the argument that early cannabis use among adolescents serves as a gateway to other illicit drugs, with cannabis inflicting lasting harm on the brain. Cannabis use impairs cognitive function, diminishes socialization skills, and leaves users struggling to build social capital, maintain employment, or access adequate healthcare.

Peterson et al. (2010) present the "Criminalization Hypothesis," which posits that individuals with mental illness often become ensnared in the legal system due to insufficient mental health resources in their communities (as cited by Willis et al., 2021, p. 118). Willis et al. (2021) argue that the scarcity of mental health facilities and services fosters conditions for criminal behavior. Individuals with untreated mental health issues are frequently arrested for perceived social norm violations rather than receiving proper care, leading to cycles of repeated arrests. "Repeated re-incarceration is sometimes inappropriately used for those in emotional crisis or even for those who were seemingly noncompliant with treatment" (p. 119).

Arresting individuals, exhibiting potential violence presents a challenge, as police discretion becomes constrained in these situations. Officers are often faced with the complex task of ensuring the safety and rights of all parties involved in a mental health crisis, an endeavor that demands careful judgment to determine the best solution. This task requires leadership, knowledge, and confidence. Leadership means taking appropriate charge of the situation, regardless of rank or position. Knowledge involves understanding how to judiciously apply laws, rules, and regulations to unique circumstances. Confidence entails making decisions without hesitation and being accountable for them.

For example, police officers were dispatched to a disturbance involving a son with a history of mental health issues that was reported by his mother. Upon arrival, the officers found the son shouting and threatening harm to family members. He was visibly enraged, and his mother explained that he had been undergoing mental health treatment but had stopped taking his prescribed medication. She expressed that she did not want him to return to jail, where he had previously been held due to similar events. After unsuccessfully attempting to take him to a healthcare facility herself, she called the police for assistance.

The officers tried to calm the son, encouraging him to accompany them to the hospital for treatment, but he refused, becoming even more agitated and attempted to harm his family members. The police officers on the scene called for backup. With the assistance of additional personnel, they took the son into custody after a physical struggle. Initially, he was taken to the police station, but Sherwin intervened, instructing the officers to instead bring him to the hospital for emergency care.

At the hospital, the son refused to sign treatment consent forms, creating a dilemma. The hospital did not want to admit him without consent. The watch commander was reluctant to assign an officer to guard him if he stayed, and did not want him held in the police lock-up. Sherwin instructed the officers to bring the mother to the hospital so she could authorize her son's treatment. Sherwin instructed the police officers to complete an incident report and file an arrest report. Upon completion of the reports, Sherwin requested the watch commander's approval to release the son without charges. This approach safeguarded everyone's rights, allowed the son to receive medical care, and relieved the family of immediate danger. However, this highlights an underlying issue; the critical need for reinstituting mental health facilities to better address such situations.

Another unfortunate outcome of police encounters with citizens experiencing mental health crises tied to illicit drug use is the lasting stigma. This stigma becomes a significant barrier to employment and reintegration with individuals often facing "employer discrimination…a criminal record, limited formal education or job skills, and chronic homelessness" (Richardson et al., 2015, p. 687). These obstacles largely prevent those affected from achieving social acceptance and stability. Furthermore, the stigma's polarizing effects deepen over time, leading to cycles of vulnerability and violence that become the norm in disorganized neighborhoods which ultimately result in repeated police-citizen encounters.

Deadly force lies at the heart of the defund police debate. Using deadly force is a profoundly traumatic experience for a police officer; causing serious injury or death is never part of an officer's professional goal. When police-citizen encounters lead to severe injury or loss of life, they undergo extensive investigation and oversight, often with the potential for the officer(s) to face criminal charges. Such incidents leave families and friends emotionally devastated, while many in society react to incomplete details of the event. Premature judgments can quickly escalate into anger, hatred, and even violence. We've all seen instances where a fact is reported without full context, where the fact of an event is given, but not the truth behind why it happened. Having experienced both sides of police-citizen encounters, Sherwin shares a story as an example to justify his perspective.

The Wayward Son (As told by Sherwin)

I was working the afternoon shift, 3 to 11 pm, as a field training officer on a cold winter night. The recruit I was training that night was experiencing his first day as a police officer working on the street. He graduated from the police academy the day prior. Although it had been a busy shift, it was mostly uneventful. We were nearing the end of our tour of duty when, around 11:10 p.m., I decided to head back to the police station for a check-off roll call. The check-off roll call ends the day of work. It is always a welcome part of the day regardless of the shift because it is the precursor for the time to head home and unwind. Everyone has their own way of decompressing, and each shift lends itself to different routines. Normally, I'd go to the gym, but after an afternoon shift, all I want is to relax. The thought of heading home, taking a shower, eating a sandwich, and sipping a cold beer always puts me in a good mood. But on this night, things went in a different direction from the anticipated peaceful conclusion.

There are two types of calls that make the hairs on the back of your neck stand up: a domestic disturbance and the infamous last-minute call right as you're about to wrap up your shift. That night, we hit the jackpot. Just as we were heading back, the dispatcher's voice came through: "On your way in, handle a domestic disturbance involving a teenage son." My stomach turned as I responded with a reluctant "10-4."

The assignment was literally on our route back to the police station, which, at that time, was just three blocks from the station. I reassured the new officer that this should be quick. When we rang the doorbell, a middle-aged woman opened the door while appearing upset. She introduced herself as the mother of a disobedient seventeen-year-old and invited us inside. As we stepped into the living room, I quickly assessed the room and the people in it. My senses were high alert to danger.

The mother introduced us to her mother, who sat quietly in an armchair, composed but observant. She pointed toward her son. He was a tall, slender young man who stood nearby, visibly agitated and vocalizing some choice vulgarities toward his mother. She explained her concern about her son's recent rebellious attitude and his resistance to her attempts to correct and discipline him. She informed us that her son dropped out of high school and started hanging around with some questionable characters living in the neighborhood. Emotions had come to a head that night, and she'd had enough. She wanted her son arrested. Grandma, though silent through the arguing, nodded in agreement and acknowledged that she was afraid of her grandson's constant angry outbursts and defiance.

As police officers, the last thing we want to do is to make an arrest that involves a family dispute, especially when children are involved. There were no signs of injury or immediate threats, either visible or reported. I suggested that the son cool off for the night, and after a few choice words, he stomped off to his upstairs bedroom. I advised the mother to call 9-11 again if the situation escalated. That suggestion angered her even more.

The mother was beside herself with anger, insisting that her son should be arrested. I tried to reason with the mother, but she wouldn't back down. All I wanted was to finish up and go home, but I reluctantly climbed the stairs, knocked on the son's closed bedroom door, and waited. The son didn't respond or open the door, which was honestly a relief. I went back downstairs and told the mother that the door was locked and that her son was probably sleeping. The mother shot me a look of absolute disdain, stormed up the stairs, kicked the bedroom door open, barged in, grabbed her son by the ear, and marched him down to the dining room, shouting at me, "Now, lock him up!" Her tone of voice and directness reminded me of my Marine Corps drill instructor. I didn't argue with her.

After the mother signed the complaint, I informed her son that he was under arrest. I turned him around and had him stand against the dining room wall to perform a search before cuffing him. However, I never got the chance. All hell broke loose.

With swift precision, the son turned from the wall, swinging his clasped hands toward me to strike me. I quickly ducked, narrowly avoiding the blow, and responded with a strike to his face. He staggered back, hitting his head against the dining room wall as blood spurted from his nose. But it didn't stop him. He continued his attack. My earlier suspicions were now confirmed: he was high on something. It's common for those on stimulants to feel no pain, and he certainly didn't. We stumbled into the living room, locked in a relentless struggle like two gladiators in combat.

Just as the clash felt endless, two gunshots suddenly echoed through the room, filling the air with the sharp scent of cordite. The son froze, took a step, then dropped to his knees, releasing a knife from his clenched hands; a razor-sharp boning knife that I hadn't seen. I thought we'd been boxing. My partner, the recruit, had fired the shots. This was a very emotionally traumatic experience, especially his first day on the job. I immediately called for an ambulance, and the son was taken to the county hospital.

The use of deadly force is one of the most emotionally fraught situations for any police officer, and this was no exception. An officer-involved shooting requires a thorough investigation. Every high-ranking supervisor in the police department arrives at the scene, while the crime lab meticulously processes evidence and detectives conduct their inquiries. Forensic procedures were extensive: the recruit's gun was sent to the lab, blood spatter and bullet trajectory analyses were performed, and the scene was documented with photos, sketches, and detailed notes. An Assistant State's Attorney (ASA) also arrived. He meticulously interviewed everyone present at the time of the shooting. Unfortunately, the ASA assigned to this case had a clear bias for police. He wanted me and the recruit to be guilty of unlawfully shooting the son. This is antithetical to his obligation to conduct a fair and impartial investigation. The mother, grandmother, recruit, and I were separated and placed in different rooms for interviews which is standard procedure for any investigation. However, I had a strong feeling that the ASA wanted to charge me with a crime as his interview with me felt more like an interrogation especially when the ASA read me my Miranda rights before we began.

Hours later, the ASA burst into my room and told me I was "a lucky man." I already knew that, but not in the way he meant. I was lucky to be alive, lucky that the son survived, and lucky the son hadn't managed to kill me. But that wasn't the ASA's point. He clarified that I was "lucky" because I wasn't going to jail. According to the ASA, the only reason I wasn't facing jail time was because, when he asked the mother and grandmother whether the officers had done anything wrong, they replied yes, "They didn't kill the little m@#f@#"! Domestics – people become enraged by the love they have for each other!!

Several months later, I found myself in court testifying during the trial of the son. It was a bench trial, and the son was ultimately found guilty. Before sentencing, the judge turned to me and asked if I had anything to say in aggravation or mitigation. Surprised by the opportunity, I replied that I did. Knowing the son had spent significant time in the hospital and in rehab recovering from his injuries, I expressed that he had suffered enough and suggested the court consider leniency. Both the judge and prosecutor agreed, and the judge granted him supervision. I hoped he would take this second chance and turn his life around. Police work is full of surprises. It never ceases to amaze.

Epilogue

On a warm beautiful summer afternoon, months after the trial, my partner and I were on foot patrol during rush hour, writing citations for vehicles parked at a bus stop, when I suddenly heard my name call. I turned quickly toward the voice and saw a young man standing by the curb. He asked, "You're Sherwin, right"? I hesitated, unsure of his intentions, but responded, "Yes." I didn't recognize him at first, but then he told me his name, and I was stunned, it was the son. For a moment, I didn't know whether to reach for my gun or brace myself. He realized my discomfort and confusion and started laughing, assuring me it was okay. He was okay.

He explained that he'd been looking for me to say thank you. He'd cut ties with the negative influences that had steered him off course, graduated high school, enrolled in junior college, and even found a job. He was helping his mother with household expenses. We hugged, and he cried. I couldn't let myself cry in front of him, so as I wiped my eyes, I blamed it on the bright sunlight. Sometimes, your hunches truly do pay off. Although one reporter attempted to skew the facts and obscure the truth, the incident ultimately only made a small news column. However, the emotional toll on the recruit was profound. Months later, he took his own life.

Police officers wield significant power over people's lives, with the lawful authority to arrest citizens, thereby restricting their freedoms, and to enforce certain prohibitions on their behavior. This authority is granted through a social covenant citizens uphold with the government "toward democratic forms" (Dewey, 1954, p. 146). However, this power must be exercised consciously, with respect, dignity, and without bias. Law enforcement must embody humanistic principles; because "every community has a right to demand of all its agents, an account of their conduct" (Paine, 1999, p. 67).

All police officers receive training in the use of force which is taught by using the Deadly Force Continuum paradigm. The lawful use of deadly force serves not only as a self-defense measure but also to protect citizens whose lives may be in imminent danger. Deadly force is considered a last-resort tool. It should only be utilized when all other measures have been taken and fail to stop or prevent serious or fatal bodily harm to another person or themselves. Thus, the use of deadly force must be consistent with the "totality of the circumstances" of a police-citizen encounter. The employment of deadly force requires tempered disciplined and rational cognitive choice. Police officers do not have an obligation to utilize deadly force, but they do have an obligation to lawfully utilize force that is necessary to protect lives. Police officers are trained in both physical and verbal defense tactics to de-escalate situations effectively. The de-escalation process begins with verbal commands, progressing to physical control methods, such as using hands, batons, or tasers. When none of these tactics succeed in controlling the situation, and a clear, immediate threat to someone's life persists, officers are lawfully authorized to use deadly force.

This authority, like the "21-foot rule," does not mean that officers "must" use deadly force but that they may choose to if they perceive it as the only viable option. The 21-foot rule suggests that a person armed with a weapon while charging toward a police officer could close about 21 feet before an officer could unholster and fire their weapon to stop the threat. Although often challenged as a rule utilitarianism in court, it's intended as a guideline for police officers rather than a strict requirement thus providing opportunity for police discretion. Sherwin testified as an expert witness in a court trial where the defense lawyer representing his client questioned him on the 21-foot rule. Sherwin explained to the jury that it serves as a guideline based on the totality of the circumstances, allowing officers the discretion to use deadly force, a maxim rather than a mandate.

Several factors complicate situations where the use of force may be necessary. One of these is emotion, both on the part of the individuals involved and the responding officers. Emotions can narrow decision-making perspectives, intensifying reactions on all sides. Drug use further exacerbates the issue, as the combination of substances and heightened emotions can intensify experiences, especially for individuals with mental health conditions. Too often, "confrontations between police and people with mental health conditions arise because of breakdowns in communication between the officers and the people they are supposed to help" (Shah, 2019, p. 208). Emotions make it challenging to evaluate a situation objectively, as people react differently when emotions are running high, triggering a fight-or-flight response.

A second significant factor is the concept of "saving face." Street terms like "dissed," "punked," or "man-up" reflect the pressure for a citizen, especially a gang member to maintain respect from their associates and or neighbors. Thus, the citizens will choose to be combative however they would rather not but feel they have no alternative because they don't want to lose face. This unfortunately places police officers in a precariously perilous situation that requires decisive action to stop a threat. These situations highlight the importance of de-escalation tactics, which will be discussed in a later chapter. Officers must be adept at "reading" a scene, paying attention to body language, verbal and non-verbal cues, the setting, and the time. Here's an example to illustrate this further.

The Pickaxe vs. the Knife (As told by Sherwin)

It was a beautiful summer day, and I was working solo on the day watch, 7am to 3pm. Around noon, with the radio traffic quiet, I decided to head to the station for a quick break. As I drove along the street approaching the police station, I spotted two men facing off in the middle of the street. One man was holding a pickaxe with both hands in a fighting stance. The other man, standing directly across from the first man, was holding a large knife and waving it back and forth in a menacing way. At first glance, the appearance of both men projected the probability of imminent threat to each other's life. They were standing directly in front of a construction company where they both worked. I recognized both men as laborers employed by the construction company. I also had a memory of both men being friends. Yet here they were, weapons in hand, locked in a standoff, each posturing with their weapon in a way that looked more theatrical than genuinely threatening.

The man with the pickaxe was short, shirtless, and muscular. His opponent, tall and slender, brandished a large knife, waving it back and forth in an intimidating but reluctant manner. Neither seemed eager to make the first move, as though neither truly wanted to harm the other. I stopped my squad car, opened the door to use as a shield, and discreetly held my gun at my side, out of view. Both men turned to look at me, and I addressed the man with the pickaxe, saying, "Now don't pick on him," with a bit of a smirk. He gave me an intense look, then shook his head, threw down the pickaxe, and walked off and headed for home.

I holstered my gun, approached the second man, who was now smiling, and instructed him to return the pickaxe to the office. He thanked me. I got back to my squad car and proceeded with my original plan of driving to the police station. A few days later, I saw both men interacting with each other in a friendly manner, laughing together like the friends they were. My simple comment had given both a chance to "save face."

The Use of Force Continuum

Figure 12. Use of force (https://nuqum.com)

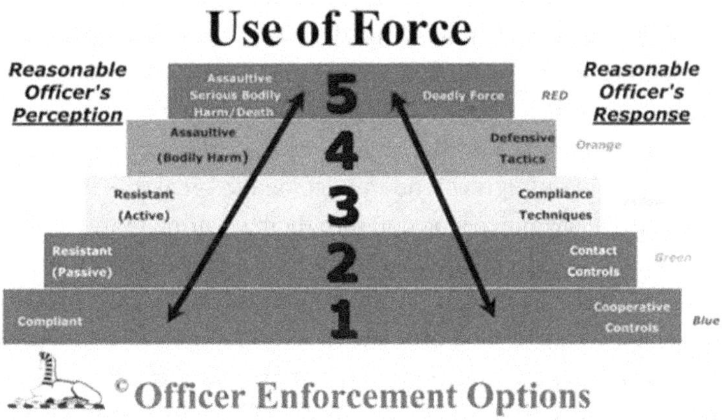

Police Officers Use of Force Chart

The Use of Force Continuum was first developed in 1970 at the Federal Law Enforcement Training Center (FLETC) to equip police officers with a structured system for objectively assessing options before, and up to, considering deadly force. This continuum provides officers with a series of measured steps to take before resorting to lethal action. The first and perhaps most crucial step is control, taking a moment to stop, look, and listen. This involves listening to what is said and unsaid. Is the person compliant? Using clear, calm voice commands based on an officer's visual and auditory observations of the scene and participants, such as the "pickaxe vs. knife" incident, is essential.

The way a police officer speaks to people is critical in determining how the situation will develop. Whether emotions will escalate or de-escalate often hinges on the tone and words the officer chooses. Shouting or using profanities to gain compliance is often counterproductive, as it may provoke rather than calm, reflecting a lack of confidence. How likely are people to respond, rather than react, to an officer using such language and tone? Here's an example to illustrate this point.

Two Brothers (As told by Sherwin)

While working day watch, I brought one of my gang members with me to the Ickes project buildings in Chicago. I had an informant who wanted to give me information about a murder suspect we were searching for. Just as we were entering one of the buildings, I heard a uniformed unit request backup from the dispatcher at a domestic disturbance call in one of the apartments in the building. I paused our mission and headed to the apartment where assistance was needed. Upon arrival, the apartment door was open, giving a clear view of the living room where several people were shouting at the two uniformed officers.

As I started to enter the apartment, a short, middle-aged man, visibly upset and in tears, walked toward me. I glanced at one of the uniformed officers, who signaled that I should let the man leave. Meanwhile, as the officers attempted to calm the situation, the shouting only grew louder. I decided to break the tension with a silly joke, which caused everyone to stop and turn their attention to me. This unexpected shift allowed the officers to regain control of the situation peacefully.

Just then, a member of the gang team came running to me, visibly distressed, to inform me that two uniformed officers on the floor above had their guns trained on two men in the hallway. I hurried up the stairs and arrived to find the officers pointing their pistols at two men standing in the hall. One was the same short man I had seen leaving the apartment below. He was crying, holding a small folding knife, and threatening to stab the man next to him. His target was a towering figure, about

6'4" and 400 pounds, shirtless and sweating profusely in the middle of January. They were brothers.

I quickly instructed the officers to holster their weapons and approached the men. Addressing the brother with the knife, I said, "Shame on you, give me that knife!" Without hesitation, he handed it over; the knife wasn't even sharp enough to cut butter. I scolded him for wanting to harm his brother. He apologized to his brother, to the officers, and to me. We arrested him and charged him with disorderly conduct.

I read the room. The short brother wasn't going to harm his sibling, nor did he truly intend to. Often, people who make loud threats are hoping the police will intervene, allowing them to save face without the situation escalating further. The big brother showed no signs of alarm and didn't adopt any defensive stance. I had little doubt that if he felt truly threatened, he could have easily handled the situation himself. In the end, everyone walked away satisfied. The next time I encountered the two brothers, they were back to normal, as though nothing had ever happened between them.

Siegel and Worrall (2018) offer a definition of deadly force and list of patterns of shootings involving deadly force,

> **Deadly Force:** The intentional use of a firearm or other instrument resulting in a high probability of death.
>
> Seven patterns related to police shootings:

1. Local and national violence levels.
2. Exposure to violence.
3. Workload.
4. Firearms availability.
5. Social conflict.
6. Administrative policies.
7. Race. (p. 269)

The use of deadly force has long been a point of contention within society and among police departments, raising questions about its lawful versus appropriate use. Just because the deadly force is legally sanctioned doesn't give officers free rein to apply it without clear justification. This is why rigorous investigations are undertaken to gather evidence that either confirms or challenges the lawfulness of its use. During Sherwin's career, he was involved in numerous investigations of officer-involved shootings, many of which included critical eyewitness accounts from citizens who questioned the actions of the police. Here is an example of what I mean.

The Hit Man (As told by Sherwin)

I was working on the second watch with my partner on a pleasant summer weekday. Around 1:30 p.m., the dispatcher assigned us to a call of shots fired by police officers in an alley. Upon arrival, we found four plainclothes tactical officers. One of the officers had been shot in the abdomen. I immediately called for paramedics. Questioning the officers, I learned that the wounded officer had been shot by a man driving a vehicle that was now situated midway in the alley. The driver of the vehicle remained seated in the driver's seat of the vehicle. Upon approaching the vehicle, I found an unresponsive man in his twenties slumped in the seat bleeding profusely. I made a second call for paramedics to assist. I saw the interior of the vehicle and noticed a 44-caliber magnum revolver resting on the dashboard.

By this time, a crowd of citizens had gathered, shouting profanities, throwing objects, and accusing the officers of assassinating the man in the vehicle. The officers explained that they had the double tee alley stacked out. They positioned themselves at the south end of the alley where they had a clear and unobstructed view of the rear of the apartment building where the suspect's girlfriend lived. The officers were waiting for this individual, a known "hit man" with a pattern of staying at his girlfriend's apartment. An informant had tipped the officers off, saying the man typically left the apartment around 1:30 p.m. and entered his car parked in a lot behind the building.

The officers observed the man leave the apartment, enter his vehicle, and drive into the alley toward them. As the vehicle approached, one of the officers, the one who was subsequently wounded, walked toward the vehicle while his team held their positions. At that moment, the driver shot the approaching officer and began to reverse the direction of his vehicle. Despite his injury, the officer ran toward the vehicle, returning the fire and ultimately hitting the driver. The vehicle stopped moving. The other officers refrained from shooting, worried about hitting their partner. After arriving at the hospital where the wounded officer was taken, I learned that the officer's Kevlar vest prevented entry of the bullet. However, the officer sustained a massive bruise and indentation of his abdomen which required a few days of hospitalization.

Though the citizens insisted that the wounded officer had fired first, forensic evidence of bullet holes in the windshield confirmed that the driver had indeed shot first, justifying the officer's use of deadly force.

A psychological term often used to describe police officers' reactions during shooting incidents is known as *excited delirium*, defined as "an overdose of adrenaline that can occur in heated confrontations with the police" (Siegel and Worrall, 2018, p. 275). Sherwin has observed this phenomenon in many shooting investigations he was involved with, such as in the Hit-Man incident, where the wounded officer couldn't recall the number of shots fired, even though he had reloaded once and fired a total of eleven rounds. This response is common, countering the Hollywood myth that officers instinctively count their shots or aim to wound. Officers are trained to shoot at the largest area of the body, known as center mass, to effectively neutralize a threat. In the heat of a real confrontation, adrenaline and excitement make it impossible to keep a steady hand or focus on counting shots or precise sight alignment; the priority is stopping the threat.

In 1985, the Supreme Court ruled in *Tennessee v. Garner*, outlawing "the indiscriminate use of deadly force." The Court determined that using deadly force against an apparently unarmed and non-dangerous fleeing felon constitutes an illegal seizure under the Fourth Amendment (Siegel and Worrall, 2018, p. 275). However, when deadly force is used, *Graham v. Connor* set a multifactor reasonableness standard, requiring that the "totality of the circumstances" be considered in determining when force is justified (McLean, Atikhan, and Alpert, 2023, p. 86). These case laws serve as guidelines in officer-involved shootings, but no one can predict their precise response in the real moment. Each day, each person, and each situation have unique variables that influence the outcome.

Emotions, work, domestic issues, and financial stress can affect everyone's mental clarity, including police officers who uniquely face the possibility of life-or-death decisions daily. Unlike most people, police officers take an oath to lawfully respond and mitigate deadly threats. People who weren't present at an incident often share opinions on how they believe it should or could have been handled. However, police officers frequently must act instinctively, relying on training and experience, with little time for deliberation. Yet even those of us who have professionally handled or investigated such incidents can sometimes watch a video, such as the footage of the George Floyd incident, and feel a sense of discomfort and disbelief at what unfolds before us.

This brings me to the case of George Floyd, which became a catalyst for calls to defund the police. To understand the Floyd incident fully, let's consider it through a different lens. According to Baker (2020), Floyd's cause of death was "cardiopulmonary arrest complicating law enforcement subdual, restraint, and neck compression." In my view, the handling of the Floyd incident was flawed from the moment police arrived. There were several actions taken, and others omitted, that should have been addressed differently. Even though not present, Sherwin's understanding is based on what he read and seen in various videos; however, with experience investigating police-citizen encounters resulting in serious injury or death, Sherwin offers a reasonable perspective on reconstructing such scenes with accuracy. Several key issues stand out that merit close examination.

George Floyd (Overview expressed by Sherwin)

The first issue concerns the counterfeit $20 bill Floyd allegedly used at a convenient store. Officers are within their lawful authority to inventory the suspected counterfeit bill, document the incident, question Floyd, and even detain him for the Secret Service. Here's how I have handled similar complaints in the past. I took control of the alleged counterfeit bill, wrote a report, and provided the reporting party with a Victim Information Notice (VIN). I took the person of interest to the police station, where I inventoried the suspect counterfeit bill, checked the person of interest for outstanding warrants, and notified the Secret Service. The secret service representative that I spoke with subsequently thanked me for the information. They had no intention of interviewing or arresting the person at that time. If the individual had no warrants and hadn't committed any other crime at the scene, they would be released without charges. The Secret Service is the agency authorized to arrest and charge individuals for counterfeiting.

The second issue concerns Floyd's demeanor. While it's understandable that the police officers at the scene wanted to question Floyd about the $20 bill, upon approaching him, they should have recognized signs of a drug-induced mental health episode. Instead of drawing their weapons, effective communication could have been a benefit to everyone involved. Remember *Flash Gordon*. Demonstrating empathy and reassuring Floyd of their intent to help might have encouraged him to calm down and cooperate. Letting him know they would get him the care he needed by taking him to a hospital could have been more effective than making demands or arguing. Think back to the incident with the brothers. An immediate call for paramedics to transport Floyd to the hospital would likely have been the more prudent choice. The interview could have taken place later.

The third issue that stands out is why Floyd was removed from the back seat of the patrol vehicle. Why not simply drive him to the hospital once he was secured in the back seat? Although Floyd was complaining, some empathy and human-centered communication skills might have helped defuse the situation. With Floyd already in the vehicle, officers had the option to transport him to the hospital quickly. Admittedly, transporting someone experiencing a drug-induced mental health episode isn't always ideal, but given the circumstances, they had him in custody and ready to go. Would it have taken longer than the nine minutes ultimately spent? I have also transported individuals with gunshot wounds, knife injuries, and drug-induced crises when paramedics or patrol wagons weren't available, prioritizing immediate hospital care above all else.

The fourth issue is the kneeling restraint. Chauvin, as an assistant and apparently senior officer on the scene, used a restraint technique authorized and taught by the Minneapolis Police Department. However, while this may explain the method's initial use, it does not justify its prolonged application under the totality of the circumstances. The extended duration of Chauvin's kneeling on Floyd has led to extensive speculation as to why he chose to maintain the position for so long. One can only wonder if Chauvin himself fully understands his decision and has since reflected on it many times.

The fifth and final issue is leadership. Numerous leadership questions arise from this incident. First, where were the supervisors? Were any notified or called by the officers on scene? If Chauvin was indeed the senior officer present, why did he choose to kneel on Floyd rather than manage the overall scene, ensuring it was secure, reassuring the public that Floyd was receiving proper medical care, and that paramedics were in route? It appeared there was no clear crime scene management or investigational oversight. The image of Floyd lying on the street, forcefully restrained by Chauvin's knee, is profoundly disturbing for anyone to observe. I've handled many scenes where clear communication with bystanders and demonstrating care for the person in custody has eased tension and concern.

This also brings me back to the moment Floyd was in the back of a police vehicle. Keeping him there and "getting out of Dodge" as quickly as possible would have minimized the risk of escalation. Lingering only intensified the situation, doing little to benefit Floyd, the police department, other police officers, or Chauvin. Another leadership issue lies with the other officers on scene. They took no proactive role in de-escalation: they could have either removed Floyd, asked Chauvin to move his knee, placed Floyd in a safer position, managed the crowd with effective communication, or called for a supervisor. Or all the above.

I recognize that my perspective here is subjective but having been on similar scenes as both a patrol officer and supervisor. I believe that strong leadership doesn't always require a supervisor, it requires proactive decision-making. Police officers, in high-stress situations like Floyd's, often need someone to step up and direct them. Police officers want to help, but sometimes they need guidance on how best to do so. As I stated above, my perspective is subjective; I was not there. Nonetheless, we all need to be held accountable for our actions but without being judged unfairly. Sometimes quick judgments can have harmful outcomes, especially if the judgment is clouded by emotions or social pressures.

"In many real-world situations, the determination of whether force is reasonable relies not on the subject's level of resistance, but on the immediacy or imminence of the threat posed by a subject" (McLean, Alikhan, and Alpert, 2023, p. 87). From the videos I reviewed and the articles I read, Floyd did not appear combative; he seemed more disoriented, another clear indicator of potential drug use that the officers should have recognized and responded to with an alternative approach. Yelling at someone experiencing a drug-induced episode is not an effective de-escalation tactic. The issues I've highlighted reflect not

only my observations but those of much of society, including police officers and other law enforcement professionals. This discrepancy between effective police practices and public confidence creates a void, one that was quickly filled by criticism from groups like Black Lives Matter (BLM), which, in response, have called for police abolition or, at minimum, defunding.

The demand to abolish or defund the police has galvanized the BLM movement to insist on being heard and supported. Protests across the nation have at times given way to radical expressions of anger, property destruction, and animosity toward the police. This movement has a polarizing effect on society, with some countering, "don't all lives matter?" However, this rebuttal misses the point. BLM focuses on the disparities in police interactions with Black citizens, raising critical questions about social justice. The movement argues that Black Americans face a higher risk of injury or death during encounters with police, solely due to their race. McLean et al. (2023) contend that while an officer's race "does not affect the uses of force" (p. 88), the "police cultural values" (p. 88) within certain departments do play a role in force application. Fryer (2017) similarly found that "Blacks and Hispanics are more than fifty percent more likely to have an interaction with police involving any use of force" (p. 4), although his study "found no evidence of racial discrimination in officer-involved shootings" (p. 5). This raises further questions about the root causes behind BLM's critique of policing practices and its calls to abolish or defund the police.

BLM Movement

Black Lives Matter "was born in the wake of widespread incidents of police brutality" and stands as "a movement that is... inclusive and democratic" (Peniel, 2017, p. 18). The turning point came with the killing of Trayvon Martin, which sparked national outrage (Hall, 2018, p. 13). However, the movement formally began following the death of Eric Garner (Hall, 2018). Watters (2017) notes that the Women's March and Black Lives Matter share parallel values and concerns, as both "were founded by women who felt angry, disillusioned, and helpless against a system that does not equally enforce the political, social, and economic rights of its members" (p. 202). Watters (2017) advocates for a union between the Women's March and Black Lives Matter to "amplify" their causes, especially around issues of "State violence... such as the disproportionate impact of police brutality on Black and Brown communities" (p. 203). According to Watters (2017), "Black people are three times more likely to be killed by police than White people" (p. 204).

Watters (2017) highlights a striking disparity in police conduct toward protesters of the Women's March compared to those of Black Lives Matter. During the Women's March, police officers were lighthearted, "willing to take selfies and march alongside... [the protesters]" (p. 205). In contrast, Black Lives Matter protesters "have been met with SWAT teams in riot gear armed with tear gas and rubber bullets" (p. 205). Dewey (1927) argues for the democratic rights individuals hold, including the fundamental right to protest, which allows individuals and groups to scrutinize facts, particularly those related to police power and physical force in police-citizen interactions. Dewey emphasizes the importance of distinguishing "between facts which condition human activity and facts which are conditioned by human activity" (p. 7) and warns that "established power has a way of legitimizing itself" (p. 80).

Thus, any protest challenging police authority risks retaliation unless thoroughly grounded in facts. Dewey also contends that the legitimacy of movements like Black Lives Matter and the Women's March is rooted in liberty and shared equality, achieved through a "community of associated action" (p. 150). The collaboration of Black Lives Matter and the Women's March symbolizes this collective effort, embodying Dewey's assertion that "associated or joint activity is a condition of the creation of a community" (p. 151). This is the essence of democracy, a system that police officers are sworn to uphold, not oppose. Regardless of jurisdiction, every police officer takes an oath to uphold the United States Constitution, impartially ensuring that each citizen's First Amendment rights to free speech and assembly are protected.

The Black Lives Matter (BLM) movement has gained international recognition for its stance against systemic racism, particularly its impact on Black communities and their relations with police. This global awakening to issues of racial and justice inequalities has galvanized people worldwide, often polarizing political landscapes. Polarization fuels fear, anger, and loyalty to specific ideologies, creating stark boundaries that leave little room for open discussion. Many countries outside the United States, such as France, have aligned with BLM in their support for minority rights and the fight against discrimination and prejudice, as noted by Lankester and Alexopoulos (2023, p. 2). However, some question the movement's foundational principles. Issar (2020) contends that BLM's ideology is rooted in Marxism, invoking the notion of "racial capitalism" (p. 2). While arguing against racial equality and systematic reform is counterproductive, genuine progress requires commitment to active listening thus internalizing the needs of others to foster sustainable solutions.

The concern over Marxist ideology, perceived as antithetical to democratic values, is echoed by Newman (2020), who highlights the BLM founders' statement, "We are trained Marxists" (p. 2), a claim that has deepened political divides and generated apprehension about the movement's broader intentions. Sowell (2023) critiques the notion of social justice, describing it as an "idiom" and arguing that in reality, "there is seldom anything resembling the equal outcomes that might be expected if all factors affecting outcomes were the same for everyone" (p. 1). Despite these critiques, BLM has brought longstanding issues of injustice in the Black community to the forefront with the George Floyd incident serving as a catalyst for exposing unhealed societal wounds. Freire (1970) cautions the oppressed: "In order for this struggle to have meaning, the oppressed must not, in seeking to regain their humanity… become in turn oppressors of the oppressors, but rather restorers of the humanity of both" (p. 44).

Whether the Minneapolis police officers' actions toward Floyd were a product of systemic racism or police culture was not substantiated in the investigation or trial. Nonetheless, the incident was profoundly painful to witness, searing into the minds and hearts of a nation, evoking deep and old wounds that continue to need healing.

Defund or Not Defund

The call to defund or abolish the police has deepened divisions, creating distinct groups with opposing views. Jackson, Fine, Bradford, and Trinkner (2023) draw on social identity theory to explain how individuals align with groups that reflect their values, shaping their perspectives on life, justice, and morality. Jackson et al. (2023) also references Blader and Tyler's (2009) "group engagement model," which posits that "people in hierarchical group settings…[embrace]…procedural…[and]… distributive justice" (p. 834). Procedural justice emphasizes treating people fairly, focusing particularly on the behavior of authority figures like the police. Distributive justice, meanwhile, emphasizes the fair allocation of community resources across all groups.

Thus, those who advocate defunding the police, such as BLM supporters, and those who oppose defunding share a similar group engagement model but apply it differently. The defund group perceives the police as untrustworthy and believes systemic or cultural racism undermines their effectiveness within Black communities. Conversely, those who oppose defunding the police argue for equitable treatment and view police actions as not racially motivated. While both groups unwittingly agree on the need for police reform, their approaches to achieving it vary significantly. Regardless of one's position, assessing the impact of defunding or supporting the police requires a careful, fact-based examination.

Glauser (2020) highlights some reasons doctors advocate for defunding the police. Doctors argue that reallocating part of police budgets toward social service organizations would better serve public health. They feel that police are not ideally suited to respond to individuals during a mental health crisis, noting that "people in crisis have better outcomes interacting with non-police response teams" (p. 1). Furthermore, doctors believe that "funding for education, health care, and other social services goes further than policing to prevent crime" (Glauser, 2020, p. 1). This stance reflects a group identity focused on preventive care and social support. However, it raises a critical question: will social workers be available and equipped to handle situations "at three o'clock in the morning when somebody's wielding a knife, and they're suffering from a mental health crisis" (Glauser, 2020, p. 1)?

Doctors underscore an important point: the need for expanded mental health care services, especially for low-income and disadvantaged communities. Their argument also underscores the importance of Crisis Intervention Team (CIT) training for police officers, a topic to be discussed in a later chapter.

Dorgan (2024) presents a contrasting view, emphasizing the drawbacks of defunding police within communities. Dorgan argues that "the $4 million cut from the St. Louis police budget, reallocated to hire social workers and support affordable housing initiatives, has led to low morale among officers, a decrease in murder case resolutions, and a rapid erosion of community support and trust" (p. 3). Alongside this, diversion programs, the release of arrestees without bond, delays in bringing arrestees to trial, and increased police accountability measures have, Dorgan contends, compromised public safety, reduced police personnel, and emboldened criminal activity. Protecting the rights of those arrested over the welfare of crime victims and the community, he argues, undermines true justice and police reform. There remains a vital need for a police presence within communities; law-abiding citizens often prefer the presence of police over that of street gangs, drug dealers, and other criminal elements (Dorgan, 2024).

Henderson and Yisrael (2021) offer seven myths about defunding the police highlighted in the defund the police (DTP) movement.

> **Myth #1: Defund means abolishment.** The Defund the Police (DTP) movement "aims to demilitarize police departments and reallocate funding to trained mental health professionals and social workers" (p. 1) to help reduce violent encounters between police and citizens during mental health interventions.
> **Myth #2: Defunding will lead to disorder.** "The best tools to establish peaceful societies are equity in education and infrastructure" (p. 2).
> **Myth #3: Police protect the public from violence.** The argument for having more "heavily funded and armed police" (p. 2) to serve and protect is antithetical to the reduction in crime.
> **Myth #4: Community programs won't work.** "Investing, developing, and supporting education and economic programs do, in fact, lead to less offenses and create more social harmony" (p. 2).
> **Myth #5: Most police work is focused on crime prevention.** "There is minimal evidence that police surveillance results in reduced crime" (p. 2).
> **Myth #6: Police officers do not need college degrees.** "Police officers that have at least two years of a college education are less likely to have misconduct complaints" (p. 3).

Myth #7: Defunding the police is a knee-jerk reaction with no research. "60 years of data indicates that increases in spending do not reduce crime". (p.3). Money is a needed asset but not the solution.

Special attention has been given to the debate around defunding the police, a multifaceted issue with diverse perspectives. To move forward productively, it's essential to approach these perspectives with openness and objectivity. As noted, defunding or not defunding the police is not a new debate; it's a longstanding issue that has evolved over many years. Yet, people are often shy away from addressing the root causes that drive the need for reform. Simply increasing funding is not enough. It can lead to further frustration and erosion of trust, hindering social healing.

This chapter has highlighted key issues in police-citizen encounters that have sometimes ended in violence or death. Two critical factors in these tragic outcomes are substance abuse and mental health crises. These issues deeply impact the dynamics of police-citizen interactions, as drug-induced mental health episodes often trigger aggressive or destructive behaviors. When individuals experience such crises, often endangering others, it's the police who are called to intervene, not a doctor, social worker, or psychologist. Police officers are summoned to a scene because of a 911 call to manage these volatile situations. Unfortunately, access to mental health and substance abuse treatment has declined, and those facing these issues frequently lack financial and social resources to address their struggles. As a result, they turn to the one resource that is certain to respond, a police officer.

One critical issue that remains unaddressed is social capital. There is substantial evidence that drug use has impaired cognition in adolescents, increasing the likelihood of mental health challenges. Illicit drug use disrupts natural development, affecting individuals' ability to navigate life successfully and make principled decisions. However, it is the lack of social capital that often drives behaviors that conflict with societal norms. While police officers cannot resolve these issues, they need the tools to approach them with justice, fairness, and equity, as these challenges are unlikely to disappear. Legalized marijuana has generated billions in state revenue, which the states are unlikely to forgo. Still, a portion of these profits should be allocated to strengthen community infrastructure, enhance mental health services, and support police reform (not defunding). Many elites and politicians have private security resources; everyday citizens do not. Citizens, the taxpayers, rely on the police for protection.

To build trust and respect between police officers and the communities they serve, we must find common ground. Police officers deserve recognition for the risks they take daily, as they step into dangerous situations each time they wear the uniform. At the same time, citizens deserve respect and acknowledgment of their dignity. Police departments need to self-reflect: are they contributing to the problem, or can they lead to developing 21st-century solutions that align with today's social values and needs? However, police departments cannot do this alone; they need the support of politicians, community leaders, doctors, and judiciary. Together, these groups can foster trust by designing effective solutions for improving police-community relationships.

Calls to defund or abolish the police stem from frustration and a sense of giving up on societal issues. Defunding is a symbolic act that reflects a lack of confidence in addressing the impacts of illicit drugs and mental health challenges. But we are better than that. We must set aside emotions, pride, and resentments, and come together as a community to develop sustainable, cooperative solutions.

SECTION-3: A RENEWED MISSION: STRENGTHENING TRUST AND PUBLIC CONFIDENCE IN THE WAKE OF SOCIAL UPHEAVAL

Social justice cannot be attained by violence. Violence kills what it intends to create. Pope John Paul II

During the height of the COVID-19 pandemic, society witnessed the 2020 "Summer of Love" through various media channels, capturing scenes of riots, looting, arson, shootings, and fatalities. Griffin (2021) reports that the Major City Chiefs Association (MCCA) recorded "8,700 protest events" and "3,692… unlawful acts of civil disobedience" (p. 2). During this period, "more than 2,035 law enforcement officers were injured" (p. 3). People were largely confined to their homes as a precaution against COVID-19, and media platforms became the main link to the outside world, offering news and entertainment to relieve the anxiety of isolation. Amid this confinement, many turned to media for stimulation and social connection, becoming increasingly dependent on it for interaction and information. Social media and news networks, however, often delivered visuals and narratives that portrayed overwhelming violence without providing context or deeper understanding. They deliberately provoked audiences with images with an obfuscated narrative that belied the truth behind them.

The Department of Homeland Security (DHS) later debunked several myths that circulated widely at the time. For example, contrary to narratives that "the Trump administration deployed federal troops… protests in Portland were peaceful until DHS expanded its presence," or that "DHS is infringing upon the rights of peaceful protesters… federal forces are invading multiple US cities including Portland and Chicago," DHS clarified these were misleading claims (Department of Homeland Security, 2021). Despite their inaccuracy, these myths were broadcast by what society regarded as reputable media sources, contributing to a climate of confusion and heightened tension during an already challenging time.

Fear, anger, and hate spread through society like a cancer, distorting how people viewed one another, particularly police officers. The shift from trust and respect for the police to widespread fear and resentment was swift, driven largely by media portrayals. Media platforms are intensely focused on police responses to various incidents, often portraying police officers as aggressors rather than providing the true context about the incident. For instance, in Chicago, when officers were assigned to protect a monument, they endured attacks with projectiles, resulting in serious injuries. Yet, much like the response to other incidents during the "Summer of Love," investigations ultimately faulted law enforcement agencies. The Chicago Inspector General criticized "the city and police department's leadership for a confused and uncoordinated response to the protests and riots that endangered the protesters and the police" (Griffin, 2021, p. 4).

This selective reporting allowed media outlets to shape a narrative that depicted police as aggressors rather than as victims responding to orchestrated attacks. The injuries sustained by officers were largely overlooked, with the storyline focusing on alleged police provocations instead. Organized groups brought objects to use as missiles against officers, arriving well-prepared with protective equipment, while Chicago police officers were limited to standard uniforms and denied adequate protection.

Griffin (2021) reports that "more than three quarters of agencies (78%) identified individuals with far-left ideologies, and over half (51%) noted individuals aligning with violent far-right ideologies" (p. 3). A video showing an organized group in Chicago changing into protective gear and retrieving projectiles before launching an assault on police officers wasn't released to the public until later. Police officers faced attacks involving "fireworks, impact weapons, and lasers aimed at their eyes" (Griffin, 2021, p. 3). Protesters employed a variety of dangerous devices, including "incendiary devices, firebombs, and firearms" (Griffin, 2021, p. 3). In some cases, police officers had to abandon police stations as they were prohibited from defending themselves or their buildings, leading to destruction, looting, and arson. Federal law enforcement officers faced similar perils while defending federal buildings. However, the media's narrative inaccurately suggested that federal troops had been deployed, fueling further public anger and distrust toward law enforcement despite this information later being debunked.

The damage to law enforcement's public image was substantial, fostering greater resentment and intensifying calls for defunding the police. Instead of empathy, appreciation, and support, police officers were criticized by media. Political leaders abstained from supporting police officers and ensuring their safety during the extremely volatile conditions.

Police officers in riot gear were depicted using tear gas, detaining individuals, and employing defensive measures against protesters, many of whom were dressed in black clothing with black head, facial coverings, and wore black backpacks. However, media coverage and video narratives largely focused on the police response itself, neglecting the reasons behind or context of these responses. While we were told the protests were peaceful, background footage in these same videos revealed scenes of fires, looting, destruction, and chaos unfolding simultaneously.

Phillips (2016) observes that violence in American history has often served as the foundation "through which...democratic values are defended and enforced" (p. 185). This theme is frequently reinforced in visual media of police officers who are depicted as rugged, streetwise figures with a tough, unyielding demeanor. This visual interpretation is intended to provoke fear. The symbolic power of the uniform, combining self-perception and the projected image of authority, shapes attitude and behavior. Reflecting on the Rockwell images discussed earlier, we see in the second, modern rendition a stark transformation: the police officer is wearing camouflaged military gear, armored vest, helmet, and a rifle slung over his shoulder, peering intensely at the youth. This visual effect amplifies a deliberate attempt to instill fear while compromising trust. Kisielius and Roedder (1983) argue that imagery stimulates cognitive reasoning that connects attitudes to behaviors. By juxtaposing Rockwell's two images, we see Zimbardo's (2007) theory come to life: how a uniformed role shapes one's identity and actions. This contrast illuminates two key elements, body language and perception, and the powerful impact of imagery on public attitudes and behavior.

Body Language

Body language conveys an image of an internalized role, consciously or subconsciously shaped through visual expression. This image is then interpreted by both the individual and the audience as a true reflection of the self. Zimbardo (2007) argues that merely putting on a police uniform can make a person feel more empowered and authoritative. For an observer, however, a police uniform, especially one as depicted in the second Rockwell rendition, can evoke a sense of threat, instilling a perception of negative, potentially harmful behavior. Such an image undermines trust and hope. For example, when a police officer, wearing mirrored sunglasses, approaches a driver during a traffic stop, it can create a critical and oppressive impression. The driver, already apprehensive, may experience heightened anxiety and distrust from the visual effect of the sunglasses which can cloud their perception of the police officer. This apprehension is detrimental to positive police-citizen interactions, emphasizing the need for officers to be mindful of their body language. On the other hand, police officers must also remain vigilant in interpreting the body language of those they interact with as a necessary measure for their own safety. Sadly, this reflects today's complex social dynamics surrounding law enforcement.

Community Perception

Television, movies, books, magazines, and news media often portray police work through a sensationalized and misleading lens that is synchronized with a skewed story line. These portrayals frequently feature "Dirty Harry" methods that are far removed from reality, leading citizens to perceive Hollywood fiction as fact and thus fostering a misleading view of police officers. Schuck and Martin (2013) note that "the reason for a given police-citizen encounter influences the resident's assessment of the quality of his or her experience" (p. 222). Communities that rely on such skewed informational sources often lack a true understanding of the various social and judicial obligations that police officers must uphold to perform their duties fairly and impartially (Barthe, Leone, & Lateano, 2013).

There is an ongoing concern about social justice in police-citizen interactions, with police officers often portrayed as uncaring, trigger-happy, and racially biased. "Race and socioeconomic status contribute disproportionately to a minority person's perception of the police" (Nordberg, Crawford, Praetorius, & Smith-Hatcher, 2016, p. 138). Many social action groups, fueled by frustration of the criminal justice system, especially their perspective of police officers, have taken to the streets in protests, some of which turned violent, as seen in the summer of 2020. In some protests, individuals, under the guise of justified rebellion, have committed acts of violence against police officers. Unfortunately, this has been with deadly consequences. In response to confrontational behaviors, police officers employ force-based tactics to counter the threats against them. The protests and the response to them create a conundrum to a social enigma of what and who is right or wrong. Citizens call for transparency and reform, politicians pledge to address these demands, and police department leaders advocate for more resources to safely manage citizen threats and reduce violent encounters.

News media outlets and other media platforms deliberately attempt to influence citizen perceptions of police officers by editing out exculpatory information and tailoring coverage to fit partisan narratives. Citizens, while absorbing information from multiple media sources and subjective accounts of police-citizen interactions, subconsciously internalize these perspectives, which can skew their understanding of the full context of an incident. This internalization influences whether they respond positively or negatively to the coverage. For instance, the widely broadcast image of an officer kneeling on George Floyd with apparent indifference projects a form of body language that invites varying interpretations. These interpretations are easily manipulated by suggestively tailored partisan narratives to influence a viewer to experience a negative perspective of what they see.

A complex social dilemma, however, remains largely unaddressed. While most agree that questionable use of force in police-citizen encounters is unacceptable, little attention has been directed toward underlying causes of these interactions. Some of these factors stem from the internal culture within police departments, while others, rarely discussed openly, are rooted in broader social failures and the shifting of political responsibilities to the police. Police departments operate under the executive branch of government, following its directives and enforcing laws established by the legislative branch. The legislative branch enacts laws to which citizens agree, either explicitly or tacitly, as part of the "Social Contract." Through elections, citizens entrust politicians with the duty to safeguard their Constitutional rights and promote social stability, education, and opportunities for personal success. When these societal foundations falter, it is not a failure of the police but a lapse in the responsibilities of elected officials and community leaders. Transforming disorganized neighborhoods into thriving communities requires collective commitment from political and community leaders, rather than from police departments alone.

The social contract implicitly promotes civic virtue by fostering a commitment to lawful "abidingness." Yankah (2013) draws on an Aristotelian view of civic virtue to argue that "the most basic civic virtue…is law abidingness" (p. 63). Law abidingness signifies a citizen's willingness to follow laws that are inherently just. For laws to earn citizens' respect and adherence, however, they must first be "worthy of respect, both in nurturing human development and cultivating a flourishing society… [otherwise]…the failure of law to respond appropriately to its own declared values instills contempt for law and threatens the rule of law" (Yankah, 2013, p. 64). Yankah emphasizes that law abidingness is crucial for maintaining community quality of life, including safety, mutual trust, and impartial law enforcement. The purpose of civic virtue, according to Aristotle, is to build a flourishing society where "the education of the young is essential…[and]…civic education…[is]…the business of the state" (Yankah, 2013, p. 64). Political leaders, therefore, play a key role in "shaping both excellent personal character and the right relationship between citizens and the law" (p. 64). These moral virtues provide a moral compass in youth, preparing them to sustain social stability. For communities to thrive, political leaders must provide equal access to resources and opportunities, especially for young people. Leaders bear a categorical responsibility to supply the foundational values, tools, and structures needed to foster a flourishing society.

Youth in society require our immediate attention and, above all, our compassion. Love is the force that can empower young people to see their worth and understand their role within society. They need to believe that they are respected members of their communities, contributing meaningfully to their stability and success. Inner-city neighborhoods, however, face high rates of unemployment, disenfranchisement, financial hardship, and crime. Failing to hold lawbreakers accountable undermines social stability and reflects an unfortunate indifference; a 'giving up' on society, especially its vulnerable demographics, while 'giving in' to short-sighted tactics. Inner-city areas remain focal points for law enforcement, yet rather than fostering positive change, police presence alone has, in some cases, fueled resentment and shame.

While police misconduct or abuse must be appropriately addressed, drug abuse and gang-related activities have intensified, overwhelming these communities. The violence surrounding these activities erodes self-esteem and a sense of worth among young people, stifling the development of civic virtue and fostering disorder. Society cannot afford to lose its youth to cycles of dysfunction; it must focus on cultivating a sense of moral responsibility. Communities, too, must commit to self-reflection, acknowledging their own roles and accountabilities, rather than placing the full burden of responsibility on external forces. This introspection is crucial to rebuild trust and promote a healthier, more unified social structure.

Sherwin contends that while police leaders can establish rules and regulations to ensure discipline and accountability, each police officer must possess remarkable leadership qualities in their professional role as police officers. Those who choose this profession should embody values that reflect genuine dedication to community unity. Police officers act as community leaders every day, serving as visible examples of civic virtue. Gaskins (2016) emphasizes, 'Police officers are community leaders – all day every day – and …are conspicuous men and women of civic virtue' (p. 1). Leadership is a crucial quality for officers, as it is the underpinning for civic virtue and fosters trust. For communities to function harmoniously, citizens must have trust in their police officers; without it, there is a risk of fostering fear, anger, and hate.

Leadership

> *When you get to the top of the mountain pull the next one up, then there'll be two of you roped together at the waist tired and proud, knowing the mountain, knowing the human force it took to bring both of you there. (Smith, as cited by Eleveld, 2003. p. 128)*

Smith's profound poetic insight reflects a fundamental truth about leadership and life through a humanistic lens: we are all here, facing life's challenges together. His metaphorical 'mountain' represents universal human struggles of pain, joy, success, failure, love, and friendship. Smith encourages us to see these shared experiences as a path to empathy, suggesting that this perspective might dissolve fear, anger, and hate, allowing us to recognize our common humanity. His perspective invites us to embrace love for humankind, a love that is often complex and difficult to give or receive. As Goff (2018) wisely observes, 'What is simple often isn't easy; what is easy often doesn't last' (p. 19). This speaks to the continuously challenging journey of fostering mutual respect and forgiveness.

For both police officers and citizens, this shared pursuit calls for teamwork, understanding, and compassion. Facing the 'mountain' together reveals the inner strengths of character that form the basis of trust and respect. Effective teamwork flourishes under good leadership, and police departments have a vital opportunity to step into that role, leading with a commitment to the spirit of love and empathy toward the communities they serve.

Leadership skills are often learned through experience and observation rather than being innate, yet they are crucial for fostering trust, respect, and enduring relationships between police officers and citizens. Police officers lacking leadership skills may face less favorable outcomes in interactions. Cunliffe and Eriksen (2011) introduce a compelling concept in *relational leadership*, which emphasizes forming meaningful community connections grounded in mutual respect and trust. This approach is vital for sustainable relationships, as it shapes 'how leaders coordinate action and socially construct identities, culture, strategy, etc.' (Cunliffe and Eriksen, 2011, p. 1429). Relational leadership also brings a humanistic perspective, valuing individuals' diverse cultures, identities, and experiences. Viewing others not merely as objects or suspects but as human beings fostering enriching empathetic interactions. Such leadership skills also bolster officers' self-esteem, actualization, and confidence, aligning with Aristotle's view that good leadership is rooted in a sound understanding of moral and ethical principles (Yankah, 2012).

When discussing leadership, Sherwin refers to every individual in law enforcement. Police officers shouldn't need constant oversight from supervisors to ensure lawful, civil interactions with citizens. Instead, each officer should be empowered with strong leadership skills, allowing them to independently handle situations in ways that foster trust, respect, and be able to withstand public scrutiny. Officers are the visible face of their departments, interacting daily with the community. They represent not only themselves but the culture and standards of their departments. When tensions arise, it is often individual police officer's, not department heads. who face citizens' frustrations and disapproval. However, those police/citizen encounters eventually influence public perception which frequently provokes the protesting of the public and political leaders.

When citizens call for defunding the police, they often seek accountability of police officers they perceive as having caused undue harm during their interactions with citizens. Yet, they still desire protection from criminal elements in their communities. The good taxpaying citizens simply want law enforcement to enforce justice lawfully.

Effective leadership should not rely on punishment to build community trust, safety, and respect. Leaders must recognize their duty to ensure justice through legal and ethical means that genuinely foster public support. To do so, police officers need discretionary authority that is grounded in strong moral and ethical virtues that focus on a universal commitment to 'good,' as Aristotle describes.

Good leadership is not just about enforcing the law; it's about embodying virtues that uphold community values. Aristotle's concept of 'affective knowledge' teaches that knowing and practicing virtues helps individuals discern right from wrong, shaping character and decision-making. As leaders, police officers' character will be held to universal standards of public opinion, state law, and ethical virtues. The value of liberal education becomes critical here, offering insights that shape a humanistic understanding of issues and instill the virtue of knowing how to make relevant moral decisions. Embracing Aristotle's Golden Mean and principles like the Six Pillars of Character helps foster balanced, ethical decision-making that resonates with communities' hopes for fairness, protection, and respect.

Josephson Institute of Ethics (2008) Six Pillars of Character (cited by Pollock, 2019. p. 27)

The "Six Pillars of Character" provides a remarkable platform for leadership virtues.

Figure 13. Aristotle's six pillars of character

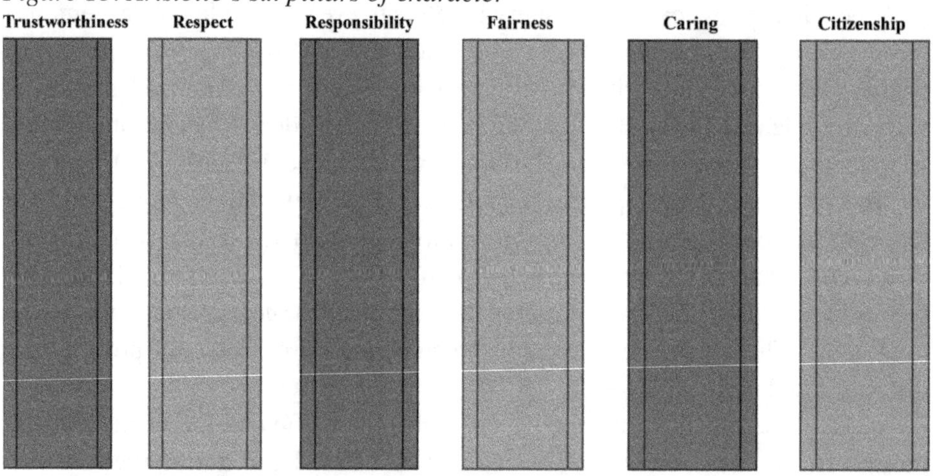

The Josephson Institute of Ethics underscores Aristotle's virtues through the Six Pillars of Character, qualities essential for all police officers to embody. As visible role models, police officers not only enforce laws but personify the ethical standards that secure society's inalienable rights. Police officers are the frontline protectors of community safety, confronting diverse and often dangerous situations. Police officers are the ones who run toward peril, frequently placing their own lives at risk. Yet, they also face public scrutiny, sometimes intensely, for decisions made under complex circumstances, even if those decisions are lawfully prudent.

Most people who choose a career in law enforcement inherently embody Aristotle's virtues. While they may not voice these principles explicitly, their actions reflect them in the way they interact with others and through their dedication to service. Tholen (2022) highlights a cautionary Aristotelian perspective on 'magnanimity,' where unchecked self-importance can make a leader appear foolish thus undermining community trust. This points to the need for leaders with authentic moral and ethical values to build sustainable bonds with their communities.

Police officers who embrace Aristotle's virtues also align with the Six Pillars of Character: trustworthiness, respect, responsibility, fairness, caring, and citizenship. These foundational values help establish an unbreakable bond between police officers and the communities they serve thus reinforcing mutual respect and safety. The following sections reflect my interpretation of each value of Aristotle's virtues as it pertains to effective law enforcement.

Trustworthiness

The virtue of trustworthiness encapsulates four significant values that are important for developing sustainable quality relationships with members of communities.

Figure 14. Trustworthiness values

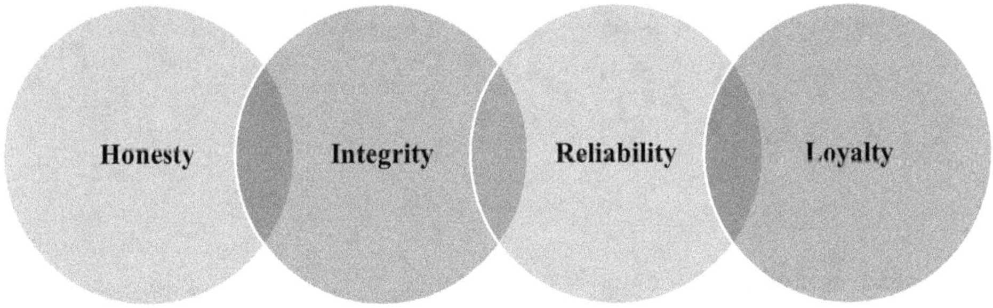

Each value interlocks to form the core foundation of trustworthiness. They are essential qualities that society expects from police officers in their interactions with the public. Society desires, and indeed demands, that police officers embody honesty. This ethical value entails truthfulness, sincerity, and transparency in their communication, whether they are engaging with victims of crimes or those accused of criminal acts. Integrity is paramount; it signifies a commitment to fairness, impartiality, and justice when interacting with citizens across diverse backgrounds, including race, culture, faith, and personal orientation. Trustworthiness cannot exist if a police officer's integrity is in question.

Moreover, police officers must exemplify reliability, a steadfast dedication to law enforcement without bias, consistently answering calls for service with impartiality and carrying out thorough and fair investigations. This reliability forms the basis of trust for both the judicial system and crime victims, ensuring that justice is rightly served, and no innocent person is wrongly charged. Lastly, loyalty is vital. Police officers must remain faithful to the communities they serve, the departments they represent, and the oaths they have sworn to uphold the Constitution. In this way, each value collectively strengthens the foundational trust between police officers and the public they protect.

Respect

Respect includes the interactional relationships of civility, dignity, tolerance, and acceptance.

Figure 15. Respect values

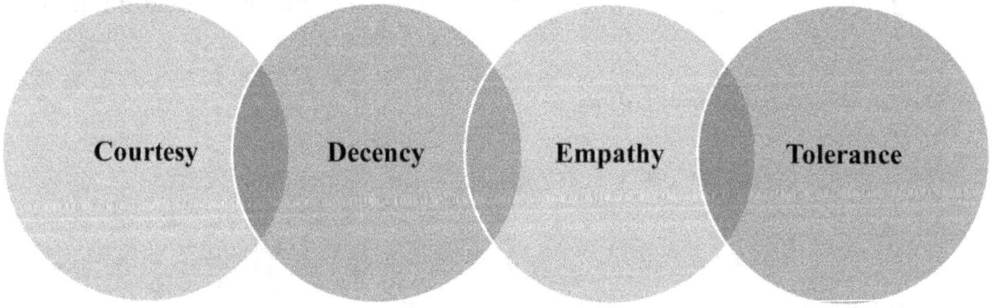

Respect in policing is demonstrated through courteous interactions, attentive listening, and treating every individual with decency and fairness. A police officers' role is not to impose punishment but to lawfully investigate with disciplined humanism, devoid of coercion or intimidation. An old policing adage encourages officers to treat each person as if they were interacting with a cherished family member, like a grandmother. This approach ensures that everyone feels valued and free to express their concerns without fear of retribution.

Respect also means safeguarding an individual's dignity; officers must avoid actions that might cause someone to 'lose face' or feel embarrassed, as this can damage their sense of worth. Empathy is crucial, especially during encounters with individuals who are experiencing emotional stress. Many interactions with the public may involve anger or hostility, yet a calm and tolerant response, combined with effective communication skills, often serves as the most powerful tool in de-escalating potential conflicts.

Finally, respect in policing involves acceptance, regardless of differences in race, faith, culture, and personal orientation. Police officers should not impose personal beliefs or moral judgments on others but instead embrace a tolerant, open-minded approach that honors the diversity and individuality of each person in society.

Responsibility

Figure 16. Responsibility values

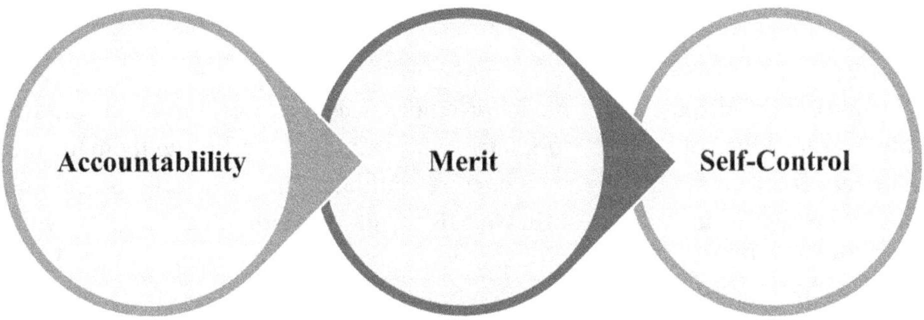

Accountability is a cornerstone of restorative justice, reflecting a person's character, leadership, and integrity. When individuals acknowledge their actions and accept responsibility, it fosters an environment of forgiveness and trust. Conversely, failure to accept accountability breeds distrust and erodes respect. This is especially relevant in the context of policing, where the decisions made by police officers have significant, sometimes life-altering impacts. For justice and equality to be upheld, it is essential that police officers are held accountable for their actions.

To embody the highest standards of accountability, police officers must strive for excellence, actively engage in learning, and adapt to changing social and legal landscapes. Continuous education, especially in the liberal arts, plays a vital role in shaping well-rounded officers who can serve as role models within their communities and police departments. Excellence requires commitment to ongoing training, education, and self-improvement, which bolsters confidence, self-esteem, and integrity.

With this foundation, officers are better equipped to exercise self-control and apply a humanistic perspective to their duties. This approach promotes forgiveness, tolerance, and objective thinking, enabling officers to respond thoughtfully to situations rather than react impulsively. By integrating these values into their work, police officers can foster stronger, more trusting relationships with the communities they serve.

Fairness

Figure 17. Fairness values

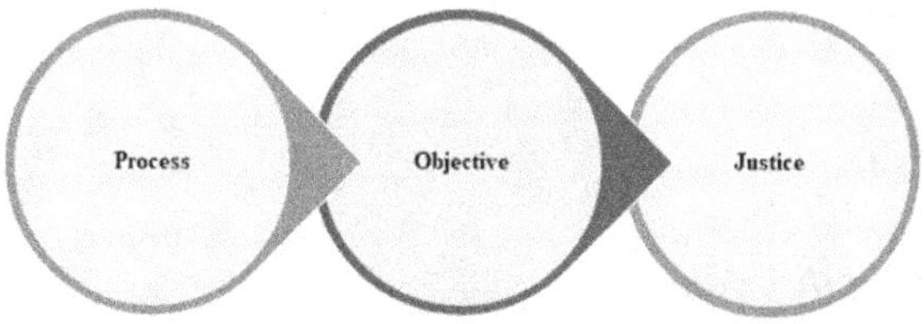

Approaching disputes as a mediator emphasizes a process-oriented mindset, empowering police officers to work fairly with individuals, allowing them to voice their concerns and facilitating negotiated resolutions. This structured process not only addresses the immediate conflict but also reinforces individuals' dignity, which builds their confidence in police officers. When people feel heard and respected, they are more likely to feel calm and be open to seeing different perspectives, fostering a productive environment for resolving disputes.

This mediation-focused approach helps reduce citizen complaints and strengthens public trust and respect for police officers. It requires police officers to remain objective, free of personal biases, and to accept individuals as they are, setting aside personal morality in favor of impartial justice. Justice is the bedrock of effective policing; without it, trust erodes, frustration grows and calls for defunding increase. When justice is upheld consistently, it prevents the buildup of fear, anger, and resentment towards law enforcement. At its core, the mission of police work is to serve justice, as it is the key to a harmonious, respectful relationship between police officers and the communities they protect.

Caring

Figure 18. Caring

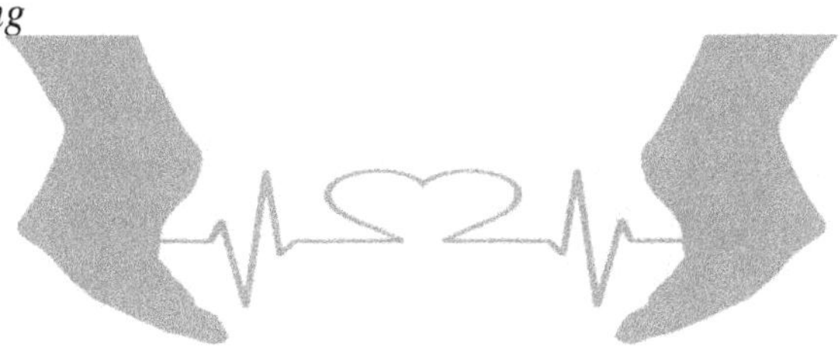

Caring embodies a profound commitment to love and humanistic fidelity. For police officers, this commitment forms the bedrock of their duty to protect citizens, fulfilling their oath to serve society with compassion and dedication. True care is not merely a job requirement, it is the essence of the law enforcement profession. Those who choose this path are called to it by a desire to uplift and protect others, especially those without a voice, security, or an advocate to champion their rights. This level of dedication is more than an occupation; it is an expression of love for humanity and an unwavering desire to make a difference.

Any officer who does not inherently embrace, internalize, and project caring for others cannot genuinely fulfill the role of a public servant. The ability to care deeply and, when necessary, to risk one's own life for the welfare of others, is a rare and invaluable quality. To witness any police officer disregarding this virtue is profoundly disheartening, as it undermines the trust and respect that the uniform represents. True service to society requires a steadfast dedication to humanity. There is no place in law enforcement for those who lack this essential commitment to care.

Citizenship

Figure 19. Citizenship

Choosing to be a police officer is a profound commitment to civic duty, rooted in the values of service, resilience, and an unyielding moral compass. This path demands a dedication to exceptional ethical standards and a willingness to embody the highest ideals of citizenship, including the sacrifice of certain personal freedoms. Police officers stand as models within their communities, undertaking the responsibility to protect justice, uphold equality, and ensure the safety of others, even when facing criticism, hostility, and intense scrutiny. This role goes beyond enforcing laws; it involves a deep, unwavering commitment to serving a public that may, at times, be skeptical or critical.

The journey to becoming a police officer often brings sacrifices on many fronts. It may strain friendships, dissolve relationships, and at times alienate family members or once-close friends. These challenges underscore the unique strength and commitment required of those who answer this call. Police officers who possess resolute moral character and a genuine love for their communities navigate these sacrifices and adversities with grace. They remain focused on their mission, rising above dissent to fulfill a civic responsibility that goes to the heart of citizenship, championing justice and protecting those who need it most.

REFERENCES

Agrawal, A., Lynskey, M. T., Madden, P. A. F., Kathleen, M. K., & Heath, A. C. (2006). A latent class analysis of illicit drug abuse/dependence: Results from the National Epidemiological Survey on alcohol and related conditions. *Department of Psychology Washington University School of Medicine.*, 102, 94–104. PMID: 17207127

Baker, A. M., (2020). Cardiopulmonary arrest complicating law enforcement subdual, restraint, and neck compression. Hennepin County Medical Examiner's Office Autopsy Report. ME NO: 20-3700, 1-13 PMID: 17207127

Baron-Cohen, S. (2011). *The Science of Evil.* Basic Books.

Battistella, G., Fornari, E., Annoni, J. M., Chtioui, H., Dao, K., Fabritius, M., Favrat, B., Mall, J. F., Maeder, P., & Giroud, C. (2014). Long-Term effects of cannabis on brain structure. *Neuropsychopharmacology : Official Publication of the American College of Neuropsychopharmacology*, 39(9), 2041–2048. DOI: 10.1038/npp.2014.67 PMID: 24633558

Benzkofer, S. (2018). Legendary lawmen, No. 8: O. W. Wilson. *Chicago Tribune.* Retrieved from: www.chicagotribune.com

Bilyk, J. (2022). SAFE-T Act boosts uncertainty around trespassing enforcement, could raise lawsuit risk for cops, property owners. Retrieved from: https://cookcountyrecord.com

Burggren, A. C., Shirazi, A., Ginder, N., & London, E. D. (2019). Cannabis effects on brain structure, function, and cognition; considerations for medical uses of cannabis and its derivatives. *The American Journal of Drug and Alcohol Abuse*, 45(6), 563–579. DOI: 10.1080/00952990.2019.1634086 PMID: 31365275

Butler, A., Zakimi, N., & Greer, A. (2022). Total systems failure: Police officers' perspectives on the impacts of the justice, health, and social service systems on people who use drugs. *Harm Reduction Journal*, 19(48), 1–13. DOI: 10.1186/s12954-022-00629-1 PMID: 35590421

Carriere, K.R., & Encinosa, W. (2017). The risks of operational militarization: Increased conflict against militarized police. Peace Economics, Peace Science and Public Policy. 23(3,13), 1-13. PMID: 17207127

Cooper, C. (1999). *Mediation & Arbitration by Patrol Police Officers.* University Press of America, Inc.

Cunliffe, A. L., & Eriksen, M. (2011). Relational leadership. *Human Relations*, 64(11), 1425–1449. DOI: 10.1177/0018726711418388

David, J. D. (2023). Police encounters for behavioral health-related reasons in rural and remote communities: A Canadian study. *Rural Sociology*, 88(1), 135–161. DOI: 10.1111/ruso.12471

Degenhardt, L., Hall, W., Warner-Smith, M., & Lynskey, M. (2024). Comparative quantification of health risks: Illicit drug use. World Health Organization. 1109-1175

Del Pozo, B., Sightes, E., Goulka, J., Ray, B., Wood, C. A., Siddiqui, S., & Beletsky, L. A. (2012). Police discretion in encounters with people who use drugs: Operationalizing the theory of planned behavior. *Harm Reduction Journal*, 18(132), 1–12. PMID: 34915910

Dewey, J. (1936). *Experience & Education*. Free Press.

Dhein, S. (2020). Different effects of cannabis abuse on adolescent and adult brain. *Pharmacology*, 105(11-12), 609–617. DOI: 10.1159/000509377 PMID: 32629444

Dorgan, M. (June 2024). Who suffers from defunding the police? This blue city has over 1,000 unsolved murders. Fox News. 1-5. Retrieved from https://nypost.com

Eleveld, M. (2003). *Pull the next one up. The Spoken Word Revolution (slam, hip hop & the poetry of a new generation)*. Sourcebooks, Inc.

Fox 32 Chicago. (2018). 50 years later: Ceremony held for victims of deadly 1968 explosion. Retrieved from https://www.fox32chicago.com/

Freire, P. (2012). *Pedagogy of the oppressed*. Bloomsbury Publishing Plc.

Fryer, R. G., Jr. (2017). An empirical analysis of racial differences in police use of force. Department of Economics, Harvard University. 1-43

Gaskins, J. (2016). Ethics in leadership: Applying Aristotle in police work. *Police (Springfield)*, 1, •••. https: wwwpolice1.com/patrol-issues/articles/

Georgieva, E., Benkova, K., Vlaeva, N., Karamalakova, Y., Miteva, R., Abrashev, H., & Nikolova, G. (2022). Is illicit substance use gender-specific? The basic points of mental and health disorders. *Toxics*, 10(7), 2–19. DOI: 10.3390/toxics10070344 PMID: 35878250

Glauser, W. (2020). Why some doctors want to defund the police. *Canadian Medical Association Journal*, 192(48), 1–2. DOI: 10.1503/cmaj.1095905 PMID: 33257333

Goff, B. (2018). *Everybody Always. Becoming Love in a World Full of Setbacks and Difficult People*. Nelson Books.

Greek, C. (2009). Documenting and framing police public interaction with citizens: A study in visual criminology. *Criminal Justice Matters*, 78(1), 18–20. DOI: 10.1080/09627250903385198

Griffen, D. (Apr 2021). After action reports on the riots of 2020. Police Law Enforcement Solutions. Retrieved from https://www.policemag.com

Grube, G. M. A. (1981). *Plator. Five Dialogues, Euthyphro, Apology, Crito, Meno, Phaedo.* Hackett Publishing Company, Inc.

Henderson, H., & Yisrael, B. (May 2021). 7 myths about "defunding the police" debunked. Brookings Institute. Retrieve from https://www.brookings.edu

Heradstvelt, O., Skogen, J. C., Hetland, J., & Hysing, M. (2017). Alcohol and illicit drug use are important factors for school-related problems among adolescents. *Frontiers in Psychology*, 8(1023), 1–11. PMID: 28676779

Hyshka, E., Anderson, J. A., & Wild, T. C. (2017). Perceived unmet need and barriers to care amongst street-involved people who use illicit drugs. *Drug and Alcohol Review*, 36(3), 295–304. DOI: 10.1111/dar.12427 PMID: 27242102

Issar, Siddhant, (2020). Listening to Black Lives Matter: racial capitalism and the critique of neoliberalism. Springer Nature Limited. 1-24 PMID: 28676779

Jackson, J., Fine, A., Bradford, B., & Trinkner, R. (2023). Social identity and support for defunding the police in the aftermath of George Floyd's murder. *Group Processes & Intergroup Relations*, 26(4), 833–858. DOI: 10.1177/13684302221128230

Jean-Davis, D. (2023). Police encounters for behavioral health-related reasons in rural and remote communities: A Canadian study. *Rural Sociology*, 88(1), 135–161. DOI: 10.1111/ruso.12471

Josephson, M. S. (2008). Character: Linchpin of leadership. *Leadership Excellence.*, 16(8), 13.

Kant, E. (1999). *Grounding for the Metaphysics Of Morals with On a Supposed Right to Lie Because of Philanthropic Concerns* (3rd ed.). Hackett Publishing Company, Inc.

Kisielius, J., & Roedder, D. L. (1983). The effects of imagery on attitude-behavior consistency. *Advances in Consumer Research. Association for Consumer Research (U. S.)*, 10, 72–74.

Lankester, L. A., and Alexopoulos, T. (2023). Black lives matter, but to whom? An examination of Nationally grounded determinants of Black Lives Matter support. International Review of Social Psychology. 36 (1): 16, 1-15

Locke, J. (1980). *Second Treatise of Government*. Hackett Publishing Company, Inc.

Mayo Clinic. (2024). Definition retrieved from https://www.mayoclinic.org/diseases-conditions/ Schizophrenia/symptoms-causes/syc-20354443

McLean, K., Alikhan, A., & Alpert, G. P. (2023). Re-examining the use of force continuum: Why resistance is not the only driver of use of force decisions. *Police Quarterly*, 26(1), 85–110. DOI: 10.1177/10986111211066353

Mellsop, G., Tapsell, R., & Holmes, P. (2019). Mental health service users' progression from illicit drug use to schizophrenia in New Zealand. *General Psychiatry*, 32(5), 32. DOI: 10.1136/gpsych-2019-100088 PMID: 31552389

Merton, R. K. (1996). *On Social Structure and Science*. The University of Chicago Press.

Munsey, B. (1980). *Moral Development, Moral Education, and Kohlberg*. Religious Education Press, Inc.

Munson, S. C. (2000). Art: Selling Norman Rockwell. *Commentary (New York, N.Y.)*, 110(2), 64–67.

Nam, Y., Wolfe, S. E., & Nix, J. (2024). Does procedural justice reduce the harmful effects of perceived ineffectiveness on police legitimacy? *Journal of Research in Crime and Delinquency*, 61(1), 124–167. DOI: 10.1177/00224278221121622

New York, N. B. C. (2022). Jose Alba murder case. Retrieved from: https://www.nbcnewyork.com › news › local › new-video.

Newman, A. (2020, October). Black lives matter: Behind the façade. *The New American Magazine*, •••, 1–5.

Nix, J., Ivanov, S., & Pickett, J. T. (2021). What does the public want police to do during pandemics? A national experiment. *Criminology & Public Policy*, 20(3), 545–571. DOI: 10.1111/1745-9133.12535 PMID: 33821153

Nordberg, A., Crawford, M. R., Practorius, R. T., & Smith Hatcher, S. (2016). Exploring minority youths' police encounters: A qualitative interpretive meta-synthesis. *Child & Adolescent Social Work Journal*, 33(2), 132–149. DOI: 10.1007/s10560-015-0415-3

Phillips, S. W. (2016). Myths, militarism and the police patrol rifle. *Policing and Society*, 26(2), 185–196. DOI: 10.1080/10439463.2014.922088

Phillips, S.W. (August 2017). Police Militarization. FBI Law Enforcement Bulletin. p.1-6.

Plato, . (1981). *Five Dialogues, Euthyphro, Apology, Crito, Meno, Phaedo*. Hackett Publishing Company.

Pollock, J. M. (2019). *Ethical Dilemmas and Decisions in Criminal Justice* (10th ed.). Cengage Learning, Inc.

Reynolds, M. (2020-21). Called to arms. *American Bar Association Journal. American Bar Association*, 106(6), 62–71.

Richardson, L. A., Long, C., DeBeck, K., Nguyen, P., Milloy, M. J. S., Wood, E., & Kerr, T. H. (2015). Socio-economic marginalization in the structural production of vulnerability to violence among people who use illicit drugs. *Journal of Epidemiology and Community Health*, 69(7), 686–692. DOI: 10.1136/jech-2014-205079 PMID: 25691275

Royal Queens Seeds Blog. (2024). Is Marijuana Stronger Than It Used To Be? Retrieved from www.royalqueenseeds.com

Sartre, J. P. (2011). *Sartre, The Transcendence of the Ego*. Routledge Classics.

Shah, P. V. (2019). A use of deadly force: People with mental health conditions and encounters with law enforcement. *Harvard Human Rights Journal*, 32, 208–221.

Siegel, L. J., & Worrall, J. L. (2018). *Introduction to Criminal Justice* (16th ed.). Cengage Learning.

Sowell, T. (2023). *Social Justice Fallacies*. Hachette Book Group.

Spotted Eagle, F. (2000). *Many Paths, Many Spirits*. Spotted Eagle and Associates.

Stringer, H. (2023, June 1). How does marijuana affect the brain? Psychological researchers examine impact on different age groups over time. *Monitor on Psychology*, 54(4). https://www.apa.org/monitor/2023/06/marijuana-effects-brain

Sweetman, P. (2003). Twenty-first century disease? Habitual reflexivity or the reflexive habitus. *The Sociological Review*, 51(4), 528–549. DOI: 10.1111/j.1467-954X.2003.00434.x

Tarm, M. (2021 – April 5). Explainer: was officer's knee on Floyd's neck authorized? Associated Press. Retrieved from https://apnews.com/hub/death-of-george-floyd

The Editors. (2014). Following Ferguson. *America Press Inc.*, 211(6), 5.

The Editors of Encyclopedia Britannica. (2024). Democratic National Convention of 1968 political event, Chicago, Illinois, United States. Article History. Retrieved from https://www.britannica.com/

Tholen, B. (2022). The virtues of the exemplary moral leader. Lessons from Aristotle's ethics. *Business Ethics, the Environment & Responsibility*, 32(2), 532–543. DOI: 10.1111/beer.12504

U.S. Department of Homeland Security. (Feb 2021). Muth vs. Fact: 50 + nights of violence, chaos and anarchy in Portland, Oregon. Retrieved from https://www.dhs.gov

Use of Force Chart. (2024). Retrieved from https://nuqum.com/Our law enforcement officers need new rules of engagement for minor crimes | NuQum.com

Willis, T., Comartin, E., Victor, G., Kern, L., & Kubiak, S. (2021). Individuals with mental illness who have multiple encounters with law enforcement. *Journal of Offender Rehabilitation*, 60(2), 117–137. DOI: 10.1080/10509674.2020.1863298

Yankah, E. N. (2012). Legal vices and civic virtue: Vice crimes, republicanism and the corruption of lawfulness. *Criminal Law and Philosophy*, 7(1), 61–82. DOI: 10.1007/s11572-012-9161-1

Zakaria, F. (2015). *Defense of a Liberal Education*. W.W. Norton & Company, Inc.

Zimabrdo, P. (2007). *The Lucifer Effect: Understanding how good people turn evil.* Random House Inc.

Chapter 3
Humanistic Training and Community Engagement for Modern Policing

ABSTRACT

Chapter three is divided into three distinct sections. The first section emphasizes the crucial role of proper training in fostering successful police/citizen relationships. The second section introduces a theory that Sherwin developed to explain its rationale and purpose within the training process. The third section addresses the ongoing criticism and disrespect faced by law enforcement and the criminal justice system. Training for police officers should be continuous, frequent, and redundant throughout their careers.

INTRODUCTION

Training for police officers should be continuous, frequent, and redundant throughout their careers. Police officers are required to be proficient in the use of their firearm. There is a mandatory yearly qualification requirement to be proficient in using their firearm. If a police officer fails to pass the qualification requirement they will be removed from service; fired. Much like a police officer's requirement to qualify with their duty firearms annually, formal training that expands their knowledge and provides them with the verbal and physical skills to confidently perform their duties must also be a requirement. This training should adhere to structured schedule with purposeful frequency. This training must be progressive, informative, timely, and should encompass more than just legal knowledge, rules, and regulations. It should integrate philosophical and sociological theories that provide police officers

DOI: 10.4018/979-8-3693-7979-0.ch003

with humanistic skills, values, and logic. This approach aims to replace hubris with empathy, all while maintaining the lawful authority and purpose of law enforcement.

Police officers are routinely exposed to situations and issues that cause stress. And there are always unknown factors that prompt a normative ethical response of "What should I do?" (Pollock, 2019). Effective training provides police officers with internal strength and confidence to respond to situations rather than react impulsively. Human nature is complex, and people respond to situations in various ways for many reasons. Training equips police officers with an understanding of why people think and act the way they do, fostering empathy and insight. Additionally, training instills self-awareness, helping police officers recognize how they appear and sound to others. This awareness allows them to self-reflect, refocus, and commit to their professional purpose. Training helps police officers remain focused on their central purpose; ensuring that their actions, methods, and values align with their role as community protectors.

In this chapter, Sherwin introduces a theory rooted in humanism, conceptualized through the imagery of *Conterminous Spheres of Dependency*. Each sphere is framed within thematic clusters, which I explain in detail throughout the chapter. These thematic clusters serve as the foundation for understanding the humanistic principles critical to law enforcement interactions. The theory operates on two key tenets:

First, it is vital that police officers are equipped with humanistic values. These values are highlighted in the themes of each sphere. These values provide guidance to police officers in their interactions with citizens for ensuring empathy, respect, and understanding. Second, the theory emphasizes the necessity of providing police officers with the essential skills to interact effectively with individuals experiencing mental health episodes.

Mental health episode calls for service have reached critical levels of urgency that require compulsory intervention. This most likely will necessitate police intervention. Therefore, it is vital that police officers receive progressively formalized training in Crisis Intervention Teams (CIT). However, for these teams to function successfully, it is paramount that the officers selected for CIT training embody humanistic values. Without this, the program risks failure in fulfilling its community obligation and purpose.

The chapter concludes by addressing the criticism and disrespect often directed at law enforcement and the criminal justice system. To explore this issue further, Sherwin introduces another theory he developed: *Fear, Anger, Hate*. This theory examines the underlying reasons why society tends to view police officers through a negative lens. While the themes of fear, anger, and hate are not new, my theory offers a fresh perspective on why these emotions persist and how they can remain unresolved. The concept of fear, anger, and hate has many causes, and while these emotions are natural, they have significant consequences when left unaddressed.

In this section, Sherwin also explores the psychological phenomenon that makes it easier for people to hate than to love, further delving into the ramifications of unresolved negative emotions.

SECTION-1: DEVELOPING TRUST THROUGH HUMANISTIC TRAINING AND CONFLICT RESOLUTION

The pathway to a career in law enforcement is stringent and thorough, requiring all applicants to undergo a demanding application process to ensure they meet high standards of integrity, aptitude, and physical agility. Minimum requirements typically include an extensive personal background check to assess the candidate's character and past conduct. A drug test to ensure compliance with health and legal standards. A cognitive proficiency test to measure mental acuity and decision-making skills. A written examination to evaluate knowledge and reasoning. And a physical agility test to confirm physical fitness for the highly stressful demands of the profession.

Figure 1. Training values

Educational requirements can vary by agency, with some law enforcement agencies requiring or preferring candidates to hold a degree in higher education, while others set varying standards based on the specific roles or responsibilities within the agency. This tailored approach to educational criteria allows each agency to align its standards with the unique needs of the communities it serves, and the manifest challenges in its jurisdiction.

After fulfilling the initial requirements, candidates move on to a police academy for comprehensive law enforcement training and indoctrination. In Illinois, training programs are standardized statewide to ensure consistent certification as peace officers, although the duration and residential requirements differ based on the agency.

For instance, recruits at the Chicago Police Academy undergo twenty-six weeks of training. Chicago police recruits attend daily classes at the training academy and go home at the end of an eight-hour regimen. Illinois State Trooper candidates train for the same period but are required to live in barracks during the week, emphasizing a more regimented, disciplined and immersive experience. Suburban police departments have slightly different arrangements. The suburban police recruits attend a fifteen-week training session at an academy near their jurisdiction, allowing them to live at home. Some suburban departments even provide a police vehicle to each recruit for transportation during training.

Academy instructors, who typically base their teaching on professional experience rather than advanced academic qualifications, guide recruits through practical and theoretical aspects of policing. Lesson plans are designed by the academies to align closely with procedures, laws, and protocols consistent with patrol duties. In some cases, lawyers are brought in to teach specific subjects such as criminal procedures, bringing specialized legal insights directly into the training curriculum. This tailored approach ensures recruits receive both practical and procedural education, preparing them for the diverse situations they will encounter in their roles as peace officers.

Recruits undergoing police academy training remain on a probationary status and can be dismissed at any point if they fail to meet minimum standards or fail academy assessments. Certain police departments, such as Chicago, also enforce a residency requirement, mandating that all police officers live within the geographic boundaries of the municipalities they work for. In these cases, new hires are given thirty days after their hiring date to comply with this requirement.

Occasionally, a recruit's background check is still in progress when they start academy training. If issues or discrepancies are identified once the background check is fully processed, the recruit may face termination, despite having already begun training. This underscores the rigorous standards and continuous scrutiny involved in the process of becoming a police officer, emphasizing the commitment to a high level of integrity and compliance with departmental rules and regulations.

Police academy training is designed to be rigorous, with daily inspections based on a strict, paramilitary disciplined environment. The formal training is structured with comprehensive instruction in areas such as law, cultural diversity, verbal judo, physical skills, and firearms proficiency. Recruits undergo weekly testing. At the conclusion of the training period recruits undergo final examinations in written knowledge, physical agility, and firearms proficiency. All the training material and examinations must comply with the mandated curriculum established by the state. Failure in any of these exams results in termination, ensuring that only those meeting all standards graduate from the academy and become State Certified Peace Officers.

Once the academy training is completed, and the recruits become police officers they enter the remaining eighteen-month probation period by being assigned to work in their police departments with a field training officer (FTO), who evaluates their progress weekly. The remaining probation period integrates practical experience, allowing the new police officers to apply what they learned in the academy to real-life situations and issues under the close supervision of an FTO. If a probationary officer fails to meet the required standards of being a police officer, they may be sent back for re-training or terminated. By the end of the probation period, successful probationary officers become full-fledged police officers.

While this process equips recruits with foundational skills and discipline for police work, it may not fully prepare them to cultivate trust and respect within the communities they serve. Building such relationships requires an ongoing commitment to humanistic values and self-improvement. An effective approach to enhancing community relations should involve integrating restorative justice practices, like mediation and de-escalation techniques, which focus on resolving conflicts with empathy and positive communication skills.

Restorative Justice

Figure 2. Restorative justice values

Restorative justice introduces an alternative approach to sustainable equality of justice that emphasizes the needs and voices of victims, focusing on accountability, healing, and closure rather than solely on punishment. Unlike traditional criminal justice processes, which prioritize punitive outcomes, restorative justice actively involves the victim, the offender, and a broader community network, including the offender's peers and victim support groups. This inclusive framework gives victims the opportunity to articulate the impact of crime on their lives and ask the offender to acknowledge their suffering through accountability.

The proper utilization of restorative justice enables victims to express their needs wherein the current traditional criminal justice system prohibits victims from doing so. Thus, victims frequently are revictimized because of having no voice in outcomes. For instance, victims, especially in sensitive cases like sexual assault, may feel re-traumatized during court proceedings, as they are subjected to probing cross-examinations that can exacerbate their suffering. Restorative justice, however, recognizes these emotional impacts, aiming to create a safe space for the victim to participate meaningfully in the justice process.

Pollock (2019) emphasizes that restorative practices facilitate a community-oriented resolution by bringing in multiple perspectives and support systems, which often leads to a deeper, more comprehensive understanding of the social implications of a crime. Thus, the person responsible for the wrongdoing is not only held accountable for their actions but is confronted by and answerable to not only the victim but to the entire community for the overarching harm they have caused. This procedure is concomitant with the Sixth Amendment of the United States Constitution. In doing so, the person who committed a crime is provided with a momentous opportunity to grasp the full extent of harm they caused the victim, family of the victim, and members of the community to experience. The proper utilization of restorative justice fosters a greater sense of resolution and closure for all who are harmed by the criminal act. As Johnstone (2011) points out, restorative justice shifts decision-making power to the victim, allowing them to help define the wrongdoing and decide on appropriate consequences. This empowerment is a stark contrast to the criminal justice system's traditional methods, which frequently leave victims feeling marginalized and their needs unmet. Ultimately, restorative justice not only offers a pathway to accountability for the offender but also promotes healing and reduces animosity, potentially transforming the justice experience into a truly reparative process for victims and their families.

Another consequence is the limited understanding of the factors that lead individuals to commit crimes. Society's leaders often struggle to fully grasp the social and cultural realities that contribute to the sense of justification felt by those who engage in criminal behavior. While Sherwin does not suggest that crime itself is justifiable, it is crucial to recognize that individuals who commit crimes frequently believe they are justified in their actions. This perception is especially significant when viewed through a sociological lens, influenced by prevailing social challenges such as disorganized neighborhoods, anomie, strain theory, labeling theory, social control, and parental efficacy

Disorganized Neighborhood

Sociologists define a disorganized neighborhood as a community marked by pervasive "income inequality, poverty, racism, and despair" (Siegel and Worrall, 2018, p. 101). Such areas are often fraught with crime and drug activity, where youths grow up in economically strained environments, increasing their susceptibility to criminal behavior. These neighborhoods are places where "school, neighborhood, and social services…are broken and ineffective" (Siegel and Worrall, 2018, p. 101). Despite the struggles and dysfunction within these communities, they foster strong social bonds among residents, particularly among youths who may turn to gangs and crime as sources of identity and belonging. Those who live in these neighborhoods frequently develop a sense that no one, whether within or outside their community, genuinely cares for them, leaving them feeling isolated and marginalized. Nonetheless, they maintain a strong resolve to survive, feeling justified in doing whatever it takes to overcome their circumstances.

Anomie

Siegel and Worrall (2018) define anomie as "the absence or weakness of rules, norms, or guidelines on what is socially or morally acceptable" (p. 100). Within disorganized neighborhoods, anomie is prevalent as residents, particularly youths, suffer from a significant lack of social capital, stable social structures, and accessible resources. This void perpetuates a pervasive sense of "normlessness," (Siegel and Worrall, 2018) where individuals feel disconnected from societal expectations and standards. Such an environment often drives deviant behavior, as the lack of clear norms and support systems can lead individuals to seek alternative means of validation and survival.

Stain Theory

Siegel and Worrall (2018) discuss Robert Merton's strain theory as an explanation for the roots of criminal behavior. According to the theory, crime can stem from "the emotional turmoil and conflict caused when people believe that they cannot achieve their desires and goals through legitimate means" (p. 103). Merton outlined five distinct categories to support his theoretical framework, each providing insight into why young people may turn to criminal activity when they perceive that societal expectations and aspirations are unattainable through lawful pathways. Sherwin highlights three of Merton's five categories.

1. Innovation – the use of innovative but illegal means to achieve success in the absence of legitimate means.
2. Retreatism – the rejection of conventional goals and choosing to live as drug users, alcoholics, and wanderers.
3. Rebellion – joining revolutionary political groups and working to change the system to one of their likings. (Merton cited by Siegel and Worrall, 2018. P. 103).

Labeling Theory

Siegel and Worrall (2018) suggest that "people become criminals when significant members of society label them as such, and they accept those labels as a personal identity" (p. 105). The labeling theory underscores how the stigmatization of youths can reinforce and deepen their ties to criminal gang enterprises. When inner-city youths are repeatedly characterized as "ruthless and uncontrollable thugs" by society, media, and politicians, these labels act as powerful reinforcements to justify their criminal actions. Such pervasive and often negative portrayals can embolden and empower these young individuals to adopt the very identities that have been assigned to them, thereby perpetuating cycles of crime and gang involvement.

Social Control

Social control, as defined by Siegel and Worrall (2018), is "the view that most people do not violate the law because of their social bonds to family, peer group, school, and other institutions. If these bonds are weakened or absent, individuals are much more likely to commit crime" (p. 107). Unfortunately, in many disorganized neighborhoods, these crucial social bonds are largely absent, weakening social control and contributing to an environment where youth crime is prevalent. This lack of social structure makes gang-related activities involving guns and drugs a common theme among youths in these communities.

Parental Efficacy

Parental efficacy, as Siegel and Worrall (2018) describe, is evident among "parents who are able to be supportive and who can therefore effectively control their children in a nonthreatening fashion" (p. 104). It encompasses nurturing love, care, and discipline, which collectively help steer children away from criminal involvement. The absence of parental efficacy has a profoundly negative impact on youths, often pushing them toward innovation in survival tactics, retreatism, and even rebellion. Many youths in disorganized neighborhoods lack this foundational support, feeling unloved and as though their thoughts or actions go unnoticed. This absence of care fosters a life outlook that feels cheap, fleeting, and devoid of meaning, diminishing their sense of self-worth and empathy and replacing it with feelings of fear, anger, and hate.

Transformative Restorative Justice

Transformative restorative justice introduces a proactive approach to reducing crime by promoting societal benefits and encouraging the growth of commerce and social welfare in disorganized neighborhoods. Instead of concentrating all resources on the aftermath of criminal behavior, this approach emphasizes prevention. Through structured educational programs in schools and community outreach, transformative restorative justice empowers youth with conflict resolution skills to address disputes nonviolently. This approach has been implemented in select communities and schools, though broader acceptance by community leaders, institutions, and the criminal justice system remains limited. A prevailing belief still exists that punishment alone can deter crime, overshadowing efforts to address its root causes. Johnstone (2011) highlights this tension, suggesting that "a clash between the values of the state bureaucracy – uniformity, regularity and predictability – and those which many see as essential to restorative justice – flexibility and creativeness" (p. 15) may be at play. Nonetheless, some school districts have embraced the potential of transformative restorative justice, initiating training programs for administrators, faculty, and staff to enhance their effectiveness in supporting restorative practices.

One initiative Sherwin has been involved with is training administrators, faculty, and social workers in mediation practices within the Valley View School District of Will County, Illinois. Sherwin brought four students, who had successfully completed a mediation course to a high school in the school district to conduct peer mediation training. The training session, which included around fifty participants of administrators, faculty, and students, was well received and has continued to remain an active part of the school's conflict resolution efforts for about four years. Additionally, Sherwin provided mediation and peacekeeping circle training to administrators, faculty, and school counselors, which has become an ongoing program. These practices foster accountability, safety, and a transformative approach to conflict prevention. The entire school community, including parents, experiences an empowering lesson in social stability, shifting focus from punitive responses to proactive, peaceful conflict resolution.

Transformative justice in this context becomes a tool for teaching students' civic responsibility through peaceful methods of reconciling conflicts, addressing bullying, and reducing discrimination. It incorporates Aristotle's six pillars of character, creating a necessary foundation of moral and ethical values within schools. Not only does this create a secure environment, but it also fosters a vibrant, supportive learning atmosphere that builds students' self-efficacy and confidence. By learning these essential skills, students are better equipped to achieve their personal and professional goals, reducing the likelihood of involvement in criminal behavior. Transformative restorative justice, at its core, is a humanistic approach, creating a lasting generational impact on social stability and promoting a utilitarian approach to community well-being.

Training Police Officers Conflict Resolution Skills

Cooper (1999) emphasizes that when police officers apply conflict resolution skills in their interactions with citizens, it results in "improved police-citizen relations…[and]…a decrease in the need for use of physical force" (p.1). Conflict resolution fosters mutual respect and understanding; when disputing parties ignore each other's perspectives, issues intensify, often culminating in fear, anger, and hatred. According to Cooper (1999), officers trained in conflict resolution are more likely to "reduce the likelihood of violent and verbal confrontation with citizens" (p.46). Cooper also makes a thought-provoking point, observing that "police departments routinely reward patrol officers for heroism when the officer shoots a suspect. However, seldom are officers rewarded who defuse and calm a situation" (p.50). For police officers and police departments to fully embrace these insights, they must be rooted in a humanistic approach that values de-escalation and conflict resolution over force, recognizing the importance of peaceful interactions as integral to effective policing.

As a mediator, Sherwin had the privilege of working with Cooper to train police officers in conflict resolution and de-escalation skills. Currently, Sherwin collaborated with a colleague, a psychology professor, to present a de-escalation workshop for students at Lewis University, incorporating many of the same methods, skills, and tools used in training police officers. One approach Cooper and Sherwin used in teaching conflict resolution to police officers was through exploring perception. In this module, the focus was on how citizens might view police officers. Trainees were shown a photograph of uniformed officers standing in line or side-by-side in various stances, and were asked to observe each officer's pose, uniform, and equipment. After a few moments, the trainees shared their emotional responses to the image. This segment encouraged cognitive processing, allowing trainees to see not only the potential threat but also to feel an emotional reaction that mirrors a lack of trust. When asked which police officer they would feel most comfortable approaching for help or directions, most trainees revealed that aspects such as stance, hand placement, and auxiliary equipment strongly influenced their comfort level more than facial expressions did. The overarching perception was one of projecting harm, hostility, and a lack of empathy (Cooper, 1999), aligning closely with findings from Zimbardo's (2007) Stanford Prison study on the behavior of prison guards.

Zimbardo (2007) argues that simply donning a uniform of authority, such as that of a prison guard, can trigger a profound psychological response known as "deindividuation" (p. 305). This phenomenon leads individuals to internalize a sense of power and authority. Zimbardo (2007) observed that this effect can erode one's moral compass, resulting in the use of harsh, oppressive measures against those under their control, further intensifying the deindividuation process. This shift, he suggests, "transforms our Apollonian nature into a Dionysian nature," where reason and restraint give way to impulsivity and unrestrained behavior (Zimbardo, 2007, p. 305).

Figure 3. Stock photo of police officers' defense line (https/www. Bing)

Figure 4. Stock photo of police officers' foot patrol (https/www.bing)

Figure 5. Stock photo of police officers' foot patrol (https/www.bing)

Every training process should be built around three core elements: need, purpose, and intended outcomes. In this context, the need is to restore the integrity of police officers, the purpose is to foster trust within the community, and the intended outcome is to strengthen police-citizen relationships. While conflict resolution training equips officers with effective de-escalation skills, one essential characteristic underpins its success: humanism. Humanism is defined as "The quality of being human; any system of thought or action based on the nature, interests, and ideals of humanity" (Webster's New World College Dictionary, 2016). Humanism can be understood through four interconnected categories: philosophical, heuristic, social justice, and competency. Together, these categories form Conterminous Spheres of Dependency developed by Sherwin. Each sphere, contained within the overarching humanistic sphere, represents a category reliant on humanism as a catalyst for sustainable intellectual growth and understanding of human interactions.

When someone engages with any category, humanism serves as the foundation for comprehending and embracing the interrelated concepts of other categories. It remains a constant motivator for acceptance and grows increasingly influential as a guiding perspective in interactions with others. Each category encompasses a humanistic component that, once internalized, fosters deeper understanding in human relationships. The more categories one comprehends, the greater their capacity for humanistic understanding, allowing for richer insights into each area. Without humanism, these categories remain inaccessible, lacking the basis for learning, understanding, or acceptance.

Figure 6. Conterminous spheres of dependency

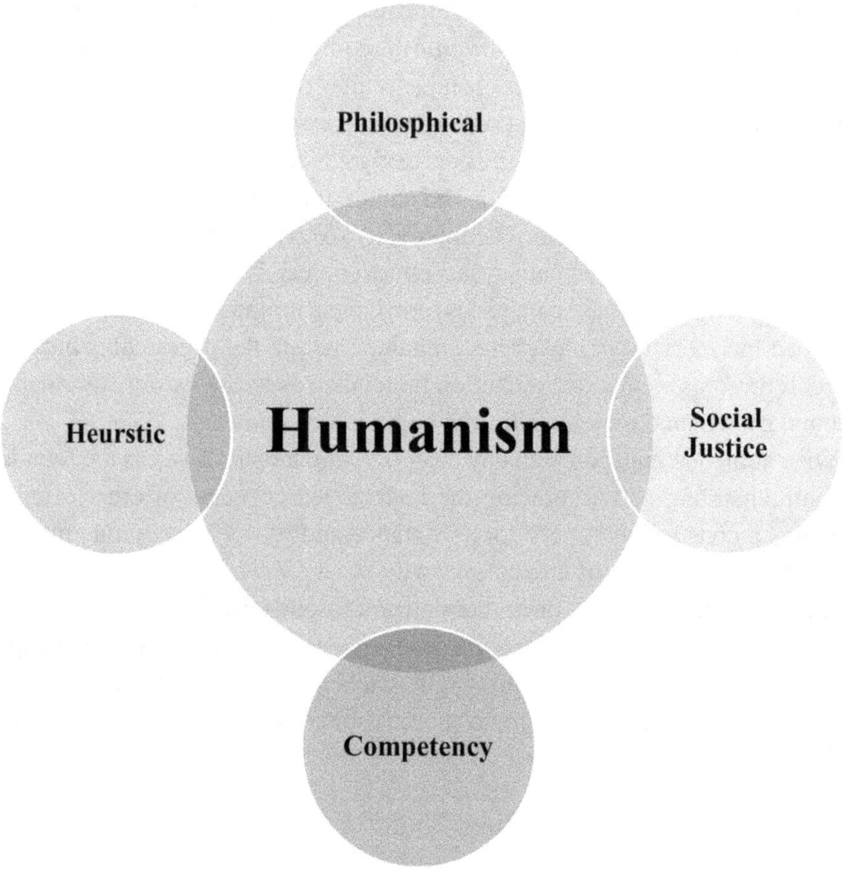

SECTION-2: THE CONTERMINOUS SPHERES THEORY: INTEGRATING EMPATHY, LEADERSHIP, AND SOCIAL JUSTICE

Evidence suggests that training is an effective approach for teaching police officers to engage with communities in a humanistic manner. Training encompasses the development of "...skills, attitudes, and general information..." (Baro & Buringame, 1999, p. 66), a viewpoint Cooper (1999) shares, emphasizing these qualities in his conflict resolution training for police officers. However, Baro & Buringame (1999) provide a compelling counterargument, noting that training is often conducted by college professors like Cooper (1999) and rooted in "...scholarly theory and research..." (p. 66). They argue that modern police training, in fact, benefits from the integration of higher education, asserting that the "...inclusion for instruction and curriculum development is a major reason why modern police training has undergone so many improvements" (Baro & Buringame, 1999, p. 66). This perspective underscores the interdependency between practical training and academic frameworks, supporting the idea that both elements are essential for fostering a more humanistic approach in policing.

Police officers are entrusted with the duty to serve and protect citizens, yet numerous incidents reveal conduct that starkly contradicts the principle of "Serving and Protecting." This issue raises pressing questions about the need for democratic solutions to police reform and rebuilding public trust, especially within African American communities, where encounters with police often seem shaped by what Eberhardt, Purdie, Goff, and Davies (2004) describe as an "...automatic stereotyping process...[where]...the mere presence of a Black man, can trigger thoughts that he is violent and criminal" (p.876). A potential remedy, long discussed but rarely implemented in full, suggests that all police officers should be required to hold a higher education degree, preferably in liberal arts with a strong emphasis on the humanities (Henion & Terrill, 2015). This proposal, while supported by some scholars, has faced resistance over the years (Vollmer, 1931; Murphy, 1965; Woska, 1978; Henion & Terrill, 2015). Bruns (2010) acknowledges its merit but notes it lacks widespread support.

Proponents argue that a liberal arts education fosters value such as "individual liberty, autonomy, and dignity" (Zakaria, 2015, p.144) and supports a "Humanitarian revolution" (Pinker, 2011, p.168) that has historically advanced empathy, minority rights, women's rights, and inclusivity. Such humanistic insights are invaluable for police officers to appreciate and respect the diversity within their communities. Unfortunately, police academy training programs do not consistently include humanistic education, leaving gaps in officers' readiness to address the full spectrum of societal diversity and the nuanced needs of the communities they serve.

In the figures below, each theme of Sherwin's Conterminous Spheres of Dependency theory is segregated into four distinctive thematic clusters, rendering a visual panorama of the essence of humanism and its core values.

Figure 7. Thematic clusters

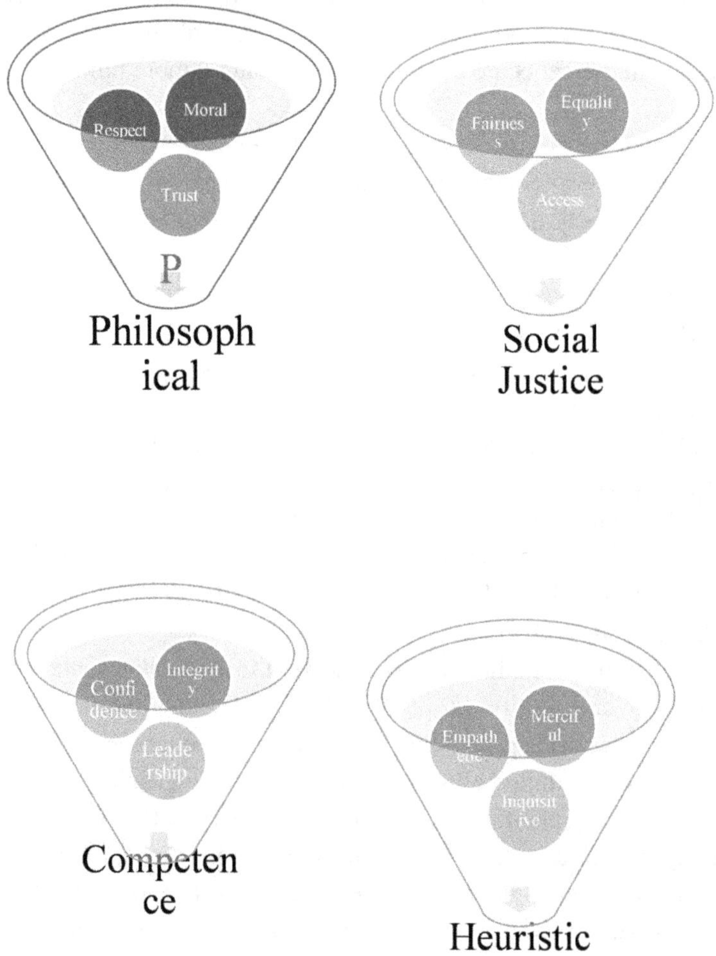

Philosophical

A philosophical outlook serves as the core foundation for cultivating trust, respect, and moral virtues. These qualities are essential for a practical and positive approach to enhancing police and citizen relationships. Police officers who adopt a philosophical framework prioritize a justice-centered perspective that ensures fairness and equality in all interactions with citizens. As Aristotle noted, "Justice...of all the virtues...is...the good of another...it does what is of advantage to others" (1962, p.114). Philosophy further promotes a sense of "rational justice," as expressed in

Rousseau's principle, "Do unto others as you would have them do unto you" (1984, p.101). Both Freire (1970) and Mill (1985) contend that respect and trust are vital for nurturing humanistic relationships, especially between those enforcing laws and the communities they serve. Therefore, trust, respect, and moral virtues are crucial values for police officers to adopt from a philosophical perspective, promoting more equitable and empathetic encounters with citizens.

Social Justice

Rousseau asserts that "there is a universal justice emanating from reason alone; but this justice, to be admitted among us, must be mutual" (2005, p. 39). His words underscore the importance of equality, where genuine choices demand equitable access. Every citizen deserves fair treatment, grounded in the fundamental rights they inherently hold. Police officers, through their oath to uphold the Constitution, commit to protecting and advocating for these rights, ensuring that the principles of fairness and justice are upheld in all their interactions with the public.

Competence

The combined virtues of confidence, leadership, and integrity are essential components of a police officer's ability to foster lasting, positive relationships within the community. Paine (1999) aptly states, "Every community has a right to demand all its agents, an account of their conduct" (p. 67). Paine's observation emphasizes the interconnected values critical for law enforcement officers. These virtues assure citizens that officers are not only competent and capable of enforcing the law with sound judgment, but that they are also trustworthy and hold themselves accountable, reinforcing the foundation of police-community trust.

Heuristic

Aristotle contemplates the role of education in developing good character, positing, "We must determine later whether the education of the individual as such, which makes a person good simply as a man [sic], is part of politics or of some other science" (1962, p. 117). Qualities like empathy, mercy, and curiosity cannot merely be imparted through reading or lectures; they must be either inherently present or cultivated through life experiences. While academic insights deepen understanding, these values are most effectively learned through lived encounters. For police officers, possessing and applying these synergistic qualities during interactions with citizens is essential for fostering trust and respect, as outlined in this thematic cluster.

Each sphere—philosophical, social justice, competence, and heuristic—encapsulates critical values that police officers must embrace to effectively engage with citizens. These thematic areas form a holistic approach, ensuring that officers are prepared not just tactically, but with a foundation of empathy, justice, and practical knowledge. Earlier chapters addressed incidents involving illicit drugs, mental health, and the use of force, underscoring the urgent need for enhanced police training in these domains. The call to defund the police often centers on perceived inadequacies in preparing officers to properly investigate and respond to mental health crises. There is merit in this argument; equipping officers with specialized training to handle these complex social challenges is essential and deserve sustained attention.

Chapter two of this book highlighted the need for specialized mental health crisis training for police officers. To strengthen this case, it is essential to present further evidence that underscores its importance. Butler, Zakimi, and Greer (2022) identify several critical issues: firstly, the shortage of mental health facilities to which police officers can refer individuals in crisis; secondly, limited access to mental health care in underserved neighborhoods; and thirdly, the political inclination to expand drug markets through policies of depenalization, decriminalization, and legalization, often seen as driving forces rather than addressing "a symptom of wider underlying issues" of illicit drug use (p. 2). These issues highlight the importance of officers having a strong foundation in the thematic spheres—philosophical, social justice, competence, and heuristic—to approach complex societal challenges with greater insight and efficacy.

There are compelling arguments for equipping police officers with intervention skills to respond effectively to mental health crises. However, implementing an intervention program involves overcoming several significant obstacles. First, determining the appropriate type of training is essential to ensure it meets the needs of both police officers and community members. Second, identifying who should receive this training—whether it's all officers or specialized units—requires strategic planning. Third, deciding how many individuals should be trained to create meaningful impact without overextending resources presents another challenge. Fourth, gaining commitment from key stakeholders, those in positions of leadership such as police officials, political figures, and medical professionals, requires a collective dedication to sustain the program. Lastly, funding remains a fundamental barrier; deciding who will finance and how to allocate a budget for such a program is crucial to its feasibility.

To address the first obstacle, del Pozo, Sightes, Goulka, Ray, Wood, Siddiqui, and Beletsky (2021) identified critical 'gaps pertaining to descriptions of training development, design, and content specific to facilitating positive police PWUD

(People Who Use Drugs) interactions' (p. 2). They suggest that training should focus on enhancing police officers' ability to understand and interpret the behavioral intentions of individuals experiencing episodes related to drug use. Specifically, by training officers in the 'Theory of Planned Behavior (TPB)' (p. 2), they argue that officers could gain a more effective framework for selecting situationally appropriate de-escalation methods, tailored to each individual encounter.

The Crisis Intervention Team (CIT) model is recognized as 'the most comprehensive model for managing episodes involving persons with mental illness' (Morabito, Socia, Wik, and Fisher, 2017, p. 32). According to Morabito et al. (2017), CIT is structured to equip a selected group of officers with specific skills in mitigation and de-escalation techniques tailored to interactions with individuals undergoing a mental health crisis. “Officers who volunteer for CIT undertake a rigorous forty-hour training program, after which they become designated 'go-to' specialists for situations involving persons with symptoms of mental illness” (Morabito et al., 2017, p. 32). Shah (2019) reinforces the effectiveness of CIT in enhancing officers' response capabilities and reducing the need for force. Notably, Shah (2019) highlights that “4,600 officers in the Miami-Dade County Police Department have completed CIT training, and the New York Police Department has integrated CIT training into its program as well” (p. 218). This robust model underscores the potential for CIT programs to become integral in police departments nationwide.

Willis, Comartin, Victor, Kern, and Kubiak (2021) discuss additional approaches to mental health crisis de-escalation training, such as the “co-responding model” (p. 120) and the “Mobile Crisis Response Team” (p. 120). The Mobile Crisis Response Team incorporates “mental health professionals, community health workers, and peers” who collaborate with police officers, crisis services, and community resources to assist individuals and their families in obtaining essential support (Willis et al., 2021, p. 120). Despite these alternatives, Willis et al. (2021) expresses a preference for the CIT training program, emphasizing that it provides a more comprehensive, skill-focused approach tailored to equipping officers with effective de-escalation techniques and immediate mental health support.

The second obstacle focuses on the importance of making the training program a voluntary choice. There are compelling reasons for this approach. Handling situations involving individuals experiencing a mental health crisis, whether due to drug effects or mental health challenges, requires individuals with specific qualities and specialized training. Shah (2019) advocates that “CIT training needs to incorporate all members of law enforcement, not just police officers” (p. 220), suggesting a broader, inclusive training model. Ideally, candidates selected for this training would exemplify the attributes and values outlined in the thematic clusters, serving as a standard for the selection process. Given the program's intensity, built on the principles represented in the Conterminous Spheres of Dependency for fostering humanistic values, those who participate must not only embody these values but also be able to internalize, model, and apply them impartially and consistently.

The third obstacle is determining how many people should be trained. This is essential for ensuring both the viability and longevity of a mental health crisis response program. Insufficient staffing could render the program ineffective and erode its support. However, the program should remain voluntary, unlike some departments, such as the New York Police Department, which aims to "make the process mandatory training for all new recruits" (Shah, 2019, p. 220). Responding to individuals in mental health crises is both psychologically and physically demanding, often requiring debriefing and decompression time afterward. Drawing from my experiences intervening in various crisis situations from individuals convinced of alien attacks to those facing potential murder-suicide scenarios, Sherwin understands the toll these interactions can take. As a peer support member with the Chicago Police Department and a Stephen Minister Leader, Sherwin recognizes the emotional rewards of offering support, yet the work can also lead to significant stress, anxiety, and, at times, depression. These are strong arguments for the necessity of debriefing and decompression to support responders effectively.

The fourth obstacle is commitment. Commitment requires buy-in, the securing of full support from leadership, politicians, and medical professionals for a mental health crisis intervention program. For example, the NYPD allocates only two hours of training for dispatchers and "has no timeline or written plan to start any…[CIT]…training" (Shah, 2019, p. 220). Furthermore, Morabito et al. (2017) note that "few departments have trained all officers" (p. 2). This obstacle persists due to several factors: the complexity and intensity of the subject matter, the need for qualified trainers, the limited number of volunteers willing to undergo rigorous training, and, critically, the varying levels of enthusiasm regarding the necessity for the training. Ensuring broad and dedicated support is vital for effective implementation and sustainability.

The final obstacle is funding. The current push to defund the police has led to significant reallocation of police department budgets, diverting resources away from critical areas. Political policies and legislation focusing on decriminalizing drugs and minor offenses as a means of reducing crime and preventing fatal police-citizen encounters, while well-intentioned, may fall short of achieving true justice or ensuring the safety and well-being of victims and law-abiding citizens. Compounding this issue, the limited availability of mental health facilities and inadequate access to drug treatment services hamper preventive initiatives and leave law enforcement in a challenging position without sufficient resources to address complex social issues effectively. Police reform cannot be realistically achieved if officers are not provided with the necessary tools and training to perform their roles adequately.

Cutting police funding without thoughtful re-investment in support structures ultimately risks compromising public safety.

In conclusion, police officers who embody humanism will help in the reform process, developed by Sherwin, and instill trust in the communities they serve and protect.

Figure 8. Reform process

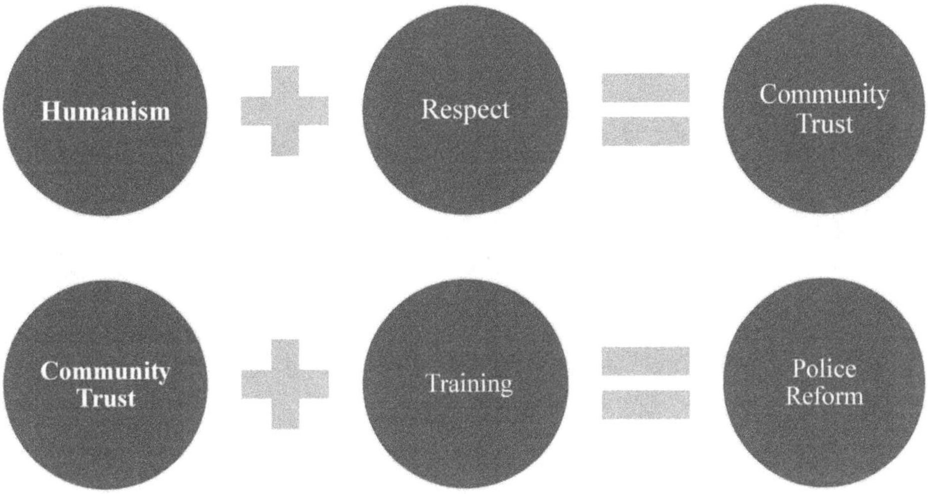

Chapter five of this book will provide a solution for these issues in a detailed and comprehensive examination of the reasons for those who choose law enforcement as a professional goal to earn a degree in criminal justice.

SECTION-3: OVERCOMING FEAR AND MISTRUST: RESPONDING TO SOCIETAL CRITICISM OF POLICING

Criticism, judgment, and disrespect often come more naturally than empathy and understanding. Years ago, Sherwin observed that people seem to "love to hate but hate to love." It seems easier to harbor resentment than to cultivate love, forgiveness, or respect. There is a tendency to seek punishment for those with whom we disagree, to demand retribution rather than reconciliation. Today, an abundance of media platforms amplifies this sentiment, frequently promoting narratives that encourage anger and division. Quick to pass judgment, many are equally quick to condemn judgment aimed at them. For individuals who are not self-actualized, this cycle can lead to feelings of unfulfillment, defensiveness, denial, and a perpetual sense of victimhood.

Fear, Anger, and Hate

Figure 9. Fear anger hate theory

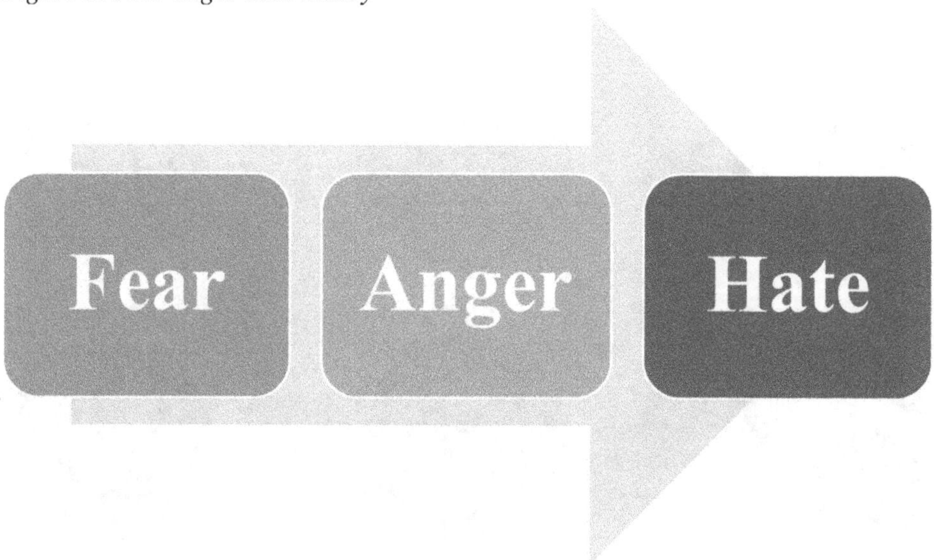

In *Webster's New World Dictionary* (2016), terms like fear, anger, and hate are defined with various nuances, encompassing both subtle and intense applications. In Sherwin's *Fear, Anger, Hate* theory, the word *fear* is interpreted primarily as the "noun agitation" and the "verb apprehension." When addressing *anger,* Sherwin focuses on aspects like "annoyance, exasperation, resentment, temper, and aggravation." For *hate,* Sherwin draws upon definitions that include the verbs "dislike greatly, regard with disgust, find intolerable," and the nouns "dislike, resentment, bad feeling, bitterness, disgust, and contempt." These definitions align closely with the dynamics of these emotions as they manifest in individual and social contexts.

Fear often arises from a lack of knowledge, understanding, and lack of self-confidence. We all encounter circumstances in life that spark some level of fear such as concerns about our children as they grow, about our health, aging, financial stability, and many other issues that appear on our life's doorstep. There's also fear of the unknown, especially toward certain people or groups based on race, culture, faith, personal orientation, etc. When we lack knowledge or hold assumptions about a person or group, uncertainty builds. Uncertainty makes us fearful and uncomfortable. That discomfort can escalate into contempt or criticism, manifesting as anger. However, this anger is often less about others and more a reflection of our internal struggle to understand or accept differences. Frustration and hostility build as we subconsciously defend our self-esteem, feeling victimized by our own lack of comprehension. This can spiral into hatred, causing us to lash out verbally or physically, viewing others as threats or adversaries.

Consider this analogy: Imagine buying a piece of furniture to assemble at home. The box is bulky and heavy, and upon opening it, you find numerous parts and a lengthy, complex instruction booklet. Confusion and self-doubt arise, sparking a sense of fear. Frustration builds as you struggle to understand the instructions, leading to anger directed at the item, the directions, the cost, and even the store. But this frustration stems from an internal reaction; your need for self-esteem feels undermined by not knowing what to do. In this state, you may overlook options like watching an instructional video or asking for help, because anger clouds your judgment. What started as confusion evolved into anger and, finally, hate.

The challenge to people is learning how to manage these fears in constructive ways. Lashing out against things that we are fearful of is antithetical to creating harmony, trust, and respect. Fear perpetuates anger while simultaneously provoking recalcitrant rebellion and polarization. When fear goes unchecked, it often evolves into anger, which can lead to hate that is directed at individuals, objects, or systems, including law enforcement and the criminal justice system. Fearful people react defensively. Someone who is in denial of truths or objective reasoning remain steadfast in their position of being "right," disregarding any corrective criticism or opposing views as they lack humility or self-confidence to acknowledge other perspectives. Finally, those who see themselves as perpetual victims believe that the world is against them, highlighting a deficit in self-actualization and the capacity to take charge of their lives. Police departments must develop sustainable solutions that eliminate the fear society has for police officers.

Hate Versus Love

The boundary between hate and love is thin, as both are powerful, emotionally driven states of mind. Because of this, people can often shift abruptly from one to the other. Emotions tend to cloud our minds, making it difficult to distinguish between fact and truth. This emotional vulnerability opens the door to influences that encourage us to harbor resentment, especially toward groups like police officers. As a result, criticism and disrespect toward law enforcement become easier to express. This follows to be true of my statement that people "love to hate" and "hate to love." This is partly because hate requires less effort; it acts like an emotional release valve. In contrast, love demands a continuous investment of energy, patience, and forgiveness, commitments that require replenishing every day.

Hate, on the other hand, becomes an easy path of surrender, a way to reject without taking on the responsibility of understanding. It doesn't require accountability or self-reflection. Love, however, calls for personal accountability, empathy, and forgiveness, qualities that involve thoughtful engagement and effort. When we love, we don't simply discard people, issues, or practices because we don't understand or agree. We take responsibility, listen, care, and extend respect, which all demand energy and willingness to be present and patient. Hate, however, allows a person to avoid these efforts, to point fingers and walk away without reflecting on their causations. In hate, a person lacks the moral compass that might lead them to the truth; it's easier to criticize and discard rather than to make the effort to understand, discern, or investigate.

Hope

In today's fast-paced and demanding world, we all strive to ensure the safety, health, security, and overall well-being of our families and ourselves. It's natural to question, "What is the purpose behind all this effort?" or "Where will all our struggles lead us?" Constantly, we are bombarded with news that tests our hopes for peace, prosperity, and a lasting, fulfilling life. Social media and news platforms often amplify societal discord, shaping our perceptions and eroding our trust, faith, and respect for one another. Unfortunately, police officers are frequently stereotyped as oppressors rather than protectors, adding to the disillusionment many feel and contributing to a cycle of misunderstanding and mistrust.

Our lives today mirror the past, with history reminding us that while circumstances evolve, fundamental challenges often remain unchanged. Social discord, crime, conflict, and skepticism toward law enforcement and the justice system have always existed, much as they do today. Yet, we cannot afford to abandon hope. Hope is essential for resilience and for crafting lasting solutions for police reform with solutions that do not involve defunding or dismantling but instead support growth and improvement. Hope is vital to our survival, shaping a sense of purpose and future. Police officers exemplify this hope, serving communities tirelessly, regardless of conditions, holidays, or crises, made evident during the COVID-19 pandemic. Haugk (1984) emphasizes the comfort in knowing that someone is always available, around the clock, in times of need (p. 149). He argues that without hope, individuals often experience increased anxiety, frustration, and despair, leading them to feel like giving up. Importantly, Haugk points out that reducing anxiety can inspire hope: "Anxiety reduction can be very hope-producing itself" (p. 149). The promise of a better world, improved police practices, and safer communities relies on maintaining hope. We must continue to believe and work toward a hopeful future; one where positive change is possible.

Love

Goff (2012) reflects on the essence of love, stating, "I used to think being loved was the greatest thing to think about, but now I know love is never satisfied just thinking about it" (p. 17). Aristotle complements this notion by presenting love as a driving force of goodness, deeply embedded in one's dedication to their work (Ward, 1968). Love plays a crucial role in fostering pride and satisfaction in one's profession, creating a genuine connection between who people are and what they do. Love is the foundation for achieving excellence, especially in law enforcement, where a love for the profession is essential for upholding humanistic values. This love cultivates self-actualization, fueling empowerment, confidence, and self-esteem. These qualities are vital for fostering community safety, respect, and trust.

Maslow (2013) suggests that a lack of self-actualization often stems from an absence of love, as people's beliefs about whether they are loved shape their sense of fulfillment. The perception of love, whether accurate or imagined, is essential, as everyone craves a love that transcends mere romantic affection. It is love rooted in a feeling of belonging, worthiness, and respect from others. This type of love bolsters self-esteem, which in turn fuels self-actualization, empowering individuals to set personal goals, experience pride, and find fulfillment. Without self-esteem and the satisfaction of this fundamental need for love, fear, anger, hate, and even disregard for others can take root. Lacking life satisfaction, people may become critical, envious, and reactive. They may distort reality through an emotional lens clouded by insecurity, causing them to lash out, either subtly or overtly, often finding camaraderie among like-minded groups and on social media.

Maslow (2013) explains that this deprivation leads people to respond defensively, with hostility towards perceived threats, "Thwarting in these freedoms will be reacted to with a threat or emergency response" (p. 8). He further argues that "any danger to them... [satisfaction of our basic needs] ...any deprivation or blocking of their free use, must be indirectly threatening to the basic needs themselves" (p. 8). This perceived deprivation often fuels disdain for institutions like law enforcement, which many view through a critical lens, as it's easier to express hate than love, especially since love requires emotional energy, confidence, and self-actualization. Without feeling loved, people may struggle with anxiety, insecurity, and heightened sensitivity, especially when faced with challenging police-citizen encounters. Love requires forgiveness, a challenging virtue for many, especially in times of tension. The onus to initiate love and trust in this dynamic rests largely on law enforcement. Through intentional training, dedicated leadership, and a transformative culture shift, police departments have an opportunity to rebuild trust by embodying the principles of love for their communities and profession, thereby fostering public confidence, respect, and support.

Feelings

The connection, or disconnect, between police officers and citizens is deeply rooted in mutual perceptions and emotional responses. For genuine change, police departments must take proactive steps to transform these feelings through authentic, community-centered outreach. Rather than dictating solutions, departments should deploy community ambassadors to engage directly with residents, asking about their specific needs and concerns regarding safety, crime prevention, and the type of support they desire from law enforcement. This approach fosters a partnership with communities, allowing residents to feel valued and heard, not simply managed.

Instead of presuming what is best for communities, it's crucial for police representatives to actively listen and learn from those they serve, establishing shared goals for safety, trust, and mutual respect. This approach is not only feasible but has a proven track record of success. As a supervisor, engaging with community leaders galvanized collaborative planning, resulting in targeted strategies that directly addressed community concerns and contributed to meaningful, positive outcomes. This cooperative model can bridge the gap between police and citizens, laying the groundwork for trust and effective policing through a genuine partnership.

One significant outcome that I experienced while using this modality was the strengthening of community relationships and the development of effective teamwork. Collaborating with community leaders built a powerful bond rooted in mutual respect, trust, and confidence. These meetings highlighted a shared commitment to community safety and welfare, creating an environment that encouraged open and honest dialogue. The result was a constructive exchange of unvarnished ideas and suggestions, laying a strong foundation for practical, sustainable solutions. When a community feels confident that its voice and input are respected and acknowledged, it fosters a sense of ownership in creating positive outcomes, a vital factor in enhancing respect and trust.

Another powerful result in utilizing this method of community building was the tangible success in reducing crime and enhancing the quality of life within the community. Sherwin recalls one particularly impactful meeting held in a church. This was significant not only because of its outcome but for the community's participation. Expecting a small meeting with the Pastor and a few church elders, Sherwin brought his entire gang team as a show of genuine commitment. Upon arrival, the Pastor warmly welcomed Sherwin and his team and led the way to the worship space where chairs were placed on the altar for us. To the surprise of Sherwin and his team, the entire congregation was present. The meeting focused on two critical issues affecting the community: gang activity and quality-of-life crimes. Community members expressed their fear and frustration of the gang members who roamed the streets, intimidating residents and openly engaging in activities like street gambling and prostitution at all hours. They voiced a strong desire to reclaim their neighborhood and sought accountability from the parents of the young offenders.

Almost every attendee contributed ideas and questions, and after several hours, Sherwin and his team left with a clear understanding of the issues and a plan of action. Within a few weeks, the efforts of Sherwin's gang team succeeded in removing the disruptive elements from the neighborhood, restoring a sense of safety and gratitude among the residents. However, a reality emerged: although Sherwin's team improved the safety of that neighborhood, those causing the issues simply relocated to another area where the new community had not yet joined forces with law enforcement. Real lasting change requires collaboration across neighborhoods, working collectively with police to achieve a safer environment. While it may seem idealistic, Sherwin believes that if citizens felt actively involved in the development of solutions and knew they could partner with law enforcement, crime could be managed and reduced significantly, instilling a sense of safety throughout communities, cities, and towns.

Currently, this ideal is far from reality, as many individuals feel threatened at the sight of a police vehicle or during a police-citizen interaction. This perception triggers an immediate critical reaction. Often, when someone is stopped by the police, whether for a traffic matter or another reason, they become defensive, angry, and disrespectful, seeing themselves as victims rather than evaluating the situation calmly. This reaction is fueled by fear, anger, hate, which prompts them to challenge police officers, sometimes accusing them of "picking on them" instead of focusing on "catching real criminals." A recurring sentiment in these interactions is, "Don't you know who I am?" Sherwin encountered numerous situations where people responded in this reactive, confrontational way. For instance...

CONCLUSION: THE WANT-A-BE (AS TOLD BY SHERWIN)

As a sergeant supervising a gang team, I once received a request for assistance from a high school principal concerned about gang members intimidating students and recruiting them into their ranks outside the school. These gang members positioned themselves around the school's perimeter, attempting to coerce students into joining their group. To address this, I assigned officers from the gang team to monitor the area for any gang-related activity. They soon observed a group of gang members engaging in intimidation tactics, bullying several high school students while displaying gang signs in a show of dominance. The officers subsequently arrested five individuals, one of whom was a high school junior. The others, all between the ages of 18 and 20, were not students.

The high school student stood out: he was small in stature, dressed in formal attire; dressed in pants, a shirt, a bow tie, large, thick glasses, and holding a briefcase. He clearly didn't fit the stereotypical image of a gang member. However, he was participating alongside the others, displaying gang signs with friends he openly admitted to associating with. The officers transported all five young men to the police station for processing. Shortly after, I received a call from the mother of the high school junior. She was quite upset, accusing the police officers of wrongful arrest and demanding her son's release. Identifying herself as a lawyer, she asserted that her son, an honor student, had no gang affiliations and that the arrest was unwarranted.

I listened to her concerns, then calmly asked if she knew her son's friends. She responded with an emphatic affirmation of knowing them well. The mother informed me that those young men were frequent guests in her home. She insisted that they had no affiliation or involvement in any gang. It was only after I shared with her that these young men were indeed documented gang members with records of serious criminal activity that her tone softened. She apologized and came to the police station to take her son home.

The lack of self-actualization clouds a person's visual sensory system thus rendering the inability to see things for what they really are. Thus, people fail to examine issues, incidents, and information critically. This failure places people in a defensive posture that makes them critical of anyone suggesting they are wrong. This defensive response contributes to people becoming protective, aggressive, and angry as now, they see themselves as victims. They suffer a loss of self-esteem and emotions like fear, anger, and hate becoming dominant. As these emotions escalate, their judgment and discernment become clouded thus, provoking individuals to respond reactively based on subconscious triggers rather than rational thought. This response is often fueled by misinformation from sources they trust that often leads to hostility. As a result, they view authority figures, such as police officers, as adversaries rather than allies, perceiving them as a threat.

The COVID-19 pandemic created a similar reaction among the public. With public spaces closed, work routines interrupted, and social interactions limited, people were ordered to keep their distance, wear masks, and remain indoors because congregating was forbidden. This environment fostered a sense of anomie, or normlessness, disrupting social norms and exacerbating feelings of isolation. For many, the inability to fulfill basic social needs led to feelings of victimization. This experience made people more defensive, hostile, and sensitive, responding to the pandemic's constraints with heightened frustration. This lack of self-actualization, stemming from disrupted social structures, mirrors the reasons behind the growing criticism and disrespect toward police officers and law enforcement as people projected their frustrations onto authority figures.

Historically, society's respect and trust for police officers has often been shaped by group affiliation and social capital, creating a compelling contrast between learning through direct experience and being influenced by hearsay. One group, comprised of self-actualized individuals, tends to examine issues thoughtfully rather than reacting impulsively. They do not see themselves as victims but rather feel empowered to critically distinguish truth from misinformation. With a foundation of social capital, this group holds an optimistic view of the world, favoring rational solutions over pessimism. Rather than stereotyping police as oppressors, they recognize the constructive role that law enforcement can play in society. They view police reform as a positive avenue for growth and modernization, understanding that all societal institutions, corporate or government, should be accountable for any harm caused. For this group, failures do not erode trust; instead, these setbacks are seen as valuable learning experiences that pave the way for sustainable solutions, improvements, and necessary reforms rather than defunding or dismantling.

In contrast, the second group relies heavily on hearsay, lacking self-actualization and often perceiving themselves as victims. The belief in their own victimhood leads them to reactively accept external narratives without critical examination. With fragile self-esteem, they are highly influenced by external opinions and seek validation and sympathy. Many in this group demand retribution and the removal of perceived threats to their need for recognition and affirmation. They desire awards and public accolades to fulfill what they see as deserved acknowledgment, stemming from a deep need for approval. Due to this vulnerability, they become critical, defensive, and quick to judge others, particularly police officers, whom they view through a lens of suspicion and opposition rather than as protectors of justice.

This perception, often fueled by stereotypes, lacks a foundation for self-awareness, leaving them easily angered and prone to aggression. They feel oppressed by societal forces, attributing this sense of repression to police officers, whom they view as obstacles to their vision of freedom and justice. Consequently, they mistrust and do not respect law enforcement, seeing it as antithetical to their interests and ideals. This group often advocates for the defunding or abolition of police, feeling threatened by what they perceive as interference in their personal freedoms, unaware that their own self-image and lack of self-actualization contribute significantly to their mistrust.

To foster unity between these two groups, there is a pressing need for a bridging effort that encourages constructive and open dialogue. This effort should be aimed at rebuilding relationships based on understanding, forgiveness, and mutual respect. Both groups must engage collaboratively, setting aside preconceived notions to genuinely listen to each other. This process should cultivate a culture of acceptance, trust, respect, and accountability, where individuals feel safe expressing their beliefs without fear of retribution or judgment.

This approach emphasizes the importance of not imposing beliefs but instead creating space for honest expression and shared perspectives. By prioritizing this respectful exchange, the foundation is set for a culture of success, one where both groups can come together to design balanced, sustainable solutions that align with society's collective needs and values. Through cooperation and understanding, a pathway emerges for achieving social harmony and a shared commitment to progress.

REFERENCES

Aristotle, . (1962). *Nicomachean ethics*. Prentice Hall.

Baro, A. L., & Burlingame, D. (1999). Law enforcement and higher education; is there an impasse? Journal of Criminal Justice Education. *Academy of Criminal Justice Sciences*, 10(1), 57–69.

Bruns, D. (2010). Reflections from the one-percent of local police departments with mandatory four-year degree requirements for the new hires: Are they diamonds in the rough? *Southwest Journal of Criminal Justice*, 7(1), 87–108.

Butler, A., Zakimi, N., & Greer, A. (2022). Total systems failure: Police officers' perspectives on the impacts of the justice, health, and social service systems on people who use drugs. *Harm Reduction Journal*, 19(48), 1–13. DOI: 10.1186/s12954-022-00629-1 PMID: 35590421

Cooper, C. (1999). *Mediation & Arbitration by Patrol Police Officers*. University Press of America, Inc.

del Pozo, B., Sightes, E., Goulka, J., Ray, B., Wood, C. A., Siddiqui, S., & Beletsky, L. A. (2021). Police discretion in encounters with people who use drugs: Operationalizing the theory of planned behavior. *Harm Reduction Journal*, 18(1), 1–32. DOI: 10.1186/s12954-021-00583-4 PMID: 34915910

Eberhardt, J. L., Purdie, V. J., Goff, P. A., & Davies, P. G. (2004). Seeing black: Race, crime, and visual processing. *Journal of Personality and Social Psychology*, 87(6), 876–893. DOI: 10.1037/0022-3514.87.6.876 PMID: 15598112

Freire, P. (1970). *Pedagogy of the oppressed*. Bloomsbury Publishing Plc.

Goff, B. (2012). *Love Does. Discover a Secretly Incredible Life in an Ordinary World*. Harper Collins Christian Publishing, Inc.

Haugk, K. C. (1984). *Christian Caregiving, a Way of Life*. Augsburg Publishing House.

Henion, A., & Terrill, W. (Feb. 2015). Do cops need college? Retrieved from https://msutoday.msu.edu/news/2015/do-cops-need-college/

Johnstone, G. (2011). *Restorative Justice, Ideas, Values, Debates* (2nd ed.). Routledge.

Maslow, A. H. (2013). *A Theory of Human Motivation. Mansfield Centre*. Martino Publishing.

Mill, J. S. (1974). *On liberty*. Penguin Books.

Morabito, M. S., Socia, K., Wik, A., & Fisher, W. H. (2017). The nature and extent of police use of force in encounters with people with behavioral health disorders. *International Journal of Law and Psychiatry*, 50, 31–37. DOI: 10.1016/j.ijlp.2016.10.001 PMID: 28029437

Murphy, M. J. (1965, March). Improving the law enforcement image. *Journal of Criminal Law and Criminology*, 56(13), 105–108.

Pain, T. (1999). *Rights of man: Dover Thrift Editions*. Dover Publications, Inc.

Pinker, S. (2011). *The better angels of our nature; why violence has declined.* Penguin Group.

Pollock, J. M. (2019). *Ethical Dilemmas and Decisions in Criminal Justice* (10th ed.). Cengage Learning, Inc.

Rousseau, J.-J. (1984). *A discourse on inequality. New York, NY: Penguin Books. Rousseau, J-J. (2005). The Social Contract.* Barnes & Noble,Inc.

Shah, P. V. (2019). The use of deadly force: People with mental health conditions and encounters with law enforcement. *Harvard Human Rights Journal*, 32, 207–221.

Siegel, L. J., & Worrall, J. L. (2018). *Introduction to Criminal Justice* (16th ed.). Cengage Learning.

Vollmer, A. (1931). Police education. *The Journal of Criminal Law and Criminology*, 22(1), 7–8.

Ward, L. R. (1968). Aristotle on criteria of moral good. *The Review of Politics*, 30(4), 476–498. DOI: 10.1017/S0034670500025195

Webster's New World College Dictionary, 2016.

Willis, T., Comartin, E., Victor, G., Kern, L., & Kubiak, S. (2021). Individuals with mental illness who have multiple encounters with law enforcement. *Journal of Offender Rehabilitation*, 60(2), 117–137. DOI: 10.1080/10509674.2020.1863298

Woska, W. J. (1978). Police officer academic standards. *Public Personnel Management*, 7(5), 312–316.

Zakaria, F. (2015). *In defense of a liberal education*. W.W. Norton & Company, Inc.

Zimabrdo, P. (2007). *The Lucifer Effect: Understanding how good people turn evil.* Random House Inc.

Chapter 4
The Evolving Role of Police Leadership and Organizational Culture

ABSTRACT

This chapter explores three critical issues that intersect with law enforcement and society which are predicated on the word "NO". The first issue focuses on police authority and the use of the word "no." There is an inherent challenge in balancing the power embedded in an authoritative role with the ability to say "no" in a way that avoids rebellion or rejection. For police officers, this requires striking a delicate balance in being firm in authority while maintaining respect and understanding. To achieve this, police officers must be devoid of hubris and grounded in practical common sense, tempered with humanistic values.

INTRODUCTION

Building on the *Conterminous Spheres of Dependency* theory introduced in Chapter Three, this chapter explores how these spheres reflect humanistic values, particularly in situations where the word "no" is used. One essential aspect of these values is the concept of "saving face." When a police officer needs to tell someone "No," the way it is delivered can lead to various outcomes. However, when the word no is employed with respect, it helps avoid humiliation and can defuse potential conflict, preventing defiance or rebellion. Sherwin offer examples from his own experiences when he employed the word "no" in police/citizen encounters, applying a humanistic approach that preserved dignity and fostered cooperation.

The second issue is the examination of the criticism and conflicts surrounding this issue.

DOI: 10.4018/979-8-3693-7979-0.ch004

Being denied something, whether material or in terms of action, prompts the question, "Why?" This questioning often touches on citizens' constitutional rights, creating a space where law enforcement must ensure that their actions are lawfully justified. The key to maintaining authority while using "no" is having clear, lawful reasoning that aligns with the rights of an individual, thus ensuring that authority is not abused but properly exercised in a manner that respects and upholds citizens' rights.

This requires police officers to use sound judgment, possess a humanistic spirit, and exercise discretion rooted in lawful methods. The lack of humanism was tragically underscored in the George Floyd incident, where the responding officers relied on authoritative power rather than humanistic discretion. By failing to de-escalate the situation, they exacerbated a social wound that sparked global outrage and rebellion. There are moments when saying "no" is clear-cut, and others when it is not. In those cases when it is not clear, it is essential to provide a lawful explanation that fosters understanding and cooperation. The ability to tell someone "No" and have them peacefully submit to the demand is a humanistic skill that must be an integral part of a police officer's character.

However, the way "no" is communicated matters just as much as the decision itself. From parents telling children "No" to signage in public spaces, the word is integral to shaping our actions, thoughts, and decisions. Yet, we are far more receptive when we understand the reasons behind it. It is crucial for police departments to recruit individuals with exceptional moral and ethical values, those who are receptive to practicing humanism in their work. Police work is not for everyone. It is an inherently stressful and challenging profession, but it is also a deeply rewarding human experience. Sherwin expresses that he loved being a police officer. Throughout his career, he had the privilege of meeting remarkable individuals, including world leaders, actors, and even Pope John Paul XXIII. But beyond these extraordinary experiences, Sherwin had the honor of working with exceptional citizens in the communities he served.

The third issue encourages society to be part of the solution rather than the problem. During Sherwin's tenure with the Chicago Police Department, he had the privilege of working with police officers from various units and departments, including federal, state, and county law enforcement agencies. The focus of all of them is to ensure equal justice for every citizen, including those who perpetrate crimes against society. Most police officers possess exceptional moral and ethical virtues, trustworthiness, professionalism, and humanistic values. Despite the negative depictions of police officers, their devotion to duty and desire to serve and protect remains undaunted. Their kindness, care, and professionalism are not always highlighted to the public, only the police/citizen encounters that have unfortunate endings. Citizen's trust and respect for police officers rarely is acknowledged by news or social media, only negative commentary of the police. Police officer's modeling of humanistic values plays a significant role with society's perception of police officers. Some public officials, media outlets, and civic leaders are frequently quick to criticize police officers, often injecting their criticisms into the public discourse without recognizing the complexity of the work police officers routinely engage in.

It is crucial that society be a part of the solution rather than part of the problem. Police officers are special people. It takes a unique individual to confront traumatic events daily, to help others, to save lives, and to risk their own safety, all while being maligned by some segments of society. Yet, police officers continue to serve and protect, without hesitation, the very people who criticize them.

SECTION-1: TRANSFORMING POLICE LEADERSHIP: THE NEED FOR HUMANISTIC AND ETHICAL COMMAND

The word "no" carries a range of meanings and can convey anything from a gentle nudge to a forceful refusal. It may represent a boundary, a law, or a punishment, delivered in various tones whether gently, critically, or even harshly. Its application may be either deliberate or indiscriminate, serving purposes that range from safety and precaution to opinion or enforcement of fact. Children, especially in the "ego" stage of psychological development, often resist the word "no," leading to tantrums or disobedience. This stage of defiance can challenge parents to exercise effective skills that guide children toward appropriate behavior. Adults, too, can react negatively to "no," perceiving it as rejection and often experiencing an emotional response. Many find it challenging to say "no" themselves, avoiding using the word either to spare someone's feelings or due to a lack of confidence in making firm decisions.

Failing to say "no" when it is warranted, however, can compromise safety or inhibit an opportunity for growth as a teaching moment. Though it can be difficult, saying "no" is often a morally responsible and loving choice. Like parents guiding their children, saying "no" can express care, respect, and a commitment to fairness and justice. It can serve as a lesson in humility, reinforcing the importance of boundaries and mutual respect. Society sometimes avoids using "no," especially with children, teaching them that everyone is a winner rather than using a "no" situation to teach them humility, to be gracious, respectful, and applaud the achievements of other people. Not everyone is a winner. Winning takes dedication, tenacity, and self-discipline. While "no" may initially cause disappointment or frustration, it is also a powerful motivator, encouraging individuals to strive harder, improve, and be a good citizen.

Countless stories illustrate how hearing "no" has not deterred people from pressing forward. Instead, it has fueled their determination to improve, to refine their skills, or to pursue their visions with renewed commitment. For some, "no" serves as a powerful motivator, pushing them to demonstrate that their ideas are viable, even revolutionary. Pioneers in various fields, whether in science, engineering, or the arts, often encountered resistance. Louis Pasteur, for example, faced criticism for deviating from established medically accepted procedure and methods, and yet his persistence led to the development of vaccines for diseases like rabies, cholera, and anthrax. Leonardo da Vinci, despite early dismissal of his innovative designs for a helicopter and solar power, laid conceptual foundations that inspired modern engineering. Similarly, artists such as Rembrandt, van Gogh, and Monet, initially disregarded as good artists, eventually shaped the very future of art. In this way, "no" can act as a catalyst, sparking creativity and perseverance. However, the power of "no" lies not just in its use but in the approach and context. When delivered thoughtfully, it can challenge and inspire without discouraging, providing a constructive push that leads to meaningful, satisfying outcomes.

The foundation of the law enforcement profession is deeply intertwined with the word "no." Police officers, wielding discretionary authority, use this word repeatedly throughout the day in various forms: during arrests, issuing citations, preventing harm, and stopping potentially dangerous situations before they escalate. The examples are numerous. Officers are entrusted by the Constitution with powers rooted in "no." They represent the only government group operating under the executive branch, that can lawfully restrain an individual's freedom of movement by telling them "No" and enforcing it. This means that police officers have the authority to utilize the word "no" while lawfully enforcing societal laws whether making arrests with or without a warrant or intervening in a situation for the purpose of maintaining order.

Yet, the word "no" is rarely welcomed by anyone, regardless of the circumstances, except when presented in a way that fosters agreement. For police officers, success often lies in making "no" more palatable, in ways that encourage individuals to accept its necessity or purpose, creating an essential "buy-in." The following example illustrates this concept of application.

Count Dracula (As told by Sherwin)

It was a crisp, clear fall night, just days before Halloween. My partner and I were on the first watch, working the midnight shift. It was a quiet weekday, the kind where activity tends to taper off after 2 a.m. My partner, a towering figure at 6'4" and 250 pounds, had a penchant for snacking, especially White Castle hamburgers. Craving a bite, he drove us over to one of their locations to indulge his taste buds. As we entered, the scent was unmistakable: the potent mixture of sizzling onions and freshly applied bleach. A distinctive pre-dawn cleaning ritual at White Castle. Even if I had been inclined toward fast food, the overwhelming bleach odor quickly dampened any temptation, so I settled contentedly with my cup of hot tea.

It was around 2:30 a.m., and my partner's hunger had been satisfied. We were patrolling our assigned beat when we overheard another unit being dispatched to a parked vehicle on a boulevard. A rather innocuous violation. Moments after the assigned police officers acknowledged the call, we heard their request for backup. Another unit replied to the request and went to the scene. With nothing else happening, and being curious, we decided to offer our services and headed over as well. Upon arrival, we found four officers on the scene. They were engaged in a heated exchange with a man whose car was parked on the boulevard. As we stepped out of our vehicle, the tension was palpable. The officers were visibly upset with the man's defiance to moving his vehicle. The officers were yelling at the man, ordering him to move his car or be arrested. My instincts kicked in; I sensed the situation was on the brink of escalation. This is never ideal for something as minor as a parking issue. My partner and I quickly approached with the purpose of calming down the situation.

As my partner and I hurried toward the scene, the sight before us was as surprising as it was oddly humorous. Behind the man in question was a sleek, glossy black Cadillac hearse parked at the curb on the boulevard. The hearse had its rear gate fully open, revealing a polished walnut casket resolutely resting inside. The casket's lid was propped up, its plush, embroidered lining made visible by the hearses interior lighting. The man causing the commotion was young, muscular, and shirtless. His upper body, arms, and face smeared in bright red paint. Tensions were running high; the officers were repeatedly ordering the recalcitrant man to move his hearse from where it was parked. The man defiantly insisted that it had to stay right where it was so that he could sleep in the casket. As I came closer to the group, frustration and irritation on both sides were getting to the breaking point, teetering dangerously close to physical confrontation.

I joined the group, looked at the painted man, and exclaimed, "Count, Count Dracula!" The crowd fell silent. The man's face shifted from frustration to surprise, and he responded, "You know who I am? You're the only one who understands!" I nodded with a knowing smile, "Of course! Everyone knows who Count Dracula is." This acknowledgment seemed to calm him, and he eagerly explained that he needed to sleep in his casket with the hearse parked precisely where it was, citing the full moon as the reason.

The moon, indeed, was casting an enchanting blue glow across the night sky. After he vented, I offered him a suggestion, reminding him that Count Dracula's powers are fully restored by the full moon. I advised him that if he wanted uninterrupted rest, he could park his hearse on the side street, where the tall trees with autumn leaves could shield him from the moon's potent rays. I pointed out an imposing Catholic church a block away, its Gothic silhouette stark against the sky, with a large cross at its spire, casting a shadow down the street. "Such proximity," I warned, "could be dangerous for the Count."

Relieved, the man thanked us all, apologizing to the officers before moving his hearse to the suggested spot under the trees. After parking the hearse, Count Dracula crawled into his casket, closed the lid, and settled in for the night. After that night, he and his hearse vanished, never to come back to the area, leaving us with an unforgettable story and a successful, peacefully resolved encounter. Vampires, they can be a little "batty"!

Humanistic skills are among the most powerful tools a police officer possesses. Effectively exercising humanistic communication skills can make the difference between the use of force and its avoidance, and between arrest and resolution. Police officers exercise considerable discretion in deciding when to arrest; most would prefer not to, unless lawfully necessary. To make a lawful arrest, police officers require probable cause, a victim, and above all, reasonable lawfulness.

As stated previously, domestic violence calls for service are the most dangerous calls for a police officer to investigate. There is always a lot of emotion in domestics. Remember my domestic violence and wayward son stories. Most police officers, have a plethora of domestic violence stories. Nonetheless, there is one moral issue involved in domestic violence that goads someone on to become violent. Infidelity. When people, regardless of who they are; their education, profession, race, culture, or personal orientation, become aware of infidelity in their relationship they become extremely impassioned and often violent. However, in cases like these, it is not uncommon that a police officer will be attacked by the victim when making an arrest. This is also true when a police officer is mandated to make an arrest, even when the victim refuses to file or sign a complaint. Many police officers have experienced the paradox of being called to enforce boundaries, only to face resistance from the very individual who sought their help. Often, these individuals want the officer to say "No" to their partner, yet resist when an arrest becomes necessary, opposing the officers' authority to act because they, the victim, do not want to be told "no". Confusing? Police work is often filled with confusing people and situations. Sometimes a police officer can never be right in the eyes of the public, especially when they tell someone "No".

Sherwin encountered numerous instances where one partner's discovery of infidelity led to intense confrontations, some resulting in serious injury, violence, or even death. These situations varied widely: some involved violent acts like mutilation, stabbing, or shooting, while others involved one partner simply calling 911, seeking the police as an advocate amid betrayal. Here's one example.

Raising Cane (As told by Sherwin)

While working on the day shift on a mild winter day, my partner and I responded to a disturbance call involving an elderly man. When we arrived at the address, we found an older gentleman sitting on the porch landing. The unsuspecting senior was warmly dressed in an overcoat, hat, scarf, gloves, and boots while holding a wooden cane. He reeked of alcohol and seemed rather agitated. As we approached him, briefly asking whether he lived there, he began shouting that we had no business there. I rang the doorbell, and soon, an elderly woman with a headscarf opened the door. After greeting her I asked if she had called the police. She confirmed she had called and promptly clarified, "I don't want you to get the wrong impression, but this man is *not* my boyfriend". She then launched into a detailed rant about wanting the senior gentleman removed from her porch. With that, she abruptly shut the door to her home.

I informed the old boss that he must leave. I informed him that it would be best to come back for a visit when he was sober. Not surprisingly, he refused my 'no" you can't stay and went into a tirade, insisting we had no right to tell him to leave. As I gently asked him to stand up, he unexpectedly began flailing his cane, striking me on my right shoulder and arm. My partner and I couldn't help but laugh as the elder continued his harmless attack, striking me several times with his cane. Eventually, my partner and I stopped laughing. I managed to disarm the hapless senior. After taking custody of his cane, I playfully scolded him. I told him he was naughty and should be ashamed of himself. I reminded him it was time to head home. After escorting him off the porch and down to the sidewalk I returned the cane to him. As the squiffy old-timer hobbled away he objurgated us, shouting profanities over his shoulder.

As the innocuous interloper shuffled off, I couldn't resist calling out, "You shouldn't be raising cane like that because you're not Abel!" but he was too absorbed in his own irritation to appreciate the joke. Clearly, humor wasn't going to bridge this 'No' moment.

SECTION-2: SHAPING ORGANIZATIONAL CULTURE: VALUES, TRUST, AND ACCOUNTABILITY IN LAW ENFORCEMENT

Dewey (1927) emphasized that in a democracy, it is essential for public officials to be held accountable for their actions through established regulations. As public officials, police officers are likewise obligated to uphold their duties to 'Serve and Protect' all citizens without prejudice. Effective service to the community demands that police officers develop strong cognitive skills, allowing them to respond thoughtfully and adaptively to a diverse array of situations.

Sir Robert Peel established the first officially recognized police department in response to public outcry over police corruption and misconduct. Recognizing the urgency of the issue, Peel restructured the police force, creating a professional organization led by seasoned leaders who enforced accountability through appropriate disciplinary actions. Peel also understood the importance of instilling humanistic values in police officers to build lasting trust and respect within the community. Today, the pursuit of reforming police conduct toward a more humanistic approach remains a crucial endeavor. Unfortunately, there have been too many police-citizen encounters that escalated into police officers' use of deadly force. These types of police-citizen occurrences have evoked numerous perspectives and criticisms from politicians, citizens, and the news media challenging the lawfulness of the police actions. These encounters damage the relationship between police and communities and have often been watershed moments for the provocation of protest movements and widespread public dissent. Although extensive literature and media coverage urge a closer examination of these interactions, politicians and police leaders are still challenged to develop meaningful, sustainable solutions that address these significantly appalling police/citizen confrontations.

Aristotle (1962) presents an essential argument for the necessity of change, noting that "…there are things which…are nevertheless changeable, as are all human things" (p.131). Applying a philosophical approach to police-citizen interactions is paramount; virtues rooted in philosophy provide the foundation for lasting police-community relations. Dewey (1927) echoes this sentiment, observing that "Bodies of men are constantly engaged in attacking and trying to change some political habits, while other bodies of men are actively supporting and justifying them" (p.6). Paradoxically, some politicians may hinder the integration of these philosophical principles that could foster more humanistic police-community relations. Nonetheless, politicians have a vital role in the philosophical shift toward a sustainable and respectful relationship between police and citizens.

Racism remains a persistent concern, especially among social justice groups like Black Lives Matter (BLM), whose criticism of African American citizens being shot and killed by police officers poses a significant impediment to restoring respect and trust between the police and citizens. This is an especially sensitive subject within African American neighborhoods and has prompted other demographics to take notice, leading to intense political outrage. Authors of numerous articles, books, and various forms of social media have confronted police departments with their indignation of their policies on the use of force and the apparent lack of humanistic values regarding the shooting deaths of African Americans during police-citizen encounters. These confrontations have resulted in manifold arguments, court cases, civil litigations, and protests throughout the United States, leaving some race-related questions unanswered. The frequency of clashes between police officers and citizens have caused a concerning sociological disconnect. Police officers view the crimes, lack of trust, and disrespect for laws and them as an affront to the safety of society. Wherein, citizens, politicians, and the media view the police officers as oppressors rather than crusaders of justice. Consequently, these clashes between police officers and citizens have manifest fear among citizens of color of being stopped by a police officer. Unfortunately, the fear, has caused anger and hate among citizens that erupts when being engaged by a police officer. The conundrum is whether police officers have the humanistic skills to interpret the fear being projected by citizens as a threat or a natural emotion because of their presence. Thus, a police officer who embodies humanistic values will understand and respond by de-escalating the situation. Wherein, a police officer who lacks humanistic values will react out of their own fear of being challenged of their authority. This can ultimately result in the use of force, including deadly force.

Barry (2005), addressing social justice concerns, sheds light on a pressing issue in African American communities: the prevalence of police arrests. Barry argues, "The high level of police surveillance (backed up by a network of informers) in the ghetto, combined with a discriminatory use of police discretion, results in a very high rate of arrests among African Americans in large cities" (p.95). Many citizens feel that police officers are overly focused on making arrests, often without substantial evidence or probable cause. This perception aligns with criticism of public schools, which, rather than relying on alternatives like peer juries, teen courts, or community-justice programs, shift disciplinary responsibilities to police officers (Adams, Blumenfeld, Castandeda, Hackman, Peters, & Zuniga, 2013, p.553). School-based police officers, hired by the school board, often conduct random locker searches, enforce discipline, and arrest students, with their performance evaluated by the number of arrests they make (Adams et al., 2013, p.552). However, the assertion that police make arbitrary arrests is disputable, and the issue has become highly political. Communities face a divided stance on the role of police in schools: saying "no" to police liaisons may reduce visible security but also potentially undermine school safety, making schools more vulnerable to violence, including active shooter incidents. Conversely, the absence of officers can lead to an atmosphere of heightened anxiety, diminishing the environment's focus on academic excellence. The word "no" here signifies a complex choice, weighing the balance between fostering a secure and supportive academic setting and preserving an environment free of heavy surveillance.

Fear of being shot by police is a pervasive concern among citizens, who often feel that officers are more focused on protecting each other than ensuring thorough and transparent investigations into such incidents. This sentiment reflects a belief that accountability within law enforcement is lacking. Roy (2009) noted a similar issue in the case of Amadou Diallo, who was fatally shot by plainclothes New York City officers. Roy questioned the ethical and moral judgment of those officers, echoing the concerns raised in the 2014 Chicago case involving Laquan McDonald, a seventeen-year-old African American male who was shot multiple times by Officer Jason Van Dyke. Many in the public questioned whether the investigation into McDonald's death was genuinely transparent or aimed at preserving police interests, fueling the perception that law enforcement supports action like those of Van Dyke.

Ward (1968) offers an Aristotelian viewpoint on public reactions, noting, "What the press, and therefore the public, tend to pick up in matters of social and moral philosophy is the negative side, and it is regarding this side that press, and public tend to get excited" (p. 479). Unfortunately, this tendency makes police officers especially vulnerable to criticism and media bias, particularly when their responses come across as heavy-handed "no" statements without an effort to employ alternative conflict resolution methods. This perception is compounded by a lack of accessible accountability measures, reinforcing fears and mistrust within communities.

For these reasons and more, citizens are often quick to question why they are being told "no" during encounters with police. They wonder about the foundation of this "no." In light of the many incidents highlighted by media and amplified by anti-police groups, coupled with a lack of self-actualization, many people feel victimized by police interactions. When individuals feel that their "freedom to speak, freedom to act without causing harm, freedom to express, freedom to investigate and seek information, freedom to defend oneself, justice, fairness, honesty, and orderliness" (Maslow, 2013, p. 8) are being infringed upon, they feel threatened. This perceived alarm triggers feelings of fear, anger, and hate, leading to a reactionary "no" in response. Citizens protest, saying, "No, we don't want the police to react this way. No, we don't want harm to be inflicted without justification. No, we don't want to be mistreated, abused, or disrespected."

To address these concerns, police departments must cultivate a culture that transforms these types of "no" into actions that build respect and trust. Police departments must embrace reform by changing agency culture to command respect, trust, confidence, and integrity. This is not a time to retreat or concede but rather to take decisive steps to restore community trust and respect. Achieving this requires leadership and political support, as well as a committed effort to recruit quality candidates who not only possess liberal arts education but who also genuinely internalize humanistic values. This doesn't imply that police officers should avoid saying "no" when warranted but rather that they should know how to deliver it in ways that de-escalate situations and foster compliance with their lawful authority.

Police officers with exceptional communication skills inherently project self-confidence, a quality that, paired with clear communication, often leads to compliance from the public. People are generally more willing to listen to and follow the directives of a police officer who exhibits these qualities, as they serve to disarm tension. Even individuals inclined to resist authority tend to respond positively to an officer who exudes calm confidence and employs strong communication techniques. Randolph (2016) underscores the significance of this skill, noting, "The ability and capacity instantaneously to create trust and respect is rarely intuitive; more frequently, it is the product of intense and meticulous training" (p. 37). This foundational training begins at the police academy but should not end there; it must be continuously reinforced as part of an ongoing professional development program throughout an officer's career.

One essential communication skill that should be integrated into police training is Nonviolent Communication (NVC), a technique that fosters respectful and effective interactions. NVC training, as emphasized by Rosenberg (2015), can equip officers with methods to de-escalate conflicts and communicate empathetically, fostering a constructive relationship with the communities they serve.

Nonviolent communication (NVC) skills empower individuals "to remain human, even under trying conditions" (Rosenberg, 2015, p. 3). Police officers equipped with NVC skills are better positioned to de-escalate emotionally charged situations without relying on force. Officers trained in these skills adopt a wholesight perspective, which fosters vigilance in remaining empathetic and unbiased during interactions with citizens. Such police officers engage in active listening, not merely hearing words, but also understanding the unspoken cues. Randolph (2016) highlights a common pitfall in listening: "we do not listen properly; we listen from a selfish perspective, based upon what we think we need to know, rather than listening in order to hear what others have to say" (p. 37). Mastering listening skills enables police officers to discern both facts and underlying truths, aligning them as defenders of justice rather than mere enforcers. This approach often leads to greater respect, trust, and compliance from citizens.

Furthermore, an essential aspect of effective communication is ensuring that interactions allow individuals to "save face." This respect for personal dignity, even in tense situations, builds a foundation for positive police-community relations and reduces the likelihood of conflict escalation.

Fisher and Ury (1981) emphasize the significance of respecting others' perspectives to help them "save face" during interactions, particularly in high-stress situations. This approach is exemplified in my handling of "Count Dracula," where Sherwin acknowledged and validated his self-identity, thereby preserving his dignity and avoiding confrontation. According to Fisher and Ury, "Face saving reflects a person's need to reconcile the stand he [sic] takes" (p. 29). These skills are crucial for mitigating fear, anger, and hate often triggered by emotionally charged encounters. However, their value extends beyond potentially violent interactions, as they are equally beneficial in everyday interactions between police officers and citizens.

Police officers should routinely employ these communication strategies, fostering respect and trust, while upholding everyone's dignity, even when saying "NO." It is essential that officers, as trained professionals, take the lead in de-escalating and bringing calm to situations without expecting or requiring citizens to possess similar skills, particularly as citizens may already be emotionally heightened. By doing so, police officers reinforce their role as peacekeepers, promoting constructive engagement and ensuring that every individual feels respected.

SECTION-3: LEADERSHIP IN ACTION: INSPIRING COMMUNITY TRUST THROUGH INTEGRITY AND RESPONSIBILITY

To Be a Cop

I think there's no higher calling in terms of a career than public service, which is a chance to make a difference in people's lives and improve the world. Jack Lew

Today's world, as portrayed across various media, is filled with images and narratives of individuals committing violent acts against others and rebelling against law enforcement. Unfortunately, this recurring theme among a small segment of offenders often casts police officers as targets for channeling their resentment. Each day, police officers face threats of being shot, stabbed, beaten, or openly defied. Diverse groups have emerged, forming coalitions to voice their grievances about perceived instances of police misuse of power. Through slogans and chants, these groups may either rally support or fuel an oppositional and disruptive attitude toward law enforcement. But is this hostility toward the police a recent societal development? Is the resistance against authority something unique to modern times? In truth, opposition to law enforcement is as old as the institution of organized policing itself.

It has always been this way. Sir Robert Peel faced public opposition stemming from a lack of humanism in the police force. Similarly, August Vollmer and Robert Murphy encountered intense criticism, prompting their advocacy for police reform. All three sought a transformation that would rebuild community trust. Their vision was of police officers embodying humanistic qualities of helping, caring, and respecting others while protecting citizens regardless of race, culture, education, or sexual orientation. Herein lies a paradox: the issue remains unchanged over time, which may offer some solace by showing it is not an isolated anomaly. However, it is equally concerning because it persists as a deeply divisive social challenge. The path to a solution is clear, education is the answer.

Peel, Vollmer, and Murphy emphasized that reform within law enforcement required reshaping society's perception of police officers. They rejected an "Us versus Them" mentality or the notion that citizens were the "enemy," as well as uniforms that projected a harsh image of dominance and authority. As self-reflective leaders, they recognized their accountability in fostering positive police-citizen relationships. Their vision for reform centered on cultivating trust, care, and respect between police officers and citizens. Peel, Vollmer, and Murphy demanded professionalism from police officers, urging them to be community leaders and role models, embodying a presence that instills respect and sets a standard for civic engagement.

Police officers, by oath, commit to being model leaders within their communities. As part of the executive branch of government, police departments hold the crucial role of upholding the law and are directly accountable to the public, positioning police officers in a role of power that, if not guided by virtues grounded in humanistic education, may amplify instances of excessive behavior. Policing is a vocation—a profession filled with individuals who possess "heart" and are ready to embrace the diverse roles required daily: building community trust, upholding justice, ensuring public safety, and protecting citizens from harm. The goal is to "Make a Difference" in ways that inspire confidence, not fear. Police officers should strive to project an image of trust and approachability, not one that resembles a militaristic presence, which can instill apprehension rather than reassurance. When police officers wear uniforms resembling military attire, as portrayed in Rockwell's second image, it sends a message that danger is near, leaving citizens to feel more threatened than protected.

Being a police officer involves facing complex, sometimes perilous situations that might make the average citizen question why anyone would choose such a profession. Sadly, a growing tide of hostile rhetoric encourages threats of physical harm against police officers, stokes violent street protests, and fosters a general disregard for respect toward law enforcement. While some may enter law enforcement primarily for the salary, medical benefits, or retirement plans, these motivations alone fall short of embodying the qualities that define a true, committed professional in law enforcement. It's the dedication to service, resilience in the face of challenges, and a commitment to upholding justice that form the foundation of what makes a good police officer.

Police officers hold a unique and often mysterious influence on human interaction; they rarely know the full impact they have on others. Therefore, it is essential to consistently approach others with respect, kindness, and fairness, an effort grounded in being true to oneself. The adage "clothes make the person" underscores this idea, and Zimbardo (2007) agrees. However, just as beauty is only surface-deep, uniforms also merely cover the person within. Zimbardo (2007) contends that people embody the roles represented by their uniforms, but the question remains: which uniform are they adopting? Is it one that signifies power and authority, or one that conveys hope, trust, and protection? Only the latter projects an image of someone willing to resolve issues, a police officer who embodies humanistic values. This is the kind of police officer communities need: one who serves and protects with diligence, respect, and dignity. Such a police officer wears a uniform that represents confidence, strong moral and ethical principles, and the guardianship of the community.

Greek's (2009) pictorial study of police officers engaging with citizens in diverse scenarios reveals a visual ethnographic narrative. He organizes his findings into two layers of perception. The first tier suggests, "The perception that police are in control of situations and, in effect, maintaining public order, is fostered by visual clues" (p.20). These visual elements include police officers dressed in uniform, the visibility of their weapons, the presence of multiple officers, and clearly marked patrol vehicles. According to Greek (2009), the public views these displays of police presence, authority, and control as typical and reassuring. Citizens tend to expect that once police officers manage a situation, there will be no risk of sudden, unjustified aggression from either the police or those involved in the incident. This visual display reinforces the notion of police officers being stabilizing figures, creating an atmosphere of safety and order.

The second tier of perception, Greek (2009) explains, is "...the perception that police are present at particular locations to assist citizens rather than control their behavior" (p.20). This impression is cultivated when police officers are in less formal attire or on horseback, bicycles, foot patrol, or Segways. Such images present police officers as friendly, approachable, and trustworthy, encouraging citizens to engage openly with them. This approach fosters a sense of partnership between police officers and the community, paving the way for collaborative efforts to address social justice concerns. Addressing these issues effectively requires a cooperative dynamic, where citizens and police officers work together toward shared goals, an endeavor that demands police officers who view their profession as an exciting, service-oriented vocation.

Police work is a calling, one that is rewarding, thrilling, and full of surprises. It should be interiorized as a vocation rather than just a career. It brings police officers face-to-face with real people, real problems, and the full spectrum of human experiences. Being a police officer offers countless chances to make a difference by helping others, providing care, offering encouragement, mentoring, and ultimately, protecting those in need. It's a job that demands courage, humility, and resilience. Performing the services and safety of police work evokes emotions that range from sadness to profound joy. Police work reveals both the light and dark sides of life, evil and goodness, sin and virtue, often in a single eight-hour shift. This exposure either strengthens a police officer's humanitarian resolve or seduces them toward the dangers of corruption. Police officers are human, and there should be consistent efforts to preserve that humanity. When police officers patrol in militarized uniforms, the image shifts from that of a compassionate protector to an intimidating and frightening oppressor. Sherwin had countless experiences that affirmed his pride in being a police officer, yet one story stands out, capturing just how deeply rewarding this work can be.

The Gift (As told by Sherwin)

It was a bright summer day, and I was working alone assigned to the day watch. Working solo didn't bother me; it reminded me of my days on the farm, spending hours in the field with time to reflect. My partner was off enjoying a day with his family. The morning was calm, and I was on preventive patrol, which I enjoyed. Police officers are well-acquainted with their beat of assignment. I knew the business owners, many of the neighbors, the ER staff at the four hospitals, the pastors of local churches, the firefighters and paramedics from the three firehouses, and, of course, many residents, especially the youth. Even the local troublemakers were familiar faces. We shared mutual respect. The radio was quiet until, suddenly, the dispatcher assigned me a confinement call on the second floor of an apartment building. It was around 10:00 a.m. The dispatcher assured me that paramedics were on route.

I had responded to confinement calls before and even assisted in delivering four babies. Still, despite the experience, I knew the urgency of the call, so I drove quickly to the scene. Once there, I took the stairs two at a time to reach the second floor and searched for the correct apartment number. I located it. When I knocked on the apartment door I heard a faint, trembling voice from inside, "Help me, I'm in the bathroom." The door was unlocked, so I entered. The apartment was clean, modestly furnished, and invitingly cozy. I quickly oriented myself, spotting the bathroom's location and headed straight toward it.

Entering the bathroom, I found a woman lying on the floor, visibly distressed, crying in pain, and unmistakably in labor. A puddle beneath her indicated that her water bag had broken. I knelt beside her, holding her hand as she explained she had come into the bathroom thinking she needed to relieve herself, only to realize her baby was on the way. There was no time to wait. I assured her that everything would be fine and that the paramedics were on the way. She told me it was time; the baby did not want to wait. I took a deep breath and told her to do the same. I prayed for guidance. I felt confident as I encouraged her to push, and with care, I guided her baby out into the world: a beautiful little girl. After gently clearing the baby's mouth, I gave her a light pat on her backside, and she let out a powerful, healthy cry that seemed to echo through the neighborhood. She made the whole world aware of her presence. I held this new life carefully in my hands, greeting her as she wailed with all the strength she had.

The mother's face lit up, tears streaming down as she reached for her daughter. I helped the new mother to the couch in the living room, where she could hold her new baby close to her. To keep things sterile, I found some newspapers, placed them on the mother and then placed her baby there and then covered the baby with more newspaper. The baby was lively, vocal, and full of life, a beautiful sight.

I knew that the umbilical cord needed to be cut soon, ideally within twenty minutes, but there was nothing in the apartment sharp enough to do the job. While continuing my search for scissors or a knife, the door swung open, and in came a familiar face, a large red-headed paramedic that I recognized from other calls for service. He was slightly out of breath, apologizing for the delay and immediately asking about the umbilical cord. When I explained that there was nothing available to cut off, he quickly surmised the urgency. Without missing a beat, he knelt beside the mother and baby and, in an unexpected but effective move, bit through the cord, skillfully severing it just in time.

His unorthodox but quick-thinking approach ensured that the mother and baby avoided the serious risk of peritonitis infection. Just then, the second paramedic arrived, this time with the full emergency medical bag and gurney in hand. As they began providing comprehensive medical assistance to the new mother and her child, I stood back, gathering details for my report. The mother, in a gentle voice, asked me my name. I responded formally, with my last name, rank, and star number, but she persisted, asking for my first name. After a brief pause, I told her, Stephen, and spelled it out to avoid the common misspelling. She looked at me, smiling, and said she would name her daughter Stephanie. I was taken aback, filled with unexpected emotion as tears welled up in my eyes.

The paramedics congratulated both of us, and as they prepared to transport the mother and her newborn daughter, Stephanie, to the hospital, the mother held my hand, expressing her heartfelt thanks. Standing there, humbled and deeply moved, I silently gave thanks to God for the strength and clarity to help in this beautiful moment, a true gift. Once they were safe on their way, I returned to my squad car to finish the report. There were no special commendations or recognition for moments like these in Englewood, just as there wasn't for the friend who, not long before, had been injured in the line of duty. To the department, it was just another day. But to me, it was a profound experience I carry with me always.

I never followed up on Stephanie's life, and I have recounted this story many times, especially to my students. I wonder often how her life has turned out, but a part of me hesitates to find out, preferring to keep that day preserved as a cherished memory, full of hope and grace.

There is often a failure to recognize that police officers are fundamentally woven into the fabric of society. They share the same human experiences as everyone else; they come from the same neighborhoods, attend the same schools, worship in the same churches, synagogues, mosques, and temples and are shaped by the same social dynamics. "They are as human as the next citizen" (Gaskins, 2016, p. 1).

Yet, those who enter the field of law enforcement typically do so with one of two distinct motivations, either to challenge authority or to serve their communities.

Some individuals enter law enforcement with a self-styled mission to "clean up" society, adopting a punitive, often harsh approach toward those they view as 'bad elements,' embodying a "Dirty Harry" mentality. This perspective is shaped by a self-righteous, pious viewpoint that sees society not as a community of individuals but as a problem needing correction. The moral entrepreneurs of society. Those with such a mindset may believe they alone understand what's best, viewing others as morally adrift or emotionally weakened by their sense of reality, thus justifying actions that sidestep rules and laws in the name of 'justice.'

Plato explores this sanctimonious stance in his account of Socrates' encounter with Euthyphro, a former student prosecuting his own father for murder. When Socrates questioned Euthyphro's motives, Euthyphro defended his actions as pious, asserting that the gods endorse such piety. Socrates then posed a critical question: "Is the pious loved by the gods because it is pious, or is it pious because it is loved by the gods?" (Plato, 1981, p. 14). Through this dialogue, Socrates emphasizes that true piety, like morality, is not simply an inherent trait but rather an understanding shaped by context and social learning.

Pollock (2019) further elucidates this, noting that "An emotionally mature person balances individual needs with others' demands; however, that development might be stunted by negative environmental influences" (p. 87). Here, Pollock references Kohlberg's stages of moral development, suggesting that rigid or misguided moral perspectives may result from limited or distorted developmental experiences, often influenced by the environments in which individuals are socialized.

Kohlberg's theory of moral development outlines three progressive stages of moral learning, suggesting that individuals internalize these stages as they form a lasting moral compass that guides their worldview into adulthood. Kohlberg emphasizes the importance of intellectual growth in moving to higher moral stages, cautioning that "one must grow intellectually to achieve a higher moral stage. One cannot skip stages" (Pollock, 2019, p. 87). Those who bypass stages may never fully reach the highest levels of moral reasoning, which are typically acquired through familial relationships, educational, and social learning contexts. Cultural norms and rationales significantly shape these moral or ethical values, as they reflect one's accumulated experiences and interpretations of right and wrong.

However, in the absence of sound leadership and amidst polarizing societal discourse, moral clarity can become compromised, leading to divisive perspectives on ethical conduct. This often results in blurred distinctions between issues of moral and ethical significance, impairing some individuals' capacity to "determine universal good," a stage few attain, and which markedly sets them apart from the majority (Pollock, 2019, p. 87). When this moral confusion arises, people, including some police officers, may feel justified in pursuing actions they perceive as righting societal wrongs, even if these actions contradict established laws or policies. They may view existing regulations as barriers to societal well-being, feeling compelled to "correct" perceived injustices, often without discretion or regard for broader humanistic values.

Sartre (2004) provides insight into this mindset through the concept of transcendental consciousness, or intentionality, where individuals act with a heightened sense of moral authority. Such individuals believe their perception of societal injustices is superior and view themselves as possessing an "I" perspective, an individualized conception of the world, detached from recognizing the independent value of other perspectives (Sartre, 2011, p. 50). Consequently, they impose their own moral and ethical frameworks on others, enforcing laws through a rigid, literal interpretation that lacks flexibility and empathy.

Police officers who choose to serve as champions of society embrace fair and impartial enforcement of the law, guided by a strong moral and ethical foundation. These officers maintain clarity in their values and make just, lawful decisions with confidence. They embody a humanistic spirit that anchors their moral compass, a quality essential for effective de-escalation in tense interactions with citizens. Possessing this moral grounding enables police officers to not only enforce laws and protect the public but also to engage in crime prevention with a commitment to justice.

Gaskins (2016) asserts, "we need to make sure officers have the skills necessary to make the best decisions in any situation they may face" (p. 1). His concern lies in how police leaders address "the glitch in human behavior" (p. 1), the variability that can affect decision-making. While rules and regulations are essential, Gaskins and others argue that police officers must inherently possess a unique blend of leadership and humanistic intention to serve as true models within the community. These qualities, often referred to as the "right stuff," are what empower officers to care deeply about community unity and social cohesion. Police officers, as Gaskins (2016) notes, "are community leaders – all day every day – and …[they]…are conspicuous men and women of civic virtue" (p. 1).

This leadership quality is indispensable for cultivating civic virtue and public trust, which in turn mitigates fear, anger, and resentment among citizens. Without this trust, societal tensions can escalate, leading to the current calls for defunding, abolishing, or reforming police departments, a demand that echoes through political discourse, social justice movements, and public opinion.

In today's social climate, there is a unique opportunity for young people to become active participants in meaningful police reform. Now is the time to join the ranks, to truly make a difference, and to contribute to the solution rather than perpetuate the problem. Sherwin encourages today's youth to stand apart from those who choose to criticize and disrespect police officers without offering constructive alternatives. Young people are better than that; they are driven by ideals of justice, fairness, equal treatment, and a desire to uplift their communities.

The youth of society should consider whether those calling for the defunding or abolition of police departments are truly acting in society's best interests. Are such individuals primarily motivated by their own unmet needs for justice, unable or unwilling to see beyond their grievances? Or do they lack the self-actualization needed to become part of the solution? Every day, society relies on the social contract, which is upheld through lawful structures designed to ensure justice for everyone, regardless of race, culture, faith, personal orientation, or political ideology.

Not everyone possesses the unique qualities required to serve the public, especially in such a challenging role as law enforcement. Becoming a police officer means facing the daily reality of putting oneself in harm's way, knowing that criticism, scrutiny, and labels of bias may accompany the duty. Such misconceptions are damaging not only to individual police officers but to the society that depends on them. Society needs good police officers. People deserve protection from threats and harm, and everyone should feel safe and confident when traveling anywhere in the United States. Everyone, young and old, should know that police officers are there to support and protect, to genuinely care for their well-being. This dedication takes heart.

Those who aspire to become police officers must bring not only education, common sense, and a strong spirit of humanistic qualities but also an unwavering commitment to working with, protecting, and serving people. Yet, above all, what is truly essential for anyone wearing the police uniform is "heart." Without heart, a police officer cannot fully embody the qualities of humanism that project care, trustworthiness, morality, ethics, or empathy. Having a heart is a vital prerequisite for anyone considering the role of police officer. It is the foundation for making morally and ethically sound decisions in every police-citizen encounter. No amount of training, education, or adherence to laws and regulations can replace the influence of the heart. Heart is the driving force behind respectful and compassionate interactions, even toward those whom police officers may need to arrest.

There may be instances in which a police encounter requires the lawful use of force; however, how a police officer conducts themself once a person is in custody speaks volumes about their character. This is the revealing moment. The point at which the true virtues of a police officer are displayed. Do they embody humanism, or are they led by reactive emotions?

Infidelity (As told by Sherwin)

One summer night while working the midnight shift, my partner and I overheard a call of distress from a fellow officer who was investigating a domestic disturbance. Responding swiftly, we arrived at the residence and found the front door wide open. Rushing up the steps and into the house, we were immediately taken aback by the scene unfolding before us. Two police officers, one a sergeant, the other a patrolman, were lying on the living room floor, visibly injured. In the center of the room stood an imposing figure: a man towering at 6'6" and weighing close to 300 pounds. His face contorted in rage, his eyes filled with tears, and his fists clenched. He was breathing heavily and seemed ready to unleash more violence.

It was obvious he had taken down the two police officers lying before us. As my partner moved to position himself behind the man, I decided to strike a blow with my baton, aiming for his chest in the hope of subduing him. It was a decision I would soon regret. The strike had the opposite effect, fueling his anger instead of calming it. Before I could react, he landed a powerful punch, sending me sprawling to the floor. In that tense moment, my partner acted decisively, leaping onto the man's back and securing a grip around his head, attempting to control him.

After recovering from the blow, I got back on my feet and delivered a swift kick to the man's shin, causing him to collapse with a heavy thud. This gave us the opening we needed to restrain him. Given his size, it took two pairs of handcuffs to secure him. Once the situation was under control, we helped the two downed police officers back to their feet. That's when I noticed another presence in the room, the wife of the man we arrested, standing off to the side, visibly shaken and crying. She tearfully confided that her husband had slapped her multiple times. My partner and I arranged for her transportation to the hospital, along with the two police officers who had been injured. Meanwhile, the man was taken to the police station by a patrol wagon.

My partner and I also returned to the police station to complete the necessary reports and processing of our gladiator. By the time we arrived, I had calmed down. I went to the lockup area and placed my weapon in the gun locker before entering the lockup where the arrestee was being held. The lockup keeper escorted the arrestee from the "Bullpen" to the desk where I was seated to finish the paperwork. As he sat down, I looked at him and, rather than jumping into formalities, I asked how he was doing. His rage had also subsided, and instead of answering, he offered an apology. I returned the courtesy and asked what had pushed him to such an intense reaction.

He opened with explaining that he had found out, upon his wife's return home that night, that she had been with another man. He confessed it wasn't the first time she'd been unfaithful, but he had warned her the last time that he would not tolerate it again. Although I did not condone his violent actions, I could empathize with the depth of hurt and betrayal he must have felt. After I gathered all the information and finished the report, I stood up to leave. To my surprise, he also rose and extended his hand, asking for forgiveness. I shook his hand. In court, the judge sentenced him to serve probation. He and his wife reconciled, and to my knowledge, the police were never called back to their home.

In my experience, individuals suffering from emotional stress, depression, or anxiety are often not truly angry at the police officers they encounter; rather, they use the interaction as an outlet for their pent-up emotions. Working in such situations, especially when violence is involved, is challenging and requires a strong humanistic approach. Yet, once the immediate threat is neutralized, it is essential for police officers to have the heart to respond with empathy and professionalism. People are more likely to forgive and understand when officers demonstrate compassion, empathy, and genuine humanism.

REFERENCES

Adams, M., Bell, L. A., Goodman, D. J., & Joshi, K. Y. (2016). *Teaching for diversity and social justice* (3rd ed.). Routledge. DOI: 10.4324/9781315775852

Aristotle, . (1962). *Nicomachean ethics*. Prentice Hall.

Barry, B. (2005). *Why Social Justice Matters*. Polity Press.

Dewey, J. (1927). *The public & its problems*. Swallow Press.

Fisher, R., & Ury, W. (1981). *Getting to Yes, Negotiating Agreement Without Giving In*. Penguin Books.

Gaskins, J. (2016). Ethics in leadership: Applying Aristotle in police work. Police 1. Retrieved From: https://wwwpolice1.com/patrol-issues/article

Greek, C. (2009). Documenting and framing police public interaction with citizens: A study in visual criminology. *Criminal Justice Matters*, 78(1), 18–20. DOI: 10.1080/09627250903385198

Maslow, A. H. (2013). *A theory of human motivation. Mansfield Centre*. Martino Publishing.

Plato, . (1981). *Five dialogues: Euthyphro, Apology, Crito, Meno, Phaedo*. Hackett Publishing Company, Inc.

Pollock, J. M. (2019). *Ethical Dilemmas and Decisions in Criminal Justice* (10th ed.). Cengage Learning, Inc.

Randolph, P. (2016). *The Psychology of Conflict – Mediating in a Diverse World*. Bloomsbury Continuum.

Rosenberg, M. B. (2015). *Nonviolent Communication, A Language of Life*. (Third Edition). PuddleDancer Press.

Roy, B. (2009). *41 Shots...and Counting; What Amadou Diallo's Story Teaches us About Policing, Race, and Justice*. Syracuse University Press.

Sartre, J.-P. (2004). *The transcendence of the ego*. Routledge. DOI: 10.4324/9780203694367

Ward, L. R. (1968). Aristotle on criteria of moral good. *The Review of Politics*, 30(4), 476–498. DOI: 10.1017/S0034670500025195

Zimbardo, P. (2007). *The Lucifer effect: understanding how good people turn evil*. Random House Inc.

Chapter 5
Education and Expertise in Law Enforcement: Developing Skilled Officers

ABSTRACT

Chapter 5 describes that the complex interplay between higher education and police reform underscores a critical need to reshape policing through transformative learning. Historically, through leaders like August Vollmer, Robert Peel, and others, he championed education as an essential component for improving police-community relations, promoting empathy, ethics, and professionalism within police departments. Vollmer's early initiatives, rooted in higher education, sought to elevate the standards of policing by integrating humanities-based curricula. These educational foundations aimed to foster trust, reduce misconduct, and establish a new ethical framework for police officers, thereby addressing systemic issues that have long plagued law enforcement. Vollmer's pioneering efforts led to the creation of the first police academy in the United States, which included formal education in liberal arts to instill humanistic values essential for police interactions.

INTRODUCTION

Sherwin utilized Vygotsky's concept of the zone of proximal development to highlight the need for transformative education within policing by developing my own theory that is applied in reverse order. Sherwin's reverse developmental transformative learning theory is predicated on reversing socially objectionable learning. In other words, unlearning biased or harmful perspectives. By collaborating with police officers who have a liberal arts background, those without such education can be exposed to humanistic values, prompting self-reflection and enhancing their ability to address social issues. This shared learning space promotes a gradual,

DOI: 10.4018/979-8-3693-7979-0.ch005

empathy-driven shift in attitudes, which is pivotal for rebuilding trust between police and citizens. This reverse zone of proximal development fosters not only individual growth but also collective transformation within police culture, where police officers learn to navigate complex social interactions more sensitively and responsively.

The broader liberal arts education equips police officers with critical skills in thinking, speaking, and writing, skills that Zakaria (2015) identifies as essential for effective communication and ethical decision-making. In challenging situations, such abilities enable police officers to engage constructively with the public, de-escalate conflicts, and approach law enforcement with a democratic ethos grounded in respect and understanding. A liberal arts curriculum, with its emphasis on cultural awareness, social justice, and ethical reflection, enriches police officers' perspectives, encouraging a shift away from an "us versus them" mentality and toward a collaborative, community-centered approach.

This transformative learning process is essential in preparing police officers for the demands of modern society, where issues of racial bias, mental health, and justice require nuanced, empathetic responses. Scholars argue that microaggressions and implicit biases are deeply rooted in social conditioning and often manifest in law enforcement practices. Through education, these biases can be critically examined, allowing police officers to move beyond prejudiced mindsets. Engaging police officers in a curriculum that challenges preconceived notions fosters accountability, self-awareness, and respect for diverse communities.

To facilitate such reform, police departments should prioritize recruiting candidates with liberal arts degrees and encourage existing police officers to pursue higher education. This approach promotes sustained, positive change, fostering a force that embodies humanistic principles. Moreover, adopting community youth programs can strengthen the police-citizen relationship by providing opportunities for police officers and community members to engage constructively. These programs foster reciprocal learning and encourage youths to view law enforcement as allies rather than adversaries, setting the stage for long-term trust and cooperation.

Ultimately, transformative learning in policing offers a sustainable model for reform, one that addresses both the personal growth of police officers and structural changes within law enforcement. By nurturing humanistic values through a liberal education, police departments can cultivate a more responsive, ethical, and effective force, capable of meeting the challenges of a diverse and evolving society. Such reform is not only achievable but necessary for fostering a future in which police officers are genuinely committed to serving and protecting all community members with respect, empathy, and integrity.

SECTION-1: RECRUITING FOR THE FUTURE: THE ROLE OF HIGHER EDUCATION AND HUMANISTIC VALUES

Vollmer and Schneider (1917) emphasized the importance of higher education for police officers, advocating for an education infused with the humanities to cultivate "...courtesy in their dealings with the public" (p. 878). Building on this idea, Wilson (1953) championed the requirement for police officers to attain a minimum of a bachelor's degree, inspired by Vollmer's original proposal to include police officers in academic programs at the University of California. This call for reform emerged in response to widespread issues within police departments, as leaders in law enforcement recognized the prevalence of misconduct. By promoting higher education, they proposed a reformation that would support a transformative praxis, one grounded in learning that encourages empathy, ethics, and professionalism in police interactions with the community.

Lyman's (1964) research highlights the influential work of Sir Robert Peel, a nineteenth-century reformer in London, England, whose approach emphasized building a trustworthy and effective police force. Peel's model of reform became a foundation for policing practices in democratic nations worldwide. At the time, the police response to community needs in London was marked by indifference and indecision, which often led to public unrest and riots. Peel attributed this unrest to a "lax police system" (Lyman, 1964, p. 151), emphasizing that a reformed, reliable police force was essential for public trust and stability. He advocated that police officer candidates should have a higher-than-average education to ensure they could serve the community responsibly and effectively. Peel's forward-thinking approach to police reform would later influence August Vollmer, further solidifying education and accountability as central to effective policing.

Oliver (2012) introduces August Vollmer as a visionary, much like Peel, sharing a background in policing. Oliver (2012) argues that Vollmer, like Peel, recognized the necessity of establishing trust between police officers and citizens. At the time, citizens were afraid of police officers and had minimal, if any, respect, confidence, or trust in them. Vollmer's vision focused on building citizen trust through higher education. He established the first police academy in the United States (Oliver, 2012). Inviting faculty members from Berkeley to teach the officers under his command, this initiative soon developed into "...an actual degree program for his police officers in higher education" (p.36). The ongoing movement toward police reform and promoting trust among citizens was strengthened by social justice awareness issues highlighted by Murphy (1965). During the late 1950s and early 1960s, the same issues of police officers' persistent misconduct that eroded citizen trust, as observed by Peel and Vollmer, continued to exist. Complaints about police officers' ineffective enforcement diminished public confidence, eroded trust, led to a lack of respect, and connections with criminal enterprises caused citizen rebellion and demands for reform (Murphy, 1965).

Considering this historical perspective, the question arises: can higher education, especially one enriched with a liberal arts foundation, truly equip police officers with the skills needed to engage collaboratively with citizens to "Serve and Protect"? For such an initiative to succeed, both citizens and police officers must engage in a community partnership grounded in mutual goals of safety, peace, and trust (Murphy, 1965). Murphy (1965) suggested that communities should take an active role rather than relying solely on the police to manage crime and ensure safety in their neighborhoods. He advocated collaborative efforts, encouraging communities and police to join forces to "...correct the illnesses of society" (p.105). According to Murphy, the cornerstone of restoring public trust in law enforcement lies in promoting higher education as a vital pathway to cultivating more understanding, empathy, and humanistic values among police officers.

A police officer's pledge to "Serve and Protect" cannot be compromised due to inadequate knowledge, sensitivity, or mindset. Understanding the unique needs of each community is central to effective policing, and police officers must transition from a stance of "us" versus "them" to one of inclusive cooperation. Murphy (1965) emphasized the importance of police officers working alongside citizens, engaging in mutual learning to truly enact change. Change itself serves as the foundation for this transformative shift among police officers, fostering deeper connections with the communities they serve.

Such a shift involves more than superficial adjustments; it requires a sincere commitment from all parties involved, reflecting the principles of transformative learning, which "...includes not only the individual's structural change, but also structural change in the social world" (Rubenson, 2011, p.55). As Merriam and Caffarella (1999) assert, "Transformative learning shapes people; they are different afterward" (p.318). Freire (1970) supports this view, contending that a "Conversion to the people requires a profound rebirth. Those who undergo it must take on a new form of existence, they can no longer remain as they were" (p.61). Freire's insight into conversion and rebirth forms the basis for integrating higher education into police training, intertwining it with social justice reform. Such deep-rooted reform within police departments hinges on this process of rebirth and transformation, strengthening accountability and a genuine commitment to social justice.

Murphy (1965) advocates higher education as the ultimate solution to restore public trust in police officers, suggesting that police recruitment efforts should actively seek candidates from college campuses. He proposes that all aspiring police officers should first obtain a baccalaureate degree, arguing that the breadth and depth of higher education prepare police officers not only for the technical aspects of policing but also for the democratic and humanistic values essential in community interactions. However, this recommendation is not universally embraced.

Dewey's (1938) insight into the transformative nature of education underscores a central theme: exploring how higher education shapes police officers' beliefs and practices. Dewey (1927) further emphasizes that democratic values are vital virtues necessary for the sustenance of society, reinforcing the value of education in nurturing a policing approach that aligns with the principles of democracy and mutual respect.

Dewey (1927) emphasizes that accountability is essential for public officials in a democratic society, advocating for regulations to ensure their conduct aligns with democratic values. As public officials, police officers must therefore be held accountable to their mandate to "Serve and Protect" all citizens impartially. Effective service requires police officers to develop cognitive skills that enable thoughtful, situational responses.

Zakaria (2015) highlights the advantages of a liberal education in cultivating these skills, with the first advantage being that it "...teaches you how to think," instilling humanistic values (p.72). Writing, according to Zakaria, is a medium that expresses a person's thoughts, fostering clarity and depth in what they wish to communicate, engaging in the philosophical debate of "...which comes first thought or language" (p.73). Writing compels individuals to make decisions, which ultimately "...brings clarity and order to your ideas" (p.74).

Zakaria's (2015) second advantage is that a liberal education "...teaches you how to speak," promoting articulate communication that allows one to understand their own mind. This process of filtering undeveloped thoughts helps logically express one's ideas to the outside world (p.75). For police officers, the skills of thinking, writing, and speaking are indispensable, as they facilitate peaceful resolutions and mutual understanding during police-citizen interactions.

Henion & Terrill (2015) suggest that higher education proves more advantageous for police officers when it includes a strong foundation in the humanities. Michelson (2016), referencing research by Rydberg & Terrill (2014), highlights that higher education can significantly aid in reducing racial biases and instances of deadly force among police officers. Bruns (2010) supports this perspective, noting that many police chiefs agree college-educated police officers tend to engage more humanely with citizens, face fewer disciplinary issues, demonstrate better problem-solving abilities, and resort to deadly force less frequently compared to their counterparts without higher education.

Cross and Fine (2022) underscore the transformative impact of education in meeting the modern call for diversified police departments capable of managing complex social issues (p. 554). They stress the importance of qualities like "communication skills, empathy, sensitivity, technological savviness, and cultural awareness" in police candidates—qualities that are nurtured through a transformative liberal arts education (Cross & Fine, 2022, p. 554). This educational background, as they suggest, equips officers with the skills necessary to navigate the increasingly nuanced and socially charged circumstances they encounter, fostering more effective and sensitive policing.

Zimbardo (2007) contends that human nature is fundamentally driven by "wanton desires, unlimited appetites, and hostile impulses" that must be transformed through education into rational, compassionate behavior (p. 297). This transformation is essential in the policing profession, where police officers' humanistic values significantly impact their ability to work constructively with community members. Maslow's (2013) theory of human motivation further supports this view, emphasizing that fulfilling self-esteem needs leads to a "feelings of self-confidence, worth, strength, capability, and adequacy of being useful and necessary in the world" (p. 7). The satisfaction of self-esteem plays a pivotal role in a police officer's disposition and conduct. A liberal education, rich in humanistic values, promotes this self-esteem, encouraging police officers to feel competent, valued, and empowered to cultivate positive and peaceful police-citizen interactions. Consequently, these educational foundations help galvanize police officers to apply skills and methods that ensure respectful, empathetic, and effective engagement with the communities they serve.

Zimbardo (2007) illustrates the transformative power of a uniform on a person's mindset, specifically in how it shifts their perception of the role they embody. In his study, students wearing prison guard uniforms shifted from compassionate, non-violent dispositions to exhibiting punitive, radical behaviors toward student prisoners, revealing how a uniform can dramatically influence conduct. From a broader transformative perspective, Mezirow (1997) defines transformative learning as "the process of effecting change in a frame of reference" (p. 5), that is, altering deeply ingrained perspectives shaped by one's life experiences. This learning reshapes the way a person interprets their identity and worldview, suggesting that shifts in external roles or attire, like a uniform, can catalyze profound internal changes in thought and behavior.

Mezirow (1997) explains that a frame of reference "is composed of two dimensions: habits of mind and point of view" (p. 5). It shapes how individuals make decisions, formulate strategies, and interpret others' actions. This framework, as Zimbardo (2007) found, can lead to harmful behaviors such as microaggressions, where a person's underlying perceptions and values within their frame of reference trigger subtle or overt psychological and physical abuses toward others. These abuses often stem from ingrained biases and assumptions, demonstrating how a person's perspective, even subconsciously, can influence their treatment of others.

Mezirow (1997) explains that habits of mind are "influenced by assumptions that constitute a set of codes" shaped by cultural, social, educational, economic, political, and psychological beliefs (p. 6). However, he differentiates habits of mind from points of view, noting that points of view shape a person's immediate perceptions of others, such as "homosexuals, welfare recipients, people of color, or women," and are more accessible to awareness and open to feedback from others (p. 6). Hearing diverse points of view, Mezirow suggests, can initiate a process of self-reflection, prompting individuals to examine and question their assumptions, potentially leading to significant personal transformation (p. 7). Imel (1998) builds on Mezirow's theory of transformative learning, asserting that individuals "must engage in critical reflection on their experiences… through a series of phases," which involve planning for action, implementing new approaches, and redefining their understanding of the world (p. 2, 3).

Preconceived frames of reference can be reshaped through educational experiences, particularly within a liberal arts curriculum. Zakaria (2015) contends that a liberal arts education teaches individuals *how* to think critically and independently. Mezirow (1997) similarly emphasizes that thinking autonomously and responsibly is a learning outcome shaped by education, fostering decision-making that is morally sound and adaptable, especially vital "for full citizenship in democracy and moral decision making in situations of rapid change" (p. 7). This autonomy serves as a crucial standard for police officers pursuing a liberal arts degree, as it provides them with the values and insights to transform prior "concepts, values, feelings... [and]...conditioned responses" (Mezirow, 1997, p. 5) into humanistic approaches that promote peaceful outcomes in their interactions.

Appiah (2015) underscores the value of a college education, emphasizing its alignment with the qualities needed for aspiring police officers. Jagiello (1971) expands on the various responsibilities in police work, from routine tasks to complex investigations, highlighting the role of the police officer as both peacemaker and a trusted figure whom all members of society can turn to for assistance. He argues that police officers should ideally hold a Bachelor of Arts with an emphasis on liberal studies, behavioral sciences, and law (p. 117). This foundation promotes an understanding of essential social values, cultural diversity, justice, and tolerance toward different races and lifestyles, which Zakaria (2015) asserts is central to a liberal arts education. This concept is further supported by Mezirow (1997), Maslow (2013), and Vygotsky (1978). Vygotsky's (1978) concept of the zone of proximal development reinforces the idea that learning in a cohort environment on campus nurtures transformative values, enhancing lifelong understanding and acceptance. Higher education thus broadens perspectives, fostering tolerance, fairness, and equality, while transformative learning instills a self-reflective commitment to uphold these values.

Transformative learning requires "critical reflection and reflective discourse" (Merriam, 2004), a process that empowers individuals to cultivate rational thinking and promotes perceptions that are "more inclusive, discriminating, open, emotionally capable of change, and reflective" (Merriam, 2004, p. 61). This learning approach acts as a pivotal force, equipping police officers with the competence to integrate the pedagogical insights gained through higher education, preparing them to meet the evolving social demands of the community. A foundational willingness to change is essential to effectively cultivate the humanistic qualities and attributes that align with the needs of modern policing. del Carmen, Butler, & Odo (2006) suggest two primary goals: first, enhancing the professional status of law enforcement as a respected career, and second, improving the effectiveness of officers (p. 210). While challenges persist, potential solutions lie in the roles played by both politicians and the media.

The Problem

Many politicians are often more focused on gaining votes than on genuinely understanding the underlying issues or accepting accountability. Blaming, criticizing, and broadly labeling all police officers as societal "monsters" has harmful consequences. When politicians assume they know more about police work than those trained and experienced in it, and when they restrict police officers from performing their duties, it harms not only the police officers but also the community and society at large. Such restrictions can empower criminals and undermine public safety. Policies like releasing individuals charged with serious crimes without bail or choosing not to prosecute, under a misguided approach to restorative justice, harm victims, honest citizens, and demoralize dedicated police officers.

The media frequently contributes to these issues by rushing to portray incidents involving police officers in a negative light, often prioritizing sensationalism over thorough investigation and truth. Such portrayals can undermine the credibility of police officers, their departments, and the criminal justice system. Police officers have an obligation to thoroughly investigate crimes, seek the truth, gather evidence, arrest suspects, and present the accused in court. It is within the court's purview, not the bidding of politicians, the media, or law enforcement, to determine a person's guilt or the legality of police actions. Police officers are responsible for collecting evidence that reveals the truth, while it is the role of politicians and the media to observe, ensure justice is served, and refrain from dictating or subverting due process.

Suggestion

It may be challenging, but police officers, politicians, and the media need to cultivate respect for one another and collaborate as allies rather than adversaries. Each group must embody leadership, accountability, and trustworthiness. Strong leadership is essential here. Good leaders know how to build a culture of acceptance, equip their teams with the necessary tools, and act as coaches and mentors. Virtuous leaders show respect, patience, and wisdom, strengthening unity rather than division. Effective leaders delegate with guidance and trust, bringing people together and creating a shared sense of purpose.

True leadership is built on knowledge, experience, and humanistic skills. Leaders with heart, deplete of hubris, prioritize the well-being of their team while remaining focused on the greater good: societal welfare and the protection of victims. Wise leaders ensure their teams have both the practical tools and emotional support to perform their roles effectively and to maintain their physical and mental health. When these conditions are met, society reaps the benefits, and the calls to defund or abolish policing will diminish. This vision is not only achievable but also profoundly valuable. Our communities, especially the next generation, are far too precious to abandon. With a collective spirit and a willingness to work together, we can ensure that police officers represent the best of humanity, carrying a deep, heartfelt commitment to serving and protecting all members of society.

SECTION-2: BALANCING KNOWLEDGE, SKILLS, AND ETHICS FOR EFFECTIVE POLICING

Figure 1. Altered transformative learning matrix

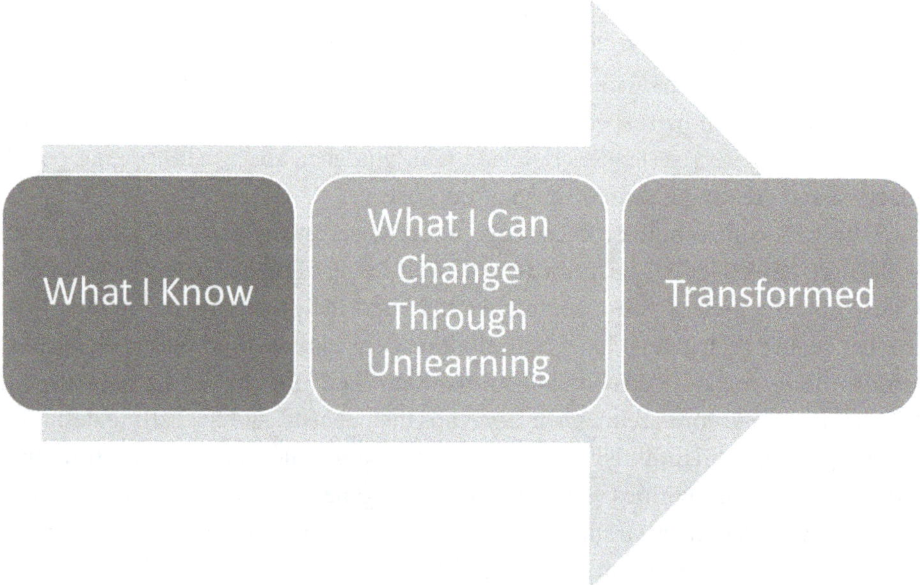

Altered Transformative Learning

In Sherwin's theory of transformative learning, he argues that transformation can be intentionally reversed, encouraging unlearning to alter established ways of thinking. This involves revisiting and reconsidering ingrained biases, rather than exclusively learning new concepts around social values or cultural diversity. Zuniga highlights the power of dialogue in transformative education, suggesting the value of "...bringing college students together to talk and learn from each other" (as cited in Adams et al., 2013, p.635), enabling them to bridge differences and build understanding around issues of culture, race, gender, faith, and orientation. This approach centers on unlearning past prejudices rooted in early social conditioning, thereby providing a pathway to humanistic values.

To illustrate, one might observe children playing harmoniously, unaware of racial or cultural distinctions, simply enjoying the experience of connection and fun. Unfortunately, at some formative stage, children often learn to focus on and judge these differences whether through familial influence, societal norms, or peer dynamics. By engaging in alternative transformative unlearning, individuals can dismantle these biases formed in childhood, replacing them with inclusive and mutual respect. This altered approach to transformative learning seeks to undo biases formed through early experiences and social learning, advancing a humanistic perspective that promotes deeper empathy and understanding in diverse social interactions.

The zone of proximal development used in a reverse order for adults raises a compelling dynamic learning perspective. Vygotsky (1978) argues that the development of learning is achieved through a peer process, learning from others, fostering the dynamic of those without a liberal arts degree learning from those with a liberal arts degree. A liberal arts education exposes the learner to a variety of humanistic ideas, skills, and values. "Thus, learning is a necessary and universal aspect of the process of developing culturally organized, specifically human, psychological functions" (Vygotsky, 1978, p.90). Integrating police officers with a liberal arts degree in higher education with peers who do not have a liberal arts degree has a twofold effect. The first effect is the re-learning process provided by the exposure to humanistic values, encouraging the learner to self-reflect and develop a new perspective on a variety of social issues. This process enables the learner to utilize humanistic values that restores trust between police officers and citizens. The second effect is the influence of modeling humanistic values among peers, creating a zone of proximal development among peers while working together, stimulating a growth in development in humanistic values that transforms habits of mind, points of view, and stimulates autonomy. Through an alternative transformative learning process old biases can be replaced with humanistic values that encourage the utilization of peaceful outcomes during police/citizen encounters. This can be a watershed for essential assurance in sustainable police reform.

Current application requirements to become a police officer does not require that all candidates must have a degree in higher education that is predicated on a liberal arts curriculum. This poses a training challenge. Police academies must have an alternative transformative curriculum synthesized with humanistic outcomes. And the training academies must have instructors with humanistic pedagogical qualifications to transform micro-aggressions, ingrained prejudices, fears, and biases. These are essential elements needed to reverse early learned stereotypes and return individuals to a mindset unmarked by issues of race and cultural diversity. Thus, bringing forth the openness they may have once possessed as children. This challenge is at the heart of liberal education, even as many students increasingly turn toward STEM programs, which often lack an explicit focus on humanistic values. Zakaria (2015) underscores this need for balance, advocating for a harmony between technology and the liberal arts, where humanistic values are preserved and promoted alongside scientific and technical advancement.

Vollmer advanced his vision for humanistic values in policing by inviting Berkeley University professors to teach at the police academy, providing police officers with a chance to unlearn ingrained habits, fears, and biases, thus enhancing professionalism and respect in police-community relations (as cited in Oliver, 2012, p. 36). This approach to transformative learning aligns with the insights of Vygotsky (1978), Dewey (1938), Maslow (2013), and Mezirow (1997), who each argue that education can reshape cognitive skills, especially in youth, by fostering an environment for critical reflection and growth. Zimbardo (2007), however, posits that even adult values and mindsets can be altered through a reversal process, akin to what is depicted in an "altered transformative learning matrix" (e.g., Figure 1), which serves to deconstruct biases and rebuild constructive perspectives. This aligns with two foundational theories that support the potential for unlearning and reorientation within adult transformative learning.

Zakaria (2015) argues that higher education serves as a transformative force, equipping individuals with critical thinking and effective communication skills. The core mission of higher education is to reshape and expand students' perspectives. Students entering college bring with them a foundation of knowledge, beliefs, and values shaped by previous social experiences and formal education. However, higher education immerses them in a broad array of new, often challenging, ideas and theories, exposing them to diverse viewpoints and critical analysis. This exposure encourages students to refine their thinking and, ideally, prepares them to take on leadership roles across various fields, including police work, where such qualities are essential.

Those who doubt or critique the concept of altered transformative learning might start by questioning the very purpose of higher education. Why do people seek it out? Fundamentally, learning aims to reshape our thinking, often through a process of unlearning outdated or biased perspectives. A liberal arts degree, for instance, introduces students to philosophers who challenge established ethical and moral values, encouraging deep reflection. This curriculum also exposes students to diverse cultures, urging them to see people and ideas through new lenses that prioritize reality over myth or stereotype. Such a transformation is not unlike the experience of a military boot camp, where individuals undergo a structured process of rebuilding their mindset and values to become renewed versions of themselves. Through the liberal arts, students learn to rethink and broaden their worldviews, becoming more adaptable, empathetic, and resilient in an increasingly complex society.

One argument has remained unwavering over time: the need for police reform. Community and political leaders consistently urge police department heads to transform their police officers to align with evolving social needs and values. Cit izens frequently challenge police leadership and politicians alike, demanding that all police officers are trained in humanistic principles and practices. In response, police departments often implement training programs aimed at promoting these values and meeting social justice needs within a dynamic society. However, budgetary constraints, compounded by union demands and limitations, have led to the scaling back or even complete elimination of many of these programs over time. The programs that do exist often only last if funding is allocated. This points to a need for a more sustainable solution to promote positive police-citizen interactions. The solution has been apparent all along, though often obscured by disagreements and resistance between police leadership and policymakers: prioritize hiring police candidates who hold a liberal arts degree.

From the Heart

Police officers must embody foundational humanistic values, foremost among them being "heart." Heart is the essence of all humanistic skills, the force that drives a police officer to genuinely care, forgive, and foster respect and trust within the community. In Sherwin's experiences, both professionally and personally, he discovered that the key to effective mitigation is wholehearted engagement in each situation. Without heart, a police officer may miss the deeper issues, the voices that reveal needs, express pain, or plead for attention and understanding. This goes beyond empathy and isn't about sympathy; it's about fully committing to listening and acting as an agent of support. A police officer with heart is dedicated to truly serving and protecting, advocating for those who might otherwise feel unseen or unheard. When a police officer brings heart into their role as a public servant, they become a vessel through which the right words and insights naturally arise, helping to guide transformative, positive outcomes.

Being "humanistic" is not merely a skill but a mindset rooted in ethical values, cultivated through transformative learning in a higher education setting (Carlan & Byxbe, 1999). This mindset requires "heart"—the willingness to engage deeply with humanistic development. For a police officer, applying jurisprudence ethically and morally demands this heart. True toughness lies in the ability to empathize without condoning wrongful actions. Zakaria (2015) emphasizes that liberal education broadens humanistic viewpoints, encouraging individuals to think compassionately, assess situations thoughtfully, and know when to be firm and when to be gentle. Heart equips a police officer with the capacity "to think" (Zakaria, 2015), enabling them to discern and respond appropriately in their interactions.

SECTION-3: SUSTAINING EXCELLENCE: ONGOING TRAINING, ADAPTATION, AND LEADERSHIP DEVELOPMENT

Academic requirements and training standards for police departments vary significantly. Currently, there is no universal requirement for police officers to hold a four-year degree, let alone one in liberal arts. In some departments within the Chicago area, candidates need only a high school diploma. Other departments may require candidates to have at least two years of higher education, though there is no stipulation on the field of study. Candidates might have a degree in any discipline, including fields unrelated to law enforcement. Police departments generally do not mandate specific areas of study in their academic requirements.

A Need to Transform

What is the goal of police departments in the 21st century? Are they responding to social disorders out of fear, relying on measures of control and dominance? Or are they beginning to recognize the need for a more tolerant, empathetic, and forgiving approach? Do they view civil unrest surrounding social justice issues as an assault on law enforcement, or are they instead reflecting on whether they contribute to these societal problems? Interestingly, insight into this question can be drawn from an unexpected source: the conflict resolution practices of the Sioux Native American tribes.

In 2002, as a mediator, Sherwin had the privilege of working remotely with Spotted Eagle, a Sioux Native American civil rights lawyer. She introduced Sherwin to the profound way in which the Sioux community addresses internal conflict. When someone commits a crime within the tribe, they are summoned to a gathering where the entire community forms a circle around the accused. Standing in the center of the community circle, the malefactor faces the community for members to collectively examine the reasons for the commission of the offense.

A unique aspect of the Sioux approach is the community's sense of implicit accountability. Instead of solely condemning the offender, the community examines its own responsibility in the transgression, asking themselves what they might have neglected to do or have done that could have contributed to this act against the victim, community, and their traditional values. To Sioux, a crime against one member is a crime against all. A crime perpetrated against one member of the tribe is a violation of the tribe's social contract, a promise that no member of the tribe willfully violates without cause. This communal introspection, coupled with a desire for reform, provides invaluable insight into how to prevent future harm.

The empathy embodied by the Sioux community in this process is foundational to their concept of justice and reform. They understand that without empathy, fear, anger, and hate are quick to emerge. As Baron-Cohen (2011) posits, the absence of empathy can become a catalyst for what we perceive as evil. The Sioux's approach models a compassionate, reformative form of justice that seeks healing rather than punishment, fostering accountability through understanding rather than through coercion.

Zimbardo's (2007) exploration into human behavior underscores a troubling phenomenon: the ease with which individuals can succumb to hate and even engage in harmful acts toward others. This is not a novel concept. As discussed in an earlier chapter, Plato (1981) illuminates the seductive pull toward hatred through a philosophical lens in a dialogue with Socrates, who investigates its underlying motivations by examining the concept of piety. Socrates confronts Euthyphro about prosecuting his own father for murder. Euthyphro defends his choice, claiming that it aligns with pious duty. Socrates' primary objective in this inquiry is to prove the ethical foundation of Euthyphro's decision, whether it is grounded in deontological principles (adherence to duty) or teleological reasoning (consideration of outcomes). Through this examination, Socrates sheds light on the potential for moral reasoning to become entangled with personal motives and societal pressures, which can easily lead one astray from truth.

A Categorical Imperative

Nietzsche (1966) provides a philosophical insight into moral virtue, casting light on Socrates' challenge: "Even apart from the value of such claims as 'there is a categorical imperative in us,' one can still always ask: what does such a claim tell us about the man who makes it" (p. 99). This reflection aligns with Baron-Cohen's (2011) argument that a lack of empathy erodes, or even annihilates, one's sense of humanity toward others, whether in personal or professional contexts. When empathy is absent, an emotional void opens, inviting contempt that overshadows compassion, tolerance, and understanding. This is a crucial lesson not only for Euthyphro but for police officers as well. Engaging in a reflective discourse on the influence of police officers' military-style attire and its impact on public perception could serve as a foundation for fostering accountability in their interactions with the community. The second Rockwell image, portrayed in an earlier chapter, raises two thought-provoking questions: does such an image encourage hostility, an inclination toward harm or animosity. Secondly, are police officers themselves resistant to such a potential descent? Through this introspection, the discussion challenges both the image police officers project and their awareness of its influence on community relations.

Merton's (1996) strain theory, rooted in Émile Durkheim's concept of anomie, offers a valuable sociological framework for understanding human behavior under strain. According to Merton, individuals in situations of intense stress or crisis often respond through one of five adaptive strategies: conformity, ritualism, retreatism, rebellion, or innovation (pp. 139-151). Police officers, regularly facing situations that put their lives in danger, are not immune to this emotional strain, which can impact their behavior, including the rationale behind wearing military-style apparel. It's plausible that police officers, too, might exhibit responses aligned with Merton's strain theory. This raises a critical question: do police officers, like the Sioux, engage the community to examine mutual accountability, or do police departments instead claim a categorical imperative in enforcing the law in a utilitarian manner? What may appear as a categorical imperative could, in fact, stem from internal motivations shaped by fear, anger, and hate. When this becomes the case, the visual impact intensifies, projecting an image of authority that may, consciously or unconsciously, convey an intimidating shadow of control and oppression.

Among those who dislike oppression are many who like to oppress. Napoleon Bonaparte

Mirrored Oppression

Freire (1970) cautions against the transformation of the oppressed into oppressors, highlighting how easily one may adopt an oppressive role. He contends that a lack of education advances negative qualities such as cruelty, absence of empathy, and eventual oppression. In this cycle, the oppressor often responds to the resistance of the oppressed with force, rationalizing brutality to maintain control. Freire's view, much like Socrates', is that education cultivates empathy, ethical reasoning, and moral discernment, thus guiding individuals to interact compassionately with others. Just as Socrates encouraged Euthyphro to critically explore the concept of piety through reasoned discourse, Freire sees education as the essential pathway for freeing individuals from the grip of oppression.

This raises an essential question for police officers who wear military-style attire and gear: does this visually striking clothing inadvertently project a stance of dominance that could appear oppressive? It is known that we often embody the persona that our clothing represents, shaping our actions in line with the identity it conveys. Freire argues that education offers a path to eliminating such oppressive inclinations. Teaching the humanities, he suggests, equips individuals to examine social issues, diverse perspectives, and human interactions with an open mind, less prone to bias. A liberal arts education, therefore, provides a humanistic pathway, enabling police officers to approach their role with empathy, cultural awareness, and a commitment to ethical service.

Education is a process of overcoming natural inclination and substituting in its place habits acquired under external pressure. John Dewey

Education: The Transformative Answer

Dewey's (1938) perspective on education as a foundation for future readiness suggests that learning serves to "overcome natural inclination and substitute in its place habits acquired under external pressure" (p.17). This view underlines the importance of police departments practicing accountability and examining their approach toward citizens, communities, and the perceived necessity of militarization. When police departments, feeling pressured, choose militarization, they adopt a teleological approach, focusing on ends rather than means. Dewey's insights reinforce that opting out of an educational approach limits the ability to create thoughtful, conflict-resolving strategies. He cautions that ignoring education in decision-making results in consequences beyond mere "lack of preparation" (p.48).

Dewey's emphasis on the role of education in preparing for future challenges suggests that police departments could adopt educational foundations to form rational, acceptable approaches to community protection thus avoiding reliance on forceful measures. He argues that "attentive care must be devoted to the conditions which give each present experience a worthwhile meaning" (p.49), indicating that education builds the capacity to address issues with empathy and understanding, rather than with tactics that risk community trust. Through an educational lens, police departments can nurture practices that inspire care, hope, and trust, thus strengthening their relationship with the communities they serve.

Henion and Terrill (2015) advocate for higher education in law enforcement, emphasizing that a curriculum grounded in humanities is particularly beneficial. Michelson (2016) cites a study by Rydberg and Terrill (2014), which reveals that higher education among police officers is linked to reduced racial bias and a lower propensity for using deadly force. Bruns (2010) also supports this perspective, noting that numerous police chiefs observe college-educated officers engaging in more compassionate interactions with citizens, receiving fewer disciplinary actions, demonstrating stronger problem-solving skills, and resorting to deadly force less frequently compared to officers without higher education.

In 1917, Vollmer and Schneider emphasized the importance of higher education for police officers, particularly through exposure to the humanities, to enrich "courtesy in their dealings with the public" (p.878). Building on this, Wilson (1953) later championed higher education as a critical component of police reform, aligning with Vollmer's recommendation for police officers to study at the University of California. Wilson asserted that Vollmer's vision aimed for all police officers to hold at least a bachelor's degree, which he believed essential for raising ethical standards within law enforcement. As concerns about police misconduct intensified, law enforcement leaders increasingly saw higher education as a transformative tool, advocating for reform through educational advancement to cultivate a more accountable and professional police force.

Zakaria (2015) contends that a liberal education brings forth an understanding of human vulnerabilities, providing a comprehensive perspective for interacting with others to foster a balanced, utilitarian social contract. He argues that without a foundation in liberal education, true change is impeded. Society's progress stalls, people lack insight into essential social values, and the cultivation of moral and ethical principles is compromised. For police departments, reform rooted in a liberal education is essential; without it, there is a diminished capacity for effective problem-solving, the development of trust-building strategies, and the assurance of community safety. Zakaria (2015) suggests that a liberal education enables the exploration of constructive, humanistic approaches to public needs and challenges, moving beyond a reductive "fight fire with fire" response.

A liberal arts degree encompasses a wide range of philosophical courses that reinforce and cultivate humanistic values. This curriculum engages students with themes of diversity, moral and ethical principles, and ideals that encourage humanistic perspectives. Its purpose is to challenge and reshape pre-existing beliefs and biases that conflict with humanism, guiding students through a process of "unlearning" via an altered transformative learning framework. Vygotsky's (1978) zone of proximal development theory is central here, emphasizing the importance of learning collaboratively, which resonates with Zakaria's (2015) view that liberal education nurtures critical thinking. Furthermore, Zimbardo's (2007) concept of reverse transformative learning supports this by promoting a heuristic, experience-based approach to education. Through this comprehensive liberal arts experience, individuals are encouraged to discard socially harmful preconceptions and adopt a more humanistic, empathetic worldview.

The selection of police candidates traditionally seeks individuals regarded as the most respected in their communities. Children often aspire to become police officers, admiring them as role models, which strengthens the ambition to pursue a career in law enforcement. This admiration supports a compelling case for establishing recruitment qualifications that mandate a liberal arts degree for police applicants, and for encouraging veteran officers to pursue this education as well. The benefits of a liberal arts degree are profound; it fosters a learning approach grounded in humanistic values that are essential for building lasting, positive relationships between police and the community. Police departments can take a transformative step by recognizing the need for police officers to obtain a liberal arts degree, laying a foundation for trust and respect. This educational pathway promotes openness and mutual understanding, enabling police officers to engage in sustainable, respectful interactions with citizens. This approach aligns with Vygotsky's (1978) zone of proximal development, where both police and citizens learn from each other, further fostering respect and trust.

A police officer's commitment to "Serving and Protecting" must remain steadfast, free from deficits in knowledge, sensitivity, or attitude. Understanding and addressing a community's needs is central to effective policing, requiring officers to move from an "us" versus "them" mentality toward a collaborative, inclusive approach. Murphy (1965) recognized that impactful change is possible when police work in partnership with citizens, learning from each other to foster real transformation. Such change serves as a foundation for a deeper conversion within the ranks of law enforcement, one that transcends individual transformation and prompts structural shifts within society (Rubenson, 2011, p. 55). As Merriam & Caffarella (1999) note, "Transformative learning shapes people; they are different afterward" (p. 318). Freire (1970) echoes this sentiment, emphasizing that "Conversion to the people requires a profound rebirth" that fundamentally changes one's way of being (p. 61). This notion of rebirth and transformation is critical for police officers who are both college-educated and aligned with social justice reform, pointing to a need for structural reforms within police departments. Such reforms are achievable only through the type of conversion and renewal that Freire champions, that is, one that centers on accountability and a commitment to social justice.

Police Officers and Youths

Bronfenbrenner (2005) posits that human development unfolds through interactions centered on "people, objects, and symbols" (p. 177). Core values of humanism, respect, dignity, and professionalism, are essential in fostering community relations programs that help police officers reconnect with their communities, building lasting bonds of trust and mutual respect. Developing grassroots programs focused on youth engagement within communities is crucial. Such initiatives offer broad benefits, including encouraging positive police-youth relationships, reducing youth crime, preventing gang involvement and drug use, and boosting youths' self efficacy and self-esteem. Additional impacts include reducing school dropout rates, increasing enrollment in higher education, and strengthening long-term relationships between police and adult community members. Through these community relations programs, police officers act as external sources of learning and support, helping to nurture healthier, safer communities.

Bronfenbrenner (2005) highlights that "development involves interaction between" individuals and their environment, such as youth programs, noting that this "interaction implies a two-way activity" (p.177). Community programs foster active engagement between police officers and youth, initiating a reciprocal learning process that unfolds gradually. This transformative interaction allows both parties, police officers and youth, to grow and learn over time. According to Bronfenbrenner, "Human development takes place through processes of progressively more complex reciprocal interaction between an active evolving biopsychological human organism and the persons, objects, and symbols in its immediate environment." For this interaction to be truly impactful, it must be consistent, occurring "on a regular basis over extended periods of time" (p.178). This sustained engagement is essential in facilitating meaningful and lasting developmental changes.

Bronfenbrenner (2005) suggests that the impact of community youth programs is "greater in disadvantaged and disorganized environments" (p.181). However, this does not imply that youth programs should be limited to these areas or that community policing initiatives are unnecessary elsewhere. Both youth and community policing programs serve as valuable foundations for fostering sustainable, transformative relationships between police officers and the community. Bronfenbrenner (2005) further explores the potential for transformative learning by addressing the influence of peer pressure: "At all age levels, pressure from peers to engage in aggressive behavior is difficult to resist. Now, if the peer group can propel its members into antisocial acts, what about the opposite? Can peers also be a force for inducing constructive behavior?" (p.205). This insight highlights the importance of community programs that harness the power of positive peer influence to encourage constructive and cooperative behavior.

Bronfenbrenner (2005) explores how involving youths alongside adults in addressing "the problems and tasks of society" (p.207) can serve as a powerful mechanism to reduce negative behaviors. He argues that youths thrive when they are part of partnerships working toward shared, overarching goals, as this structure bolsters self-efficacy and self-esteem by fulfilling their needs for love and acceptance from adults. This principle is especially relevant in the context of police-youth interactions. Bronfenbrenner emphasizes that youth and community policing programs are essential and universally needed, underscoring that "the need for such programs is not restricted to the nation's poor" (p.208). These initiatives offer police officers opportunities to build enduring, positive relationships within communities and go beyond mere crime prevention, helping to create a culture of mutual respect and understanding between law enforcement and the public.

For social justice reform to thrive and cultivate a sustainable quality of life, it is essential to actively involve the youth in partnerships with police officers and community adults. Bronfenbrenner (2005) notes that "the principal purpose of these programs is not remedial education but giving children and their families, from all levels of society, a sense of dignity, purpose, and meaningful activities" (p.208). Youth and community policing programs can also play a crucial role in helping senior citizens reclaim their dignity and sense of self-worth. These programs encourage young community members to offer comfort and assistance to senior citizens, creating meaningful intergenerational connections. Additionally, as Bronfenbrenner (2005) suggests, "participation in constructive activities on behalf of others may also reduce the growing tendencies to aggressive and antisocial behavior" (p.208). This collaborative approach not only reinforces community bonds but also channels youth energy into positive, socially constructive paths.

The second theory integrated into the altered transformative learning matrix emphasizes conflict resolution and mediation. Police officers with a liberal arts background have often been exposed to philosophical and psychological concepts that form the foundation of conflict resolution. However, this educational background does not exclude officers without a liberal arts degree from acquiring these skills. Both groups with and without liberal arts education stand to gain significantly from learning conflict resolution and mediation techniques, which are invaluable during police and citizen interactions. This approach is not intended to replace the necessary use of force in situations where there is an immediate threat to life or bodily harm. Instead, it equips officers with tools to de-escalate situations, thus potentially reducing the frequency and urgency with which force is applied.

Mending Social Injustice

The 21st century remains marked by persistent social injustices, many stemming from a learning process that has yet to fully embrace humanistic philosophies. Racial bias, unfortunately, endures as a pervasive issue, influencing various aspects of cultural and social diversity and perpetuating inequities. Microaggressions are subtle, often insidious forms of discrimination. They are embedded within social interactions and can manifest through innuendos, omissions, rituals, euphemisms, and hidden biases. As learned behaviors, microaggressions can be unlearned and thus are open to transformation. While some critics doubt the possibility of genuine change, questioning whether anyone can truly be transformed, such skepticism runs counter to the fundamental purpose of education. Addressing these complex transformative issues involves two key steps: first, recognizing the need to confront and transform biases, and second, implementing an altered transformative learning experience. Conflict resolution, as an advanced and intellectually rigorous curriculum, addresses these needs by fostering commitment, confidence, and professionalism within a humanistic framework.

Recognizing the need to transform bias is crucial, as it is often deeply ingrained and subjective, which compromises self-awareness. Many individuals fail to recognize their own biases because they do not have the tools for self-reflection or understanding. When confronted with examples of bias, they may immediately deny it, often citing personal relationships with people from marginalized groups as evidence of their lack of bias. This response reflects a lens clouded by subjective emotions, which prevents them from understanding the lived realities of those who experience bias. Biases can be so deeply embedded in behavior and thought that individuals may perceive their actions or words toward others as entirely normal. Zimbardo's (2007) Stanford Prison Experiment underscores this phenomenon, where students playing the role of prison guards were blind to their own biases and lacked empathy for the "prisoners." These students failed to see how oppressive their actions were, highlighting how easy it is for individuals to perpetuate harm without awareness. A liberal arts degree plays a significant role in advancing social justice awareness and helps filter out racial biases by offering the tools to critically analyze and challenge preconceived notions. Furthermore, a curriculum focused on conflict resolution equips individuals with the cognitive and emotional skills needed to unlearn racial biases and replace them with a deeper, more inclusive acceptance of all people, regardless of race, gender, culture, faith, or sexual orientation.

Sartre (1984) suggests that failing to truly see and understand others for who they are can lead to assumptions that foster prejudices and biases, manifesting in indifference, desire, hate, and even sadism toward them (p. 494). Randolph (2016) echoes this notion, arguing that conflict resolution offers a transformative learning opportunity that helps mitigate these biases and prejudices. By introducing humanistic methods to interact with empathy, conflict resolution teaches individuals how to engage with others in a manner that promotes understanding rather than division. A well-designed conflict resolution curriculum exposes learners to a wide array of social justice issues and values, helping to cultivate a deeper sense of empathy and awareness. Additionally, it emphasizes the importance of self-esteem, which not only empowers individuals but also fosters more respectful and constructive interactions, both in personal and professional settings.

Self-esteem is crucial for police officers to maintain. Without it, gaining trust and respect from the community would be incredibly difficult, if not impossible. Just as police officers must have a healthy sense of self-esteem, they must also recognize that citizens require recognition of their own self-worth. Many police/citizen interactions are rooted in issues of self-esteem, and officers need to be aware of when "saving face" is important to de-escalating situations that could otherwise lead to unnecessary use of force. This principle applies not only in interactions between police officers and citizens but also in disputes between citizens themselves. Randolph (2016) argues that a rigid stance that ignores the importance of self-esteem, or the need to save face, can result in humiliation that triggers violent reactions, either from a police officer or a citizen. Randolph (2016) illustrates this concept using the metaphor of "The Golden Bridge," an ancient Chinese strategy offered by a general facing an enemy. He explains: "If the enemy is provided with a dignified exit route from the dispute, it will be able to "save face' and thereby maintain its self-esteem. If the enemy encounters nothing but shame and dishonor in defeat, it will have little option but to fight, for it is only through fighting that it believes it can regain its self-esteem" (p. 76). This highlights the importance of empathy and respect in conflict resolution, particularly in sensitive situations involving police officers and citizens.

Police officers must provide an exit route for themselves and the citizens they interact with. Self-esteem plays a pivotal role in police/citizen encounters, as it offers an opportunity for police officers to use conflict resolution techniques to de-escalate situations that might otherwise lead to the use of force, including excessive force. Cooper (1999) argues that conflict resolution curriculum exposes officers to diverse communities, cultures, racial biases, and a variety of social and personal values. The central purpose of teaching conflict resolution and mediation is to equip police officers with the skills to engage in a "win-win process" (p. 6). Cooper (1999) further asserts that utilizing conflict resolution not only reduces allegations of police misconduct but also fosters community trust and respect, enhances self-esteem, and builds confidence. As a result, conflict resolution helps to cultivate sustainable relationships between police officers and citizens, while simultaneously decreasing police/citizen encounters that escalate into the use of force.

Conflict resolution curriculum emphasizes the importance of empathy. Police officers must embody empathy during their interactions with citizens to better serve and protect the community. It is crucial that police officers project humanistic values, with empathy at the core, as this factor fosters trust and respect. This does not undermine their authority; rather, it strengthens their authority and power because they will be seen as fair and just. When police officers treat people with humanity and understanding, they can significantly reduce, if not eliminate, violence during police/citizen encounters, fostering a safer environment for all.

Police officers, especially those working in major metropolitan departments, frequently encounter situations involving citizens exhibiting symptoms of mental disorders. Individuals affected by drug abuse, birth complications, domestic violence, or other psychological trauma are often the subjects of police calls for service. LaGrange (2003) studied the outcomes of police officers with higher education versus those without, specifically in situations involving individuals with mental disorders. The study provides evidence that a liberal arts curriculum in higher education equips police officers with the cognitive discernment needed to apply effective methods for de-escalating emotionally traumatic situations. As Zakaria (2015) argues, a liberal arts education helps police officers "think" before responding, which can ultimately reduce the likelihood of misconduct.

Past and current incidents involving police and citizens highlight the critical need for police officers to be grounded in knowledge, skills, and humanism; qualities nurtured through a liberal arts curriculum in higher education. Police officers are expected to understand laws and theories, but it is one thing to know them by name or to be able to recite definitions, and quite another to apply them effectively in real-world situations. To ensure impartial jurisprudence, empathy, restraint, and care, officers must be able to judiciously apply legal and sociological theories to the issues they face. This ability is directly linked to a police officer's self-confidence, which is essential for earning the trust of the community. Self-confidence, in turn, is developed through the knowledge and critical thinking skills gained from a liberal arts education.

REFERENCES

Adams, M., Bell, L. A., Goodman, D. J., & Joshi, K. Y. (2016). *Teaching for diversity and social justice* (3rd ed.). Routledge. DOI: 10.4324/9781315775852

Appiah, K. A. (2015). What is the point of college? The New York Times Magazine, The Education Issue. Retrieved from http://nyti.ms/1Q1GgQh 1-6.

Baron-Cohen, S. (2011). *The science of evil: On empathy and the origins of sin*. Basic Books.

Bronfenbrenner, U. (2005). *Making human beings human, bioecological perspectives on human development*. Sage Publicaions, Inc.

Bruns, D. (2010). Reflections from the one-percent of local police departments with mandatory four-year degree requirements for the new hires: Are they diamonds in the rough? *Southwest Journal of Criminal Justice*, 7(1), 87–108.

Carlan, P., & Byxbe, F. (2000). The promise of humanistic policing: Is higher education living up to societal expectation? *American Journal of Criminal Justice*, 24(2), 235–243. DOI: 10.1007/BF02887595

Cooper, C. (1999). *Mediation & arbitration by patrol police officers*. University Press of America, Inc.

Cross, A. R., & Fine, A. D. (2022). Police-related social media exposure and adolescents' interest in becoming a police officer. *Police Practice and Research*, 23(5), 553–568. DOI: 10.1080/15614263.2021.2017932

del Carmen, A., Butler, R. R., & Odo, J. C. (2006). Criminology and criminal justice through the lenses of the law enforcement community: An Attitudinal assessment. *Criminal Justice Studies*, 19(2), 209–222. DOI: 10.1080/14786010600764583

Dewey, J. (1927). *The public & its problems. New York, NY: Swallow PressDewey, J. (1938). Experience & education*. Free Press.

Freire, P. (1970). *Pedagogy of the oppressed*. Bloomsbury Academic.

Henion, A., & Terrill, W. (Feb. 2015). Do cops need college? Retrieved from https://msutoday.msu.edu/news/2015/do-cops-need-college/

Imel, S. (1998). Transformative learning in adulthood, Eric Digests, 200, 1-7. Retrieved from www.eric.ed.gov

Jagiello, R. J. (1971). College education for the patrolman - necessity or irrelevance? *The Journal of Criminal Law, Criminology, and Police Science*, 62(1), 114–121. DOI: 10.2307/1142134

LaGrange, T. C. (2003). The role of police education in handling cases of mental disorder. *Criminal Justice Review*, 28(1), 88–112. DOI: 10.1177/073401680302800106

Lyman, J. L. (1964). The Metropolitan Police Act of 1829: An analysis of certain events influencing the passage and character of the Metropolitan Police Act in England. *The Journal of Criminal Law, Criminology, and Police Science*, 55(18), 141–154. DOI: 10.2307/1140471

Maslow, A. H. (2013). *A theory of human motivation. Mansfield Centre*. Martino Publishing.

Merriam, S. B. (2004). The role of cognitive development in Mezirow's transformational learning theory. *Adult Education Quarterly*, 55(1), 60–68. DOI: 10.1177/0741713604268891

Merriam, S. B., & Caffarella, R. S. (1999). *Learning in adulthood; a comprehensive guide* (2nd ed.). Jossey-Bass Publishers.

Merton, R. K. (1996). *On social structure and science*. The University of Chicago Press.

Mezirow, J. (1997). Transformative learning theory to practice. *New Directions for Adult and Continuing Education*, 74(74), 5–12. DOI: 10.1002/ace.7401

Michelson, R. (2016). Why cops should pursue higher education. (March), 1-3. Retrieved from PoliceOne.Com. DOI: 10.1002/ace.7401

Murphy, M. J. (1965, March). Improving the law enforcement image. *Journal of Criminal Law and Criminology*, 56(13), 105–108.

Nietzsche, F. (1989). *Beyond good and evil: prelude to a philosophy of the future*. Vintage Books.

Oliver, W. M. (2012, November). Historian's Corner. ACJS today. *Academy of Criminal Justice Sciences*, 37(5), 34–40.

Plato, . (1981). *Five dialogues: Euthyphro, Apology, Crito, Meno, Phaedo*. Hackett Publishing Company, Inc.

Randolph, P. (2016). *The psychology of conflict: mediating in a diverse world* Bloomsbury Publishing Plc.

Rubenson, K. (2011). *Adult learning and education*. Academic Press.

Rydberg, J., & Terrill, W. (2010). The effect of higher education on police behavior. *Police Quarterly*, 13(1), 92–120. DOI: 10.1177/1098611109357325

Vollmer, A., & Schneider, A. (1917). The school for police as planned at Berkeley. *Journal of the American Institute of Criminal Law and Criminology*, 7(6), 877–898. DOI: 10.2307/1133670

Vygotsky, L. S. (1978). *Mind in society. The development of higher psychological processes*. Harvard University Press.

Wilson, O. W. (1953). Police science: August Vollmer. *The Journal of Criminal Law, Criminology, and Police Science*, 44(1), 91–103. DOI: 10.2307/1139476

Zakaria, F. (2015). *In defense of a liberal education*. W.W. Norton & Company, Inc.

Zimbardo, P. (2007). *The Lucifer effect: understanding how good people turn evil*. Random House Inc.

Chapter 6
Crisis Management and De-Escalation Tactics

ABSTRACT

Chapter 6 examines the significance of social media; its effects and pivotal role in shaping public opinion. This became especially apparent during the George Floyd incident, when Minneapolis Police Officer Derek Chauvin kneeled on Floyd's neck for nearly nine minutes, as bystanders stood by, witnessing the incident in disbelief. Cellphones were used to capture video footage of the incident, instantly broadcasting the interaction between Floyd and Chauvin to a global audience before any news network had become aware of the event. The video post quickly went viral, drawing widespread reactions of disbelief, anger, and calls for protest.

INTRODUCTION

The ability of social media to rapidly disseminate information across a vast social media network, creating immediate public awareness, has a profound impact. It galvanizes a wide range of responses and reactions, often evoking strong emotions. When police misconduct, abuse, or questionable use of force is captured on video and shared across social media platforms, it significantly influences public perception of law enforcement. The widespread visibility of these events can lead to fear, anger, and hate, undermining the trust and respect people have for police officers.

However, despite its potential for harm, social media also has positive aspects. It provides a platform for transparency, accountability, and engagement, allowing police departments to communicate directly with the public, share information, and demonstrate their commitment to serving and protecting the community. Social media also provides an opportunity for police officers to highlight their positive actions and community outreach, offering the public a more balanced perspective of their work.

DOI: 10.4018/979-8-3693-7979-0.ch006

Many police departments have recognized the positive potential of social media to help rebuild, restructure, and reform their relationships with the communities they serve. By using social media as a communication tool, police departments can provide citizens with public service announcements, share details about positive interactions, highlight community events, and inform the public about various police initiatives. These platforms are managed by a dedicated team of officers and are designed to encourage community engagement, including feedback, suggestions, and complaints. In this way, social media serves as a bridge, creating a more direct and relatable relationship between police officers and the communities they protect.

However, social media also presents significant challenges. Content on these platforms can easily be manipulated or fabricated, intentionally damaging police-community relations. With the widespread and immediate access to social media, individuals with malicious intent can spread misinformation, tarnishing the reputation of police officers and citizens. Such false narratives and imagery can cause irreparable harm to someone's character, career, and community standing, as the damage caused by a viral post or video is difficult to undo. Once misinformation spreads, it becomes perceived as truth, leading to public disillusionment and support for actions like defunding or abolishing the police.

The consequences of misinformation can be far-reaching, potentially inciting public discourse that undermines the legitimacy of law enforcement. Without the proper context or clarification, a video or social media post can perpetuate a false narrative, making it harder for police departments to correct misconceptions. The long-lasting impact of such misinformation is often felt in the form of heightened tensions, public unrest, and divisiveness.

Thus, while social media holds tremendous value in enhancing community policing efforts, it must be approached with a strong moral and ethical framework. The responsible use of these platforms is crucial in fostering trust, transparency, and accountability within the community, ensuring that the narrative shared reflects the truth and promotes constructive dialogue.

SECTION-1: UNDERSTANDING CRISIS INTERVENTION: MENTAL HEALTH, SUBSTANCE USE, AND PUBLIC SAFETY

Technology now offers real-time information on incidents involving police and citizen interactions through a variety of social media platforms such as Instagram, X (formerly Twitter), YouTube, Tik Toc, Facebook, etc. These platforms often display concerning and questionable instances of force employed by police officers. While it is true that some media coverage may omit important context or details of an incident, it is undeniable that these portrayals often provoke public outcry and fuel social justice movements that advocate for police reform. The central question arises: does social media have a negative or positive impact on 21st-century policing? Moreover, a critical inquiry is whether police officers' use of social media can enhance their image of humanistic qualities and contribute to increased trust and respect of the community. As Dewey (1927) aptly stated, "The more sincerely we appeal to facts, the greater the importance of the distinction between facts which condition human activity and facts which are conditioned by human activity" (p. 7).

Social media videos and narratives depicting police/citizen encounters, especially those involving the use of force, including deadly force, have sparked significant public debate and division between society and police officers. These incidents have fueled public outcry, with citizens and politicians calling for reform or even the defunding of police departments. The result has been a considerable erosion of respect and trust for police officers, prompting police leaders to reimagine their departments' image through a community policing framework. Beshears (2017) suggests that re-establishing trust and respect can be achieved by leveraging "new social media networks between police and local communities" (p. 490). These networks can provide an effective nexus for information exchange between law enforcement and the public. Beshears (2017) emphasizes that to rebuild public trust, police departments "must keep the public informed of police efforts and needs" (p. 490).

Colbran (2020) supports this perspective, arguing that social media also offers police the opportunity for independence from traditional media by enabling press officers to share "good news" stories on social media platforms, thus countering the negative narratives often portrayed in mainstream media. The portrayal of "bad news" on social media, especially in the context of police/citizen encounters, is compelling and emotionally charged. It captures attention and stimulates emotions due to its focus on police behavior. Maj and Lewandowsky (2020) further explore this idea, noting that "images attract attention effectively... [as they] ...enhance a message and make it more salient" (p. 2), with graphic material amplifying its reach to a larger audience. The goal of such imagery is to elicit emotional reactions from viewers, which, according to Maj and Lewandowsky (2020), "significantly influence the interpretation of the message conveyed" (p. 2).

There are two key elements influencing the psychological effects of these messages: first, "the verbal message evokes beliefs," and second, "nonverbal aspects (e.g., photos) influence emotions" (p. 2). Maj and Lewandowsky (2020) also highlight that images promoting a controversial cause can "strongly influence attitudes ... [that] ... can last for several days" (p. 2). This powerful impact of visual and verbal communication can also work to the advantage of police departments using social media to promote a more humanistic image of their officers and their work.

Videos have become powerful tools for marketing and shaping social agendas, often using imagery to influence consumer behavior and attitudes. Images are strategically crafted to appeal to a targeted audience, creating a desire to purchase products that promise to enhance personal attributes such as attractiveness, strength, and youthfulness. The fashion industry, for instance, promotes narcissistic behavior by stimulating hedonistic desires, leading individuals to reflect on their appearance such as clothing, physicality, and hygiene. This type of imagery, showcased on social media, television, and in movies, fuels cosmetic trends, driving people to seek glamour through fashionable clothing, flawless skin, and gleaming white teeth.

Movies and television further amplify this effect, casting actors in roles that convey power and authority, reinforcing the influence of imagery on societal perceptions. Video games also play a significant role in shaping behavior, using graphically seductive visuals to captivate players, stimulating their dopamine neurotransmitters and keeping them engaged for extended periods. In their 1983 study, Kisielius and Roedder explore the impact of imagery on consumer behavior, highlighting how imagery can shape both behavior and attitudes. They suggest that understanding the role of imagery is crucial, emphasizing two key purposes: first, the intention behind projecting the image, and second, the expected behaviors and attitudes that result from it.

The projection of negative imagery, particularly through social media, has significantly affected how police officers are perceived by the public. Videos of police/citizen encounters shared on platforms such as Instagram, Facebook, Tik-Tok, and X (Twitter) have contributed to a widespread erosion of trust and respect for law enforcement. These videos, often highlighting contentious or aggressive interactions, have cast doubt on the legitimacy of police authority and their right to enforce the law, leading to general mistrust within communities. This negative portrayal has not only diminished the public's confidence in police officers, but it has also deeply impacted criminal justice students who aspire to enter law enforcement. These future professionals are increasingly concerned about the potential ramifications because of hyperbole proselytized to impugn all police officers for the questionable actions of a few. And for creating an image that is perceived as socially unacceptable, let alone unlawful. No one wants to be punished for doing their job, especially when they are employing acceptable measures that predicate on methods consistent with the spirit of lawfulness. Nonetheless, quick judgement based on emotion rather than evidence that proves beyond a reasonable doubt the truth about an incident whether involving a police officer or citizen is an egregious injustice. Criminal justice students, and students with other majors in higher education are grappling with committing to pursue law enforcement as a profession. The socially amplified public criticism of police officers, the vitriol, humiliation, lack of political endorsement, probability of disciplinary action, civil suits, and possibility of being criminally charged are daunting issues to consider. As Cross and Fine (2022) point out, this fear of negative exposure can deter students from fully committing to a career in law enforcement, fearing the consequences of missteps in a highly scrutinized environment.

Social media platforms have rapidly evolved, providing more advanced technological tools that allow for quicker and broader exposure to incidents of police/citizen encounters, especially those involving citizens of color where the use of force is perceived as unjustified or excessive (Cross and Fine, 2022). This widespread dissemination has led to a shift in public opinion, with social media playing a pivotal role in shaping societal views on law enforcement. One of the most significant impacts is the increased exposure of adolescents to police-related social media content.

According to Cross and Fine (2022), "Adolescents, in particular, may be disproportionately exposed to police-related content" (p. 556). When young people repeatedly see videos of police officers misusing their authority on social media, it can create a lasting mistrust and lack of respect for law enforcement. This negative exposure may also influence their career choices, with many adolescents potentially steering away from law enforcement as a profession, thereby eroding a pool of potential candidates who could contribute positively to the field.

This concern is supported by a study in which participants were shown police body camera footage depicting either a procedurally just or unjust police interaction. Those who watched the lawful interaction reported higher levels of trust and confidence in the police, whereas those who viewed the unjust interaction video displayed lower levels of trust (Maguire et al., 2017, as cited by Cross and Fine, 2022). Additionally, Adorian and Ricciardelli (2021) support this argument, noting that social media's role in divulging police/citizen encounters often projects negative and undesirable images that impact public sentiment. Mawby (2012) suggests that such events "threaten to undermine police legitimacy" (as cited by Adorian and Ricciardelli, 2021, p. 64), which speaks to the broader consequences of these incidents being broadcast publicly.

Social media's ability to disseminate information rapidly creates an environment where users not only receive the information but also engage with others in real-time. This creates a shared space for collective interpretation, criticism, and conclusions about police/citizen incidents. As Adorian and Ricciardelli (2021) point out, the exposure of police officers to public scrutiny through social media is akin to Goffman's dramaturgy theory, which frames this exposure as putting police officers on the "front stage." What once may have remained private or behind the scenes, is now open to the public eye, making police officers vulnerable to assessment by external parties. As Goldsmith (2015) argues, "as police actions become more vulnerable to external assessment, their own claims to acting consistently, fairly and without corruption become more fragile and tenuous" (as cited by Adorian and Ricciardelli, 2021, p.

64). This heightened scrutiny can have serious implications for the legitimacy of police officers and the public's trust in their ability to act justly and without bias.

Adorian and Ricciardelli (2021) reference Lee and McGovern's (2013) theoretical perspectives, which argue that social media serves as a lens through which the public views police officers' "front stage" interactions with citizens, often in the form of highly visible, brief moments. This imagery and the limited narrative that accompanies it offer only a partial glimpse of an incident, leaving the public with an incomplete picture. Despite this, social media platforms quickly disseminate these fragmented narratives, leading the audience to form opinions based on what is presented, which may lack the full context or truth of the situation. This rapid, ubiquitous sharing of information allows for the swift formation of public opinion, significantly influencing society's view of law enforcement.

Given their highly recognizable uniforms and constant presence in the community, police officers are continuously exposed to scrutiny through social media. Whether responding to a traffic stop, crime scene, emergency call, or even mediating a neighborhood dispute, police officers are regularly on the "front stage" of public life, with every interaction spotlighted under the social microscope. This creates an environment where their actions, and the perceptions of those actions, are often amplified. Consequently, police officers are frequently tested on their ability to project a humanistic approach, demonstrating empathy, respect, and professionalism, even under the intense scrutiny that accompanies their role in society.

The simplicity and honesty of young children's perception of police officers is a poignant reminder of the purity with which they view the world. Children, especially in their early years, see officers as protectors, someone to turn to when in need. Sherwin has fond memories of walking through housing projects where young children would eagerly approach him, reaching out to hold his hand as they both conversed. Their trust was unwavering, a testament to the untainted way they viewed the role of a police officer in their community. Yet, Sherwin also experienced the painful contrast when working with children who were victims of heinous crimes. These children, despite their trauma, would reach out, holding Sherwin's hand as they bravely shared their stories in an unvarnished discourse.

Beyond these interactions with children, Sherwin also had countless conversations with teenagers, sometimes offering advice as a mentor, other times simply listening as they navigated the complexities of adolescence. Likewise, adults within the community, troubled by issues in their neighborhoods, would approach Sherwin with a desire to be heard. Even members of gangs, often seen as antagonists by moral entrepreneurs. would approach Sherwin, wanting nothing more than to engage in a candid conversation about the struggles they were facing. These moments were an invaluable reminder of the power of simply listening and offering a compassionate ear.

Officer Camp (As told by Sherwin)

About two weeks after the funeral for one of my gang team members, James Camp, who was tragically killed in the line of duty, a couple of teams arrested some familiar faces, gang members who were arrested for trafficking drugs. The police officers of my team brought the arrestees to our office, which was on the second floor of the police station. We were working on the second watch, the day watch, and I was at my desk completing some administrative responsibilities. The suspects were secured to the metal rings on the walls while sitting on an adjacent bench while being processed for their arrest.

One of the malefactors, a towering figure known as "Big Man" who weighed around 400 lbs., asked me how I was doing. I mumbled that I was fine, trying to keep my emotions in check. But he didn't stop there. He asked again, and I gave the same response. Finally, he said, "Sarge, I want to know how you're feeling about Officer Camp."

He continued, saying he was concerned because he and his associates respected me and my gang team. He spoke about how, even though they knew their actions were criminal, they had to do what they could to survive. He said he understood that we were just doing our jobs too, and he respected that. When I realized the depth of his words and the raw compassion he expressed, I got choked up. Here was a person, someone who we had interacted with numerous times, arrested even, yet he didn't harbor hate for us. Instead, he respected us. It was moments like this that made me realize how fortunate I was to have the best Gang Team in the Chicago Police Department working with me.

Mawby (1999) "Underscores the importance of a healthy police-media relationship as it adds transparency and visibility" (Cited by Grygiel and Lysak, 2021. p. 999).

Many people have told Sherwin that times have changed, that things on the street are different now. Sherwin understands their perspective but does not agree. The truth is things have always been the way they are. This is a sad reality. No one has truly changed the poor living conditions within the inner cities, or the criminal entrepreneurship to survive in them. Only the nuance of political rhetoric has changed to continue inhibiting the rehabilitation of the inner-city neighborhoods. The experiences of the survivors in those communities may feel new to them, but they are not historically new.

Historical Reflection (As told by Sherwin)

Reflecting on my thirty-eight years with the Chicago Police Department, I have so much experience that I would take another book to write about. But for the sake of making a point I have highlighted a few examples that defend my position about whether things have changed or just perceived through a different lens.

During my time working in the Chicago Police Department, it was common to be shot at, threatened with a gun, knife, or other makeshift weapons daily. I'm small in stature, and many people assumed that I would be an easy target, someone they could fight and overpower easily. However, my Marine Corps training and boxing experience proved them wrong. I remember every spring, on the first warm day of the season, when I worked in Englewood, the streets were literally filled with people shooting firearms. After being promoted to sergeant and voluntarily working on my day-off, I was assigned to work at the Robert Taylor projects. It was the Fourth of July. When I arrived at the police station there were several people, from their high-rise balconies, shooting their guns at the police station. To make my holiday experience even brighter someone had set the squad car I was assigned to on fire. A pool car was brought in for me. It was a routine occurrence to receive calls from the fire department and paramedic personnel who were under siege from gunfire or had been beaten and stabbed while responding to emergencies. When I worked in Englewood the yearly murder rate was always high contributing to the total city murder rate of nearly a thousand each year for several years. One year, the City of Chicago hit that grim milestone of a thousand. But that was just one police district out of twenty-five. Other districts reported similar, if not higher, numbers. Today there are twenty-two.

As a young police officer, I was once assigned to work the patrol wagon during the summer, on the afternoon watch. We had a body to transport to the morgue. Upon arriving, we were shocked to find many bodies stacked on the receiving dock because the morgue had run out of space. We had no choice but to leave the body we transported on the dock adding to the already macabre display of human carnage. I witnessed the growth of criminal gang enterprises, the various street gangs at war with one another, recruiting and killing with impunity. Throughout my career, I investigated the deaths of many police officers who were killed in the line of duty as well as those who took their own lives.

I have many stories, many incidents, but the point I'm trying to make is that the violence and social unrest we see today is nothing new. That is a sad truth. What's even more tragic is that, despite the years of escalating violence, there has been little to no legitimate effort to develop sustainable solutions to mitigate crime and violence.

These are the issues that were once relegated to the “Back Stage,” hidden from public view, but are now being thrust onto the “Front Stage” through the power of social media. Once these incidents are made public, they inevitably provoke outrage. The blame, anger, and erosion of trust and respect are directed at the police because they are the ones in the spotlight during these events. Police officers have become “amongst the most watched institutions in our contemporary society” (Adorian & Ricciardelli, 2021, p. 65).

Accountability

The issue, however, is not solely a problem within the police force; it is also a broader social problem. Community leaders must recognize their own role in this dynamic and be held accountable as well. The solution cannot rest solely on the shoulders of law enforcement; rather, the police and the community must work together, putting aside their differences, and agreeing to unite as a team. Mutual respect, trust, humility, and forgiveness are necessary qualities for both groups. It is only through this collaborative effort that we can begin to find solutions to improve police/citizen relationships and, ultimately, strengthen the community.

SECTION-2: CRISIS INTERVENTION TEAMS (CIT): BEST PRACTICES AND IMPLEMENTATION

While it may be debatable whether police departments still actively engage in community policing as originally conceived, it remains a valuable and effective method for fostering collaboration between citizens and law enforcement. In some cases, police departments have restructured their community policing programs, replacing police officers with civilian employees to manage non-police functions. In other instances, community policing has been completely phased out. Roberg & Bonn (2004) argue that police officers with higher education, particularly those with a liberal arts background, are more likely to develop effective strategies for working with the community and addressing social issues in a constructive and empathetic manner.

Community policing requires police officers to have strong collaborative skills. These are the same skills that Horton & Freire (1999) advocated for, encouraging both the community and police officers to work together, collaborate, and learn from one another. This process aligns closely with Vygotsky's (1978) concept of the zone of proximal development. According to del Carmen, Butler, & Odo (2006), “community policing emphasizes values such as autonomy and problem-solving, attributes commonly associated with higher education” (p. 211).

Trottier (2015) argues that community policing and social media share similar goals, such as soliciting public input and feedback, as well as making police departments more visible to the public (p. 534). Collaboration between police and citizens through social media initiatives can be beneficial in promoting safety, reducing crime, and addressing potential threats to communities. Hu, Rodgers, and Lovrich (2018) also support the idea that social media enhances community policing. They argue that "digital media, with its internet connectivity and widespread use of smartphones, facilitates the quick sharing of information, allowing for timely feedback on messages" (p. 545).

The advantages of digital media in community policing are clear. First, messages can be shared across multiple platforms simultaneously. Second, a large audience can be reached, and third, information can circulate rapidly through high-speed digital loops. Hu et al. (2018) demonstrate the effectiveness of digital media through a story about an "NYPD officer who bought a pair of shoes for a homeless person. The story went viral, gaining 30,000 new followers in one day, receiving over 612,000 likes and 48,000 comments" (Cited by Lieberman et al., 2013, p. 546). This illustrates the significant impact digital media can have in building community trust and reinforcing positive interactions between police officers and the public.

All the essential community policing skills outlined by Eck & Knutsson (2014) are inherently linked to the need for higher education, particularly a liberal arts education. One crucial factor that determines the success of community policing is leadership. For community policing to thrive, leadership plays two key roles: first, it must authorize community policing initiatives, and second, it must actively engage in the program, showing "buy-in." No matter how much training or education a police officer has, without the support and endorsement of leadership, the program can become dysfunctional or even fade out completely. Woods (2000) emphasizes the importance of leadership in sustaining community policing, stating that "implementation of community policing is based largely on the vision of leaders of the department" (p. 41).

While social media can serve as a surrogate tool for community policing, Bullock (2018) contends that "social media are not transforming the nature of routine police-citizen communications... [and are] less effective on police practices" (p. 248). Bullock (2018) points out that some leaders in police departments are "opposed" to regularly using social media, while others "struggle to see a role for social media within the organization" (p. 249). This resistance to change is compounded by the fact that "police departments are generally quite resistant to change, and implementation issues often persist for quite some time" (Brainard & McNutt, 2010, cited by Hu, Rodgers, & Lovrich, 2018, p. 250). Hu et al. (2018) highlights a concerning hypocrisy in how social media is embraced by some police departments. While certain agencies have fully adopted social media as a resource for providing community service and cultivating a competent, reliable, trustworthy, and humanistic image of their officers, "many other police agencies are likely to start using social media largely because they observe their peers doing so and wish to maintain the appearance of being up to date" (p. 547). This indicates a lack of genuine commitment to social media's potential in fostering better police-community relationships.

Bullock (2018) raises an important concern about controlling media output and whether proper oversight is in place to monitor the information shared with the public. Without adequate monitoring, the reputation of an organization could be compromised, putting it at risk. This is especially true when individual police officers use social media platforms to express their personal opinions or share details about incidents involving police/citizen encounters. Any false, biased, or inaccurate information shared could jeopardize the credibility of the entire police department, even if the information was not sanctioned by department leadership. Trottier (2015) builds on this concern, warning police departments and their officers about the use of social media platforms, such as X, Tik-Tok, and Facebook, for disseminating information. These platforms are often treated as "open sources," meaning the content shared becomes a public record with lasting longevity and can be used as open-source intelligence.

Trottier (2015) highlights a potential causational issue that could create tension within police cultures, where the extraction of data from "open" and "social" sources requires partnerships with public and private entities. This partnership could raise concerns regarding privacy, security, and the potential for misuse of the information (p. 532). The integration of social media into policing, without clear guidelines and effective oversight, could lead to unintended consequences and undermine the integrity of police work.

Nonetheless, community policing has not fully achieved its intended goals of improving communication between police and citizens. As Bullock (2018) states, "In short, traditional forms of community engagement activity have done little to promote the desired outcomes of increased participation, transparency, and accountability" (p. 247). When community policing was first introduced, its primary goals were to foster a collaborative working relationship between the police and the community. The aim was for both parties to work together to develop initiatives that would prevent and reduce criminal activity within neighborhoods. This was meant to be a goal-oriented process where community members could voice their needs and demands for improving the quality of life in their areas. Community policing was designed as a system to galvanize community engagement, creating a cooperative partnership between citizens and police to develop strategies focused on crime prevention and enhancing community safety.

Ralph and Robinson (2023) encourage police departments to leverage social media platforms as tools for promoting sustainable respect and trust within communities. Wood (2020) builds on this argument, asserting that "social media has the potential to increase police accountability and erode police legitimacy" (p. 42). Wood (2020) further highlights that social media offers a unique opportunity to provide "insight" into the daily tasks of police work, giving the public a closer look at the realities officers face. Wood also suggests that social media serves as a stage for engaging in "image management or 'image work'," which includes public relations strategies designed to promote, project, and protect the police image" (p. 42).

Figure 1. Stock images (https://www.bing.com/images)

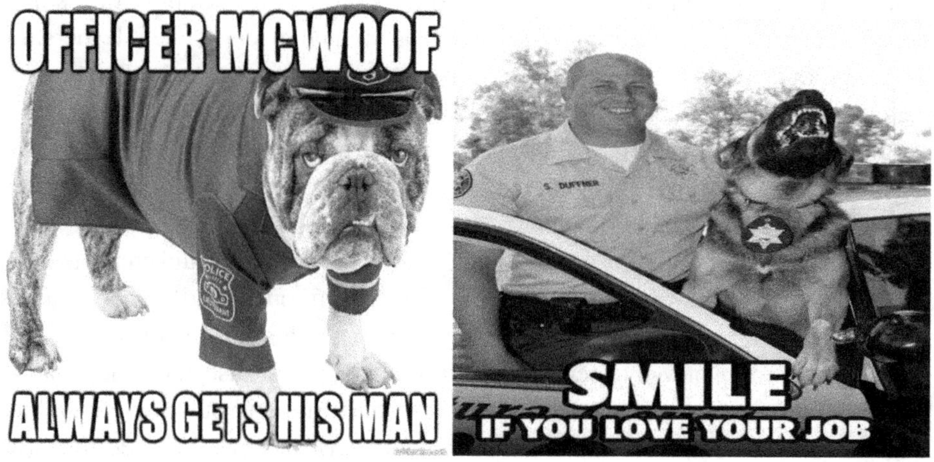

To maintain sustainably favorable relationships with the community, police officers must be vigilant in providing continuous, informative, and transparent content on social media. While the ongoing advancement of technology supporting social media platforms has played a crucial role in improving police/citizen relationships, Ralph and Robinson (2023) caution that a key challenge lies in the "lack of trained personnel involved in managing social media accounts" (p. 243). Brainard and McNutt (2010) also note that "asking police officers to serve as online facilitators is difficult, as it is not part of the traditional role of a police officer or part of their basic law enforcement academy training" (cited by Hu et al., 2018, p. 250). Without the necessary human resources to create, manage, and monitor a trustworthy social media platform that aligns with enhancing a positive police image, the goal of regaining community respect, trust, and support will likely falter. Achieving this goal will require a team of officers with expertise in digital technology, marketing platforms, and digital aesthetics. This undertaking also carries a financial burden, as taxpayers must fund such an initiative. Thus, the debate over whether to defund or reform the police continues to be a contentious social issue.

Another issue raised by Bullock (2018) is the risk associated with using social media to promote a positive image of the police. Social media platforms, while powerful tools for engagement, can also undermine this image. For instance, a police department might post a commentary that is later taken out of context, with someone claiming to be offended by a latent, harmful message. Wood (2020) expands on this risk by pointing out that the use of "cute memes" by police departments, designed to generate positive community engagement, can be met with criticism. These memes are often dismissed as a waste of police resources and are sometimes viewed as attempts to distract from more serious concerns, such as police misconduct, excessive force, and militarization. Critics argue that the use of police animals in these memes contributes to what they perceive as a "weaponized cuteness" intended to soften the public's view of the police (Wood, 2020, p. 52). Some even claim that these images misrepresent the reality of policing, presenting a subjective narrative that is seen as an "animalized form of police terror" (Wood, 2020, p. 53). Unfortunately, the rapid pace of criticism on social media often leads to misinterpretations and manipulations of information, with individuals projecting their own fears, anger, and biases, thus clouding the true intent or message behind the images.

Community safety and protection remain the core focus of justice and equality. Communities depend on the police to safeguard them from criminal activity. But equally important, communities need truth and accountability, they don't need to be fed a spin or narrative that undermines their intelligence. Social media platforms offer police departments a valuable opportunity to build trust within the community by demonstrating their commitment to lawful and humanistic policing practices. Police departments must take proactive steps to create public confidence, not through knee-jerk reactions meant to appease, but through clear, sincere actions that communicate accountability. When the public sees that police officers are operating with integrity and in accordance with the law, their concerns will be alleviated. Here is an example of what I mean.

The Robbery (As told by Sherwin)

Before I supervised a gang team, I worked as a patrol sergeant, overseeing several police units within a designated area of my assigned police district. One summer afternoon, while working the third watch (afternoons), the 911 dispatcher assigned a unit to an armed robbery in progress at a newsstand located in the Hyde Park community of Chicago. As I responded to the call, I heard the assigned unit broadcast a description of the suspect and direction of flight, along with a warning that the individual was armed with a handgun. Several officers responded to the call, and one alerted the assisting units that they were pursuing the suspect into a parking lot of a mini-mall just two blocks from the newsstand. The pursuit culminated with the suspect turning toward the pursuing officer and firing his gun at him. The officer returned fire, wounding the suspect, who subsequently fell to the ground.

I arrived shortly afterward to find several police officers standing around the injured suspect, who was lying on the pavement, along with the police officer who fired his weapon. There were several angry citizens yelling at the police officers for not attending to the medical needs of the suspect while he lied on the ground. I immediately called for paramedics, secured the crime scene, and had the officer who shot the suspect taken to the police station. Meanwhile, I addressed the angry onlookers, providing them with a brief account of the incident. Their anger quickly subsided, and a sense of calm and comfort spread as they saw the suspect being properly attended to and recognized that the situation was being managed with order and discipline. They needed reassurance that everything was under control, and that the situation was being handled with proportionate and disciplined responses. This reassured them, alleviated their fears, and helped to restore trust and respect.

Social media presents an opportunity for police departments to project an image of confident, resourceful, respectful, and trustworthy police officers whose primary goal is the protection and safety of citizens. This is the essence of policing and the categorical imperative of every law enforcement professional. However, social media alone is not sufficient to alleviate the tensions and concerns citizens may have regarding police officers. None of the social media platforms can work effectively unless the police officers behind them embody the humanistic qualities necessary to engage with citizens such as humility, empathy, and a genuine commitment to ensuring equal justice for all. This takes heart, not a nonchalant or detached approach, as Hu et al. (2018) noted, but a sincere concern for the well-being of the communities they serve and the moral and ethical standards by which they uphold the law.

Social media can serve as a tool to facilitate police and citizen cooperation, but it should not be utilized as a substitute for trustworthiness. While social media technology provides a variety of platforms to enhance the image of police officers, it cannot replace the deep connections made through direct, face-to-face interaction. Social media is inherently impersonal and detached, whereas real human engagement involves physical presence. People need to meet, speak, and interact in real-time to build true trust and respect. Though social media can encourage citizens to report, advise, and inform police officers anonymously, it cannot replace the quality of interpersonal connections. Real trust and respect are forged when people physically meet and experience one another's genuine qualities. An analogy to this argument is "online dating." While everything may appear ideal through the social media platform, the in-person meeting is the critical moment that determines whether the online persona matches reality.

SECTION-3: EFFECTIVE DE-ESCALATION STRATEGIES: BRIDGING CONFLICT AND BUILDING UNDERSTANDING

There has always been historical tension between the police and the media. Police officers are often faced with situations that require split-second decisions, which are sometimes made more from reaction than thoughtful response, leading to outcomes that are less than ideal. While I do not condone poor decision-making, I have learned from investigating numerous incidents, crimes, and allegations that one should never accept things at face value when determining guilt, wrongdoing, or innocence. There is the fact, and then there is the truth behind that fact. The truth is what we should all be striving for, not sensationalism intended to promote a specific opinion or bias. The result of any situation or incident doesn't fully explain why or how the outcome occurred. To truly understand a situation, we must seek the deeper truth behind the facts. The evidence that either proves or disproves a fact.

Unfortunately, technology has become a force that further divides society, challenging social media platforms to create a more inclusive, human-centered environment that is sensitive to diversity while advocating for a consistent and resolute doctrine. Police officers are not immune to the societal ills amplified by technology, and as such, they too require significant changes to uphold humanistic values. Many individuals are manipulated by various sources into believing that all police officers are inherently bad and should therefore be criticized and disrespected. This merely encourages hate toward police officers, portraying them as being indiscriminately harmful to everyone. This transformation from love to hate is facilitated by persuasive narratives that prey on people's emotions, turning hearts against individuals, institutions, groups, or entire professions like law enforcement.

Today, the shift from reasoned judgment to biased perception becomes alarmingly easy. People are increasingly visual learners, addicted to their electronic devices, which offer an endless flow of information, contacts, and opportunities for anonymous interactions. This digital dependency undermines the process of self-actualization, as people no longer need to engage in more thoughtful, reflective forms of learning or even read in-depth to understand complex issues. The result is a fractured society where the truth is often oversimplified, and genuine understanding is lost in the noise of constant connectivity.

People are enticed, seduced, and manipulated by the power of visual effects. They are told what to think, how to think, and how to react. Constantly bombarded with unreliable, manufactured, and misleading information, they are led to believe these sources are accurate, resourceful, and trustworthy. The dissemination of such skewed information is often a deliberate strategy, designed to satisfy personal agendas and manipulate the public's perception. However, not all media content, whether on social media or traditional platforms, is intentionally deceitful. The motives behind the information shared can vary, depending on the purpose of the individual or organization behind it.

In law enforcement, it is well known that witnesses to a crime frequently offer differing versions of events. Even victims may struggle to provide accurate descriptions of the perpetrator or the incident itself. This is why a detailed investigation requires critical examination of information and evidence to separate facts from perception, to discern the truth. Many people are presented with a version of an event via various forms of media platforms, accompanied by a narrative that often reflects personal conjecture rather than objective truth. We witnessed this firsthand during the "Summer of Love," when reporters stood in front of burning buildings and riots, telling the public that everything was fine and that it was a peaceful protest. The assassination attempts on former President Trump during his rally in Butler, Pennsylvania, on July 13, 2024, serves as another example. The variety of witness accounts and opinions expressed in the media during that event demonstrated how easily sensationalized narratives can be disseminated, often without knowing all the facts.

This lack of objectivity in media reporting fosters sensationalism, stoking public emotions and creating social unrest that can result in tragic consequences, including heightened police-citizen conflicts. A historical example of such distortion is the infamous Wayne Williams murder case. This case nearly sparked mass riots and posed a significant risk to the integrity of the investigation. In both historical and modern contexts, the rush to judgment fueled by media narratives often hinders our ability to understand the full scope of events, leading to uninformed reactions and prolonged societal divisions.

Figure 2. Stock Wayne Williams photo (https://www.bing.com/images)

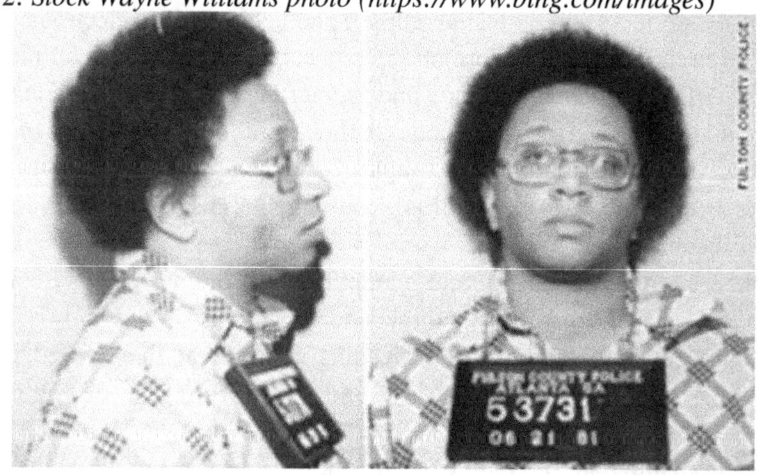

Wayne Williams, a resident of Atlanta, Georgia, became a prime suspect in a high-profile serial murder investigation conducted by the Atlanta Task Force. Over a 22-month period beginning in July 1979, there were 30 Black children and young men reported missing or found dead under suspicious circumstances in the Atlanta area. This series of murders sparked widespread social unrest; with many people believing the deaths were racially motivated. The severity of the situation led the Fulton County District Attorney to request assistance from the Federal Bureau of Investigation (FBI) (Saferstein and Roy, 2021).

Most of the victims' bodies were discovered either in or near the Chattahoochee River in Atlanta. During the investigation, a key piece of evidence was discovered: "a number of yellowish-green nylon fibers and some violet acetate fibers on the bodies and clothing of the murder victims whose bodies had been recovered" (Saferstein and Roy, 2021, p. 272). In February 1981, a news article revealed that several different fiber types had been found on two of the murder victims, which was publicized in an Atlanta newspaper. This disclosure, though meant to inform the public, posed significant legal ramifications for the ongoing investigation.

The premature revelation of such confidential details compromised the integrity of the investigation. The untenable zealous reporting influenced the perpetrator to change the method of disposing of the partially clothed bodies in wooded areas to dumping them into the Chattahoochee River without clothing. This severely hindered the collection of physical evidence, particularly the crucial fiber evidence. The reporter's egotistical hubris in leaking confidential information about the fiber evidence could have jeopardized the chances for justice and closure for the victims' families. Despite this setback, and the offender's adjusted disposal methods, the evidence still pointed to Wayne Williams. He was arrested in June 1981, charged with two counts of murder, and ultimately found guilty. Williams is currently serving a life sentence in prison, but this case remains a stark example of how public media exposure can interfere with the justice process and alter the course of criminal investigations (Saferstein and Roy, 2021).

Sherwin has been involved with many investigations and incidents throughout his professional career and during the time while he was in the Marine Corps serving in Vietnam when news reporters wrote stories for their agencies about those incidents. However, one incident that makes a relative point regarding the influence of public opinion involved a personal circumstance Sherwin experienced.

Plane vs. Soybean Field (As told by Sherwin)

It was a warm and beautiful day in July 1999, and I was nearing the completion of my flying lessons. I was being trained in a Cessna 172, taking off from Midway Airport in Chicago with my instructor onboard. We spent the day practicing landings and take-offs at various small local airports. At one point, I flew to Howell Airport in New Lenox, Illinois, a small, uncontrolled airfield situated in the middle of farmland.

After landing and making the necessary adjustments to the aircraft, I prepared for takeoff. As my air speed accelerated to about 55 mph the aircraft quickly ascended to about 600 feet when the engine stopped running. While this wasn't an uncommon occurrence during training, the engine failed to restart, which was not common. Ahead of me was a barn, and to my left, a vast field of soybeans. The field appeared to be the safer option, so the logical decision was to land there. Unfortunately, the landing wasn't as smooth as planned. The Cessna hit the ground hard, causing the landing gear to break off and ultimately flipping the aircraft over. In the chaos, my hands went through the windshield, but miraculously, my instructor and I both walked away without serious injury. We exited the plane safely, thankful for seatbelts and that the situation wasn't worse.

After what I considered a successful landing, but others contended it to be a crash, I went back inside the aircraft to retrieve my flight bag and cellphone. While retrieving my gear I made sure the ignition was off. It wasn't until a farmer's wife came out to check on us that I realized the severity of the situation. At first, she ran away in fear but quickly returned with large white bath towels, wrapping them around my hands to stop the bleeding. That was when I truly understood that my hands were injured. I was later transported to a hospital where, in the emergency room, I received over thirty-two stitches in each hand. Thankfully, my instructor was uninjured, though she was understandably upset, especially since neither of us knew why the engine had failed to restart.

The National Transportation Safety Board (NTSB) investigated and determined that the cause was mechanical failure, concluding that there was no pilot error. Despite this, the incident made national and local news, but the media misrepresented several key facts. They falsely reported that one of my arms had been severed and exaggerated other injuries sustained by both me and the flight instructor. Our families were horrified, with some even believing we had both perished in the incident.

We refused to meet with the media, though I'm not sure if anyone at the hospital was interviewed. Regardless, the reporters printed and broadcasted a narrative based on incomplete and inaccurate information. This experience was deeply disturbing, as it highlighted how easily misinformation can spread. It also brought to light how police officers are often subjected to similar misrepresentations when an incident occurs. The rush to quickly publish or report something, without verifying its accuracy, can lead to significant harm in shaping public opinion, especially when it concerns law enforcement. This serves as a reminder of the powerful impact that media can have on perception, for better or worse.

Grygiel and Lysak (2021) emphasize key concerns related to how media platforms are used in the context of police incidents. One major theme they address is the concept of *Gatekeeping*, which plays a crucial role in determining which stories make it to the public. Gatekeeping involves a process of selecting, filtering, and crafting the vast amounts of information that are generated daily, shaping the limited number of messages that reach the audience. As Shoemaker and Vos (2009) and Vos and Finneman (2017) describe, gatekeeping is about filtering news content through various layers, and it is often guided by subjective judgments and perceived priorities, ultimately influencing what the public is allowed to know. Grygiel and Lysak (2021) further argue that these gatekeeping practices are not neutral; they are influenced by the biases and underlying purposes of those in control of the information, thereby potentially skewing the narrative and shaping public opinion in ways that align with specific agendas and biases.

The second theme, as highlighted by Grygiel and Lysak (2021), focuses on the role of *routines* in media gatekeeping. They argue that gatekeepers often operate in a "mechanical" manner, relying on established routines and practices to decide what information is included in the news. These routines are shaped by the social and organizational norms within individual media outlets, rather than by a standardized policy of verification. As a result, there is a lack of consistent and rigorous practices for verifying information before it is reported. This is especially concerning when it involves social media content, which is frequently used in news broadcasts without sufficient vetting. As Grygiel and Lysak (2021) cite from Adornato (2016), a nationwide survey of television news directors revealed that 40 percent of them admitted that their organizations did not have formal procedures in place to verify social media content before it was aired. This highlights a significant gap in journalistic accountability and raises questions about the credibility of news sources that rely on information that they depend on to have been properly vetted.

Reports and videos that portray a police/citizen encounter only present a part of the story, the *fact* that an event occurred. To understand the *truth* of that fact requires deeper self-reflection and examination. Simply watching a video of an incident doesn't always allow us to absorb every detail, especially when the event unfolds rapidly. For example, in Sherwin's experience with the "Wayward Son," he didn't initially see the knife because his focus was fixated on what he believed was happening, a physical fight with fists. This moment of distraction illustrates the challenge in truly understanding what's happening in the full context of a situation.

In media coverage, there's a tendency to report quickly or to take things out of context to fit a narrative, often influenced by a personal bias. When media outlets show a video and then narrate it, they're not simply showing the raw footage, they're guiding the viewer to see things through a media lens. This has become a significant ethical issue. Are we watching the video based on the facts of what is happening, or are we being influenced by what someone else tells us to believe? As viewers, we are often witnesses to only a fraction of the event, not the full context that leads up to or follows the moment. Without understanding the broader context, we can't truly grasp why certain actions took place.

Police/citizen encounters are frequently shared through social media, often captured on someone's cellphone during the heat of a physical altercation, without providing the context or understanding of how or why the situation escalated. This is not an argument against holding police accountable for their actions, but rather an entreaty to withhold judgment until all the facts are known. Too often, social media and news outlets present police/citizen encounters with inherent bias, only for it to later emerge that the police actions were justified and lawful in mitigating the situation. However, by that time, the damage is already done. Public perception of the police has been tarnished, and the trust and respect of the community have been diminished.

Colbran (2020) highlights the discord between the police and the media, noting that journalists often take quotes out of context, fueling distrust and resentment toward law enforcement. This, combined with the national press's reluctance to highlight positive police work, has only exacerbated the strain between police officers and the news media. The lack of cooperation and mutual respect is a social concern, as it negatively impacts the image of police officers and their relationship with the public.

The power of a media platform is vast and multifaceted, it can unify, inspire hope, and provide transparency. However, it can also be used for manipulation, opinion, and to create division. Whether used by traditional networks or social media platforms, the potential for misuse is significant. Without proper oversight, the consequences can be dangerous and irresponsible. Legitimate media outlets that projects and or reports any content for public airing must be managed by a team of professionals who embody humanistic values, ensuring trust, accountability, and transparency in their reporting. This too must be a priority for police departments to do the same internal vetting of media they air to the public.

Nonetheless, Sherwin has always strived to maintain a good relationship with the media. As with any profession or vocation, there are individuals who fail to adhere to a moral or ethical code. This creates challenges for the majority who are committed to doing the right thing, as we, too, are judged by the actions of a few. Good working relationships are essential for everyone. No one truly works in isolation, even if they might believe they do. Ultimately, we all rely on the support and assistance of others to achieve successful outcomes. We must recognize that respect is not something we should demand; it is something we must earn. Respect is earned through our actions, not granted automatically. Additionally, we need to be more forgiving, less sensitive, and open to constructive criticism. Criticism is healthy, helpful, and provides an opportunity for growth and improvement.

REFERENCES

Adorian, M., & Ricciardelli, R. (2021). Synoptic prudentialism: The police, social media, and bureaucratic resistance. *Canadian Journal of Sociology*, 45(1), 59–84. DOI: 10.29173/cjs29727

Beshears, M. L. (2017). Effectiveness of police social media use. *American Journal of Criminal Justice*, 42(3), 489–501. DOI: 10.1007/s12103-016-9380-4

Bullock, K. (2018). The police use of social media: Transformation or normalisation? *Social Policy and Society*, 17(2), 245–258. DOI: 10.1017/S1474746417000112

Bullock, K. (2018). (Re)presenting 'order' online: The construction of police presentational strategies on social media. *Policing and Society*, 28(3), 345–359. DOI: 10.1080/10439463.2016.1177529

Colbran, M. P. (2020). Policing, social media and the new media landscape: Can the police and the traditional media ever successfully bypass each other. *Policing and Society*, 30(3), 295–309. DOI: 10.1080/10439463.2018.1532426

Cross, A. R., & Fine, A. D. (2022). Police-related social media exposure and adolescents' interest in becoming a police officer. *Police Practice and Research*, 23(5), 553–568. DOI: 10.1080/15614263.2021.2017932

del Carmen, A., Butler, R. R., & Odo, J. C. (2006). Criminology and criminal justice through the lenses of the law enforcement community: An Attitudinal assessment. *Criminal Justice Studies*, 19(2), 209–222. DOI: 10.1080/14786010600764583

Eck, J. E., & Knutsson, J. (2014). Community policing defined (COPS), Community Oriented Policing Service, U.S. Department of Justice, 15, 79-114. Retrieved from www.cops.us.doj.gov

Fielding, N. G. (2023). Police communications and social media. *European Journal of Criminology*, 20(1), 316–334. DOI: 10.1177/1477370821998969

Grygiel, J., & Lysak, S. (2021). Police social media and broadcast news: An investigation into the impact of police use of Facebook on journalist's gatekeeping role. *Journalism Practice*, 15(7), 994–1011. DOI: 10.1080/17512786.2020.1759123

Horton, M., & Freire, P. (1999). *We make the road by Walking*. Temple University Press.

Hu, X., Rodgers, K., & Lovrich, R. P. (2018). We are more than crime fighters: Social media images of police departments. *Police Quarterly*, 21(4), 544–572. DOI: 10.1177/1098611118783991

Kisielius, J., & Roedder, D. L. (1983). The effects of imagery on attitude-behavior consistency. *Advances in Consumer Research. Association for Consumer Research (U. S.)*, 10(1), 72–74.

Maj, K., & Lewandowsky, S. (2020). Is bad news on TV tickers good news? The effects of voiceover and visual elements in video on viewer's assessment. *PLoS One*, 15(4), 1–18. DOI: 10.1371/journal.pone.0231313 PMID: 32294122

Ralph, L., & Robinson, P. (2023). Assessing police social media practices through a democratic policing lens. *International Journal of Police Science & Management*, 25(3), 237–249. DOI: 10.1177/14613557231169391

Roberg, R., & Bonn, S. (2004). Higher education and policing: Where are we now? *Policing*, 27(4), 469–486. DOI: 10.1108/13639510410566226

Saferstein, R., & Roy, T. (2021). *Criminalistics, An Introduction to Forensic Science*. Pearson Education Inc.

Trottier, D. (2015). Open source intelligence, social media and law enforcement: Visions, constraints, and critiques. *European Journal of Cultural Studies*, 18(4-5), 530–547. DOI: 10.1177/1367549415577396

Vygotsky, L. S. (1978). *Mind in society. The development of higher psychological processes*. Harvard University Press.

Wood, M. A. (2020). Policing's meme strategy: Understanding the rise of police social media engagement work. *Current Issues in Criminal Justice*, 32(1), 40–58. DOI: 10.1080/10345329.2019.1658695

Woods, M. J. (2000, December). Interpersonal communication for police officers: Using needs assessment to prepare for skeptical trainees. *Business Communication Quarterly*, 63(4), 40–48. DOI: 10.1177/108056990006300404

Chapter 7
Integrating AI Into Restorative Justice and Conflict Resolution

ABSTRACT

In this chapter we see that artificial intelligence (AI) has rapidly evolved into a crucial tool for enhancing various aspects of law enforcement, bringing significant potential to improve efficiency, accuracy, and decision-making processes. Defined by John McCarthy in the 1950s as "the science and engineering of creating intelligent machines," AI encompasses various methods allowing machines to emulate human problem-solving and data analysis capabilities, enabling applications across fields as diverse as healthcare, finance, and criminal justice.

INTRODUCTION

There are two major forms of artificial intelligence: good old-fashioned AI and current AI. It's important to distinguish between these two forms because they employ different methodologies. Good old-fashioned AI, which spanned from the 1950s to the 1990s, was rule-based and utilized languages such as Prolog and Lisp. This era marked the beginning of expert systems. In contrast, current AI relies on machine learning, deep neural networks (also known as deep learning), large language models, and generative AI. The current AI algorithms, which are frequently based on historical data, can unintentionally reinforce biases and social inequalities present in the original datasets. Predictive policing, for instance, may lead to over-policing in certain communities, perpetuating systemic biases if not carefully managed. Concerns around transparency and accountability are also significant, as AI's "black box" nature complicates understanding the decision-making processes

DOI: 10.4018/979-8-3693-7979-0.ch007

behind certain outputs. In applications such as loan approvals or sentencing predictions, lack of transparency and traceability can erode public trust and hinder the ability to contest or understand AI-driven outcomes.

In the realm of law enforcement, AI is particularly transformative. Within law enforcement, AI's machine learning algorithms analyze massive datasets to identify patterns, from facial recognition to fraud detection, assisting in crime prevention and enhancing public safety measures. For instance, advancements in facial recognition software aid in accurately identifying individuals in real-time, enabling officers to track suspects or missing people more efficiently. AI-driven image analysis tools surpass human limitations, identifying faces, weapons, and complex events such as accidents or crimes with high precision. Collaborative projects, such as those funded by the National Institute of Justice (NIJ), highlight ongoing research to optimize AI's functionality for identifying individuals across diverse conditions, even with partial or poor-quality images, as seen in partnerships with institutions like Carnegie Mellon University. The development of scene analysis, which provides contextual object and event recognition, further enhances real-time monitoring and investigative capabilities, allowing law enforcement to intervene proactively.

Another promising application is in DNA and forensic analysis. AI has revolutionized DNA identification by enabling the detection of complex DNA mixtures and facilitating reexamination of aged DNA evidence, thus unlocking leads in previously unsolved cases. Additionally, AI's predictive capabilities are employed in gunshot detection and sound analysis, where AI can assess audio characteristics to identify firearms, determine shot frequency, and differentiate between sound sources—providing essential data for law enforcement investigations. AI's anticipatory tools further extend to recidivism prediction, where algorithms analyze vast databases to assess reoffending risks, assisting officers in resource allocation and case prioritization. However, while AI's integration into law enforcement promises efficiency and effectiveness, it also raises ethical concerns.

The ethical challenges in AI use for law enforcement have prompted calls for a multi-dimensional approach, encompassing technical solutions, regulatory oversight, and public education. Techniques like interpretable machine learning, fairness-aware algorithms, and regular audits are essential to address bias, ensure transparency, and maintain accountability. Furthermore, a collaborative approach, involving interdisciplinary research and input from affected communities, can guide the ethical deployment of AI in ways that prioritize societal values and legal compliance.

Ultimately, AI in law enforcement offers transformative potential to improve investigative accuracy, enhance public safety, and optimize resource allocation. Yet, addressing ethical concerns is crucial to ensuring AI's responsible application. By balancing technological innovation with ethical considerations, law enforcement agencies can leverage AI to better serve and protect communities while fostering trust and accountability.

SECTION-1: AI IN COMMUNITY RELATIONS: STRENGTHENING TRUST THROUGH DATA-DRIVEN APPROACHES

Artificial intelligence (AI) is a constantly evolving discipline within the realm of computer science. In the 1950s, John McCarthy, known as the pioneer of AI, described it as "the science and engineering of creating intelligent machines" (refer to the "A Brief History of Artificial Intelligence" sidebar). In simple terms, AI enables machines to independently sense and react to their surroundings and execute tasks that would normally require human cognitive and decision-making abilities without direct human involvement (Rigano, 2019).

One aspect of human intelligence is problem-solving. Unlike humans, AI's machine learning involves AI algorithms that are programmed to solve complex problems and execute tasks. These AI algorithms can analyze data, such as medical scans or market trends, and make decisions based on patterns and AI algorithms. This can have a significant impact in various fields, including criminal justice. With these advanced AI algorithms, machines can understand complex data sets and recognize patterns, such as identifying individuals from images or predicting stock market trends. This ability to analyze data and make decisions opens numerous possibilities for industries to streamline processes and make informed decisions (Marr, 2016).

Artificial intelligence is currently being explored as a tool for promoting safety in various capacities. A specific example of AI in action is its use in facial recognition, a technology that is now widely utilized by both public and private sectors (see sidebar, "The National Artificial Intelligence Research and Development Strategic Plan") (National Science, 2016). Law enforcement officers often use facial images to establish the identity and whereabouts of individuals. However, this process is time-consuming and prone to human error, as analysts must sift through many images and videos. Unlike humans, machines do not tire, which is why initiatives like the Intelligence Advanced Research Projects Activity's Janus project are testing AI algorithms that can accurately distinguish between different individuals based on their facial features, emulating the capabilities of a human analyst (Janus, 2024).

The United States government is actively pursuing ways to improve public safety by incorporating advanced technology into transportation systems. With a focus on enhancing efficiency and reducing accidents, the Department of Transportation is researching and implementing automatic traffic accident detection systems using video surveillance (Zhang and Bruce, 2004). This technology has the potential to greatly benefit a variety of locations, weather conditions, and traffic situations. In addition, AI algorithms are being utilized in the field of medicine for interpreting radiological images, which have the potential to impact the criminal justice and medical examiner communities (Arndt, 2017). Furthermore, AI has also been investigated in other fields related to forensic science, such as DNA analysis, opening new possibilities for advancement and understanding in this field (Rigano, 2019).

The emergence of AI has paved the way for its integration in detecting fraudulent activities as well (Jaokar, 2017). Companies, including PayPal, have embraced this technology and are constantly updating their AI algorithms with large amounts of data to anticipate and identify suspicious trends and adapt to new patterns (Knorr, 2015). NIJ chooses to allocate its support in AI research toward four significant fields: augmented reality simulations, behavioral analysis, risk assessment, and insider threat detection.

The criminal justice and law enforcement industries rely on video and image analysis to gather intel on individuals, items, and events to assist with criminal inquiries. Yet, this type of analysis can be extremely time-consuming and necessitates a substantial allocation of skilled personnel. Human error is a common issue in video and image analysis due to the vast amount of data, rapid advancements in technology, and a shortage of competent staff trained in handling this data (Rigano, 2019).

Artificial intelligence tools can outperform human capabilities and act as experts in various tasks. Unlike traditional software AI algorithms, which are restricted to predetermined criteria like eye shape and color, AI algorithms for video and image processing can learn and create their own intricate facial recognition parameters. This allows them to surpass human limitations and accurately identify faces, weapons, and other objects, as well as detect complex events such as accidents and crimes (Rigano, 2019).

To meet the demands of the criminal justice and law enforcement sectors, National Institute of Justice (NIJ) has made significant investments in various aspects to enhance data gathering, imaging, and analysis processes. Furthermore, they strive to enhance contextual information for improved accuracy and efficiency (Rigano, 2019).

An ongoing research project at the University of Texas at Dallas, in collaboration with the FBI and the National Institute of Standards and Technology and funded by NIJ, is investigating the capabilities of AI in terms of speed. The study specifically focuses on facial identification and aims to determine how AI algorithms compare to human facial examiners when given a time limit of 30 seconds. Initial findings suggest that AI algorithms developed in 2017 display similar performance to human examiners, highlighting the potential for AI to supplement and improve the accuracy and productivity of facial identification (Phillips, 2017).

Furthermore, Carnegie Mellon University is receiving funding from the NIJ to develop advanced AI algorithms that will enhance the detection, recognition, and identification of individuals. This effort specifically focuses on improving image analysis capabilities for faces that are captured at various angles or in situations where the individual's face is partially obstructed by objects such as masks or helmets. Additionally, the university's researchers are striving to overcome challenges posed by low-quality facial images with poor resolution and low light levels, which can make facial matching challenging. These AI algorithms are currently being evaluated by the NIJ's test and evaluation center (Carnegie Mellon University, 2013).

Dartmouth College researchers are utilizing advanced AI algorithms to improve the recognition of low-quality images or video. By intentionally degrading high-quality images and comparing them to low-quality ones, they can develop a better understanding of how to identify features in degraded images. This technique has proved successful in deciphering license plates and aiding investigations. The resulting mathematical representations are then compared to low-quality license plate images to assist in identification (DeGrade, 2016).

Another area of focus is the concept of "scene analysis," which involves generating written descriptions that depict the connections between objects (humans, locations, and items) in a sequence of images to provide context. For instance, a description might read, "A weapon is being drawn by an individual and fired into a storefront window." The aim is to recognize objects and activities that can assist in identifying ongoing crimes for real-time monitoring and intervention, as well as to aid in post-event investigations. Across multiple scenes, scene analysis can highlight potentially significant occurrences that law enforcement may need to observe, verify, and pursue. A team of researchers at the University of Central Florida, in collaboration with the Orlando Police Department, is utilizing NIJ funding to develop AI algorithms for detecting objects in videos, like people, vehicles, weapons, and structures, without the need for human involvement. They are also creating AI algorithms for detecting events, such as car accidents and acts of violence (NJR, 2015).

One notable function of AI is its capacity to forecast actions and decisions. Instead of simply identifying crime in real-time, the University of Houston has utilized NIJ funds to create AI algorithms that allow for ongoing surveillance to detect suspicious and illegal behavior across a network of cameras. This specific research focuses on utilizing attire, physical characteristics, movement patterns, and directional forecasting to target and track individuals of interest through a variety of camera feeds and visual data (NJR, 2009).

Artificial intelligence has the potential to greatly aid law enforcement by streamlining and enhancing the handling of scientific data and evidence. One specific area where it has shown significant promise is in forensic DNA analysis, revolutionizing the capabilities of the criminal justice field in recent years (Rigano, 2019).

The transfer of biological matter, such as blood, saliva, semen, and skin cells, can occur during the commission of criminal acts through contact with individuals and objects. With advancements in DNA technology, forensic experts are now able to detect and analyze DNA evidence at even lower levels, including degraded or previously unusable samples. In fact, aged DNA evidence from past violent crimes, such as sexual assaults and unsolved murders, is now being re-examined in labs. This enhanced sensitivity also brings new challenges for crime labs, as it increases the potential for detecting DNA from multiple sources, even in minimal amounts. This presents the difficulty of interpreting DNA mixtures and identifying individual profiles, which is critical for providing important leads for law enforcement (Rigano, 2019).

The advancement of AI could potentially assist in tackling this issue. The process of DNA analysis generates a vast amount of intricate information in electronic form, revealing complex patterns that may exceed human comprehension but could prove valuable as technology becomes more sophisticated. A collaborative effort between Syracuse University, Onondaga County Center for Forensic Sciences, and the New York City Office of Chief Medical Examiner's Department of Forensic Biology was undertaken to investigate a new machine learning-based technique for separating mixed DNA samples. Through the support of an NIJ research grant, the team merged traditional methods used by human analysts with data mining and AI algorithms. This combination proved beneficial in identifying individual DNA profiles, mitigating the limitations that may arise when using a single approach. It is crucial to continually assess the use of AI in this area, as there are various factors that may impact its success in distinguishing DNA donors. Nevertheless, research has shown that AI has the potential to aid in these intricate analyses (NJR, 2014).

The emergence of identifying patterns in gunshot analysis opens new opportunities for the application of AI algorithms. For example, the NIJ funded a project by Cadre Research Labs, LLC, which centers on the analysis of gunshot audio recordings from various types of devices. This project is based on the recognition that the characteristics of gunshot recordings can be influenced by several factors such as firearm type, ammunition type, scene layout, and recording device (NIJ, 2016a). With a carefully constructed mathematical model, Cadre's team of experts is working towards developing AI algorithms that can accurately identify gunshots, distinguish between muzzle blasts and shock waves, determine the timing between shots, identify the number of firearms involved, match specific shots to their respective firearms, and estimate the likelihood of class and caliber. These advancements could greatly benefit law enforcement agencies in their investigative efforts (NIJ, 2016b).

Anticipatory examination involves a multifaceted procedure utilizing substantial amounts of information to project and develop potential conclusions. In the field of criminology, the responsibility primarily lies with police officers, probation practitioners, and other specialized professionals who must acquire extensive knowledge over time. This work requires a significant investment of time and is prone to personal biases and errors (NIJ, 2016c). In other words, law enforcement agencies, particularly police departments, can hire data scientists and analytics experts. These technical staff members, who are familiar with machine learning and artificial intelligence, can help save time and reduce mistakes in the process.

AI technology has the potential to revolutionize the legal field by utilizing vast amounts of data on laws, social dynamics, and media to make informed decisions on legal cases, criminal activities, and identifying individuals at risk. Researchers at the University of Pittsburgh, supported by the NIJ, are currently developing innovative computational methods for interpreting statutes, which could greatly enhance the efficiency and accuracy of legal professionals. Utilizing machine learning AI algorithms, the team aims to create a computer program that can identify key statements crucial for statutory interpretation. The ultimate objective is to create a prototype expert system to aid in the interpretation and automatic handling of cybercrime cases (NIJ, 2016d).

Artificial intelligence is not only capable of analyzing large amounts of data, but it can also be utilized in the criminal justice system to predict potential criminal recidivism. A team of researchers at the Research Triangle Institute, in collaboration with the Durham Police Department and the Anne Arundel County (Maryland) Sheriff's Office, have worked on a new automated warrant service system for the North Carolina Statewide Warrant Repository. With the support of the NIJ, this team was utilizing advanced AI algorithms to analyze over 340,000 warrant records. Using decision trees and survival analysis, the AI algorithms can determine the likelihood of when a desired event may occur and predict the risk of reoffending offenders with open warrants. This innovative approach will assist practitioners in effectively managing warrant backlogs. Additionally, the system will have a geographical component, allowing for the identification and pursuit of high-risk absconders and others with active warrants, leading to a more efficient use of resources (NIJ, 2015).

Artificial intelligence technology has the potential to detect and identify elderly abuse victims who may be experiencing physical or financial mistreatment. Funded by the National Institute of Justice, a team of researchers at the University of Texas Health Science Center at Houston utilized AI algorithms to examine cases of elder victimization. Through this method, the AI algorithms can discern key factors such as the victim's identity, the perpetrator's involvement, and the impact of the environment on the different types of elder abuse, specifically financial exploitation. These AI algorithms are also capable of distinguishing between instances of "pure" financial exploitation, where the victim only experiences financial harm, and "hybrid" financial exploitation, which includes other forms of abuse such as physical violence or neglect. The researchers aim to develop user-friendly online applications that will allow professionals to accurately assess the likelihood of financial exploitation and take swift action to prevent it (NIJ, 2013).

Ultimately, artificial intelligence is now being utilized for the purpose of detecting potential victims of violent crime through the analysis of their behavior and connections. The collaboration between the Chicago Police Department and the Illinois Institute of Technology saw success in identifying individuals at risk by utilizing AI algorithms to group and analyzing social networks. As a result, this research, funded by NIJ, has been integrated into the Chicago Police Department's Violence Reduction Strategy, further reinforcing its effectiveness (NIJ, 2011).

In recent years, AI has gained widespread attention for its potential to revolutionize various industries. Governments and companies around the world are investing in AI, citing its ability to enhance personalization and convenience. Despite the widespread excitement, concerns have been raised by civil rights groups, particularly regarding using AI in law enforcement (Mozur, 2019). Facial recognition technology has been criticized for its potential to be used as a tool for authoritarian control and perpetuation of racial bias (FRVT, 2019). To address these issues, companies like IBM and Amazon have made decisions to discontinue or restrict the use of their facial recognition platforms in law enforcement (Statt, 2020). While there are promising possibilities for AI in criminal justice, the negative repercussions of this technology also need to be carefully considered. It is important to avoid overhyping the short-term impacts of AI and instead consider its long-term effects, as futurist Roy Amara reminds us (Ratcliffe, 2016).

For example, recently the U.S. Immigration and Customs Enforcement (ICE) faces significant challenges in identifying illegal immigrants. In this context, AI can play a crucial role in locating these individuals across the country. One method ICE could utilize is gait analysis (Levine et al., 2012), which allows for the assessment of human movement. Gait analysis systematically studies how individuals walk, employing AI tools alongside instrumentation that measures body and muscle movement. While ICE officers may find it difficult to stop individuals on the street to check for documents, gait analysis could provide insights into those who may behave differently in public settings, helping to identify potential illegal immigrants based on their walking patterns.

Many people mistakenly believe that AI is a single, modern technology. However, this is not the case. AI is a combination of computer science methods that have been studied since the 1950s (NRC, 1997). It is difficult to define AI accurately, but it can generally be described as an area of computer science that aims to create machines with human-like intelligence. There are numerous approaches to developing AI, and it encompasses various functions such as machine vision, predictive analytics, natural language processing, autonomous robotics, and robotic process automation. The details of these functionalities and potential applications in law enforcement are discussed in the first segment of this series, which provides examples of their use in this field (Redden et al., 2020).

New advancements in artificial intelligence have the capacity to greatly influence various aspects of both internal and external law enforcement procedures. Law enforcement officials must adopt a design mindset when assessing these AI-based tools. Design thinking involves thoroughly comprehending the issue at hand, its surroundings, and limitations before determining the most optimal solution (Linke, 2017).

In general, the use of AI can offer valuable assistance to law enforcement by aiding in decision-making and task execution. These advanced solutions prioritize optimizing efficiency, implementing data-driven practices, and enhancing capabilities for targeted assignments and choices (Redden et al., 2020).

One essential aspect of design thinking is determining the potential benefits of incorporating AI in law enforcement, such as streamlining tasks or improving decision-making. It is important to carefully consider the degree of AI involvement in these processes, ranging from simple assistance for the user to full automation (Redden et al., 2020).

Instead of hastily implementing AI, law enforcement officials should carefully assess all potential solutions, regardless of whether they involve AI or not, to determine which one is most suitable for their specific needs. Every aspect of daily law enforcement operations must be analyzed individually, considering its own distinct context and limitations (Redden et al., 2020).

SECTION-2: AI-DRIVEN TOOLS FOR CONFLICT RESOLUTION: INNOVATIONS IN MEDIATION AND DE-ESCALATION

Innovative uses of AI continue to emerge in the law enforcement sector, helping in decision-making and task completion. As with any new advancement, careful consideration of the potential benefits and costs of implementing AI is crucial for agencies (Redden et al., 2020).

While AI technology is gaining some attention in the realm of law enforcement, it is not yet a widely adopted tool. However, there are several agencies that are starting to explore the potential of AI and advanced robotics. This section aims to showcase various AI-based products and services that are currently available, to generate discussion among law enforcement officials about the feasibility and impact of incorporating these technologies (Redden et al., 2020).

Automatic License Plate Recognition (ALPR) technology has been utilized by both law enforcement and private companies for a significant amount of time now (Roberts and Casanova, 2012). With continual advancements in AI-powered machine vision technology, the capabilities of ALPRs have greatly improved, and their costs have decreased. As a result, the utilization of ALPRs has expanded to various new use cases for both law enforcement and private companies. These include creating virtual boundaries to monitor vehicle movement and issuing automated tickets for red light violations. It is safe to say that ALPRs remain one of the most common forms of machine vision technology used in law enforcement (Kaplan, 2019).

Besides automatic license plate recognition systems, there has been significant progress in video surveillance and other security camera technology. Manufacturers have incorporated AI features, such as deep neural network capable chips, into their cameras. This allows for AI algorithms to be processed directly on the camera's hardware, saving money and increasing efficiency due to reduced reliance on cloud processing and lower bandwidth needs (Faggella, 2019). This AI-enabled hardware has also been employed in law enforcement for tasks such as real-time detection of weapons and facial recognition in crowded public locations (Nytimes, 2018; XeroEyes, 2020).

Even though redaction is commonly associated with public disclosure, AI technology has the potential to address unconscious prejudice in the criminal justice system. An instance of this is the implementation of AI redaction by the San Francisco District Attorney to remove racial and personal details of suspects and victims from police reports. The aim is to ensure fair charging decisions by preventing any discriminatory influences (Queally, 2019).

Gunshot detection technology has evolved with the incorporation of artificial intelligence into the systems. Many law enforcement agencies in numerous cities have adopted advanced acoustic gunshot detectors, such as ShotSpotter®, to detect and map gunshots. One emerging startup, Aegis, has taken it a step further by utilizing visual recognition to identify potential gunshots before they occur. The effectiveness of these AI-driven systems is a key area of research for the National Institute of Justice, although it is not the sole focus of their evaluations (CUNY, 2020; Lawrence et al., 2019). A recent study by Cheng et al. (2023) explored the use of AI deep learning models to classify entry and exit gunshot wounds in digital color images. Their findings demonstrated that these models can accurately distinguish between entrance and exit gunshot wounds in digital images.

Thorn, a nonprofit organization, has developed a unique approach to tackling human trafficking and child predators. Utilizing Amazon's facial recognition technology, they scour the internet and dark web for images of missing children. This innovative use of AI demonstrates how technology can work alongside, rather than replace traditional law enforcement methods. It's important to note that even with the help of technology in locating victims, capturing offenders and rescuing those in danger still relies on traditional policing tactics (Simonite, 2019).

Different strategies are being implemented to combat the distribution of child pornography and capture individuals who prey on children (Video Fingerprints, 2014). In partnership with Thorn and various other organizations, Microsoft has created Project Artemis, a tool designed to detect communication patterns commonly used by predators in online chat rooms to groom and target minors. Furthermore, certain internet monitoring companies that cater to the public have expanded their efforts by collaborating with law enforcement agencies to detect and apprehend child predators (Bark Newsroom, 2020).

The rise in usage of body cameras among law enforcement agencies has resulted in a growing need for video redaction (MCCA, 2016). In some cases, identifying information is intentionally removed from police body cam footage before it is made available to the public, either by regulation or personal choice. Specific timeframes for the release of body cam recordings may even be mandated by states. However, the process of manually redacting can be time-consuming, with 10 minutes needed for just 2 minutes of footage (Peace Officers, 2018). As a result, many police agencies are turning to AI-based solutions for video redaction, with companies like Microsoft, academic researchers, and technology vendors actively working on developing these solutions (Gada, 2018; Sah et al., 2017).

The use of AI technology in transcription has greatly enhanced the accuracy and efficiency of reporting for law enforcement. Thanks to automatic speech recognition software, officers no longer need to type out their reports but can instead use voice-to-text dictation tools. This saves valuable time and can also help prevent errors, such as incorrectly identifying voices in witness testimonies or interrogations, as the advanced AI system is able to accurately transcribe audio and video materials (DLE, 2020).

The use of computer-aided dispatch (CAD) systems by law enforcement and emergency medical services (EMS) agencies is becoming increasingly common. These systems allow for the collection of data from incoming calls, aiding in resource deployment decisions and streamlining reporting processes. Some providers, including RapidDeploy, are going above and beyond by incorporating advanced technologies like AI and analytics into their CAD software. With the integration of AI, these systems have the potential to optimize resource allocation and save time and money. By analyzing historic data, making predictions, and automating workflows, AI can help inform decision-making and even adapt its recommendations in real time. This exciting development could revolutionize the way CAD systems are utilized by law enforcement and EMS agencies (Redden et al., 2020).

Predictive policing and hotspot mapping have been utilized for many years to optimize resources. However, new advancements in technology, specifically AI, have been integrated into these systems to enhance their predictive capabilities. AI is primarily used to bolster both place-based and individual-based predictive models. While place-based predictive policing focuses on identifying high-risk areas and times for crime and disorder, individual-based predictive policing considers a person's criminal history to determine their likelihood of being involved in future law enforcement-related incidents, either as a victim or offender. Despite these models being useful, they also have their limitations, such as the potential for reinforcing systemic biases and over-policing certain communities. Furthermore, AI can also utilize crime databases to identify patterns and connections between crimes, potentially identifying perpetrators or predicting their likelihood of committing multiple offenses based on past data (Baron, 2019).

Public safety agencies frequently need to transmit vital information to the community, which includes issuing public announcements and catering to individual inquiries. The continuous development of natural language processing technology has enabled the use of advanced and intelligent systems in managing customized communication. For instance, virtual chatbots have gained commercial popularity in aiding customer service operations. These chatbots show potential in enhancing interactions between law enforcement and civilians. As seen in an example, the Los Angeles Police Department integrated a virtual chatbot into their website to assist prospective police recruits with their queries. Similarly, in Georgia and Indiana, officials are currently piloting a community engagement chatbot developed by civitasAI. This chatbot can not only assist with emergency services but also address common questions and provide information on available resources and referrals (Redden et al., 2020; Norris, 2019).

In 2018, the Department of Justice gave a grant to the City of San Francisco Police Department (SFPD), Justice & Security Strategies, Inc. (JSS) and Stanford University (SU) to enhance their methods of solving homicide cases using advanced technology. Their project involves analyzing a vast database of homicide cases spanning over two decades (1990-2010) which consists of over 6,000 handwritten files to identify patterns that contribute to high clearance and conviction rates. The team intends to develop and evaluate a cutting-edge investigative tool that utilizes deep learning AI algorithms to aid in their investigations (Redden et al., 2020).

SECTION-3: CHALLENGES AND ETHICAL CONSIDERATIONS OF AI IN RESTORATIVE JUSTICE

Today, AI algorithms play an integral role in essential services and infrastructures. People regularly encounter recommendation systems, which use AI algorithms to suggest songs, movies, products, and even potential friends (Paraschakis 2017; Perra and Rocha 2019; Milano et al. 2020). Similarly, AI algorithms are also utilized in various industries, such as schools, hospitals, financial institutions, courts, local governments, and national governments, to assist in decision-making processes (Obermeyer et al. 2019; Zhou et al. 2019; Morley et al. 2019a, b; Lee and Floridi 2020; Aggarwal 2020; Green and Chen 2019; Yu and Du 2019; Eubanks 2017;

Lewis 2019; Labati et al. 2016; Hauer 2019; Taddeo and Floridi 2018a; Taddeo et al. 2019; Roberts et al. 2019), demonstrating the increasing reliance on AI algorithms in vital operations.

The potential benefits of AI algorithms for improving individual and societal well-being should not overshadow the ethical concerns they bring (Floridi and Taddeo 2016). It is important to recognize that AI algorithms are not morally neutral. For instance, the seemingly objective outputs of translation and search engine AI algorithms often perpetuate gendered language (Larson 2017; Prates et al. 2019). Similar bias has been observed in AI algorithmic advertising, with men being targeted more frequently for high-paying and STEM-related positions (Datta et al. 2015; Lambrecht and Tucker 2019). Furthermore, the use of prediction AI algorithms in managing healthcare data for millions of patients in the United States has exacerbated existing disparities, resulting in better care for white patients compared to their black counterparts (Obermeyer et al. 2019). Despite ongoing discussions and efforts to address these issues, the number of AI algorithmic systems causing ethical concerns only continues to increase.

Since 2012, the field of artificial intelligence (AI) has experienced significant progress and has garnered significant attention from various stakeholders (Perrault et al. 2019). One emerging area of research has been the examination of ethical considerations surrounding AI algorithms, with a particular focus on issues of fairness, accountability, and transparency (Lee 2018; Hoffmann et al. 2018; Shin and Park 2019). The Digital Ethics Lab's previous study from 2016 provided a comprehensive overview of these concerns (Mittelstadt et al. 2016). However, with the fast-paced developments in this field, it has become necessary to update and enhance that research to address new ethical challenges and potential solutions.

The study of ethics surrounding AI algorithms has significantly grown in recent years, sparked by the involvement of government entities, non-profits, and corporations in discussions of "fair" and "ethical" artificial intelligence (AI) and AI algorithms (Sandvig et al. 2016; Binns 2018; Selbst et al. 2019; Wong 2019; Ochigame 2019). There has been a substantial increase in the amount and quality of research on this topic as a result. This article presents an updated analysis of the ethics of AI algorithms, incorporating new insights and references that were previously overlooked. The scope of the analysis has been expanded to include AI for social good.

With the rapid advancement and integration of AI algorithms, particularly in the realm of machine learning (ML) and artificial intelligence (AI), significant ethical concerns have surfaced. These concerns are not merely abstract philosophical issues; they have real-world implications affecting everyone from individual users to entire societal structures. Mittelstadt et al. (2016) delineate these concerns into six categories within a conceptual map, providing a comprehensive framework to address the ethical challenges in AI algorithmic practices. These concerns are divided into epistemic and normative categories, with traceability acting as a bridge between the two. Epistemic concerns are those related to knowledge, beliefs, and the justification of data. AI algorithms, especially those utilizing ML, often generate outputs that carry specific epistemic challenges.

AI algorithms can produce results that are not definitive. This occurs due to the probabilistic nature of many ML AI algorithms, which rely on statistical methods to arrive at conclusions. While these methods can provide likely outcomes, they often do not offer absolute certainty. In critical areas such as healthcare, law enforcement, and financial services, inconclusive evidence can complicate decision-making processes. For example, in healthcare, an AI algorithm predicting the likelihood of a disease might only offer a probability rather than a concrete diagnosis. This lack of conclusiveness can delay treatment or lead to unnecessary procedures.

Another significant concern is the opacity of AI algorithmic decisions. This inscrutability arises because many AI algorithms, particularly deep learning architectures, operate as 'black boxes' where the internal workings are not easily understood. Even for experts, dissecting and comprehending the decision pathways in these models can be challenging. This lack of transparency can erode trust and make it difficult to hold decision-makers accountable. If a loan application is rejected based on an inscrutable AI algorithm, the applicant won't know why or how to rectify their application, leading to frustration and potential accusations of bias.

The presence of incorrect or misleading information is another epistemic concern. AI algorithms are designed based on training data, and if this data is flawed, biased, or outdated, the AI algorithm can generate erroneous results. For instance, a predictive policing AI algorithm trained on biased historical crime data may perpetuate and even amplify existing biases, leading to disproportionate targeting of certain communities. Misguided evidence not only undermines the credibility of AI algorithmic systems but can also cause significant harm if acted upon.

Normative concerns revolve around the values, ethics, and societal norms that AI algorithms should adhere to. AI algorithms can produce biased or discriminatory outcomes, often reflecting the prejudices present in their training data. This issue is particularly problematic as it can perpetuate and institutionalize existing social inequalities. For example, hiring AI algorithms trained on company data reflecting historical gender biases may continue to favor male candidates over equally qualified female candidates. Addressing unfair outcomes requires deliberate efforts in data collection, preprocessing, and the integration of fairness-aware AI algorithms that actively mitigate bias.

AI algorithms can have transformative effects on society, often in ways that are unpredictable and sometimes detrimental. The widespread use of social media AI algorithms, for instance, has transformed how information is disseminated and consumed, with significant implications for public discourse and democracy. These

AI algorithms can create echo chambers, filter bubbles, and even propagate misinformation, altering public perception and behavior. Understanding and managing the transformative effects of AI algorithms involves not only technical solutions but also policy and regulatory measures to ensure they promote positive societal outcomes.

Situated at the intersection of epistemic and normative concerns, traceability is about ensuring transparency and accountability in AI algorithmic decisions. Traceability allows both the understanding of how decisions are made (epistemic) and the attribution of responsibility for those decisions (normative). This becomes crucial in scenarios where AI algorithms influence significant outcomes, such as judicial decisions or autonomous driving. Implementing traceability mechanisms entails logging data, maintaining decision paths, and documenting the rationale behind AI algorithmic choices. This would enable stakeholders to audit, understand, and if necessary, contest AI algorithmic decisions.

Dealing with these ethical concerns requires a multi-faceted approach, integrating technical, regulatory, and societal perspectives. Developing methods such as interpretable machine learning models that provide insights into their decision-making processes. Techniques like SHAP (SHapley Additive exPlanations) and LIME (Local Interpretable Model-agnostic Explanations) can help make model predictions more understandable.

Implementing fairness-aware AI algorithms and techniques that identify and mitigate biases in training data. This can involve diverse and representative data collection, adversarial debiasing, and fairness constraints during model training. Governments and regulatory bodies need to establish clear guidelines and frameworks to govern the use of AI algorithms. This includes data protection laws, AI algorithmic transparency mandates, and anti-discrimination laws that ensure fair and accountable use of AI algorithms. Regular audits conducted by independent bodies to assess the ethical implications of deployed AI algorithms. These audits can evaluate AI algorithms for bias, fairness, transparency, and compliance with regulatory standards. Educating the public about the functioning and implications of AI algorithms. This enables informed engagement and empowers individuals to recognize and challenge unfair practices.

Involving diverse stakeholders, including affected communities, civil society organizations, and industry experts, in the development and deployment processes of AI algorithms. This ensures that different perspectives are considered, and ethical values are integrated from the outset. Encouraging interdisciplinary research that brings together computer scientists, ethicists, sociologists, and legal scholars. This collaborative approach can uncover deeper insights and innovative solutions to address the ethical challenges posed by AI algorithms.

AI algorithms should not be static; continuous monitoring and adaptation are necessary to ensure they remain aligned with societal values and ethical standards. This involves ongoing research, development, and iterative improvements based on feedback and real-world observations. As the influence of AI algorithms continues to expand across various domains, addressing the ethical concerns they raise becomes increasingly critical. Mittelstadt et al.'s conceptual map provides a valuable framework for understanding and tackling these issues, highlighting the need for comprehensive and multi-dimensional strategies. By combining technical innovations, regulatory measures, societal interventions, and interdisciplinary research, stakeholders can work towards developing and deploying AI algorithms that are not only effective but also ethically sound good.

REFERENCES

Savvides, Marios. (2018). A Simultaneous Low Resolution and Off-Pose Angle Face Matching AI algorithm as an Investigative Lead Generative Tool for Law Enforcement" at Carnegie Mellon University, NIJ award number 2013-IJ-CX-K005. DOI: 10.1515/popets-2015-0007

Aggarwal, N. (2020) The norms of AI algorithmic credit scoring. *SSRN Electron J.* DOI: 10.2139/ssrn.3569083

Arndt, R.Z.(2017). "Artificial Intelligence Takes on Medical Imaging," Transportation Hub (July 8, 2017).

Bark in the News: Bark Newsroom: Bark Parental Control App. (n.d.). Retrieved April 1, 2020, from https://www.bark.us/blog/newsroom/

Baron, E. (2019, March 11). Predictive Policing Using AI Tested by Bay Area Cops. Retrieved April 1, 2020, from https://www.govtech.com/public-safety/Predictive-Policing-Using-AI-Tested-by-Bay-Area Cops.html

Cheng, J., Schmidt, C., Wilson, A., Wang, Z., Hao, W., Pantanowitz, J., Morris, C., Tashjian, R., & Pantanowitz, L. (2023, December 30). Artificial intelligence for human gunshot wound classification. *Journal of Pathology Informatics*, 15, 100361. DOI: 10.1016/j.jpi.2023.100361 PMID: 38234590

Mozur, Paul. (2018, July 8). Inside China's Dystopian Dreams: A.I., Shame and Lots of Cameras. *The New York Times*. https://www.nytimes.com/2018/07/08/business/china-surveillance technology.html

Datta, A., Tschantz, M. C., & Datta, A. (2015). Automated experiments on Ad privacy settings. *Proceedings on Privacy Enhancing Technologies. Privacy Enhancing Technologies Symposium*, 2015(1), 92–112. DOI: 10.1515/popets-2015-0007

DeGrade. (2016). It" at Dartmouth College, NIJ award number 2016-R2-CX-0012.

Dragon Law Enforcement—Speed Incident Reporting by Voice. (n.d.). Retrieved April 1, 2020, from https://www.nuancc.com/dragon/industry/dragon-law-enforcement.html

Eubanks, V. (2017). *Automating inequality: how high-tech tools profile, police, and punish the poor* (1st ed.). St. Martin's Press.

Face, R. V. T. (FRVT) Part 3: Demographic Effects (December 2019). Retrieved March 27, 2020, from https://nvlpubs.nist.gov/nistpubs/ir/2019/NIST.IR.8280.pdf

Faggella, D. (2019, February 2). AI for Crime Prevention and Detection—5 Current Applications. Retrieved April 1, 2020, from https://emerj.com/ai-sector-overviews/ai-crime-prevention-5-current applications/

Floridi, L., & Taddeo, M. (2016). What is data ethics? *Philosophical Transactions. Series A, Mathematical, Physical, and Engineering Sciences*, 374(2083), 20160360. DOI: 10.1098/rsta.2016.0360 PMID: 28336805

Gada, M. (2018, February 22). Using AI to automatically redact faces in videos. Retrieved April 1, 2020, from https://azure.microsoft.com/en-us/blog/using-ai-to-automatically-redact-faces-in-videos/

Green, B., & Chen, Y. (2019) Disparate interactions: an AI algorithm-in-the-loop analysis of fairness in risk assessments. In: Proceedings of the Conference on Fairness, Accountability, and Transparency—FAT*'19, 90–99. Atlanta, GA, USA: ACM Press. DOI: 10.1145/3287560.3287563

Hauer, T. (2019). Society caught in a labyrinth of AI algorithms: Disputes, promises, and limitations of the new order of things. *Society*, 56(3), 222–230. DOI: 10.1007/s12115-019-00358-5

Jaokar, A. (2017). Artificial Intelligence in Fraud Detection," Envision Blog, March 15, 2017.

Kaplan, J. (2019, July 10). Who's Using License Plate Cameras to Track Cars? Cops, Landlords, and Your Neighbors. Retrieved April 1, 2020, from https://slate.com/technology/2019/07/automatic-license plate-readers-hoa-police-openalpr.html

Knorr, E. (2015, April 13). How PayPal Beats the Bad Guys with Machine Learning," Ahead of the Curve. *InfoWorld*.

Labati, R. D., Genovese, A., Muñoz, E., Piuri, V., Scotti, F., & Sforza, G. (2016). Biometric recognition in automated border control: A survey. *ACM Computing Surveys*, 49(2), 1–39. DOI: 10.1145/2933241

Lambrecht, A., & Tucker, C. (2019). AI algorithmic bias? An empirical study of apparent gender-based discrimination in the display of STEM career ads. *Management Science*, 65(7), 2966–2981. DOI: 10.1287/mnsc.2018.3093

Larson, B. (2017) Gender as a variable in natural-language processing: ethical considerations. In: *Proceedings of the First ACL Workshop on Ethics in Natural Language Processing*, 1–11. Valencia, Spain: Association for Computational Linguistics. DOI: 10.18653/v1/W17-1601

Lawrence, D., La Vigne, N., & Thompson, P. (2019, September) Evaluation of Gunshot Detection Technology to Aid in the Reduction of Firearms Violence. Retrieved April 3, 2020, from https://nij.ojp.gov/ library/publications/evaluation-gunshot-detection-technology-aid-reduction-firearms-violence

Lee, M. S., & Floridi, L. (2020) AI algorithmic fairness in mortgage lending: from absolute conditions to relational trade-offs. *SSRN Electron J.* https://doi.org/DOI: 10.2139/ssrn.3559407

Levine, D. F., Richards, J., & Whittle, M. (2012). *Whittle's Gait Analysis Whittle's Gait Analysis Elsevier Health Sciences.*

Lewis, D. (2019) Social Credit case study: city citizen scores in Xiamen and Fuzhou. Medium: Berkman Klein Center Collection. 8 October 2019. https://medium.com/ berkmanklein-center/social-credit-case-study-city-citizen-scores-in-xiamen-and -fuzhou-2a65feb2bbb3. Accessed 10 Oct 2020

Linke, R. (2017) Design thinking, explained. Retrieved April 7, 2020, from https:// mitsloan.mit.edu/ideas-made-to-matter/design-thinking-explained

Major Cities Chiefs Association. (March 2016). Annual Report '15. Retrieved April 1, 2020, from https://www.majorcitieschiefs.com/pdf/news/annual_report_2015.pdf

Marr, B. (2016, December 8). What Is the Difference Between Deep Learning, Machine Learning and AI? *Forbes.*

Milano, S., Taddeo, M., & Floridi, L. (2020). Recommender systems and their ethical challenges. *AI & Society*, 35(4), 957–967. Advance online publication. DOI: 10.1007/s00146-020-00950-y

Mittelstadt, B. D., Allo, P., Taddeo, M., Wachter, S., & Floridi, L. (2016). The ethics of algorithms: Mapping the debate. *Big Data & Society*, 3(2), 2053951716679679. Advance online publication. DOI: 10.1177/2053951716679679

Morley, J., Floridi, L., Kinsey, L., & Elhalal, A. (2019). From what to how: An initial review of publicly available AI ethics tools, methods and research to translate principles into practices. *Science and Engineering Ethics.* Advance online publication. DOI: 10.1007/s11948-019-00165-5 PMID: 31828533

Morley, J., Machado, C., Burr, C., Cowls, J., Taddeo, M., & Floridi, L. (2019) The debate on the ethics of AI in healthcare: a reconstruction and critical review. *SSRN Electron J.* DOI: 10.2139/ssrn.3486518

Mozur, P. (2019, April 14). One Month, 500,000 Face Scans: How China Is Using A.I. to Profile a Minority. Retrieved April 1, 2020, from https://www.nytimes.com/2019/04/14/technology/china surveillance-artificial-intelligence-racial-profiling.html

Na, Z., Zhang, C.-T., Lv, H.-Y., Hao, C.-X., Li, T.-J., Zhu, J.-J., & Zhu, H.. (2019). Concordance study between IBM Watson for oncology and clinical practice for patients with cancer in China. *The Oncologist*, 24(6), 812–819. DOI: 10.1634/theoncologist.2018-0255 PMID: 30181315

National Research Council, Commission on Physical Sciences, Mathematics, Applications, Naval Studies Board, Panel on Computer Science, & Artificial Intelligence. (1997). Computer Science and Artificial Intelligence. National Academies Press. DOI: 10.17226/5812

National Science and Technology Council and the Networking and Information Technology Research and Development Subcommittee. (October 2016). The National Artificial Intelligence Research and Development Strategic Plan, Washington, DC: Office of Science and Technology Policy, https://www.nitrd.gov/PUBS/national_ai_rd_ strategic_plan.pdf

NIJ, (2011). Chicago Police Predictive Policing Demonstration and Evaluation Project" at the Chicago Police Department and Illinois Institute of Technology, NIJ award number 2011-IJ-CX-K014.

NIJ, (2013). Exploring Elder Financial Exploitation Victimization" at the University of Texas Health Science Center at Houston, NIJ award number 2013-IJ-CX-0050.

NIJ. (2015). "Applying Data Science to Justice Systems: The North Carolina Statewide Warrant Repository (NCAWARE)" at RTI International, NIJ award number 2015-IJ-CX-K016.

NIJ. (2016a). Detailed Information for Award 2016-DN-BX-0183," National Institute of Justice, https://external.ojp.usdoj. gov/selector/awardDetail?awardNumber=2016 DN-BX-0183&fiscalYear=2016&applicationNum ber=2016-90227-IL-IJ&programOffice=NIJ&po=NIJ.

NIJ. (2016b). Development of Computational Methods for the Audio Analysis of Gunshots" at Cadre Research Labs, LLC, NIJ award number 2016-DN-BX-0183.

NIJ. (2016c). Effects of Human Factors on the Accuracy of Fingerprint Analysis," National Institute of Justice, https://nij.gov/topics/forensics/evidence/ impression/Pages/human-factors.aspx

NIJ. (2016d). A Recommendation System for Statutory Interpretation in Cybercrime" at the University of Pittsburgh, NIJ award number 2016-R2-CX-0010.

NJR. 2009. Learning Models for Predictive Behavioral Intent and Activity Analysis in Wide Area Video Surveillance" at the University of Houston, NIJ award number 2009-MU-MU-K004.

NJR. 2014. A Hybrid Machine Learning Approach for DNA Mixture Interpretation" at Syracuse University, NIJ award number 2014-DN-BX-K029.

NJR., 2015. Studying the Impact of Video Analytics for Pre, Live and Post Event Analysis on Outcomes of Criminal Justice" at the University of Central Florida, NIJ award number 2015-R2-CX-K025.

Norris, D. (2019, June 19). Artificial Intelligence and Community-Police Relations. Retrieved April 1, 2020, from https://www.policechiefmagazine.org/ai-community-police-relations/

Obermeyer, Z., Powers, B., Vogeli, C., & Mullainathan, S. (2019). Dissecting racial bias in an AI algorithm used to manage the health of populations. *Science*, 366(6464), 447–453. DOI: 10.1126/science.aax2342 PMID: 31649194

Officers, P. Video and Audio Recordings: Disclosure. AB-748/Chapter 960. (September 2018). California. https://leginfo.legislature.ca.gov/faces/billTextClient.xhtml?bill_id=201720180AB748

Paraschakis, D. (2017) Towards an ethical recommendation framework. In: 2017 11th International Conference on Research Challenges in Information Science (RCIS), 211–20. Brighton, United Kingdom: IEEE. DOI: 10.1109/RCIS.2017.7956539

Perra, N., & Rocha, L. E. C. (2019). Modelling opinion dynamics in the age of AI algorithmic personalisation. *Scientific Reports*, 9(1), 7261. DOI: 10.1038/s41598-019-43830-2 PMID: 31086228

Phillips, P. J. (2017). A Cross Benchmark Assessment of a Deep Convolutional Neural Network for Face Recognition," paper presented at the 12th IEEE International Conference on Automatic Face & Gesture Recognition, 2017, 705-710. DOI: 10.1109/FG.2017.89

Prates, M. O. R., Avelar, P. H., & Lamb, L. C. (2019). Assessing gender bias in machine translation: A case study with google translate. *Neural Computing & Applications*. Advance online publication. DOI: 10.1007/s00521-019-04144-6

Queally, J. (2019, June 12). San Francisco D.A. Unveils Program Aimed At Removing Implicit Bias from Prosecutions. Retrieved April 1, 2020, from https://www.latimes.com/local/lanow/la-me-san francisco-da-prosecutions-implicit-bias-software-20190612-story.html

Ratcliffe, S. (Ed.). (2016). *Oxford essential quotations*. Oxford University Press. DOI: 10.1093/acref/9780191826719.001.0001

Redden, J., Aagaard, B., Taniguchi, T., & the Criminal Justice Testing and Evaluation Consortium. (2020). Artificial Intelligence in Law Enforcement. U.S. Department of Justice, National Institute of Justice, Office of Justice Programs. https://cjtec.org/

Rigano, C. (2019). Using Artificial Intelligence to Address Criminal Justice Needs, NIJ Journal 280, January 2019, https:// www.nij.gov/journals/280/Pages/using -artificial intelligence-to-address-criminal-justice-needs.aspx.

Roberts, D., & Casanova, M. (2012, September) Automated License Plate Recognition (ALPR) Use by Law Enforcement: Policy and Operational Guide, Summary. Retrieved April 3, 2020, from https://www. ncjrs.gov/pdffiles1/nij/grants/239605.pdf

Roberts, H., Cowls, J., Morley, J., Taddeo, M., Wang, V., & Floridi, L. (2019) The Chinese approach to artificial intelligence: an analysis of policy and regulation. *SSRN Electron J*. DOI: 10.2139/ssrn.3469784

Sah, S., Shringi, A., Ptucha, R., Burry, A. M., & Loce, R. P. (2017, July 20). Video Redaction: A Survey and Comparison of Enabling Technologies. Retrieved April 1, 2020, from https://www.spiedigitallibrary. org/journals/journal-of-electronic-imaging/volume-26/issue-05/051406/Video-redaction-a-survey-and-comparison-of-enabling-technologies/10.1117/1.JEI.26.5.051406.full?SSO=1

Simonite, T. (2019, June 18). How Facial Recognition Is Fighting Child Sex Trafficking. Retrieved April 1, 2020, from https://www.wired.com/story/how-facial -recognition-fighting-child-sex-trafficking

Statt, N. (2020). Amazon Bans Police from Using its Facial Recognition Technology for the Next Year. The Verge. Retrieved from https://www.theverge.com/2020/6/10/ 21287101/amazon-rekognition facial-recognition-police-ban-one-year-ai-racial-bias

Taddeo, M., & Floridi, L. (2018a). Regulate artificial intelligence to avert cyber arms race. *Nature*, 556(7701), 296–298. DOI: 10.1038/d41586-018-04602-6 PMID: 29662138

Taddeo, M., McCutcheon, T., & Floridi, L. (2019). Trusting artificial intelligence in cybersecurity is a double-edged sword. *Nature Machine Intelligence*, 1(12), 557–560. DOI: 10.1038/s42256-019-0109-1

The Intelligence Advanced Research Projects Activity. "Janus," Washington, DC: Office of the Director of National Intelligence, https://www.iarpa.gov/index.php/ research-programs/janus

Video Fingerprints Could Help Fight Child Porn. (2014, April 30). Retrieved April 1, 2020, from https://www.nbcnews.com/tech/security/video-fingerprints-could-help-fight-child-porn-n93521

Yu, M., & Du, G. (2019) Why are Chinese courts turning to AI? The Diplomat. 19 January 2019. https://thediplomat.com/2019/01/why-are-chinese-courts-turning-to-ai/. Accessed 24 Aug 2020

Zhang, Y., & Bruce, L. M. (2004). *Mississippi Transportation Research Center: Automated Accident Detection at Intersections (Project Number: FHWA/MS-DOT-RD-04-150)*. Mississippi Department of Transportation and U.S. Department of Transportation Federal Highway Administration, March.

Chapter 8
AI and Community Partnerships for Enhanced Public Safety

ABSTRACT

Chapter 8 shows that the integration of artificial intelligence (AI) in law enforcement is advancing rapidly, driven by technologies like 5G, the Internet of Things, autonomous vehicles, and robotics. These developments promise significant enhancements in police operations but also necessitate careful ethical examination. AI applications—ranging from facial recognition to predictive policing—are transforming traditional methods, offering tools that can streamline data analysis, automate processes, and support critical decision-making. However, the potential of AI to alter the social landscape of law enforcement is accompanied by ethical concerns, particularly around privacy, transparency, accountability, and bias.

INTRODUCTION

For effective AI implementation, law enforcement leaders must evaluate not only the technical feasibility of these technologies but also their ethical and operational impacts. Emphasizing data reliability, technical and ethical soundness, and alignment with existing workflows is crucial. This triadic approach can increase the likelihood of responsible AI adoption. Transparent and ongoing dialogue with communities is equally essential, as public perceptions of fairness and safety shape AI's acceptability. Legal and social frameworks are still evolving, as demonstrated

DOI: 10.4018/979-8-3693-7979-0.ch008

by cases like California's ban on facial recognition technology in law enforcement due to ethical apprehensions.

AI systems inherently reflect the values and choices of their designers and may perpetuate societal biases, often unintentionally. Issues arise when training data—derived from biased or incomplete datasets—leads to discriminatory outcomes, as with predictive policing models that can disproportionately target specific demographics. The Biden administration's recent Executive Order (E.O. 14110) underscores the U.S. government's commitment to addressing AI-related civil rights concerns. The order mandates guidelines for AI use in federal law enforcement, emphasizing civil rights protection, accountability, and the prevention of AI-driven discrimination.

The reliance on AI for data-driven decision-making raises further questions about human oversight and accountability. AI algorithms are increasingly tasked with making complex judgments based on large datasets, often bypassing human intervention. While machine learning can enhance objectivity, it may also obscure the ethical implications of automated decisions. Human accountability becomes challenging, especially when AI operates as a "black box," producing outputs that are difficult to interpret or justify. Critics argue that law enforcement must preserve a balance, using AI as a complement rather than a substitute for human judgment.

One of the most pressing concerns is AI's potential to amplify existing biases within the criminal justice system. AI algorithms can unintentionally replicate social biases embedded in training data, reinforcing inequality. For example, risk assessment tools such as COMPAS have faced scrutiny for using flawed metrics that result in biased predictions for marginalized communities. This phenomenon, termed "bias by proxy," illustrates the difficulty of achieving fairness in AI systems even when sensitive data is excluded. Bias mitigation strategies, such as using synthetic data, diverse datasets, and transparency in AI development, are necessary to create more equitable systems.

A sociotechnical framework that considers both technological and social contexts is essential to mitigate AI biases in law enforcement. Five key ethical pitfalls in AI implementation include: 1) neglecting the holistic system within which AI operates, 2) misapplying AI solutions across different contexts, 3) oversimplifying social concepts like fairness, 4) failing to consider the behavioral impact of AI on existing social systems, and 5) overlooking non-technological solutions. To address these pitfalls, law enforcement agencies need cross-disciplinary collaboration, integrating insights from computer science, ethics, and social sciences.

As AI-driven decision-making becomes more embedded in law enforcement, achieving ethical accountability and public trust will require ongoing efforts. Measures such as transparent reporting, rigorous bias audits, and community engagement can help ensure that AI systems serve justice equitably. The goal should be an

AI-enabled law enforcement landscape that augments human capabilities without compromising ethical standards or social equality.

SECTION-1: AI IN COLLABORATION: BRIDGING POLICE AND COMMUNITY FOR PROACTIVE SOLUTIONS

The use of artificial intelligence in law enforcement is rapidly expanding with the advancement of technologies like Internet of Things, 5G, autonomous vehicles, and robotics. There are ongoing discussions among the United Nations and other international organizations on the potential use and impact of AI in law enforcement. And while some may think of these applications as something for the distant future, they may be closer at hand than previously thought. For example, Dubai is currently experimenting with robotic cops, technology companies are working on voice-activated digital assistants for police operations, and China is already using their vast network of surveillance cameras for detecting criminals and preventing crimes. Additionally, the National Institute of Justice is actively funding various AI research projects that focus on areas such as analyzing video and images, DNA analysis, gunshot detection, and crime prediction (Redden et al., 2020; Rigano, 2018; Westrope, 2019).

Three AI Considerations for Law Enforcement Leaders: First, prioritizing the evaluation of technical feasibility, ethical considerations, and operational achievability when proposing AI solutions can greatly enhance the likelihood of a successful implementation. Police leaders can increase the chances of success by considering three crucial components when proposing AI applications: (1) the technical aspect, including data reliability and storage systems; (2) ethical implications, considering both advantages and disadvantages and ensuring alignment among all parties involved; and (3) practical feasibility, guaranteeing seamless integration of technology with existing workflows. Further elaboration on these factors is available in the first installment of this series. Failure to consider these aspects can greatly hinder the effectiveness of AI implementations (Redden et al., 2020).

Second, the community should engage in continuous and transparent conversations regarding the implementation of AI in law enforcement. The implementation of AI in law enforcement has sparked complex and critical discussions that may result in varying responses from different communities, states, and countries. Ethical concerns must be considered when utilizing AI solutions, such as fairness, liability, transparency, security, and privacy. Certain communities may opt to prohibit the use of specific technologies in law enforcement due to ethical apprehensions, as seen in California's decision to ban FRTs for law enforcement use in 2019 (Metz, 2019).

Third, there are instances where discussions revolving around ethics are being left behind as technology continues to rapidly advance. Conversations about what is technically possible often overshadow discussions about ethical considerations. For instance, singer Taylor Swift has implemented facial recognition technology (FRT) for security and marketing purposes at her concerts without informing her fans. Numerous schools in the United States are also implementing FRT in the hopes of improving safety and security. Meanwhile, the Chinese government has taken things to another level by extensively deploying FRT and other surveillance technologies to monitor its citizens, including equipping police with mobile facial recognition units disguised as eyeglasses. It is crucial for law enforcement agencies to not only utilize cutting-edge AI-driven methods, but also actively engage in ethical discussions with the community. The first brief in this series offers insight into ethical considerations and provides key questions to aid criminal justice leaders and decision-makers in assessing potential impacts of AI solutions on the community and other stakeholders (Canon, 2019; Chin, 2018; Mozur and Krolik, 2019; Simonite and Barber, 2019).

The rise of artificial intelligence (AI) usage has been witnessed in various domains, including the field of law enforcement. This form of intelligence is often described as computerized mechanisms that function in ways that mimic human thought processes. According to U.S. legislation, AI is characterized as a machine-based system capable of predicting, recommending, or influencing real or digital environments based on specified human objectives. These intelligent systems rely on a combination of machine and human-generated inputs to: (A) detect and analyze real and virtual surroundings; (B) process this information to create models in an automated manner; and (C) utilize these models to generate options for information or action (Finklea, 2023).

AI encompasses a wide range of technologies and practical applications. While still not widely utilized in the field of law enforcement, researchers have suggested that incorporating AI into existing tools could greatly enhance the capabilities and effectiveness of law enforcement activities. This can be witnessed through various examples, such as:

- Automating the issuance of red-light violation tickets by utilizing machine vision with automated license plate readers.
- Real-time facial recognition of potential suspects using specialized AI-enabled hardware in security cameras.
- AI-powered facial recognition technology and text analysis tools can assist in identifying potential crimes like human trafficking by scanning online advertisements.

- Security cameras equipped with AI-powered software can be used to detect weapons and alert authorities before any shots are fired, in addition to detecting gunshots themselves.
- Using AI-enabled redaction capabilities to reduce potential biases in officers' reports by removing identifying characteristics like race, which could affect the charges pressed by prosecutors.
- Body-worn cameras can also employ AI-driven software to blur out faces or sensitive footage before making it accessible to the public.
- Incorporating AI into automated speech recognition software can accurately identify speakers' voices in audiovisual materials, such as witness testimonies and interrogations.
- AI-enhanced CAD systems can improve resource allocation for first responders by utilizing historical data, making predictions, and streamlining workflow.
- AI can also be used in conjunction with predictive policing models to identify high-risk individuals and areas prone to criminal activity.
- Law enforcement agencies can also utilize AI to better communicate with the public by implementing chatbots to respond to queries and disseminate emergency information (Finklea, 2023).

There has been a growing amount of discourse surrounding the utilization of AI in law enforcement, particularly regarding its potential for perpetuating biases. One viewpoint posits that the data used to train these systems may contain inherent biases, resulting in biased AI outcomes. Additionally, there are concerns that relying too heavily on AI technology may cause law enforcement to overlook contradictory evidence. To address these issues, some suggest implementing stricter oversight measures to evaluate and mitigate potential shortcomings (Finklea, 2023).

On October 30, 2023, the Biden administration introduced Executive Order (E.O.) 14110, addressing concerns surrounding the development and use of Artificial Intelligence (AI). This E.O. aims to create a comprehensive strategy for effectively managing AI, covering key areas such as safety, security, innovation, worker support, equity, individual rights, privacy, federal use, and global leadership. This move highlights the government's commitment to promoting responsible and safe application of AI technology (Finklea, 2023).

E.O. 14110 addresses concerns about potential discrimination resulting from the use of AI and instructs federal law enforcement on how to handle it. (In relation to this, E.O. 14074 from May 25, 2022, focused on establishing accountability for federal law enforcement and criminal justice practices to increase public trust and safety.) Directives outlined in E.O. 14110 include the following:

- The Attorney General (AG) is responsible for coordinating and supporting the enforcement of federal laws related to discrimination and the protection of civil rights and liberties regarding AI. The Department of Justice's Civil Rights Division will also collaborate with other federal civil rights offices to assess ways to prevent and address discrimination in automated systems, such as AI algorithmic discrimination.
- The AG, together with the Homeland Security Secretary and Office of Science and Technology Policy Director, will submit a report to the President on the use of AI in the criminal justice system. The report will cover the potential benefits of AI for law enforcement, while upholding privacy and civil rights protections. It will also provide recommendations on best practices for law enforcement, including guidelines on AI usage, to address concerns raised in E.O. 14074 regarding the use of "facial recognition technology, other biometric technologies, predictive AI algorithms, and data storage and access related to these technologies."
- The interagency working group established by E.O. 14074 will share best practices for recruiting law enforcement professionals with expertise in AI and training them on responsible AI usage. The AG and Homeland Security Secretary may review these practices and provide recommendations for state, local, tribal, and territorial law enforcement agencies.
- The AG will assess the Justice Department's ability to handle cases of law enforcement violating civil rights by AI and will work on improving training for federal law enforcement officers and prosecutors (Finklea, 2023).

Government officials responsible for regulating executive branch actions regarding the use of AI to ensure fairness and justice may not only review the dedicated aspects of E.O. 14110 pertaining to federal law enforcement but also consider other factors such as the establishment of industry guidelines for AI that could impact its usage in law enforcement. Additionally, they may contemplate the implementation of unique standards for AI utilization in the criminal justice field and potentially impose AI-specific mandates for criminal justice agencies receiving federal funding. Furthermore, policymakers could engage in ongoing deliberations surrounding the inclusion of certain AI technologies, like facial recognition, within the law enforcement arsenal (Finklea, 2023).

SECTION-2: STRENGTHENING COALITIONS WITH AI: REAL-TIME DATA FOR COMMUNITY-LED INITIATIVES

In modern information-driven societies, tasks and choices that were traditionally handled by humans are increasingly becoming the domain of AI algorithms. These AI algorithms are not only advising but often make decisions on data interpretation and resulting actions. There are numerous instances of this shift. AI algorithms used for profiling and classification shape and control how individuals and groups are perceived and managed (Floridi, 2012). Recommendation systems guide users on various activities including exercise routines, shopping choices, navigation routes, and contact suggestions (Vries, 2010: 81). Data mining AI algorithms show potential in elucidating behavioral patterns from the data influx produced by the 'Internet of Things' (Portmess and Tower, 2014).

Online services rely heavily on personalization and filtering AI algorithms to curate information access (Newell and Marabelli, 2015; Taddeo and Floridi, 2015). Machine learning AI algorithms proactively detect misleading or biased information from the moment it is created, such as with Wikipedia's Objective Revision Evaluation Service. These examples underscore the growing role of AI algorithms in shaping our understanding of and interaction with our environment and each other. AI models that are built based on fitted algorithms inherently carry values (Brey and Soraker, 2009; Wiener, 1988). It is important to distinguish between algorithms and fitted algorithms. The algorithms themselves do not inherently possess values or biases. However, when algorithms are trained on data that is value-laden, imbalanced, or biased, they can be influenced by those training data. Their operational guidelines are set by developers and configured by users, emphasizing certain values and interests over others (cf. Friedman and Nissenbaum, 1996; Johnson, 2006; Kraemer et al., 2011; Nakamura, 2013). However, adhering to these guidelines does not ensure ethical behavior. Profiling AI algorithms can inadvertently discriminate against marginalized groups (Barocas and Selbst, 2015; Birrer, 2005), as observed in online advertisement targeting based on perceived ethnicity (Sweeney, 2013).

Evaluating the ethical impact of an AI algorithm is challenging for several reasons. Assessing human influence on AI algorithm design and configuration requires investigating extended, multi-user development cycles. Even with adequate resources, problems and implicit values may only become evident when a problematic use case arises. Learning AI algorithms, often cited as the future of analytics (Tutt, 2016), add uncertainty due to their ability to modify operational parameters and decision rules on the fly (Burrell, 2016). It may be challenging to determine whether an issue is an isolated bug or indicative of a systemic problem in these complex, adaptive systems. As AI algorithms become more sophisticated and interact with one another's outputs, these challenges will intensify (Tutt, 2016). The disconnect between AI algorithm design, operation, and our ethical comprehension of these systems can lead to significant consequences for individuals, groups, and entire societal segments. We address two primary questions: what types of ethical concerns do AI algorithms raise? And how do these concerns specifically relate to AI algorithms, rather than to technologies based on AI algorithms?

To explore the ethical dimensions of AI algorithms, specific terminology needs to be clarified. The term 'AI algorithm' is interpreted differently across fields like computer science, mathematics, and general discussion. As Hill notes, any procedural method can be deemed an 'AI algorithm' in media and public conversations, such as those recommending potential partners or identifying financial trends, implying they can be either correct or incorrect (Hill, 2015). Academic critiques often lack technical specificity when defining 'AI algorithm' (Burrell, 2016; Kitchin, 2016), using it not in the mathematical sense but in terms of implementation in software or systems. To properly address 'ethics of AI algorithms,' we must differentiate formal definitions from popular uses of 'AI algorithms.' Hill's (2015) rigorous definition describes an AI algorithm as a finite, abstract, effective, compound control designed to achieve a specific purpose under certain conditions. However, our inquiry extends beyond this to encompass how AI algorithms are implemented and executed, making everyday usage relevant. In public dialogue, 'AI algorithm' refers not just to mathematical constructions but also their applications and implementations.

When an AI algorithm is adjusted for a specific task or data set, its mathematical basis remains unchanged; the operation is merely fine-tuned for issues, making it illogical to separate the ethical considerations of AI algorithms from their practical applications in technology and systems. This chapter examines ethical concerns arising from AI algorithms defined in public discourse, spanning mathematical constructs, technological implementations, and specific configurations. When discussing specific implementations or configurations, we focus on issues linked to the AI algorithm's function, rather than broader issues related to the entire system. The broad public use of 'AI algorithm,' described by Hill as any procedural method, makes it challenging to map all relevant artefacts.

Public interest currently centers on AI algorithms making decisions—ranging from interpreting data to suggesting actions—which increasingly substitute or augment human analysis due to the complexity and volume of data. We are especially interested in AI algorithms that make generally reliable, yet subjective decisions based on complex rules, often challenging human understanding and predictability. AI algorithms automating routine tasks, such as in manufacturing, are outside our scope.

Decision-making AI algorithms appear in various domains, from simple decision models (Levenson and Pettrey, 1994) to intricate profiling AI algorithms (Hildebrandt, 2008). Contemporary examples include online agents operating tasks for users (Kim et al., 2014), dispute resolution AI algorithms replacing human mediators (Raymond, 2014; Shackelford and Raymond, 2014), recommendation systems personalizing content (Barnet, 2009), clinical decision aids for healthcare professionals (Diamond et al., 1987; Mazoue, 1990), and predictive policing tools.

Data analytics demonstrate the use of AI algorithms for understanding vast data streams. Analytics supports immediate user needs and long-term strategic planning, identifying relationships within large datasets (Floridi, 2012). It has enabled new inquiries, from behavioral studies using 'scraped' data (Lomborg and Bechmann, 2014) to predict future behaviors in policing, credit scoring, and employment (Zarsky, 2016). Analytics shows how AI algorithms can challenge human decision-making, especially with high-dimensional data used for tasks like risk stratification, previously done by humans but redefined through complex, quantitative logic.

Ethical issues arise from the complexity and opacity of AI algorithms' operations. Traditionally, AI algorithms required manually programmed decision rules, but many now employ machine learning, allowing them to create patterns and models from data to make effective predictions (Van Otterlo, 2013). Machine learning imparts some autonomy to AI algorithms, as seen in classification tasks where a 'learner' develops a classifier to generalize beyond training data (Domingos, 2012). Image recognition, for example, learns to classify objects in pictures autonomously. Machine learning can be supervised, learning from labeled inputs, or unsupervised, defining models from inputs without predefined labels (Schermer, 2011; Van Otterlo, 2013). This autonomy and uncertainty in decision-making rules make it hard to predict or explain decisions, complicating the identification of ethical issues in AI algorithm design and operation.

Many advocates for the automation of human decision-making by asserting that AI algorithms are unbiased (Bozdag, 2013; Naik and Bhide, 2014). However, this assumption is flawed, as research has shown that information technologies and AI algorithm development inherently carry normative elements (Bozdag, 2013; Friedman and Nissenbaum, 1996; Kraemer et al., 2011; Macnish, 2012; Newell and Marabelli, 2015: 6; Tene and Polonetsky, 2013b). Numerous studies have highlighted how biases emerge in AI algorithms and the evidence they generate. Since AI algorithms are designed and built by humans, they intrinsically reflect the preferences and values of their creators. The process of AI algorithm development is far from neutral; it involves multiple potential choices rather than a single, objectively correct path (Johnson, 2006). Consequently, the programmers' values, whether intentional or not, become embedded in the code (Macnish, 2012: 158). Detecting underlying biases in AI algorithms and their resulting models is challenging without understanding the development history (Friedman and Nissenbaum, 1996; Hildebrandt, 2011; Morek, 2006). According to Friedman and Nissenbaum (1996), biases can originate from

(1) pre-existing social values within the society where the technology was created, (2) technical limitations, and (3) the use context.

For example, individual designers can intentionally incorporate social biases into system design, such as adjusting search engine rankings manually (Goldman, 2006). Social bias can also be unintentional, merely reflecting wider cultural or organizational norms. Machine learning AI algorithms trained on human-annotated data can unintentionally learn the biases embedded in that data (Diakopoulos, 2015). Technical biases arise from the inherent constraints, errors, or specific design decisions of the technology, which can inadvertently favor certain groups (Friedman and Nissenbaum, 1996). Examples include a bias favoring companies early in an alphabetical listing or errors in creating random number generators that skew results. Data flaws also introduce biases into AI algorithms, hiding these inaccuracies in the outputs and resulting models (Barocas and Selbst, 2015; Romei and Ruggieri, 2014).

SECTION-3: SUCCESS STORIES: HOW AI-SUPPORTED PARTNERSHIPS IMPROVE SAFETY AND TRUST

Coders are primarily engaged in ensuring that their AI algorithms fulfill their intended functions. Therefore, the mindset guiding coders is critical to comprehending how bias emerges in AI algorithms and their decision-making processes. Some experts describe the prevailing mentality in AI algorithm development as "AI algorithmic formalism," characterized by strict adherence to established rules and structures (Green and Viljoen 2020, 21). Although this perspective aids in the abstraction and definition of analytical methods, it often overlooks the intricate social realities of the world (Katell et al. 2020). Consequently, AI algorithms that aim to be 'neutral' might inadvertently reinforce existing social dynamics (Green and Viljoen 2020, 20) while creating a facade of accuracy (Karppi 2018; Selbst et al. 2019). Because of such issues, the application of AI algorithms is sometimes scrutinized (Selbst et al. 2019; Mayson 2019; Katell et al. 2020; Abebe et al. 2020). For instance, many researchers are increasingly critical of AI algorithm-based risk assessment tools in judicial contexts (Berk et al. 2018; Abebe et al. 2020). Some experts highlight the limitations of abstraction in avoiding unintended biases in AI algorithms and advocate for developing a sociotechnical framework to enhance AI algorithmic fairness (Edwards and Veale 2017; Selbst et al. 2019; Wong 2019; Katell et al. 2020; Abebe et al. 2020). In this vein, Selbst et al. (2019, 60–63) identify five principal "traps" or failures in accounting for the social contexts where AI algorithm's function, which endure due to the lack of a sociotechnical perspective.

1. Failing to model the entire system that will enforce a social criterion like fairness.

2. Misunderstanding the harmful implications when AI algorithmic solutions designed for one context are applied to another.
3. Overlooking the comprehensive meaning of social concepts such as fairness, which is complex and cannot be resolved solely through mathematical models.
4. Ignoring how technology changes the behaviors and inherent values of pre-existing social systems.
5. Neglecting the possibility that non-technological solutions might be the best approach to certain problems.

The term 'bias' typically has negative connotations but is used here to mean "a deviation from a standard" (Danks and London 2017, 4692), which can arise at any point during the AI algorithm's design, development, or deployment phases. Bias often originates from the data used to train an AI algorithm (Shah 2018); this can occur through selectively sampled data or data that mirrors current societal biases (Diakopoulos and Koliska 2017; Danks and London 2017; Binns 2018; Malhotra et al. 2018). For example, morally problematic structural inequalities that disadvantage specific ethnic groups may be invisible in the data and therefore not addressed (Nobles 2018; Benjamin 2019). Moreover, the data collected to train AI algorithms is rarely gathered "according to any specific experimental design" (Olhede and Wolfe 2018, 3) and is often used despite potential inaccuracy, bias, or poor representation of the population under study (Richardson et al. 2019).

One strategy to address this issue is to intentionally omit certain data variables from influencing AI algorithmic decisions. Anti-discrimination and data protection laws often restrict or ban the processing of statistically significant sensitive attributes, such as gender or race, to reduce the chance of unfair discrimination. Nevertheless, even if protections for specific groups are programmed into an AI algorithm, unanticipated biases can still emerge, such as when language models reflect predominantly male-oriented texts (Fuster et al. 2017; Doshi-Velez and Kim 2017). Even if bias is anticipated and protected characteristics are removed from the data, unforeseen proxies for these variables may still allow biases to reappear, creating what is known as "bias by proxy," which is challenging to identify and prevent (Fuster et al. 2017; Gillis and Spiess 2019). Simultaneously, utilizing statistically biased estimators in AI algorithmic processing might be advantageous in counteracting training data bias. Here, one problematic bias can be balanced by another or through the introduction of a compensatory bias during AI algorithmic interpretation (Danks and London 2017). More straightforward methods to lessen data bias include testing AI algorithms in various contexts and with different datasets (Shah 2018).

Publishing a model, its datasets, and metadata (including provenance) for external review can also help rectify hidden or unintended biases (Shah 2018). Additionally, synthetic data generated using reinforcement learning or generative adversarial networks (GANs) provides a way to tackle certain data bias issues (Floridi 2019a; Xu et al. 2018). Fair data creation using GANs can enhance the diversity of datasets for computer vision AI algorithms (Xu et al. 2018). For example, StyleGAN2 (Karras et al. 2019) is adept at creating high-quality images of fictional human faces, which is beneficial in producing varied datasets of human faces, a resource many facial recognition systems currently lack (Obermeyer et al. 2019; Kortylewski et al. 2019; Harwell 2020). Incorrect deployment of an AI algorithm can also lead to unwanted bias. An instance of this is transfer context bias, where a correctly functioning AI algorithm yields biased results when applied in a different setting. For example, using a healthcare AI algorithm designed for a research hospital in a rural clinic without the same resources can result in flawed resource allocation decisions (Danks and London 2017). Similarly, Grgić-Hlača et al. (2018) describe vicious cycles created by AI algorithms when incorrect sequential assessments are made. For instance, with the COMPAS risk-assessment tool, one criterion is the criminal history of a defendant's friends, which can lead to a cycle where defendants associated with criminals are predicted to reoffend, thus exacerbating criminal records within a group based on correlation alone (Grgić-Hlača et al. 2018; Richardson et al. 2019). High-profile cases of AI algorithmic bias, such as the scrutiny of the COMPAS system (Angwin et al. 2016), have heightened awareness of AI algorithmic fairness. The task of defining and achieving AI algorithmic fairness has become increasingly significant in both academia and industry, as evidenced by the surge of papers, workshops, and conferences centered around fairness, accountability, and transparency (FAT) (Hoffmann et al. 2018; Ekstrand and Levy 2018; Shin and Park 2019). The next section delves into key topics and contributions in this area.

Emergent bias arises from advancements in knowledge or alterations in the characteristics of the system's intended users and stakeholders (Friedman and Nissenbaum, 1996). For instance, Clinical Decision Support Systems (CDSS) inherently favor treatments that are embedded within their framework. Although this bias is related to the user, it can surprisingly originate from the AI algorithm's decision-making rules instead of any explicitly programmed structure (Hajian and Domingo-Ferrer, 2013; Kamiran and Calders, 2010). Human oversight can sometimes mitigate such biases in AI algorithmic decisions (Raymond, 2014). Furthermore, interpreting AI algorithmic outputs involves understanding what actions to take based on the AI algorithm's indications. For behavioral data, 'objective' correlations may reflect the interpreter's unconscious motivations, specific emotions, intentional decisions, socio-economic contexts, or geographic and demographic factors (Hildebrandt, 2011). Interpreting these correlations in any of these contexts requires additional validation, as statistical models don't inherently convey meaning. Different metrics reveal aspects of individuals and groups that may not be evident otherwise (Lupton, 2014). Therefore, if an observer's interpretation accurately mirrors the actor's perspective, devoid of the interpreter's biases, is not always valid.

REFERENCES

Abebe, R., Barocas, S., Kleinberg, J., Levy, K., Raghavan, M., & Robinson, D. G. (2020) Roles for computing in social change. https://arxiv .org/ pdf/1912.04883. pdf. Accessed 24 Aug 2020

Angwin, J., Larson, J., Mattu, S., & Lauren, K. (2016) Machine bias. https:// www .propu blica. org/artic le/machi ne-bias-risk-asses sment s-in criminal-sentencing. Accessed 24 Aug 2020

Barocas, S., & Selbst, A. D. (2015) Big data's disparate impact. SSRN Scholarly Paper, Rochester, NY: Social Science Research Network. Available at: https://papers .ssrn.com/abstract=2477899 (accessed 16 October 2015).

Benjamin, R. (2019) Race after technology: abolitionist tools for the new jim code. Polity, Medford Benjamin R (2020) 2020 Vision: reimagining the default settings of technology and society. https://iclr.cc/virtu al_2020/speak er_3. html. Accessed 24 Aug 2020

Berk, R., Heidari, H., Jabbari, S., Kearns, M., & Roth, A. (2018). Fairness in criminal justice risk assessments: The state of the art. *Sociological Methods & Research*. Advance online publication. DOI: 10.1177/0049124118782533

Binns, R. (2018) Fairness in machine learning: lessons from political philosophy. ArXiv:1712.03586. http://arxiv .org/abs/1712.03586. Accessed 24 Aug 2020

Birrer, F. A. J. (2005). Data mining to combat terrorism and the roots of privacy concerns. *Ethics and Information Technology*, 7(4), 211–220. DOI: 10.1007/s10676-006-0010-6

Bozdag, E. (2013). Bias in AI algorithmic filtering and personalization. *Ethics and Information Technology*, 15(3), 209–227. DOI: 10.1007/s10676-013-9321-6

Brey, P., & Soraker, J. H. (2009). *Philosophy of Computing and Information Technology*. Elsevier. DOI: 10.1016/B978-0-444-51667-1.50051-3

Burrell, J. (2016). How the machine 'thinks:' Understanding opacity in machine learning AI algorithms. *Big Data & Society*, 3(1), 1–12. DOI: 10.1177/2053951715622512

Canon, G. (2019, February 15). How Taylor Swift Showed Us the Scary Future Of Facial Recognition. Retrieved April 1, 2020, from https://www.theguardian.com/technology/2019/feb/15/how-taylor swift-showed-us-the-scary-future-of-facial-recognition

Chin, J. (2018, February 7). Chinese Police Add Facial-Recognition Glasses to Surveillance Arsenal. Retrieved April 1, 2020, from https://www.wsj.com/articles/chinese-police-go-robocop-with-facial recognition-glasses-1518004353

Danks, D., & London, A. J. (2017) AI algorithmic bias in autonomous systems. In: Proceedings of the Twenty-Sixth International Joint Confer ence on Artificial Intelligence, 4691–97. Melbourne, Australia: International Joint Conferences on Artificial Intelligence Organi zation. DOI: 10.24963/ijcai.2017/654

Diakopoulos, N. (2015). AI algorithmic accountability: Journalistic investigation of computational power structures. *Digital Journalism (Abingdon, England)*, 3(3), 398–415. DOI: 10.1080/21670811.2014.976411

Diakopoulos, N., & Koliska, M. (2017). AI algorithmic transparency in the news media. *Digital Journalism (Abingdon, England)*, 5(7), 809–828. DOI: 10.1080/21670811.2016.1208053

Diamond, G. A., Pollock, B. H., & Work, J. W. (1987). Clinician decisions and computers. *Journal of the American College of Cardiology*, 9(6), 1385–1396. DOI: 10.1016/S0735-1097(87)80482-5 PMID: 3584725

Domingos, P. (2012). A few useful things to know about machine learning. *Communications of the ACM*, 55(10), 78–87. DOI: 10.1145/2347736.2347755

Doshi-Velez, F., & Kim, B. (2017) Towards a rigorous science of inter pretable machine learning. ArXiv:1702.08608. http://arxiv.org/ abs/1702.08608. Accessed 24 Aug 2020

Edwards, L., & Veale, M. (2017) Slave to the AI algorithm? Why a right to explanationn is probably not the remedy you are looking for. *SSRN Electron J.* DOI: 10.2139/ssrn.2972855

Finklea, K. (2023). Law Enforcement Use of Artificial Intelligence and Directives in the 2023 Executive Order, Pecialist in Domestic Security, Congressional Research Service. https://crsreports.congress.gov IN12289

Floridi, L. (2012). Big data and their epistemological challenge. *Philosophy & Technology*, 25(4), 435–437. DOI: 10.1007/s13347-012-0093-4

Floridi, L. (2019a). What the near future of artificial intelligence could be. *Philosophy & Technology*, 32(1), 1–15. DOI: 10.1007/s13347-019-00345-y PMID: 33717860

Friedman, B., & Nissenbaum, H. (1996). Bias in computer systems. [TOIS]. *ACM Transactions on Information Systems*, 14(3), 330–347. DOI: 10.1145/230538.230561

Fuster, A., Goldsmith-Pinkham, P., Ramadorai, T., & Walther, A. (2017) Predictably unequal? The effects of machine learning on credit markets. *SSRN Electron J.* DOI: 10.2139/ssrn.3072038

Gillis, T. B., & Spiess, J. (2019). Big data and discrimination. Univ Chicago Law Rev 459 Grant MJ, Booth A (2009) Types and associated methodologies: A typology of reviews. *Health Information and Libraries Journal*, 26(2), 91–108. DOI: 10.1111/j.1471-1842.2009.00848.x

Green, B., & Viljoen, S. (2020) AI algorithmic realism: expanding the bounda ries of AI algorithmic thought. In: Proceedings of the 2020 Confer ence on Fairness, Accountability, and Transparency, 19–31. Bar celona Spain: ACM. DOI: 10.1145/3351095.3372840

Grgić-Hlača, N., Redmiles, E. M., Gummadi, K. P., & Weller, A. (2018) Human perceptions of fairness in AI algorithmic decision making: a case study of criminal risk prediction. ArXiv:1802.09548. http://arxiv .org/abs/1802.09548. Accessed 24 Aug 2020

Harwell, D. (2020) Dating apps need women. advertisers need diversity. AI companies offer a solution: fake people. Washington Post

Hildebrandt, M. (2008). Defining profiling: A new type of knowledge? In M. Hildebrandt & S. Gutwirth (Eds.), Profiling the European Citizen the Netherlands (pp. 17–45). Springer., Available at https://link.springer.com/chapter/10.1007/978-1-4020-6914-7_2, Retrieved May 14, 2015, from. DOI: 10.1007/978-1-4020-6914-7_2

Hildebrandt, M. (2011). Who needs stories if you can get the data? ISPs in the era of big number crunching. *Philosophy & Technology*, 24(4), 371–390. DOI: 10.1007/s13347-011-0041-8

Hill, R. K. (2015). What an AI algorithm is. *Philosophy & Technology*, 29(1), 35–59. DOI: 10.1007/s13347-014-0184-5

Johnson, J. A. (2006) Technology and pragmatism: From value neutrality to value criticality. SSRN Scholarly Paper, Rochester, NY: Social Science Research Network. Available at: https://papers.ssrn.com/abstract=2154654 (accessed 24 August 2015). DOI: 10.2139/ssrn.2154654

Kamiran, F., & Calders, T. (2010) Classification with no discrimination by preferential sampling. In: Proceedings of the 19th machine learning conf. Belgium and the Netherlands, Leuven, Belgium. Available at: http://wwwis.win.tue.nl/tcalders/pubs/benelearn2010 (accessed 24 August 2015).

Karppi, T. (2018). The computer said so: On the ethics, effectiveness, and cultural techniques of predictive policing. *Social Media + Society*, 4(2), 205630511876829. DOI: 10.1177/2056305118768296

Karras, T., Laine, S., & Aila, T. (2019) A style-based generator architecture for generative adversarial networks. ArXiv:1812.04948. http:// arxiv.org/abs/1812.04948. Accessed 24 Aug 2020 DOI: 10.1109/CVPR.2019.00453

Katell, M., Young, M., Dailey, D., Herman, B., Guetler, V., Tam, A., Binz, C., Raz, D., & Krafft, P. M. (2020) Toward Situated interventions for AI algorithmic equity: lessons from the field. In: *Proceedings of the 2020 Conference on Fairness, Accountability, and Transparency*, 45–55. Barcelona Spain: ACM. DOI: 10.1145/3351095.3372874

Kim, H., Giacomin, J., & Macredie, R. (2014). A qualitative study of stakeholders' perspectives on the social network service environment. *International Journal of Human-Computer Interaction*, 30(12), 965–976. DOI: 10.1080/10447318.2014.925383

Kitchin, R. (2016). Thinking critically about and researching AI algorithms. *Information Communication and Society*, 20(1), 14–29. DOI: 10.1080/1369118X.2016.1154087

Kortylewski, A., Egger, B., Schneider, A., Gerig, T., & Morel-Forster, F. Vet ter T (2019) Analyzing and Reducing the damage of dataset bias to face recognition with synthetic data. http://openaccess. thecv f.com/conte nt_CVPRW _2019/html/BEFA/ Korty lewsk i_Analy zing_and_Reduc ing_the_Damag e_of_Datas et_Bias_to_Face_ CVPRW_2019_paper.html. Accessed 24 Aug 2020

Kraemer, F., van Overveld, K., & Peterson, M. (2011). Is there an ethics of AI algorithms? *Ethics and Information Technology*, 13(3), 251–260. DOI: 10.1007/ s10676-010-9233-7

Lomborg, S., & Bechmann, A. (2014). Using APIs for data collection on social media. *The Information Society*, 30(4), 256–265. DOI: 10.1080/01972243.2014.915276

Macnish, K. (2012). Unblinking eyes: The ethics of automating surveillance. *Ethics and Information Technology*, 14(2), 151–167. DOI: 10.1007/s10676-012-9291-0

Malhotra, C., Kotwal, V., & Dalal, S. (2018). *Ethical framework for machine learning. In: 2018 ITU Kaleidoscope: machine learning for a 5G Future (ITU K), 1–8.* IEEE., DOI: 10.23919/ITU-WT.2018.8597767

Mayson, S. G. (2019) 'Bias In, Bias Out'. Yale Law Journal, no. 128. https://paper s.ssrn.com/sol3/paper s.cfm?abstr act_id=32570 04. Accessed 24 Aug 2020

Mazoue, J. G. (1990). Diagnosis without doctors. *The Journal of Medicine and Philosophy*, 15(6), 559–579. DOI: 10.1093/jmp/15.6.559 PMID: 2290071

Metz, R. (2019, September 13). California Lawmakers Ban Facial-Recognition Software from Police Body Cams. Retrieved March 28, 2020, from https://www.cnn.com/2019/09/12/tech/california-body cam-facial-recognition-ban/index.html

Morek, R. (2006). Regulatory framework for online dispute resolution: A critical view. *University ofToledo Law Review. University ofToledo. College ofLaw*, 38, 163.

Mozur, P., & Krolik, A. (2019, December 17). A Surveillance Net Blankets China's Cities, Giving Police Vast Powers. Retrieved April 1, 2020, from https://www.nytimes.com/2019/12/17/technology/china surveillance.html

Nakamura, L. (2013). *Cybertypes: Race, Ethnicity, and Identity on the Internet*. Routledge. DOI: 10.4324/9780203699188

Newell, S., & Marabelli, M. (2015). Strategic opportunities (and challenges) of AI algorithmic decision-making: A call for action on the long-term societal effects of 'datification'. *The Journal of Strategic Information Systems*, 24(1), 3–14. DOI: 10.1016/j.jsis.2015.02.001

Nobles, A. (2018). *AI algorithms of oppression: how search engines rein force racism*. New York University Press. DOI: 10.18574/nyu/9781479833641.001.0001

Obermeyer Z, Powers B, Vogeli C, Mullainathan S (2019) Dissecting racial bias in an AI algorithm used to manage the health of popula tions. Science 366(6464):447–453. https://doi.org/ ce.aax2342DOI: 10.1126/scien

Olhede, S. C., & Wolfe, P. J. (2018). The growing ubiquity of AI algorithms in society: Implications, impacts and innovations. Philos Trans R Soc A Math Phys. *Engineering and Science*, 376(2128), 20170364. DOI: 10.1098/rsta.2017.0364 PMID: 30082309

Portmess, L., & Tower, S. (2014). Data barns, ambient intelligence and cloud computing: The tacit epistemology and linguistic representation of Big Data. *Ethics and Information Technology*, 17(1), 1–9. DOI: 10.1007/s10676-014-9357-2

Raymond, A. (2014) The dilemma of private justice systems: Big data sources, the cloud and predictive analytics. Northwestern Journal of International Law & Business, Forthcoming. Available at: https://papers.ssrn.com/sol3/papers.cfm?abstract_id=2469291 (accessed 22 July 2015).

Richardson, R., Schultz, J., & Crawford, K. (2019) Dirty data, bad predic tions: how civil rights violations impact police data, predictive policing systems, and justice. https://paper s.ssrn.com/sol3/paper s.cfm?abstract_id=3333423. Accessed 24 Aug 2020

Rigano, C. (2018). Using Artificial Intelligence to Address Criminal Justice Needs," October 8, 2018, nij.ojp.gov: https://nij.ojp.gov/topics/articles/using-artificial -intelligence-address-criminal-justice needs

Romei, A., & Ruggieri, S. (2014). A multidisciplinary survey on discrimination analysis. *The Knowledge Engineering Review*, 29(5), 582–638. DOI: 10.1017/S0269888913000039

Selbst, A. D., Boyd, D., Friedler, S. A., Venkatasubramanian, S., & Vertesi, J. (2019) Fairness and abstraction in sociotechnical systems. In: Proceedings of the Conference on Fairness, Accountability, and Transparency—FAT* '19, 59–68. Atlanta, GA, USA: ACM Press. DOI: 10.1145/3287560.3287598

Shackelford, S. J., & Raymond, A. H. (2014). Building the virtual courthouse: Ethical considerations for design, implementation, and regulation in the world of Odr. *Wisconsin Law Review*, (3), 615–657.

Shah, H. (2018). AI algorithmic transparency in the news media. *Philos Trans R Soc A: Math Phys Eng Sci*, 376(2128), 20170364. DOI: 10.1098/rsta.2017.0362 PMID: 30082307

Simonite, T., & Barber, G. (2019, October 17). The Delicate Ethics of Using Facial Recognition in Schools. Retrieved April 1, 2020, from https://www.wired.com/story/delicate-ethics-facial-recognition schools/

Sweeney L (2013) Discrimination in online ad delivery. Queue 11(3): 10:10–10:29.

Taddeo, M., & Floridi, L. (2015). The debate on the moral responsibilities of online service providers. *Science and Engineering Ethics*, •••, 1–29. PMID: 26613596

Tutt, A. (2016) An FDA for AI algorithms. SSRN Scholarly Paper, Rochester, NY: Social Science Research Network. Available at: https://papers.ssrn.com/abstract=2747994 (accessed 13 April 2016). DOI: 10.2139/ssrn.2747994

Van Otterlo, M. (2013) A machine learning view on profiling. In: Hildebrandt M and de Vries K (eds) Privacy, Due Process and the Computational Turn-Philosophers of Law Meet Philosophers of Technology. Abingdon: Routledge, pp. 41–64.

Westrope, A. (2019, October 25). New Radio Brings AI Voice Assistant to Law Enforcement. Retrieved April 1, 2020, from https://www.govtech.com/biz/New-Radio-Brings-AI-Voice-Assistant-to-Law Enforcement.html

Wiener, N. (1988). *The Human Use of Human Beings: Cybernetics and Society*. Da Capo Press.

Xu, D., Yuan, S., Zhang, L., & Wu, X. (2018). *FairGAN: fairness-aware gen erative adversarial networks. In: 2018 IEEE International Confer ence on Big Data (Big Data), 570–75*. IEEE., DOI: 10.1109/BigData.2018.8622525

Zarsky, T. (2016). The trouble with AI algorithmic decisions an analytic road map to examine efficiency and fairness in automated and opaque decision making. *Science, Technology & Human Values*, 41(1), 118–132. DOI: 10.1177/0162243915605575

Chapter 9
Ethical and Professional Challenges of AI Integration in Policing

In Chapter 9 we discuss that the integration of artificial intelligence (AI) in law enforcement holds transformative potential, yet requires rigorous training, comprehensive regulations, and robust ethical safeguards to ensure its responsible use. AI applications—such as video analytics, facial recognition, and predictive algorithms—are paving new paths for crime prevention and investigation by enabling real-time data processing and analysis. The adoption of robotics and drones for surveillance and public safety adds another dimension, reducing risks to both officers and the public. These technologies enhance investigative capacities and potentially foster public trust through improved accuracy and efficiency.

INTRODUCTION

However, to realize the benefits of AI without compromising ethical standards, law enforcement agencies must navigate complex considerations around privacy, community engagement, and transparency.

The deployment of AI in criminal justice necessitates frameworks that prevent bias and promote fairness. Central to this effort are AI algorithmic fairness definitions, which address issues of disparate treatment and disparate impact—concepts that reflect both direct and indirect biases. Researchers propose varied fairness metrics, including anti-classification, calibration, and statistical parity, each offering unique insights yet often conflicting with one another. For instance, while excluding protected attributes like race may reduce direct discrimination, it can inadvertently introduce bias through proxy variables like ZIP codes. Thus, law enforcement agencies must adopt nuanced fairness approaches that reflect both legal and societal

DOI: 10.4018/979-8-3693-7979-0.ch009

values, integrating third-party oversight or community-driven models to monitor and mitigate biases.

Achieving transparency and accountability in AI implementations is paramount. The opaque nature of many machine learning algorithms can lead to "black box" scenarios where the logic behind decisions remains inaccessible. This lack of transparency complicates accountability, often allowing agencies or developers to attribute errors or biases to the AI itself rather than addressing systemic flaws. Enhanced transparency can be achieved by involving communities in design processes, using participatory frameworks like Responsible Research and Innovation (RRI), and aligning AI decisions with societal values through the "Society-in-the-Loop" model, which allows for ongoing public input and accountability. Such approaches help maintain user autonomy and trust, essential in high-stakes areas like law enforcement where AI decisions can impact civil rights.

Privacy and data protection are critical concerns as AI-driven profiling and prediction systems increasingly rely on vast datasets, often with limited user control. To address privacy risks, technologies like differential privacy and Europe's General Data Protection Regulation (GDPR) offer frameworks for managing data responsibly. These tools balance the need for data-driven insights with privacy protections, allowing law enforcement to use sensitive data in ways that respect individual autonomy. This balance is particularly important in contexts where data sharing varies by situational norms, such as medical diagnostics versus job recruitment, highlighting the need for flexible privacy standards.

Accountability for AI-driven decisions extends beyond technical solutions and requires a shift toward collective moral responsibility. As AI tools become enmeshed within complex social networks, the challenge of assigning blame or rectifying errors grows. Models for shared accountability propose that all agents involved in an AI network—human or machine—be held responsible based on their contributions to outcomes. This approach emphasizes rectifying mistakes and enhancing ethical operations, moving away from punitive measures and toward fostering a culture of responsible AI use.

In summary, AI's potential in law enforcement is vast, offering advancements in efficiency, safety, and investigative precision. However, the deployment of AI technologies must be underpinned by strong regulatory frameworks, continuous public engagement, and clear accountability structures. Policymakers, law enforcement agencies, and communities must collaborate to develop AI systems that not only enhance public safety but also uphold ethical standards, protect individual rights, and maintain public trust.

SECTION-1: NAVIGATING ETHICAL DILEMMAS: AI BIAS, PRIVACY, AND THE LIMITS OF TECHNOLOGY

Each passing day brings the opportunity for innovative AI solutions in the realm of criminal justice, opening doors for future advancements to aid the legal system and ultimately enhance public safety. By utilizing advanced video analytics, including facial recognition, multiple location detection, and object and activity recognition, potential crimes can be identified and prevented through thorough movement and pattern analysis. Additionally, with the rise of modern technology such as cameras and social media, AI has the capability to uncover otherwise undetectable crimes and aid law enforcement in investigating potential criminal activity, instilling greater community trust in the justice system. Furthermore, AI has the potential to revolutionize crime laboratories and enhance complex DNA mixture analysis (Rigano, 2019).

Analyzing data using patterns could potentially be utilized to impede, diminish, and take legal action against unlawful activities and the individuals behind them. Utilizing AI algorithms may also aid in preventing innocent people from becoming involved in criminal activities and aid law enforcement officials in protecting the community in unprecedented ways (Rigano, 2019).

The use of AI technology can greatly benefit law enforcement by providing them with a better understanding of specific situations and circumstances. This, in turn, can help to ensure the safety and well-being of police officers, who will have access to more accurate information when responding to potentially hazardous situations. With the integration of robotics and drones, there is also potential for public safety surveillance to be improved. These innovative technologies can be incorporated into overall public safety systems and offer a safe and effective alternative to putting both law enforcement and the public at risk. Additionally, robotics and drones can be utilized in recovery operations and provide crucial insights, ultimately enhancing the capabilities of criminal justice professionals in ways that have yet to be explored (Rigano, 2019).

Through the implementation of advanced technology such as AI and predictive analytics, coupled with the use of computer-assisted response and real-time surveillance networks, law enforcement agencies can enhance their ability to effectively address incidents, proactively mitigate potential threats, allocate resources wisely, and conduct more thorough investigations of criminal behavior. The integration of AI into our criminal justice landscape holds tremendous potential in assisting investigators and improving overall public safety (Rigano, 2019).

The implementation of AI and advanced robotics in policing remains limited at present, yet several law enforcement agencies are currently exploring the potential of these innovations. As technology progresses, such as the advancements in AI,

5G, and autonomous vehicles, the possibilities for utilizing AI in law enforcement will undoubtedly expand (Redden et al., 2020).

This chapter presents various real-world examples, industry advancements, and technology providers to showcase the application of AI in law enforcement agencies. The intention is to spark a continuous conversation among law enforcement leaders on ways to enhance policing strategies (Redden et al., 2020).

Artificial intelligence (AI) has the potential to revolutionize the way law enforcement agencies operate. By leveraging advanced technologies, AI can streamline processes, utilize data in a more strategic manner, and enhance overall capabilities. However, the key lies in identifying suitable applications of AI that align with the specific requirements and ethical standards of each agency and their respective communities. This remains a significant challenge to overcome (Redden et al., 2020).

It is essential for authorities, neighborhoods, and the justice system to engage in continued discussions regarding the compromises between individual privacy and societal protection considering the advancements in surveillance and investigation brought about by AI (Redden et al., 2020).

SECTION-2: UPHOLDING MORALITY IN AI-DRIVEN POLICING: ENSURING TRANSPARENCY AND INTEGRITY

There is a broad consensus on the significance of ensuring AI algorithmic fairness, notably to counteract the dangers of both direct and indirect biases—termed 'disparate treatment' and 'disparate impact' under US law—stemming from AI algorithmic decisions (Barocas and Selbst 2016; Grgić-Hlača et al. 2018; Green and Chen 2019). However, researchers have not yet reached an agreement about the definition, metrics, and criteria for AI algorithmic fairness (Gajane and Pechenizkiy 2018; Saxena et al. 2019; Lee 2018; Milano et al. 2020). Wong (2019) highlights there are up to 21 varying definitions of fairness in academic writings, many of which contradict each other (Doshi-Velez and Kim 2017). It is evident that defining, measuring, and applying different standards of AI algorithmic fairness carries many subtleties. For example, fairness in AI algorithms can be interpreted at the group or individual level (Doshi-Velez and Kim, 2017).

Current discourse often references four main conceptualizations of AI algorithmic fairness (see Kleinberg et al. 2016; Corbett-Davies and Goel 2018): 1. Anti-classification, which means not explicitly using protected attributes like race and gender in decision-making processes; 2. Classification parity, which deems a model fair if performance metrics like false positive and false negative rates are equal across all protected groups; 3. Calibration, which assesses fairness based on how well an AI algorithm's predictions align across protected groups; 4. Statistical parity, which refers to ensuring equal average probability estimates for all members of protected groups. Nonetheless, these widely accepted fairness definitions have their limitations and are often incompatible (Kleinberg et al. 2016). Take anti-classification as an example, wherein eliminating characteristics like race, gender, and religion from training datasets doesn't necessarily prevent discrimination because seemingly neutral data points, such as ZIP codes, can serve as proxies for these characteristics (Edwards and Veale 2017). In some cases, it's essential to consider protected characteristics to make just decisions. For instance, disregarding gender in recidivism predictions would result in disproportionately high-risk scores for women due to their lower reoffending rates (Corbett-Davies and Goel 2018). Binns (2018) emphasizes the necessity of considering the historical and sociological context, which is often absent from data presented to AI algorithms but is crucial for determining contextually suitable fairness approaches.

Furthermore, AI algorithmic models can produce unexpected results that defy human intuition. For example, as noted by Grgić-Hlača et al. (2018), incorporating features that are perceived to promote fairness can sometimes increase AI algorithmic racism and reduce accuracy. Regarding strategies for enhancing AI algorithmic fairness, Veale and Binns (2017) and Katell et al. (2020) propose two main approaches. The first approach involves third-party intervention, where an external entity monitors data on sensitive characteristics to identify and mitigate bias. The second approach is a collaborative, community-driven method that leverages practical ML and modeling experiences (Veale and Binns 2017; Katell et al. 2020). These approaches are not mutually exclusive; they may offer different benefits depending on the context and could be beneficial when combined.

Despite the significant influence of AI algorithmic decisions on people's lives and the importance of choosing the right fairness measures, surprisingly little attention has been given to capturing public opinions on this matter (Lee et al. 2017; Saxena et al. 2019; Binns 2018). Researching public perceptions of AI algorithmic fairness definitions, Saxena et al. (2019) observed that in loan decision contexts, people prefer a "calibrated fairness definition" or merit-based selection over "treating similar people similarly" and support the principle of affirmative action. Similarly, Lee (2018) provides evidence that people view AI algorithmic decisions as less fair and trustworthy in tasks that require inherently human skills. In a related study on understandability and transparency of AI algorithms, Webb et al. (2019) found that moral considerations regarding fairness were consistent among participants, who emphasized the importance of comprehending the deployment context and the complexities of AI algorithmic consequences (Webb et al. 2019). Burke (2017) advocates for a multi-stakeholder, multi-sided approach to fairness in recommender systems, considering the interests of various system stakeholders beyond the users.

Understanding public views on AI algorithmic fairness would aid in creating AI algorithms that align with societal fairness principles (Saxena et al., 2019). Aligning AI algorithm design decisions with reasons acceptable to those most adversely affected and remaining open to adjustments based on new insights (Wong, 2019) is essential for enhancing the social impact of AI algorithms. However, fairness measures are often insufficient when applied to marginalized groups already experiencing economic, social, and political disadvantage (Benjamin 2019; Winner 1980). As Benjamin (2019) points out, we cannot simply "optimize around" existing power dynamics.

SECTION-3: AI AND PROFESSIONALISM: BALANCING TECHNOLOGY WITH HUMAN JUDGMENT AND COMPASSION

The outlook of artificial intelligence is rapidly becoming a permanent fixture in society, and advancements in technology will undoubtedly continue. However, the criminal justice sector faces numerous challenges, such as constrained budgets and a lack of trust from the community. Despite these obstacles, AI presents valuable opportunities for enhancing the criminal justice system, if ethical considerations, technical feasibility, and operational limitations are carefully considered. It is essential for decision-makers to have a thorough understanding of data requirements and utilize a design thinking approach when evaluating potential applications for AI tools. This series of briefs seeks to educate decision-makers on the current state of AI in the criminal justice landscape and the steps necessary to effectively and unbiasedly incorporate emerging AI technologies (Redden et al., 2020).

The NIJ remains dedicated to funding various AI research initiatives spanning across public safety video and image analysis, DNA analysis, gunshot detection, and crime forecasting. As the use of AI for criminal justice purposes becomes more widespread, collaboration among different countries and states could be beneficial for learning and progress. However, effective implementation of AI technologies in the field of criminal justice will require significant investment, careful evaluation, and ongoing dedication from those in positions of power. If utilized correctly, these AI tools have the potential to enhance efficiency, cut costs, and broaden the capabilities of criminal justice systems in various use cases (Rigano, 2018).

The combined effects of AI algorithms have ignited debates concerning the level of independence available to users. Discussions by scholars such as Ananny and Crawford (2018), Beer (2017), and others highlight that AI algorithm-driven services are embedded within a web of intricate social and technological issues (Shin and Park 2019). This complexity can impede user autonomy, which is limited due to: (1) the widespread and assertive nature of learning AI algorithms that influence choices (Yang et al. 2018; Taddeo and Floridi 2018b); (2) users' insufficient understanding of AI algorithms; and (3) users' lack of control over or ability to contest AI algorithmic outcomes (Rubel et al. 2019). In the context of AI ethics, Yang et al. (2018) emphasize that AI should bolster rather than diminish human dignity and self-determination, despite its predictive capabilities and subtle behavioral nudges.

Concerns about how AI algorithms might steer user decisions have gained significant attention. Ethical principles for AI, including those from the European Group on Ethics in Science and New Technologies and the UK's House of Lords Artificial Intelligence Committee, stress the need for AI algorithmic systems to support rather than undermine user autonomy (Floridi and Cowls 2019). Notably, Floridi and Cowls (2019) argue that AI algorithms should be constrained and subject to reversal. The Beijing AI Principles, a framework established by a coalition of Chinese academia and industry, also underscore the importance of respecting human autonomy (Roberts et al. 2020).

Understanding AI algorithms is a significant obstacle for users, as these systems often lack features that would help users grasp and utilize them effectively (Shin and Park 2019, 279). This challenge is crucial in discussions on balancing user decision-making with AI algorithmic assistance (Floridi et al. 2018). The issue is exacerbated by the opaque nature of AI algorithmic decision-making processes, which frequently bypass input from all relevant stakeholders and are often marked by structural inequalities (Ananny and Crawford 2018).

Responsible Research and Innovation (RRI) promotes 'participatory design' as an approach to ensure that AI algorithms reflect user values and protect their autonomy (Whitman et al. 2018; Katell et al. 2020). This involves incorporating participants' tacit knowledge and experience into the design process (Whitman et al. 2018). Rahwan's 'Society-in-the-Loop' concept (2018) allows societal stakeholders to influence AI algorithmic systems before they are deployed and to modify or reverse their decisions to maintain an "AI algorithmic social contract" that aligns with collective values.

Informational privacy is deeply connected to user autonomy (Cohen 2000; Rössler 2015), enabling essential activities such as free thought and communication (Rachels 1975; Allen 2011). However, the increasing role of AI algorithms in daily life has diminished individuals' control over their personal data and its uses. The extensive data required for AI algorithmic profiling and prediction—central to recommender systems—raises significant privacy issues. Profiles are continuously updated with new data, often inferred from groups like the individual (Paraschakis 2018), involving characteristics like location and behavioral patterns (Chakraborty et al. 2019). Consequently, safeguarding group privacy is essential for securing individual privacy.

The lack of transparency around data usage and profiling can lead to a loss of autonomy. Integrating users into the design process of recommender systems can lead to more accurate and inclusive profiling, which supports user self-determination (Milano et al. 2020). Context-specific improvements in AI algorithmic design, bolstered by stakeholder feedback, align with RRI principles and enhance user autonomy (Whitman et al. 2018). Knowledge about data ownership and usage can guide users in balancing informational privacy with processing benefits, which vary by context (Sloan and Warner 2018).

In contexts like medical diagnostics, users may be more willing to share personal data than in job recruitment scenarios. Norms for information coordination can adapt to these context-specific needs, reducing individual burdens (Sloan and Warner 2018). The EU's General Data Protection Regulation has set foundational standards for these norms. Advances in differential privacy offer new methods for protecting user data while maintaining model quality and reducing software complexity (Abadi et al. 2016; Wang et al. 2017; Xian et al. 2017). These technologies allow for secure data sharing, preventing re-identification and ensuring privacy even for sensitive data, such as genomic information (Wang et al. 2017). For example, differential privacy enabled a major dataset release by Social Science One and Facebook for research on the societal impacts of social media (King and Persily 2020).

The limited transparency and explainability of various ML AI algorithms pose significant challenges in holding them accountable and morally responsible for their actions. Reddy et al. (2019) point out that these shortcomings often blur the lines between an AI algorithm's limitations and the broader ethical, legal, and institutional frameworks in which they function. This issue is not unique to machine learning, as even traditional, linear AI algorithms face difficulties in providing adequate accountability in today's complex sociotechnical landscapes. The intricate nature of data brokerage also complicates tracing the origins of any given piece of data, often due to trade secret protections, fragmented data markets, and the intermingling of synthesized and genuine data (Crain 2018).

ML AI algorithms' inherent complexity and fluidity can lead to "agency laundering," where individuals or organizations distance themselves from morally questionable actions by attributing blame to the AI algorithm (Rubel et al. 2019). One stark instance is Facebook's automated system inadvertently endorsing anti-Semitic categories, a scenario where Facebook deflected responsibility by blaming the AI algorithm (Rubel et al. 2019). This highlights a broader issue in the processing and commercializing of massive personal data sets, which has historical precedents in technology misuse (Wiener 1950; Klee 1996; Benjamin 2019). Limited AI algorithmic explanations exacerbate these problems, leading experts to sometimes unquestioningly accept AI algorithmic suggestions (Karppi 2018).

The intertwining of human and artificial agents in distributed systems further complicates pinpointing responsibility (Floridi 2016). Shah (2018) suggests that ethical oversight can mitigate this risk, proposing bodies dedicated to monitoring AI algorithmic ethics. However, relying solely on such committees is impractical (Lipworth et al. 2017). Some experts argue that these measures are often superficial, potentially resulting in "ethics bluewashing" where the appearance of ethical standards is prioritized over substantial practices (Floridi 2019b). Furthermore, "ethics dumping" occurs when unethical practices are exported to countries with lax regulations, only to be reimported later (Floridi 2019b).

Establishing accountability for AI algorithms can be tackled through normative interventions. Ananny and Crawford (2018) emphasize the importance of public discourse facilitated by AI algorithm providers. Dignum et al. (2018) argue that accountability should be rooted in convention. Buhmann et al. (2019) draw from the seven principles by the Association for Computing Machinery, recommending that organizations should maintain responsibility for their AI algorithms through awareness, validation, and testing. Decision-making concerning AI algorithm deployment should consider contextual and desirability factors to foster a more accountable AI algorithmic culture (Vedder and Naudts 2017).

Interactive forums and stakeholder engagement could aid in achieving this accountability (Buhmann et al. 2019). Binns (2018) explores the concept of "public reason" and advocates for a public framework to evaluate AI algorithmic decisions as rigorously as human decisions. Floridi (2016) suggests a model where full moral responsibility is ascribed to all agents in a network based on their causal involvement, employing concepts from network theory, jurisprudence, and epistemic logic. This model shifts the focus from intentionality and punishment towards rectifying errors and enhancing the ethical functioning of the network.

REFERENCES

Abadi, M., Chu, A., Goodfellow, I., McMahan, H. B., Mironov, I., Talwar, K., & Zhang, L. (2016) Deep learning with differential privacy. In: Proceedings of the 2016 ACM SIGSAC Conference on Computer and Communications Security, pp 308–18. Vienna Austria: ACM. . Accessed 24 Aug 2020DOI: 10.1145/2976749.2978318

Ananny, M., & Crawford, K. (2018). Seeing without knowing: Limitations of the transparency ideal and its application to AI algorithmic accountability. *New Media & Society*, 20(3), 973–989. DOI: 10.1177/1461444816676645

Ananny, M., & Crawford, K. (2018). Seeing without knowing: Limitations of the transparency ideal and its application to AI algorithmic accountability. *New Media & Society*, 20(3), 973–989. DOI: 10.1177/1461444816676645

Barocas, S., & Selbst, A. D. (2016) Big data's disparate impact. *SSRN Electron J.* DOI: 10.2139/ssrn.2477899

Beer, D. (2017). The social power of AI algorithms. *Information Communication and Society*, 20(1), 1–13. DOI: 10.1080/1369118X.2016.1216147

Benjamin, R. (2019). *Race after technology: abolitionist tools for the new jim code*. Polity.

Binns, R. (2018) Fairness in machine learning: lessons from political philosophy. ArXiv:1712.03586. http://arxiv.org/abs/1712.03586. Accessed 24 Aug 2020

Buhmann, A., Paßmann, J., & Fieseler, C. (2019). Managing AI algorithmic accountability: Balancing reputational concerns, engagement strategies, and the potential of rational discourse. *Journal of Business Ethics*. Advance online publication. DOI: 10.1007/s10551-019-04226-4

Chakraborty, A., Patro, G. K., Ganguly, N., Gummadi, K. P., & Loiseau, P. (2019) Equality of voice: towards fair representation in crowdsourced top-K recommendations. In: Proceedings of the Conference on Fairness, Accountability, and Transparency—FAT* '19, 129–38. Atlanta, GA, USA: ACM Press. DOI: 10.1145/3287560.3287570

Cohen, J. (2000) Examined lives: informational privacy and the subject as object. Georgetown Law Faculty Publications and Other Works, January. https://scholarship.law.georgetown.edu/facpub/810. Accessed 24 Aug 2020

Corbett-Davies, S., & Goel, S. (2018) The measure and mismeasure of fairness: a critical review of fair machine learning. ArXiv:1808.00023. http://arxiv.org/abs/1808.00023. Accessed 24 Aug 2020

Crain, M. (2018). The limits of transparency: Data brokers and commodification. *New Media & Society*, 20(1), 88–104. DOI: 10.1177/1461444816657096

Doshi-Velez, F., & Kim, B. (2017) Towards a rigorous science of interpretable machine learning. ArXiv:1702.08608. http://arxiv.org/abs/1702.08608. Accessed 24 Aug 2020

Edwards, L., & Veale, M. (2017) Slave to the AI algorithm? Why a right to explanationn is probably not the remedy you are looking for. *SSRN Electron J*. DOI: 10.2139/ssrn.2972855

Floridi, L. (2016). Faultless responsibility: On the nature and allocation of moral responsibility for distributed moral actions. Philos Trans R Soc A Math Phys. *Engineering and Science*, 374(2083), 20160112. DOI: 10.1098/rsta.2016.0112 PMID: 28336791

Floridi, L., & Cowls, J. (2019). A unified framework of five principles for ai in society. *Harvard Data Science Review*. Advance online publication. DOI: 10.1162/99608f92.8cd550d1

Gajane, P., & Pechenizkiy, M. (2018) On formalizing fairness in prediction with machine learning. ArXiv:1710.03184. http://arxiv.org/abs/1710.03184. Accessed 24 Aug 2020

Green, B., & Chen, Y. (2019) Disparate interactions: an AI algorithm-in-the-loop analysis of fairness in risk assessments. In: Proceedings of the Conference on Fairness, Accountability, and Transparency—FAT*'19, 90–99. Atlanta, GA, USA: ACM Press. DOI: 10.1145/3287560.3287563

Grgić-Hlača, N., Redmiles, E. M., Gummadi, K. P., & Weller, A. (2018) Human perceptions of fairness in AI algorithmic decision making: a case study of criminal risk prediction. ArXiv:1802.09548. http://arxiv.org/abs/1802.09548. Accessed 24 Aug 2020

Katell, M., Young, M., Dailey, D., Herman, B., Guetler, V., Tam, A., Binz, C., Raz, D., & Krafft, P. M. (2020) Toward situated interventions for AI algorithmic equity: lessons from the field. In: *Proceedings of the 2020 Conference on Fairness, Accountability, and Transparency*, 45–55. Barcelona Spain: ACM. DOI: 10.1145/3351095.3372874

King, G. & Persily, N. (2020) Unprecedented Facebook URLs dataset now available for academic research through social science one. In *Social Media for Joint Experimental, Survey, and Observational Data Collection: The Case of VKontakte.*

Klee, R. (1996). *Introduction to the philosophy of science: cutting nature at its seams.* Oxford University Press.

Kleinberg, J., Mullainathan, S., & Raghavan, M. (2016) Inherent trade-offs in the fair determination of risk scores. ArXiv:1609.05807. http://arxiv.org/abs/1609.05807. Accessed 24 Aug 2020

Lee, M. K. (2018). Understanding perception of AI algorithmic decisions: Fairness, trust, and emotion in response to AI algorithmic management. *Big Data & Society*, 5(1), 205395171875668. DOI: 10.1177/2053951718756684

Lee, M. K., Kim, J. T., & Lizarondo, L. (2017) A human-centered approach to AI algorithmic services: considerations for fair and motivating smart community service management that allocates donations to non-profit organizations. In: Proceedings of the 2017 CHI Conference on Human Factors in Computing Systems—CHI '17, 3365–76. Denver, Colorado, USA: ACM Press. DOI: 10.1145/3025453.3025884

Lipworth, W., Mason, P. H., Kerridge, I., & Ioannidis, J. P. A. (2017). Ethics and epistemology in big data research. *Journal of Bioethical Inquiry*, 14(4), 489–500. DOI: 10.1007/s11673-017-9771-3 PMID: 28321561

Milano, S., Taddeo, M., & Floridi, L. (2020). Recommender systems and their ethical challenges. *AI & Society*, 35(4), 957–967. Advance online publication. DOI: 10.1007/s00146-020-00950-y

Rachels, J. (1975). Why privacy is important. *Philosophy & Public Affairs*, 4(4), 323–333.

Rahwan, I. (2018). Society-in-the-loop: Programming the AI algorithmic social contract. *Ethics and Information Technology*, 20(1), 5–14. DOI: 10.1007/s10676-017-9430-8

Redden, J., Aagaard, B., Taniguchi, T., & the Criminal Justice Testing and Evaluation Consortium. (2020). Artificial Intelligence in Law Enforcement. U.S. Department of Justice, National Institute of Justice, Office of Justice Programs. https://cjtec.org/

Reddy, E., Cakici, B., & Ballestero, A. (2019). Beyond mystery: Putting AI algorithmic accountability in context. *Big Data & Society*, 6(1), 205395171982685. DOI: 10.1177/2053951719826856

Rigano, C. (2018). Using Artificial Intelligence to Address Criminal Justice Needs," October 8, 2018, nij.ojp.gov: https://nij.ojp.gov/topics/articles/using-artificial -intelligence-address-criminal-justice needs.

Rigano, C. (2019). Using Artificial Intelligence to Address Criminal Justice Needs," NIJ Journal 280, January 2019, https:// www.nij.gov/journals/280/Pages/using -artificial intelligence-to-address-criminal-justice-needs.aspx.

Roberts, H., Cowls, J., Morley, J., Taddeo, M., Wang, V., & Floridi, L. (2020). The Chinese approach to artificial intelligence: An analysis of policy, ethics, and regulation. *AI & Society*. Advance online publication. DOI: 10.1007/s00146-020-00992-2

Rössler, B. (2015) The value of privacy. https://philpapers.org/rec/ROSTVO-9. Accessed 24 Aug 2020

Saxena, N., Huang, K., DeFilippis, E., Radanovic, G., Parkes, D., & Liu, Y. (2019) How do fairness definitions fare? Examining public attitudes towards AI algorithmic definitions of fairness. ArXiv:1811.03654. http://arxiv.org/abs/1811.03654. Accessed 24 Aug 2020

Shin, D., & Park, Y. J. (2019). Role of fairness, accountability, and transparency in AI algorithmic affordance. *Computers in Human Behavior*, 98(September), 277–284. DOI: 10.1016/j.chb.2019.04.019

Sloan, R. H., & Warner, R. (2018). When is an AI algorithm transparent? predictive analytics, privacy, and public policy. *IEEE Security and Privacy*, 16(3), 18–25. DOI: 10.1109/MSP.2018.2701166

Taddeo, M., & Floridi, L. (2018b). How AI can be a force for good. *Science*, 361(6404), 751–752. DOI: 10.1126/science.aat5991 PMID: 30139858

Veale, M., & Binns, R. (2017). Fairer machine learning in the real world: Mitigating discrimination without collecting sensitive data. *Big Data & Society*, 4(2), 205395171774353. DOI: 10.1177/2053951717743530

Vedder, A., & Naudts, L. (2017). Accountability for the use of AI algorithms in a big data environment. *International Review of Law Computers & Technology*, 31(2), 206–224. DOI: 10.1080/13600869.2017.1298547

Wang, S., Jiang, X., Singh, S., Marmor, R., Bonomi, L., Fox, D., Dow, M., & Ohno-Machado, L. (2017). Genome privacy: challenges, technical approaches to mitigate risk, and ethical considerations in the united states: genome privacy in biomedical research. *Annals of the New York Academy of Sciences*, 1387(1), 73–83. DOI: 10.1111/nyas.13259 PMID: 27681358

Webb, H., Patel, M., & Rovatsos, M.. (2019). "It would be pretty immoral to choose a random AI algorithm": Opening up AI algorithmic interpretability and transparency. *J Inform Commun Ethics Soc*, 17(2), 210–228. DOI: 10.1108/JICES-11-2018-0092

Whitman, M., Hsiang, C.-y., & Roark, K. (2018) Potential for participatory big data ethics and AI algorithm design: a scoping mapping review. In: Proceedings of the 15th Participatory Design Conference on Short Papers, Situated Actions, Workshops and Tutorial—PDC '18, 1–6. Hasselt and Genk, Belgium: ACM Press. DOI: 10.1145/3210604.3210644

Wiener, N (1950) The human use of human beings.

Winner, L. (1980). Do artifacts have politics? *Modern Techn Probl Oppor*, 109(1), 121–136.

Wong, P.-H. (2019). Democratizing AI algorithmic fairness. *Philosophy & Technology*. Advance online publication. DOI: 10.1007/s13347-019-00355-w

Yang, G.-Z., Bellingham, J., Dupont, P. E., Fischer, P., Floridi, L., Full, R., Jacobstein, R., Kumar, V., McNutt, M., Merrifield, R., Nelson, B. J., Scassellati, B., Taddeo, M., Taylor, R., Veloso, M., Wang, Z. L., & Wood, R. (2018). The grand challenges of science robotics. *Science Robotics*, 3(14), eaar7650. Advance online publication. DOI: 10.1126/scirobotics.aar7650 PMID: 33141701

Chapter 10
Conclusion:
AI and the Future of Policing and Public Trust

ABSTRACT

The authors acknowledge the necessity for police reform but emphasize the importance of gaining a deeper understanding of police culture and the challenges police officers face daily while serving and protecting. Rather than resorting to stereotypical opinions that degrade the character of police officers, there needs to be a recognition of the complexities of their work. Most police officers are dedicated public servants who take great pride in their professional roles, despite the negative and disparaging commentary they often face. Most police officers continue to do their best to ensure justice and uphold their duty to serve and protect. Most police officers are hardworking dedicated civil servants. They too are very critical of police officers who besmirch the good name of law enforcement as those who do so also disgrace the good police officers who dedicate their lives to serve and protect.

INTRODUCTION

At the same time, it is essential to understand the valid concerns of society regarding negative interactions between police officers and citizens. Criticism is easy, but offering support, listening to differing perspectives, and working together to develop solutions is more challenging. One key issue is the reluctance to hear the word "no", a response that often triggers defensiveness rather than productive dia-

DOI: 10.4018/979-8-3693-7979-0.ch010

logue. Simply saying "no" does not solve the problem. Both members of society and police department leaders must work toward mutual understanding and cooperation.

As Fisher and Ury (1981) implore the significance in not only understanding the thinking of society but respecting its perspectives. Police officers must be flexible and open to criticism to work in tandem with civic leaders to productively solve problems in the community and methods of appropriate and lawful policing. This collaboration is essential for developing a cooperative relationship. By striving to understand one another's perspectives, both groups can come together to establish sustainable solutions that cultivate trust and collaboration.

Society and police departments must reach a "YES" agreement. An agreement where each side understands and values of the other's perspective, rather than defaulting to a "NO." Citizens and police officers rely on each other for society to function safely and effectively. For this to happen, both groups must work together, as a team, to address challenges and find solutions, rather than deepening the divide between them. Restoring mutual trust and respect is essential for a safe society. Both sides must set aside their hubris and be open to listening and learning from one another.

SECTION-1: PROPOSED SOLUTIONS

When society and law enforcement can engage in meaningful dialogue and understand each other's needs, they can cultivate the respect and trust required for a functional relationship. Citizens rightly demand that police officers approach their work with empathy and humanistic perspectives. The authors of this book fully support that demand and present a set of solutions aimed at rebuilding and revitalizing the relationship between law enforcement and the community. These proposed solutions serve multiple purposes, and we recommend the following:

1. Require all law enforcement candidates to earn a bachelor's degree with a liberal arts pedagogy prior to entering the police academy. This ensures that police officers are equipped with not only legal knowledge, but also the humanistic values necessary for community interactions.
2. Demilitarize police departments. This involves reducing the use of military-style equipment and tactics, fostering community-centered policing, and emphasizing de-escalation techniques.
3. Crisis Intervention Teams (CIT): All police officers should undergo a forty-hour crisis intervention training to establish an active and well-supported CIT available 24/7, 365 days a year. This would provide officers with the necessary tools to confidently work with situations involving mental health crises to have a positive outcome, not another George Floyd incident.

4. Establish a dedicated social media team within police departments to interact with communities. This team would focus on transparent communication, providing updates, answering questions, and sharing positive police-community interactions.
5. Police academy training must stress and model a humanistic pedagogy. Training should go beyond basic law enforcement techniques, incorporating social, psychological, and philosophical lessons that focus on empathy, ethics, and community engagement.
6. Implement artificial intelligence to enhance policing practices, such as crime scene reconstruction, evidence analysis, and predictive policing. AI tools can help reduce biases, improve efficiency, and support officers in their daily work.

These solutions are intended to foster a more humane, empathetic, and effective law enforcement system that works in harmony with the communities it serves. By adopting these strategies, police departments can begin to rebuild trust, respect, and cooperation with the public to ensure a safer and more just society for all. However, to accomplish the implementation of these proposed suggestions there needs to be two significant tenets: leadership and willingness.

Police officials, politicians, and community principals need to take a leadership role that is dedicated to improving not only police departments by providing tools, resources, and training that optimizes the advancement of humanistic police/citizen encounters but ensuring the execution of its sustained compliance.

There must be a willingness, buy-in, of all participants to ensure the credibility of the proposed solutions implementation. It is one thing to implement them but another to believe in and encourage the sustainability of them. That means that all police officers, from rank and file to administrators of police departments are not only committed to the success of the reform but that politicians and community principals are also. This requires team effort as well as funding, both of which require a dedicated willingness.

Transformation requires collaborative effort, tenacity, dedication, and forgiveness to reach its intended goal. Successful rebuilding of respect and trust in police/citizen relationships is a worthwhile goal. A goal that will shape the minds of the youth, inspiring them to take pride in their communities, law enforcement, and especially in themselves.

When you ask how high is this mountain with a compulsion to know where you stand in relationship to other peaks, look down to where from you came up and see the rope that's tied to your waist tied to the next man's waist, tied to the next woman's waist, tied to the first man's waist, to first woman's waist and pull the rope!(Smith, as cited by Eleveld, 2003. p. 129).

SECTION-2: ACHIEVING SUSTAINABLE POLICING: AI, PUBLIC TRUST, AND COLLABORATIVE LEADERSHIP

The above chapters illustrate how the proposed organizational map (refer to the 'Map of the ethics of AI algorithms' section) can systematize the current academic conversation about ethical concerns related to AI algorithms, based on epistemic and ethical principles. Like the concept of 'perpetual beta' in software development, the map can be continuously updated as new ethical issues emerge or as existing categories are further subdivided. Our goal has been to outline the contemporary academic landscape regarding AI ethics and to suggest a tool for future scholarly work that helps bridge terminological and disciplinary gaps. We hope that this map will enhance the clarity with which ethical issues in AI algorithms are articulated, while also emphasizing the inherent limitations of purely methodological, technical, or social remedies to the challenges posed by AI algorithms. The multidimensional nature of ethical concerns with AI algorithms, as highlighted by the map, necessitates equally complex solutions. Although the map offers a foundational structure, it requires further elaboration as practical implementations and critical studies of AI algorithms become more common.

The themes identified in previous sections of this document highlight the current state of AI algorithmic ethics as mapped. AI algorithms significantly alter how personal identity is constructed and managed, influencing privacy and data protection measures. Typically, informational privacy is closely tied to identifiability; an individual enjoys privacy to the extent that they control their personal data. As AI algorithms minimize the importance of identifiability, a new theory of privacy is needed that aligns with this reduced emphasis. Van Wel and Royakkers (2004) advocate for a rethinking of personal data, suggesting that privacy protections should extend to 'group characteristics' when these are used instead of individual traits. Further research is needed to understand how privacy functions at the group level absent identifiability (e.g., Mittelstadt and Floridi, 2016; Taylor et al., 2017). Moreover, practical mechanisms to enforce privacy in data analytics are necessary, such as privacy-preserving data mining techniques that do not require individual, identifiable records (Agrawal and Srikant, 2000; Fule and Roddick, 2004).

Efforts to detect discrimination in data mining (Barocas, 2014; Calders and Verwer, 2010; Hajian et al., 2012) have focused mainly on illegal discrimination, but more comprehensive harm detection mechanisms are essential due to the potential for AI algorithms to indirectly or subtly disadvantage users (Sandvig et al., 2014; Tufekci, 2015). AI algorithmic discrimination may not always align with human-observable characteristics.

In terms of traceability, two primary challenges to assigning responsibility for AI algorithms are underexplored. First, although much has been written about the moral responsibility and agency of AI algorithms, there is limited focus on distribution of responsibility among human and AI algorithmic actors (cf. Simon, 2015). Existing literature discusses the moral agency of AI algorithms but omits strategies for attributing blame or responsibility within complex networks of human and machine actors. Second, significant trust in AI algorithms can lead to diminished responsibility among human users who may 'hide behind the computer' and presume automated processes are inherently correct (Zarsky, 2016: 121). Delegating decisions to AI algorithms can shift responsibility away from human decision-makers, leading to scenarios like those in bureaucratic systems where reduced personal accountability can result in otherwise unjustifiable actions (Arendt, 1971). In interdisciplinary projects involving multiple stakeholders, each party may assume the others will handle ethical responsibilities (Davis et al., 2013). Machine learning introduces an additional complexity that can dilute the blame attributable to designers due to the gap between human intention and AI algorithm-driven actions. More research is needed to examine the prevalence of these effects and to develop strategies to mitigate the inappropriate rationalization of harmful actions.

Lastly, when AI algorithms malfunction, the need for responsibility attribution becomes critical. Unethical AI algorithms can be viewed as malfunctioning software that does not perform as intended. Distinctions between design errors (types) and operational errors (tokens), as well as between failures to operate as intended (dysfunction) and unwanted side-effects (misfunction) (Floridi et al., 2014), help clarify the ethical implications of an AI algorithm's performance. These distinctions highlight the multifarious interaction between intended and actual behavior, implying different responsibilities for developers, users, and the AI algorithms. Additional research is essential for assigning responsibility for dysfunction and misfunction in large, complex development teams, and for defining resilience to malfunction as an ethical standard in AI algorithm design. Machine learning presents unique challenges, as achieving correct behavior does not guarantee the absence of errors or harmful actions (cf. Burrell, 2016). For instance, AI algorithms, especially those in robotics, should be designed to allow safe interruptions without encouraging deceitful behavior to avoid such interruptions (Orseau and Armstrong, 2016).

Transparency is a recognized requirement for traceability, but operationalizing it remains challenging, particularly for machine learning. Making an AI algorithm's code transparent does not ensure ethical conduct. The challenge data controllers face is illustrated by regulatory or methodological requirements for AI algorithms to be explainable or interpretable (Tutt, 2016). AI algorithmic auditing, conducted either internally by data processors or externally by regulators (Pasquale, 2015; Tutt, 2016; Zarsky, 2016), or by empirical researchers (Kitchin, 2016; Neyland,

2016), is one avenue toward explainability. Approaches such as ex post audit studies (Adler et al., 2016; Diakopoulos, 2015; Romei and Ruggieri, 2014; Sandvig et al., 2014), reflexive ethnographic methods (Neyland, 2016) and embedding reporting mechanisms into the AI algorithm itself (Vellido et al., 2012) are all necessary for verifying proper AI algorithm function. For analytics AI algorithms with significant human impact, auditing can help create a procedural record of decisions to identify issues or detect biases. Broadly applicable, minimally invasive auditing techniques need further development to enhance transparency and interpretability in machine learning (e.g., Kim et al., 2015; Lou et al., 2013).

Addressing these challenges involves collaboration among researchers, developers, and policymakers. Moreover, as the EU General Data Protection Regulation (GDPR) comes into effect, translating policy into practical regulatory measures becomes increasingly critical. This regulation outlines various responsibilities for data controllers and rights for data subjects concerning AI algorithmic decision-making. For example, data controllers must conduct data protection impact assessments and clearly communicate the risks of their profiling methods (Art. 35(3)(a), 13(2)(f), 14(2)(g)). Data subjects must be informed using clear language and have the right to contest automated decisions. However, the regulation's vague language implies that its effectiveness will depend on future judicial interpretations and supervisory authorities. Further, normative guidelines and practical mechanisms are necessary to implement these new rights and responsibilities effectively.

This regulation could disrupt data-intensive industries due to the requirement for 'explainability,' which involves balancing the rights of data subjects with the operational burdens placed on data controllers. Additionally, restricting specific automated methods may be necessary to comply with GDPR transparency requirements (Tutt, 2016; Zarsky, 2016). Similar restrictions exist in the US Credit Reporting Act, limiting machine learning in credit scoring (Burrell, 2016), by requiring reasons for credit denial to be provided to consumers.

REFERENCES

Adler, P., Falk, C., Friedler, S. A., ... (2016) Auditing black-box models by obscuring features. arXiv:1602.07043 [cs, stat]. Available at: http://arxiv.org/abs/1602.07043 (accessed 5 March 2016).

Agrawal, R., & Srikant, R. (2000). Privacy-preserving data mining. ACM Sigmod Record. ACM., Available at https://dl.acm.org/citation.cfm?id=335438, Retrieved August 20, 2015, from.

Arendt, H. (1971). *Eichmann in Jerusalem: A Report on the Banality of Evil.* Viking Press.

Barocas, S. (2014) Data mining and the discourse on discrimination. Available at: https://dataethics.github.io/proceedings/DataMiningandtheDiscourseOnDiscrimination.pdf (accessed 20 December 2015).

Burrell, J. (2016). How the machine 'thinks:' Understanding opacity in machine learning AI algorithms. *Big Data & Society*, 3(1), 1–12. DOI: 10.1177/2053951715622512

Calders, T., & Verwer, S. (2010). Three naive Bayes approaches for discrimination-free classification. *Data Mining and Knowledge Discovery*, 21(2), 277–292. DOI: 10.1007/s10618-010-0190-x

Davis, M., Kumiega, A., & Van Vliet, B. (2013). Ethics, finance, and automation: A preliminary survey of problems in high frequency trading. *Science and Engineering Ethics*, 19(3), 851–874. DOI: 10.1007/s11948-012-9412-5 PMID: 23138232

Diakopoulos, N. (2015). AI algorithmic accountability: Journalistic investigation of computational power structures. *Digital Journalism (Abingdon, England)*, 3(3), 398–415. DOI: 10.1080/21670811.2014.976411

Eleveld, M. (2003). *The Spoken Word Revolution: (slam, hip hop & the poetry of a new generation).* Sourcebooks, Inc.

European Commission. (2012) Regulation of the European Parliament and of the Council on the Protection of Individuals with regard to the processing of personal data and on the free movement of such data (General Data Protection Regulation). Brussels: European Commission. Available at: https://ec.europa.eu/justice/data-protection/document/review2012/com_2012_11_en.pdf (accessed 2 April 2013).

Fisher, R., & Ury, W. (1981). *Getting to Yes, Negotiating Agreement Without Giving In.* Penguin Books.

Floridi, L., Fresco, N., & Primiero, G. (2014). On malfunctioning software. *Synthese*, 192(4), 1199–1220. DOI: 10.1007/s11229-014-0610-3

Fule, P., & Roddick, J. F. (2004). Detecting privacy and ethical sensitivity in data mining results. In Proceedings of the 27th Australasian conference on computer science–Volume 26 (pp. 159–166). Australian Computer Society, Inc., Available at https://dl.acm.org/citation.cfm?id=979942, Retrieved August 24, 2015, from.

Hajian, S., Monreale, A., Pedreschi, D., ... (2012). Injecting discrimination and privacy awareness into pattern discovery. In Data mining workshops (ICDMW), 2012 IEEE 12th international conference on (pp. 360–369). IEEE., Available at https://ieeexplore.ieee.org/xpls/abs_all.jsp?arnumber=6406463, Retrieved November 3, 2015, from. DOI: 10.1109/ICDMW.2012.51

Kim, B., Patel, K., & Rostamizadeh, A.. (2015). *Scalable and interpretable data representation for high-dimensional, complex data*. AAAI. DOI: 10.1609/aaai.v29i1.9474

Lou, Y., Caruana, R., & Gehrke, J.. (2013) Accurate intelligible models with pairwise interactions. In: *Proceedings of the 19th ACM SIGKDD international conference on knowledge discovery and data mining*. Chicago, USA, ACM, pp. 623–631. DOI: 10.1145/2487575.2487579

Mittelstadt, B. D., & Floridi, L. (2016). The ethics of big data: Current and foreseeable issues in biomedical contexts. *Science and Engineering Ethics*, 22(2), 303–341. DOI: 10.1007/s11948-015-9652-2 PMID: 26002496

Orseau, L., & Armstrong, S. (2016) Safely interruptible agents. Available at: http://intelligence.org/files/Interruptibility.pdf (accessed 12 September 2016).

Pasquale, F. (2015). *The Black Box Society: The Secret AI algorithms that Control Money and Information*. Harvard University Press. DOI: 10.4159/harvard.9780674736061

Romei, A., & Ruggieri, S. (2014). A multidisciplinary survey on discrimination analysis. *The Knowledge Engineering Review*, 29(5), 582–638. DOI: 10.1017/S0269888913000039

Sandvig, C., Hamilton, K., Karahalios, K., ... (2014) Auditing AI algorithms: Research methods for detecting discrimination on internet platforms. Data and Discrimination: Converting Critical Concerns into Productive Inquiry. Available at: http://social.cs.uiuc.edu/papers/pdfs/ICA2014 Sandvig.pdf (accessed 13 February 2016).

Simon, J. (2015). Distributed epistemic responsibility in a hyper-connected era. In L. Floridi (Ed.), The Onlife Manifesto (pp. 145–159). Springer International Publishing., Available at https://link.springer.com/chapter/10.1007/978-3-319-04093-6_17, Retrieved June 17, 2016, from.

Taylor, L., Floridi, L., & van der Sloot, B. (Eds.). (2017). *Group Privacy: New Challenges of Data Technologies* (1st ed.). Springer. DOI: 10.1007/978-3-319-46608-8

Tufekci, Z. (2015). AI algorithmic harms beyond Facebook and Google: Emergent challenges of computational agency. *Journal on Telecommunications & High Technology Law*, 13, 203.

Tutt, A. (2016) An FDA for AI algorithms. SSRN Scholarly Paper. Rochester, NY: Social Science Research Network. Available at: https://papers.ssrn.com/abstract=2747994 (accessed 13 April 2016). DOI: 10.2139/ssrn.2747994

Tutt, A. (2016) An FDA for AI algorithms. SSRN Scholarly Paper. Rochester, NY: Social Science Research Network. Available at: https://papers.ssrn.com/abstract=2747994 (accessed 13 April 2016). DOI: 10.2139/ssrn.2747994

Van Wel, L., & Royakkers, L. (2004). Ethical issues in web data mining. *Ethics and Information Technology*, 6(2), 129–140. DOI: 10.1023/B:ETIN.0000047476.05912.3d

Vellido, A., Martín-Guerrero, J. D., & Lisboa, P. J. (2012) Making machine learning models interpretable. In: ESANN 2012 proceedings, Bruges, Belgium, pp. 163–172.

Zarsky, T. (2016). The trouble with AI algorithmic decisions: An analytic road map to examine efficiency and fairness in automated and opaque decision making. *Science, Technology & Human Values*, 41(1), 118–132. DOI: 10.1177/0162243915605575

Compilation of References

Abadi, M., Chu, A., Goodfellow, I., McMahan, H. B., Mironov, I., Talwar, K., & Zhang, L. (2016) Deep learning with differential privacy. In: Proceedings of the 2016 ACM SIGSAC Conference on Computer and Communications Security, pp 308–18. Vienna Austria: ACM. . Accessed 24 Aug 2020DOI: 10.1145/2976749.2978318

Abebe, R., Barocas, S., Kleinberg, J., Levy, K., Raghavan, M., & Robinson, D. G. (2020) Roles for computing in social change. https://arxiv .org/ pdf/1912.04883. pdf. Accessed 24 Aug 2020

Adams, M., Bell, L. A., Goodman, D. J., & Joshi, K. Y. (2016). *Teaching for diversity and social justice* (3rd ed.). Routledge. DOI: 10.4324/9781315775852

Adler, P., Falk, C., Friedler, S. A., ... (2016) Auditing black-box models by obscuring features. arXiv:1602.07043 [cs, stat]. Available at: http://arxiv.org/abs/1602 .07043 (accessed 5 March 2016).

Adorian, M., & Ricciardelli, R. (2021). Synoptic prudentialism: The police, social media, and bureaucratic resistance. *Canadian Journal of Sociology*, 45(1), 59–84. DOI: 10.29173/cjs29727

Aggarwal, N. (2020) The norms of AI algorithmic credit scoring. *SSRN Electron J*. DOI: 10.2139/ssrn.3569083

Agrawal, R., & Srikant, R. (2000). Privacy-preserving data mining. ACM Sigmod Record. ACM., Available at https://dl.acm.org/citation.cfm?id=335438, Retrieved August 20, 2015, from.

Agrawal, A., Lynskey, M. T., Madden, P. A. F., Kathleen, M. K., & Heath, A. C. (2006). A latent class analysis of illicit drug abuse/dependence: Results from the National Epidemiological Survey on alcohol and related conditions. *Department of Psychology Washington University School of Medicine.*, 102, 94–104. PMID: 17207127

Anany, M., & Crawford, K. (2018). Seeing without knowing: Limitations of the transparency ideal and its application to AI algorithmic accountability. *New Media & Society*, 20(3), 973–989. DOI: 10.1177/1461444816676645

Angwin, J., Larson, J., Mattu, S., & Lauren, K. (2016) Machine bias. https:// www .propu blica. org/artic le/machi ne-bias-risk-asses sment s-in criminal-sentencing. Accessed 24 Aug 2020

Appiah, K. A. (2015). What is the point of college? The New York Times Magazine, The Education Issue. Retrieved from http://nyti.ms/1Q1GgQh 1-6.

Arendt, H. (1971). *Eichmann in Jerusalem: A Report on the Banality of Evil.* Viking Press.

Aristotle, . (1962). *Nicomachean ethics.* Prentice Hall.

Arndt, R.Z.(2017). "Artificial Intelligence Takes on Medical Imaging," Transportation Hub (July 8, 2017).

Baker, A. M., (2020). Cardiopulmonary arrest complicating law enforcement subdual, restraint, and neck compression. Hennepin County Medical Examiner's Office Autopsy Report. ME NO: 20-3700, 1-13 PMID: 17207127

Bark in the News: Bark Newsroom: Bark Parental Control App. (n.d.). Retrieved April 1, 2020, from https://www.bark.us/blog/newsroom/

Baro, A. L., & Burlingame, D. (1999). Law enforcement and higher education; is there an impasse? Journal of Criminal Justice Education. *Academy of Criminal Justice Sciences*, 10(1), 57–69.

Barocas, S. (2014) Data mining and the discourse on discrimination. Available at: https://dataethics.github.io/proceedings/DataMiningandtheDiscourseOnDiscrimination.pdf (accessed 20 December 2015).

Barocas, S., & Selbst, A. D. (2015) Big data's disparate impact. SSRN Scholarly Paper, Rochester, NY: Social Science Research Network. Available at: https://papers.ssrn.com/abstract=2477899 (accessed 16 October 2015).

Barocas, S., & Selbst, A. D. (2016) Big data's disparate impact. *SSRN Electron J.* DOI: 10.2139/ssrn.2477899

Baron, E. (2019, March 11). Predictive Policing Using AI Tested by Bay Area Cops. Retrieved April 1, 2020, from https://www.govtech.com/public-safety/Predictive-Policing-Using-AI-Tested-by-Bay-Area Cops.html

Baron-Cohen, S. (2011). *The Science of Evil.* Basic Books.

Baron-Cohen, S. (2011). *The science of evil: On empathy and the origins of sin.* Basic Books.

Barry, B. (2005). *Why Social Justice Matters.* Polity Press.

Battistella, G., Fornari, E., Annoni, J. M., Chtioui, H., Dao, K., Fabritius, M., Favrat, B., Mall, J. F., Maeder, P., & Giroud, C. (2014). Long-Term effects of cannabis on brain structure. *Neuropsychopharmacology : Official Publication of the American College ofNeuropsychopharmacology*, 39(9), 2041–2048. DOI: 10.1038/npp.2014.67 PMID: 24633558

Beer, D. (2017). The social power of AI algorithms. *Information Communication and Society*, 20(1), 1–13. DOI: 10.1080/1369118X.2016.1216147

Benjamin, R. (2019) Race after technology: abolitionist tools for the new jim code. Polity, Medford Benjamin R (2020) 2020 Vision: reimagining the default settings of technology and society. https://iclr.cc/virtu al_2020/speak er_3. html. Accessed 24 Aug 2020

Benjamin, R. (2019). *Race after technology: abolitionist tools for the new jim code.* Polity.

Benzkofer, S. (2018). Legendary lawmen, No. 8: O. W. Wilson. *Chicago Tribune.* Retrieved from: www.chicagotribune.com

Berk, R., Heidari, H., Jabbari, S., Kearns, M., & Roth, A. (2018). Fairness in criminal justice risk assessments: The state of the art. *Sociological Methods & Research.* Advance online publication. DOI: 10.1177/0049124118782533

Beshears, M. L. (2017). Effectiveness of police social media use. *American Journal of Criminal Justice*, 42(3), 489–501. DOI: 10.1007/s12103-016-9380-4

Bilyk, J. (2022). SAFE-T Act boosts uncertainty around trespassing enforcement, could raise lawsuit risk for cops, property owners. Retrieved from: https://cookcountyrecord.com

Binns, R. (2018) Fairness in machine learning: lessons from political philosophy. ArXiv:1712.03586. http://arxiv .org/abs/1712.03586. Accessed 24 Aug 2020

Binns, R. (2018) Fairness in machine learning: lessons from political philosophy. ArXiv:1712.03586. http://arxiv.org/abs/1712.03586. Accessed 24 Aug 2020

Birrer, F. A. J. (2005). Data mining to combat terrorism and the roots of privacy concerns. *Ethics and Information Technology*, 7(4), 211–220. DOI: 10.1007/s10676-006-0010-6

Bozdag, E. (2013). Bias in AI algorithmic filtering and personalization. *Ethics and Information Technology*, 15(3), 209–227. DOI: 10.1007/s10676-013-9321-6

Brey, P., & Soraker, J. H. (2009). *Philosophy of Computing and Information Technology*. Elsevier. DOI: 10.1016/B978-0-444-51667-1.50051-3

Bronfenbrenner, U. (2005). *Making human beings human, bioecological perspectives on human development.* Sage Publicaions, Inc.

Bruns, D. (2010). Reflections from the one-percent of local police departments with mandatory four-year degree requirements for the new hires: Are they diamonds in the rough? *Southwest Journal of Criminal Justice*, 7(1), 87–108.

Buhmann, A., Paßmann, J., & Fieseler, C. (2019). Managing AI algorithmic accountability: Balancing reputational concerns, engagement strategies, and the potential of rational discourse. *Journal of Business Ethics*. Advance online publication. DOI: 10.1007/s10551-019-04226-4

Bullock, K. (2018). (Re)presenting 'order' online: The construction of police presentational strategies on social media. *Policing and Society*, 28(3), 345–359. DOI: 10.1080/10439463.2016.1177529

Bullock, K. (2018). The police use of social media: Transformation or normalisation? *Social Policy and Society*, 17(2), 245–258. DOI: 10.1017/S1474746417000112

Burggren, A. C., Shirazi, A., Ginder, N., & London, E. D. (2019). Cannabis effects on brain structure, function, and cognition; considerations for medical uses of cannabis and its derivatives. *The American Journal of Drug and Alcohol Abuse*, 45(6), 563–579. DOI: 10.1080/00952990.2019.1634086 PMID: 31365275

Burrell, J. (2016). How the machine 'thinks:' Understanding opacity in machine learning AI algorithms. *Big Data & Society*, 3(1), 1–12. DOI: 10.1177/2053951715622512

Butler, A., Zakimi, N., & Greer, A. (2022). Total systems failure: Police officers' perspectives on the impacts of the justice, health, and social service systems on people who use drugs. *Harm Reduction Journal*, 19(48), 1–13. DOI: 10.1186/s12954-022-00629-1 PMID: 35590421

Calders, T., & Verwer, S. (2010). Three naive Bayes approaches for discrimination-free classification. *Data Mining and Knowledge Discovery*, 21(2), 277–292. DOI: 10.1007/s10618-010-0190-x

Canon, G. (2019, February 15). How Taylor Swift Showed Us the Scary Future Of Facial Recognition. Retrieved April 1, 2020, from https://www.theguardian.com/technology/2019/feb/15/how-taylor swift-showed-us-the-scary-future-of-facial-recognition

Carlan, P., & Byxbe, F. (2000). The promise of humanistic policing: Is higher education living up to societal expectation? *American Journal of Criminal Justice*, 24(2), 235–243. DOI: 10.1007/BF02887595

Carriere, K.R., & Encinosa, W. (2017). The risks of operational militarization: Increased conflict against militarized police. Peace Economics, Peace Science and Public Policy. 23(3,13), 1-13. PMID: 17207127

Chakraborty, A., Patro, G. K., Ganguly, N., Gummadi, K. P., & Loiseau, P. (2019) Equality of voice: towards fair representation in crowdsourced top-K recommendations. In: Proceedings of the Conference on Fairness, Accountability, and Transparency—FAT* '19, 129–38. Atlanta, GA, USA: ACM Press. DOI: 10.1145/3287560.3287570

Cheng, J., Schmidt, C., Wilson, A., Wang, Z., Hao, W., Pantanowitz, J., Morris, C., Tashjian, R., & Pantanowitz, L. (2023, December 30). Artificial intelligence for human gunshot wound classification. *Journal of Pathology Informatics*, 15, 100361. DOI: 10.1016/j.jpi.2023.100361 PMID: 38234590

Chin, J. (2018, February 7). Chinese Police Add Facial-Recognition Glasses to Surveillance Arsenal. Retrieved April 1, 2020, from https://www.wsj.com/articles/chinese-police-go-robocop-with-facial recognition-glasses-1518004353

Cohen, J. (2000) Examined lives: informational privacy and the subject as object. Georgetown Law Faculty Publications and Other Works, January. https://scholarship.law.georgetown.edu/facpub/810. Accessed 24 Aug 2020

Colbran, M. P. (2020). Policing, social media and the new media landscape: Can the police and the traditional media ever successfully bypass each other. *Policing and Society*, 30(3), 295–309. DOI: 10.1080/10439463.2018.1532426

Cooper, C. (1999). *Mediation & arbitration by patrol police officers*. University Press of America, Inc.

Cooper, C. (1999). *Mediation & Arbitration by Patrol Police Officers*. University Press of America, Inc.

Corbett-Davies, S., & Goel, S. (2018) The measure and mismeasure of fairness: a critical review of fair machine learning. ArXiv:1808.00023. http://arxiv.org/abs/1808.00023. Accessed 24 Aug 2020

Crain, M. (2018). The limits of transparency: Data brokers and commodification. *New Media & Society*, 20(1), 88–104. DOI: 10.1177/1461444816657096

Cross, A. R., & Fine, A. D. (2022). Police-related social media exposure and adolescents' interest in becoming a police officer. *Police Practice and Research*, 23(5), 553–568. DOI: 10.1080/15614263.2021.2017932

Cunliffe, A. L., & Eriksen, M. (2011). Relational leadership. *Human Relations*, 64(11), 1425–1449. DOI: 10.1177/0018726711418388

Danks, D., & London, A. J. (2017) AI algorithmic bias in autonomous systems. In: Proceedings of the Twenty-Sixth International Joint Confer ence on Artificial Intelligence, 4691–97. Melbourne, Australia: International Joint Conferences on Artificial Intelligence Organi zation. DOI: 10.24963/ijcai.2017/654

David, J. D. (2023). Police encounters for behavioral health-related reasons in rural and remote communities: A Canadian study. *Rural Sociology*, 88(1), 135–161. DOI: 10.1111/ruso.12471

Davis, M., Kumiega, A., & Van Vliet, B. (2013). Ethics, finance, and automation: A preliminary survey of problems in high frequency trading. *Science and Engineering Ethics*, 19(3), 851–874. DOI: 10.1007/s11948-012-9412-5 PMID: 23138232

Degenhardt, L., Hall, W., Warner-Smith, M., & Lynskey, M. (2024). Comparative quantification of health risks: Illicit drug use. World Health Organization. 1109-1175

DeGrade. (2016). It" at Dartmouth College, NIJ award number 2016-R2-CX-0012.

del Carmen, A., Butler, R. R., & Odo, J. C. (2006). Criminology and criminal justice through the lenses of the law enforcement community: An Attitudinal assessment. *Criminal Justice Studies*, 19(2), 209–222. DOI: 10.1080/14786010600764583

Del Pozo, B., Sightes, E., Goulka, J., Ray, B., Wood, C. A., Siddiqui, S., & Beletsky, L. A. (2012). Police discretion in encounters with people who use drugs: Operationalizing the theory of planned behavior. *Harm Reduction Journal*, 18(132), 1–12. PMID: 34915910

Dewey, J. (1927). *The public & its problems. New York, NY: Swallow PressDewey, J. (1938). Experience & education*. Free Press.

Dewey, J. (1927). *The public & its problems*. Swallow Press.

Dewey, J. (1936). *Experience & Education*. Free Press.

Dhein, S. (2020). Different effects of cannabis abuse on adolescent and adult brain. *Pharmacology*, 105(11-12), 609–617. DOI: 10.1159/000509377 PMID: 32629444

Diakopoulos, N. (2015). AI algorithmic accountability: Journalistic investigation of computational power structures. *Digital Journalism (Abingdon, England)*, 3(3), 398–415. DOI: 10.1080/21670811.2014.976411

Diakopoulos, N., & Koliska, M. (2017). AI algorithmic transparency in the news media. *Digital Journalism (Abingdon, England)*, 5(7), 809–828. DOI: 10.1080/21670811.2016.1208053

Diamond, G. A., Pollock, B. H., & Work, J. W. (1987). Clinician decisions and computers. *Journal of the American College of Cardiology*, 9(6), 1385–1396. DOI: 10.1016/S0735-1097(87)80482-5 PMID: 3584725

Domingos, P. (2012). A few useful things to know about machine learning. *Communications of the ACM*, 55(10), 78–87. DOI: 10.1145/2347736.2347755

Dorgan, M. (June 2024). Who suffers from defunding the police? This blue city has over 1,000 unsolved murders. Fox News. 1-5. Retrieved from https://nypost.com

Doshi-Velez, F., & Kim, B. (2017) Towards a rigorous science of inter pretable machine learning. ArXiv:1702.08608. http://arxiv.org/ abs/1702.08608. Accessed 24 Aug 2020

Doshi-Velez, F., & Kim, B. (2017) Towards a rigorous science of interpretable machine learning. ArXiv:1702.08608. http://arxiv.org/abs/1702.08608. Accessed 24 Aug 2020

Dragon Law Enforcement—Speed Incident Reporting by Voice. (n.d.). Retrieved April 1, 2020, from https://www.nuance.com/dragon/industry/dragon-law-enforcement .html

Eberhardt, J. L., Purdie, V. J., Goff, P. A., & Davies, P. G. (2004). Seeing black: Race, crime, and visual processing. *Journal of Personality and Social Psychology*, 87(6), 876–893. DOI: 10.1037/0022-3514.87.6.876 PMID: 15598112

Eck, J. E., & Knutsson, J. (2014). Community policing defined (COPS), Community Oriented Policing Service, U.S. Department of Justice, 15, 79-114. Retrieved from www.cops.us.doj.gov

Edwards, L., & Veale, M. (2017) Slave to the AI algorithm? Why a right to explanationn is probably not the remedy you are looking for. *SSRN Electron J*. DOI: 10.2139/ssrn.2972855

Eleveld, M. (2003). *Pull the next one up. The Spoken Word Revolution (slam, hip hop & the poetry of a new generation)*. Sourcebooks, Inc.

Eleveld, M. (2003). *The Spoken Word Revolution: (slam, hip hop & the poetry of a new generation)*. Sourcebooks, Inc.

Eubanks, V. (2017). *Automating inequality: how high-tech tools profile, police, and punish the poor* (1st ed.). St. Martin's Press.

European Commission. (2012) Regulation of the European Parliament and of the Council on the Protection of Individuals with regard to the processing of personal data and on the free movement of such data (General Data Protection Regulation). Brussels: European Commission. Available at: https://ec.europa.eu/justice/data-protection/document/review2012/com_2012_11_en.pdf (accessed 2 April 2013).

Face, R. V. T. (FRVT) Part 3: Demographic Effects (December 2019). Retrieved March 27, 2020, from https://nvlpubs.nist.gov/nistpubs/ir/2019/NIST.IR.8280.pdf

Faggella, D. (2019, February 2). AI for Crime Prevention and Detection—5 Current Applications. Retrieved April 1, 2020, from https://emerj.com/ai-sector-overviews/ai-crime-prevention-5-current applications/

Fielding, N. G. (2023). Police communications and social media. *European Journal of Criminology*, 20(1), 316–334. DOI: 10.1177/1477370821998969

Finklea, K. (2023). Law Enforcement Use of Artificial Intelligence and Directives in the 2023 Executive Order, Pecialist in Domestic Security, Congressional Research Service. https://crsreports.congress.gov IN12289

Fisher, R., & Ury, W. (1981). *Getting to Yes, Negotiating Agreement Without Giving In*. Penguin Books.

Floridi, L. (2012). Big data and their epistemological challenge. *Philosophy & Technology*, 25(4), 435–437. DOI: 10.1007/s13347-012-0093-4

Floridi, L. (2016). Faultless responsibility: On the nature and allocation of moral responsibility for distributed moral actions. Philos Trans R Soc A Math Phys. *Engineering and Science*, 374(2083), 20160112. DOI: 10.1098/rsta.2016.0112 PMID: 28336791

Floridi, L. (2019a). What the near future of artificial intelligence could be. *Philosophy & Technology*, 32(1), 1–15. DOI: 10.1007/s13347-019-00345-y PMID: 33717860

Floridi, L., & Cowls, J. (2019). A unified framework of five principles for ai in society. *Harvard Data Science Review*. Advance online publication. DOI: 10.1162/99608f92.8cd550d1

Floridi, L., Fresco, N., & Primiero, G. (2014). On malfunctioning software. *Synthese*, 192(4), 1199–1220. DOI: 10.1007/s11229-014-0610-3

Floridi, L., & Taddeo, M. (2016). What is data ethics? *Philosophical Transactions. Series A, Mathematical, Physical, and Engineering Sciences*, 374(2083), 20160360. DOI: 10.1098/rsta.2016.0360 PMID: 28336805

Fox 32 Chicago. (2018). 50 years later: Ceremony held for victims of deadly 1968 explosion. Retrieved from https://www.fox32chicago.com/

Freire, P. (2012). *Pedagogy of the oppressed.* Bloomsbury Publishing Plc.

Friedman, B., & Nissenbaum, H. (1996). Bias in computer systems. [TOIS]. *ACM Transactions on Information Systems*, 14(3), 330–347. DOI: 10.1145/230538.230561

Fryer, R. G., Jr. (2017). An empirical analysis of racial differences in police use of force. Department of Economics, Harvard University. 1-43

Fule, P., & Roddick, J. F. (2004). Detecting privacy and ethical sensitivity in data mining results. In Proceedings of the 27th Australasian conference on computer science–Volume 26 (pp. 159–166). Australian Computer Society, Inc., Available at https://dl.acm.org/citation.cfm?id=979942, Retrieved August 24, 2015, from.

Fuster, A., Goldsmith-Pinkham, P., Ramadorai, T., & Walther, A. (2017) Predictably unequal? The effects of machine learning on credit markets. *SSRN Electron J.* DOI: 10.2139/ssrn.3072038

Gada, M. (2018, February 22). Using AI to automatically redact faces in videos. Retrieved April 1, 2020, from https://azure.microsoft.com/en-us/blog/using-ai-to-automatically-redact-faces-in-videos/

Gajane, P., & Pechenizkiy, M. (2018) On formalizing fairness in prediction with machine learning. ArXiv:1710.03184. http://arxiv.org/abs/1710.03184. Accessed 24 Aug 2020

Gaskins, J. (2016). Ethics in leadership: Applying Aristotle in police work. Police 1. Retrieved From: https://wwwpolice1.com/patrol-issues/article

Gaskins, J. (2016). Ethics in leadership: Applying Aristotle in police work. *Police (Springfield)*, 1, •••. https: wwwpolice1.com/patrol-issues/articles/

Georgieva, E., Benkova, K., Vlaeva, N., Karamalakova, Y., Miteva, R., Abrashev, H., & Nikolova, G. (2022). Is illicit substance use gender-specific? The basic points of mental and health disorders. *Toxics*, 10(7), 2–19. DOI: 10.3390/toxics10070344 PMID: 35878250

Gillis, T. B., & Spiess, J. (2019). Big data and discrimination. Univ Chicago Law Rev 459 Grant MJ, Booth A (2009) Types and associated methodologies: A typology of reviews. *Health Information and Libraries Journal*, 26(2), 91–108. DOI: 10.1111/j.1471-1842.2009.00848.x

Glauser, W. (2020). Why some doctors want to defund the police. *Canadian Medical Association Journal*, 192(48), 1–2. DOI: 10.1503/cmaj.1095905 PMID: 33257333

Goff, B. (2012). *Love Does. Discover a Secretly Incredible Life in an Ordinary World*. Harper Collins Christian Publishing, Inc.

Goff, B. (2018). *Everybody Always. Becoming Love in a World Full of Setbacks and Difficult People*. Nelson Books.

Greek, C. (2009). Documenting and framing police public interaction with citizens: A study in visual criminology. *Criminal Justice Matters*, 78(1), 18–20. DOI: 10.1080/09627250903385198

Green, B., & Chen, Y. (2019) Disparate interactions: an AI algorithm-in-the-loop analysis of fairness in risk assessments. In: Proceedings of the Conference on Fairness, Accountability, and Transparency—FAT*'19, 90–99. Atlanta, GA, USA: ACM Press. DOI: 10.1145/3287560.3287563

Green, B., & Viljoen, S. (2020) AI algorithmic realism: expanding the bounda ries of AI algorithmic thought. In: Proceedings of the 2020 Confer ence on Fairness, Accountability, and Transparency, 19–31. Bar celona Spain: ACM. DOI: 10.1145/3351095.3372840

Grgić-Hlača, N., Redmiles, E. M., Gummadi, K. P., & Weller, A. (2018) Human perceptions of fairness in AI algorithmic decision making: a case study of criminal risk prediction. ArXiv:1802.09548. http://arxiv .org/abs/1802.09548. Accessed 24 Aug 2020

Grgić-Hlača, N., Redmiles, E. M., Gummadi, K. P., & Weller, A. (2018) Human perceptions of fairness in AI algorithmic decision making: a case study of criminal risk prediction. ArXiv:1802.09548. http://arxiv.org/abs/1802.09548. Accessed 24 Aug 2020

Griffen, D. (Apr 2021). After action reports on the riots of 2020. Police Law Enforcement Solutions. Retrieved from https://www.policemag.com

Grube, G. M. A. (1981). *Plator. Five Dialogues, Euthyphro, Apology, Crito, Meno, Phaedo*. Hackett Publishing Company, Inc.

Grygiel, J., & Lysak, S. (2021). Police social media and broadcast news: An investigation into the impact of police use of Facebook on journalist's gatekeeping role. *Journalism Practice*, 15(7), 994–1011. DOI: 10.1080/17512786.2020.1759123

Hajian, S., Monreale, A., Pedreschi, D., ... (2012). Injecting discrimination and privacy awareness into pattern discovery. In Data mining workshops (ICDMW), 2012 IEEE 12th international conference on (pp. 360–369). IEEE., Available at https://ieeexplore.ieee.org/xpls/abs_all.jsp?arnumber=6406463, Retrieved November 3, 2015, from. DOI: 10.1109/ICDMW.2012.51

Harwell, D. (2020) Dating apps need women. advertisers need diversity. AI companies offer a solution: fake people. Washington Post

Hauer, T. (2019). Society caught in a labyrinth of AI algorithms: Disputes, promises, and limitations of the new order of things. *Society*, 56(3), 222–230. DOI: 10.1007/s12115-019-00358-5

Haugk, K. C. (1984). *Christian Caregiving, a Way of Life*. Augsburg Publishing House.

Henderson, H., & Yisrael, B. (May 2021). 7 myths about "defunding the police" debunked. Brookings Institute. Retrieve from https://www.brookings.edu

Henion, A., & Terrill, W. (Feb. 2015). Do cops need college? Retrieved from https://msutoday.msu.edu/news/2015/do-cops-need-college/

Heradstvelt, O., Skogen, J. C., Hetland, J., & Hysing, M. (2017). Alcohol and illicit drug use are important factors for school-related problems among adolescents. *Frontiers in Psychology*, 8(1023), 1–11. PMID: 28676779

Hildebrandt, M. (2008). Defining profiling: A new type of knowledge? In M. Hildebrandt & S. Gutwirth (Eds.), Profiling the European Citizen the Netherlands (pp. 17–45). Springer., Available at https://link.springer.com/chapter/10.1007/978-1-4020-6914-7_2, Retrieved May 14, 2015, from. DOI: 10.1007/978-1-4020-6914-7_2

Hildebrandt, M. (2011). Who needs stories if you can get the data? ISPs in the era of big number crunching. *Philosophy & Technology*, 24(4), 371–390. DOI: 10.1007/s13347-011-0041-8

Hill, R. K. (2015). What an AI algorithm is. *Philosophy & Technology*, 29(1), 35–59. DOI: 10.1007/s13347-014-0184-5

Horton, M., & Freire, P. (1999). *We make the road by Walking*. Temple University Press.

Hu, X., Rodgers, K., & Lovrich, R. P. (2018). We are more than crime fighters: Social media images of police departments. *Police Quarterly*, 21(4), 544–572. DOI: 10.1177/1098611118783991

Hyshka, E., Anderson, J. A., & Wild, T. C. (2017). Perceived unmet need and barriers to care amongst street-involved people who use illicit drugs. *Drug and Alcohol Review*, 36(3), 295–304. DOI: 10.1111/dar.12427 PMID: 27242102

Imel, S. (1998). Transformative learning in adulthood, Eric Digests, 200, 1-7. Retrieved from www.eric.ed.gov

Issar, Siddhant, (2020). Listening to Black Lives Matter: racial capitalism and the critique of neoliberalism. Springer Nature Limited. 1-24 PMID: 28676779

Jackson, J., Fine, A., Bradford, B., & Trinkner, R. (2023). Social identity and support for defunding the police in the aftermath of George Floyd's murder. *Group Processes & Intergroup Relations*, 26(4), 833–858. DOI: 10.1177/13684302221128230

Jagiello, R. J. (1971). College education for the patrolman - necessity or irrelevance? *The Journal of Criminal Law, Criminology, and Police Science*, 62(1), 114–121. DOI: 10.2307/1142134

Jaokar, A. (2017). Artificial Intelligence in Fraud Detection," Envision Blog, March 15, 2017.

Johnson, J. A. (2006) Technology and pragmatism: From value neutrality to value criticality. SSRN Scholarly Paper, Rochester, NY: Social Science Research Network. Available at: https://papers.ssrn.com/abstract=2154654 (accessed 24 August 2015). DOI: 10.2139/ssrn.2154654

Johnstone, G. (2011). *Restorative Justice, Ideas, Values, Debates* (2nd ed.). Routledge.

Josephson, M. S. (2008). Character: Linchpin of leadership. *Leadership Excellence.*, 16(8), 13.

Kamiran, F., & Calders, T. (2010) Classification with no discrimination by preferential sampling. In: Proceedings of the 19th machine learning conf. Belgium and the Netherlands, Leuven, Belgium. Available at: http://wwwis.win.tue.nl/tcalders/pubs/benelearn2010 (accessed 24 August 2015).

Kant, E. (1999). *Grounding for the Metaphysics Of Morals with On a Supposed Right to Lie Because of Philanthropic Concerns* (3rd ed.). Hackett Publishing Company, Inc.

Kaplan, J. (2019, July 10). Who's Using License Plate Cameras to Track Cars? Cops, Landlords, and Your Neighbors. Retrieved April 1, 2020, from https://slate.com/technology/2019/07/automatic-license plate-readers-hoa-police-openalpr.html

Karppi, T. (2018). The computer said so: On the ethics, effectiveness, and cultural techniques of predictive policing. *Social Media + Society*, 4(2), 205630511876829. DOI: 10.1177/2056305118768296

Karras, T., Laine, S., & Aila, T. (2019) A style-based generator architecture for generative adversarial networks. ArXiv:1812.04948. http:// arxiv.org/abs/1812.04948. Accessed 24 Aug 2020 DOI: 10.1109/CVPR.2019.00453

Katell, M., Young, M., Dailey, D., Herman, B., Guetler, V., Tam, A., Binz, C., Raz, D., & Krafft, P. M. (2020) Toward Situated interventions for AI algorithmic equity: lessons from the field. In: *Proceedings of the 2020 Conference on Fairness, Accountability, and Transparency*, 45–55. Barcelona Spain: ACM. DOI: 10.1145/3351095.3372874

Kim, B., Patel, K., & Rostamizadeh, A.. (2015). *Scalable and interpretable data representation for high-dimensional, complex data.* AAAI. DOI: 10.1609/aaai.v29i1.9474

Kim, H., Giacomin, J., & Macredie, R. (2014). A qualitative study of stakeholders' perspectives on the social network service environment. *International Journal of Human-Computer Interaction*, 30(12), 965–976. DOI: 10.1080/10447318.2014.925383

King, G. & Persily, N. (2020) Unprecedented Facebook URLs dataset now available for academic research through social science one. In *Social Media for Joint Experimental, Survey, and Observational Data Collection: The Case of VKontakte.*

Kisielius, J., & Roedder, D. L. (1983). The effects of imagery on attitude-behavior consistency. *Advances in Consumer Research. Association for Consumer Research (U. S.)*, 10, 72–74.

Kitchin, R. (2016). Thinking critically about and researching AI algorithms. *Information Communication and Society*, 20(1), 14–29. DOI: 10.1080/1369118X.2016.1154087

Klee, R. (1996). *Introduction to the philosophy of science: cutting nature at its seams.* Oxford University Press.

Kleinberg, J., Mullainathan, S., & Raghavan, M. (2016) Inherent trade-offs in the fair determination of risk scores. ArXiv:1609.05807. http://arxiv.org/abs/1609.05807. Accessed 24 Aug 2020

Knorr, E. (2015, April 13). How PayPal Beats the Bad Guys with Machine Learning," Ahead of the Curve. *InfoWorld.*

Kortylewski, A., Egger, B., Schneider, A., Gerig, T., & Morel-Forster, F. Vet ter T (2019) Analyzing and Reducing the damage of dataset bias to face recognition with synthetic data. http://opena ccess. thecv f.com/conte nt_CVPRW _2019/html/BEFA/ Korty lewsk i_Analy zing_and_Reduc ing_the_Damag e_of_Datas et_Bias_to_Face_ CVPRW_2019_paper.html. Accessed 24 Aug 2020

Kraemer, F., van Overveld, K., & Peterson, M. (2011). Is there an ethics of AI algorithms? *Ethics and Information Technology*, 13(3), 251–260. DOI: 10.1007/ s10676-010-9233-7

Labati, R. D., Genovese, A., Muñoz, E., Piuri, V., Scotti, F., & Sforza, G. (2016). Biometric recognition in automated border control: A survey. *ACM Computing Surveys*, 49(2), 1–39. DOI: 10.1145/2933241

LaGrange, T. C. (2003). The role of police education in handling cases of mental disorder. *Criminal Justice Review*, 28(1), 88–112. DOI: 10.1177/073401680302800106

Lambrecht, A., & Tucker, C. (2019). AI algorithmic bias? An empirical study of apparent gender-based discrimination in the display of STEM career ads. *Management Science*, 65(7), 2966–2981. DOI: 10.1287/mnsc.2018.3093

Lankester, L. A., and Alexopoulos, T. (2023). Black lives matter, but to whom? An examination of Nationally grounded determinants of Black Lives Matter support. International Review of Social Psychology. 36 (1): 16, 1-15

Larson, B. (2017) Gender as a variable in natural-language processing: ethical considerations. In: *Proceedings of the First ACL Workshop on Ethics in Natural Language Processing*, 1–11. Valencia, Spain: Association for Computational Linguistics. DOI: 10.18653/v1/W17-1601

Lawrence, D., La Vigne, N., & Thompson, P. (2019, September) Evaluation of Gunshot Detection Technology to Aid in the Reduction of Firearms Violence. Retrieved April 3, 2020, from https://nij.ojp.gov/ library/publications/evaluation-gunshot-detection-technology-aid-reduction-firearms-violence

Lee, M. K., Kim, J. T., & Lizarondo, L. (2017) A human-centered approach to AI algorithmic services: considerations for fair and motivating smart community service management that allocates donations to non-profit organizations. In: Proceedings of the 2017 CHI Conference on Human Factors in Computing Systems—CHI '17, 3365–76. Denver, Colorado, USA: ACM Press. DOI: 10.1145/3025453.3025884

Lee, M. K. (2018). Understanding perception of AI algorithmic decisions: Fairness, trust, and emotion in response to AI algorithmic management. *Big Data & Society*, 5(1), 205395171875668. DOI: 10.1177/2053951718756684

Lee, M. S., & Floridi, L. (2020) AI algorithmic fairness in mortgage lending: from absolute conditions to relational trade-offs. *SSRN Electron J.* https://doi.org/DOI: 10.2139/ssrn.3559407

Levine, D. F., Richards, J., & Whittle, M. (2012). *Whittle's Gait Analysis Whittle's Gait Analysis Elsevier Health Sciences.*

Lewis, D. (2019) Social Credit case study: city citizen scores in Xiamen and Fuzhou. Medium: Berkman Klein Center Collection. 8 October 2019. https://medium.com/berkmanklein-center/social-credit-case-study-city-citizen-scores-in-xiamen-and-fuzhou-2a65feb2bbb3. Accessed 10 Oct 2020

Linke, R. (2017) Design thinking, explained. Retrieved April 7, 2020, from https://mitsloan.mit.edu/ideas-made-to-matter/design-thinking-explained

Lipworth, W., Mason, P. H., Kerridge, I., & Ioannidis, J. P. A. (2017). Ethics and epistemology in big data research. *Journal of Bioethical Inquiry*, 14(4), 489–500. DOI: 10.1007/s11673-017-9771-3 PMID: 28321561

Locke, J. (1980). *Second Treatise of Government*. Hackett Publishing Company, Inc.

Lomborg, S., & Bechmann, A. (2014). Using APIs for data collection on social media. *The Information Society*, 30(4), 256–265. DOI: 10.1080/01972243.2014.915276

Lou, Y., Caruana, R., & Gehrke, J.. (2013) Accurate intelligible models with pairwise interactions. In: *Proceedings of the 19th ACM SIGKDD international conference on knowledge discovery and data mining*. Chicago, USA, ACM, pp. 623–631. DOI: 10.1145/2487575.2487579

Lyman, J. L. (1964). The Metropolitan Police Act of 1829: An analysis of certain events influencing the passage and character of the Metropolitan Police Act in England. *The Journal of Criminal Law, Criminology, and Police Science*, 55(18), 141–154. DOI: 10.2307/1140471

Macnish, K. (2012). Unblinking eyes: The ethics of automating surveillance. *Ethics and Information Technology*, 14(2), 151–167. DOI: 10.1007/s10676-012-9291-0

Maj, K., & Lewandowsky, S. (2020). Is bad news on TV tickers good news? The effects of voiceover and visual elements in video on viewer's assessment. *PLoS One*, 15(4), 1–18. DOI: 10.1371/journal.pone.0231313 PMID: 32294122

Major Cities Chiefs Association. (March 2016). Annual Report '15. Retrieved April 1, 2020, from https://www.majorcitieschiefs.com/pdf/news/annual_report_2015.pdf

Malhotra, C., Kotwal, V., & Dalal, S. (2018). *Ethical framework for machine learning. In: 2018 ITU Kaleidoscope: machine learning for a 5G Future (ITU K), 1–8.* IEEE., DOI: 10.23919/ITU-WT.2018.8597767

Marr, B. (2016, December 8). What Is the Difference Between Deep Learning, Machine Learning and AI? *Forbes*.

Maslow, A. H. (2013). *A theory of human motivation. Mansfield Centre*. Martino Publishing.

Maslow, A. H. (2013). *A Theory of Human Motivation. Mansfield Centre*. Martino Publishing.

Mayo Clinic. (2024). Definition retrieved from https://www.mayoclinic.org/diseases-conditions/ Schizophrenia/symptoms-causes/syc-20354443

Mayson, S. G. (2019) 'Bias In, Bias Out'. Yale Law Journal, no. 128. https://paper s.ssrn.com/sol3/paper s.cfm?abstr act_id=32570 04. Accessed 24 Aug 2020

Mazoue, J. G. (1990). Diagnosis without doctors. *The Journal of Medicine and Philosophy*, 15(6), 559–579. DOI: 10.1093/jmp/15.6.559 PMID: 2290071

McLean, K., Alikhan, A., & Alpert, G. P. (2023). Re-examining the use of force continuum: Why resistance is not the only driver of use of force decisions. *Police Quarterly*, 26(1), 85–110. DOI: 10.1177/10986111211066353

Mellsop, G., Tapsell, R., & Holmes, P. (2019). Mental health service users' progression from illicit drug use to schizophrenia in New Zealand. *General Psychiatry*, 32(5), 32. DOI: 10.1136/gpsych-2019-100088 PMID: 31552389

Merriam, S. B. (2004). The role of cognitive development in Mezirow's transformational learning theory. *Adult Education Quarterly*, 55(1), 60–68. DOI: 10.1177/0741713604268891

Merriam, S. B., & Caffarella, R. S. (1999). *Learning in adulthood; a comprehensive guide* (2nd ed.). Jossey-Bass Publishers.

Merton, R. K. (1996). *On social structure and science*. The University of Chicago Press.

Merton, R. K. (1996). *On Social Structure and Science*. The University of Chicago Press.

Metz, R. (2019, September 13). California Lawmakers Ban Facial-Recognition Software from Police Body Cams. Retrieved March 28, 2020, from https://www.cnn.com/2019/09/12/tech/california-body cam-facial-recognition-ban/index.html

Mezirow, J. (1997). Transformative learning theory to practice. *New Directions for Adult and Continuing Education*, 74(74), 5–12. DOI: 10.1002/ace.7401

Milano, S., Taddeo, M., & Floridi, L. (2020). Recommender systems and their ethical challenges. *AI & Society*, 35(4), 957–967. Advance online publication. DOI: 10.1007/s00146-020-00950-y

Mill, J. S. (1974). *On liberty*. Penguin Books.

Mittelstadt, B. D., Allo, P., Taddeo, M., Wachter, S., & Floridi, L. (2016). The ethics of algorithms: Mapping the debate. *Big Data & Society*, 3(2), 2053951716679679. Advance online publication. DOI: 10.1177/2053951716679679

Mittelstadt, B. D., & Floridi, L. (2016). The ethics of big data: Current and foreseeable issues in biomedical contexts. *Science and Engineering Ethics*, 22(2), 303–341. DOI: 10.1007/s11948-015-9652-2 PMID: 26002496

Morabito, M. S., Socia, K., Wik, A., & Fisher, W. H. (2017). The nature and extent of police use of force in encounters with people with behavioral health disorders. *International Journal of Law and Psychiatry*, 50, 31–37. DOI: 10.1016/j.ijlp.2016.10.001 PMID: 28029437

Morek, R. (2006). Regulatory framework for online dispute resolution: A critical view. *University of Toledo Law Review. University of Toledo. College of Law*, 38, 163.

Morley, J., Floridi, L., Kinsey, L., & Elhalal, A. (2019). From what to how: An initial review of publicly available AI ethics tools, methods and research to translate principles into practices. *Science and Engineering Ethics*. Advance online publication. DOI: 10.1007/s11948-019-00165-5 PMID: 31828533

Morley, J., Machado, C., Burr, C., Cowls, J., Taddeo, M., & Floridi, L. (2019) The debate on the ethics of AI in healthcare: a reconstruction and critical review. *SSRN Electron J*. DOI: 10.2139/ssrn.3486518

Mozur, P. (2019, April 14). One Month, 500,000 Face Scans: How China Is Using A.I. to Profile a Minority. Retrieved April 1, 2020, from https://www.nytimes.com/2019/04/14/technology/china surveillance-artificial-intelligence-racial-profiling.html

Mozur, P., & Krolik, A. (2019, December 17). A Surveillance Net Blankets China's Cities, Giving Police Vast Powers. Retrieved April 1, 2020, from https://www.nytimes.com/2019/12/17/technology/china surveillance.html

Mozur, Paul. (2018, July 8). Inside China's Dystopian Dreams: A.I., Shame and Lots of Cameras. *The New York Times*. https://www.nytimes.com/2018/07/08/business/china-surveillance technology.html

Munsey, B. (1980). *Moral Development, Moral Education, and Kohlberg*. Religious Education Press, Inc.

Munson, S. C. (2000). Art: Selling Norman Rockwell. *Commentary (New York, N.Y.)*, 110(2), 64–67.

Murphy, M. J. (1965, March). Improving the law enforcement image. *Journal of Criminal Law and Criminology*, 56(13), 105–108.

Nakamura, L. (2013). *Cybertypes: Race, Ethnicity, and Identity on the Internet*. Routledge. DOI: 10.4324/9780203699188

Nam, Y., Wolfe, S. E., & Nix, J. (2024). Does procedural justice reduce the harmful effects of perceived ineffectiveness on police legitimacy? *Journal of Research in Crime and Delinquency*, 61(1), 124–167. DOI: 10.1177/00224278221121622

National Research Council, Commission on Physical Sciences, Mathematics, Applications, Naval Studies Board, Panel on Computer Science, & Artificial Intelligence. (1997). Computer Science and Artificial Intelligence. National Academies Press. DOI: 10.17226/5812

National Science and Technology Council and the Networking and Information Technology Research and Development Subcommittee. (October 2016). The National Artificial Intelligence Research and Development Strategic Plan, Washington, DC: Office of Science and Technology Policy, https://www.nitrd.gov/PUBS/national_ai_rd_ strategic_plan.pdf

Na, Z., Zhang, C.-T., Lv, H.-Y., Hao, C.-X., Li, T.-J., Zhu, J.-J., & Zhu, H.. (2019). Concordance study between IBM Watson for oncology and clinical practice for patients with cancer in China. *The Oncologist*, 24(6), 812–819. DOI: 10.1634/theoncologist.2018-0255 PMID: 30181315

New York, N. B. C. (2022). Jose Alba murder case. Retrieved from: https://www.nbcnewyork.com › news › local › new-video.

Newell, S., & Marabelli, M. (2015). Strategic opportunities (and challenges) of AI algorithmic decision-making: A call for action on the long-term societal effects of 'datification'. *The Journal of Strategic Information Systems*, 24(1), 3–14. DOI: 10.1016/j.jsis.2015.02.001

Newman, A. (2020, October). Black lives matter: Behind the façade. *The New American Magazine*, •••, 1–5.

Nietzsche, F (1989). *Beyond good and evil. prelude to a philosophy of the future*. Vintage Books.

NIJ, (2011). Chicago Police Predictive Policing Demonstration and Evaluation Project" at the Chicago Police Department and Illinois Institute of Technology, NIJ award number 2011-IJ-CX-K014.

NIJ, (2013). Exploring Elder Financial Exploitation Victimization" at the University of Texas Health Science Center at Houston, NIJ award number 2013-IJ-CX-0050.

NIJ. (2015). "Applying Data Science to Justice Systems: The North Carolina Statewide Warrant Repository (NCAWARE)" at RTI International, NIJ award number 2015-IJ-CX-K016.

NIJ. (2016a). Detailed Information for Award 2016-DN-BX-0183," National Institute of Justice, https://external.ojp.usdoj. gov/selector/awardDetail?awardNumber=2016 DN-BX-0183&fiscalYear=2016&applicationNum ber=2016-90227-IL-IJ&programOffice=NIJ&po=NIJ.

NIJ. (2016b). Development of Computational Methods for the Audio Analysis of Gunshots" at Cadre Research Labs, LLC, NIJ award number 2016-DN-BX-0183.

NIJ. (2016c). Effects of Human Factors on the Accuracy of Fingerprint Analysis," National Institute of Justice, https://nij.gov/topics/forensics/evidence/ impression/ Pages/human-factors.aspx

NIJ. (2016d). A Recommendation System for Statutory Interpretation in Cybercrime" at the University of Pittsburgh, NIJ award number 2016-R2-CX-0010.

Nix, J., Ivanov, S., & Pickett, J. T. (2021). What does the public want police to do during pandemics? A national experiment. *Criminology & Public Policy*, 20(3), 545–571. DOI: 10.1111/1745-9133.12535 PMID: 33821153

NJR. 2009. Learning Models for Predictive Behavioral Intent and Activity Analysis in Wide Area Video Surveillance" at the University of Houston, NIJ award number 2009-MU-MU-K004.

NJR. 2014. A Hybrid Machine Learning Approach for DNA Mixture Interpretation" at Syracuse University, NIJ award number 2014-DN-BX-K029.

NJR., 2015. Studying the Impact of Video Analytics for Pre, Live and Post Event Analysis on Outcomes of Criminal Justice" at the University of Central Florida, NIJ award number 2015-R2-CX-K025.

Nobles, A. (2018). *AI algorithms of oppression: how search engines rein force racism*. New York University Press. DOI: 10.18574/nyu/9781479833641.001.0001

Nordberg, A., Crawford, M. R., Practorius, R. T., & Smith Hatcher, S. (2016). Exploring minority youths' police encounters: A qualitative interpretive meta-synthesis. *Child & Adolescent Social Work Journal*, 33(2), 132–149. DOI: 10.1007/s10560-015-0415-3

Norris, D. (2019, June 19). Artificial Intelligence and Community-Police Relations. Retrieved April 1, 2020, from https://www.policechiefmagazine.org/ai-community-police-relations/

Obermeyer Z, Powers B, Vogeli C, Mullainathan S (2019) Dissecting racial bias in an AI algorithm used to manage the health of popula tions. Science 366(6464):447–453. https://doi.org/ ce.aax2342DOI: 10.1126/scien

Obermeyer, Z., Powers, B., Vogeli, C., & Mullainathan, S. (2019). Dissecting racial bias in an AI algorithm used to manage the health of populations. *Science*, 366(6464), 447–453. DOI: 10.1126/science.aax2342 PMID: 31649194

Officers, P. Video and Audio Recordings: Disclosure. AB-748/Chapter 960. (September 2018). California. https://leginfo.legislature.ca.gov/faces/billTextClient.xhtml?bill_id=201720180AB748

Olhede, S. C., & Wolfe, P. J. (2018). The growing ubiquity of AI algorithms in society: Implications, impacts and innovations. Philos Trans R Soc A Math Phys. *Engineering and Science*, 376(2128), 20170364. DOI: 10.1098/rsta.2017.0364 PMID: 30082309

Oliver, W. M. (2012, November). Historian's Corner. ACJS today. *Academy of Criminal Justice Sciences*, 37(5), 34–40.

Orseau, L., & Armstrong, S. (2016) Safely interruptible agents. Available at: http://intelligence.org/files/Interruptibility.pdf (accessed 12 September 2016).

Pain, T. (1999). *Rights of man: Dover Thrift Editions*. Dover Publications, Inc.

Paraschakis, D. (2017) Towards an ethical recommendation framework. In: 2017 11th International Conference on Research Challenges in Information Science (RCIS), 211–20. Brighton, United Kingdom: IEEE. DOI: 10.1109/RCIS.2017.7956539

Pasquale, F. (2015). *The Black Box Society: The Secret AI algorithms that Control Money and Information*. Harvard University Press. DOI: 10.4159/harvard.9780674736061

Perra, N., & Rocha, L. E. C. (2019). Modelling opinion dynamics in the age of AI algorithmic personalisation. *Scientific Reports*, 9(1), 7261. DOI: 10.1038/s41598-019-43830-2 PMID: 31086228

Phillips, P. J. (2017). A Cross Benchmark Assessment of a Deep Convolutional Neural Network for Face Recognition," paper presented at the 12th IEEE International Conference on Automatic Face & Gesture Recognition, 2017, 705-710. DOI: 10.1109/FG.2017.89

Phillips, S.W. (August 2017). Police Militarization. FBI Law Enforcement Bulletin. p.1-6.

Phillips, S. W. (2016). Myths, militarism and the police patrol rifle. *Policing and Society*, 26(2), 185–196. DOI: 10.1080/10439463.2014.922088

Pinker, S. (2011). *The better angels of our nature; why violence has declined.* Penguin Group.

Plato, . (1981). *Five Dialogues, Euthyphro, Apology, Crito, Meno, Phaedo.* Hackett Publishing Company.

Plato, . (1981). *Five dialogues: Euthyphro, Apology, Crito, Meno, Phaedo.* Hackett Publishing Company, Inc.

Pollock, J. M. (2019). *Ethical Dilemmas and Decisions in Criminal Justice* (10th ed.). Cengage Learning, Inc.

Portmess, L., & Tower, S. (2014). Data barns, ambient intelligence and cloud computing: The tacit epistemology and linguistic representation of Big Data. *Ethics and Information Technology*, 17(1), 1–9. DOI: 10.1007/s10676-014-9357-2

Prates, M. O. R., Avelar, P. H., & Lamb, L. C. (2019). Assessing gender bias in machine translation: A case study with google translate. *Neural Computing & Applications.* Advance online publication. DOI: 10.1007/s00521-019-04144-6

Queally, J. (2019, June 12). San Francisco D.A. Unveils Program Aimed At Removing Implicit Bias from Prosecutions. Retrieved April 1, 2020, from https://www.latimes.com/local/lanow/la-me-san francisco-da-prosecutions-implicit-bias-software-20190612-story.html

Rachels, J. (1975). Why privacy is important. *Philosophy & Public Affairs*, 4(4), 323–333.

Rahwan, I. (2018). Society-in-the-loop: Programming the AI algorithmic social contract. *Ethics and Information Technology*, 20(1), 5–14. DOI: 10.1007/s10676-017-9430-8

Ralph, L., & Robinson, P. (2023). Assessing police social media practices through a democratic policing lens. *International Journal of Police Science & Management*, 25(3), 237–249. DOI: 10.1177/14613557231169391

Randolph, P. (2016). *The Psychology of Conflict – Mediating in a Diverse World.* Bloomsbury Continuum.

Randolph, P. (2016). *The psychology of conflict: mediating in a diverse world.* Bloomsbury Publishing Plc.

Ratcliffe, S. (Ed.). (2016). *Oxford essential quotations.* Oxford University Press. DOI: 10.1093/acref/9780191826719.001.0001

Raymond, A. (2014) The dilemma of private justice systems: Big data sources, the cloud and predictive analytics. Northwestern Journal of International Law & Business, Forthcoming. Available at: https://papers.ssrn.com/sol3/papers.cfm?abstract_id=2469291 (accessed 22 July 2015).

Redden, J., Aagaard, B., Taniguchi, T., & the Criminal Justice Testing and Evaluation Consortium. (2020). Artificial Intelligence in Law Enforcement. U.S. Department of Justice, National Institute of Justice, Office of Justice Programs. https://cjtec.org/

Reddy, E., Cakici, B., & Ballestero, A. (2019). Beyond mystery: Putting AI algorithmic accountability in context. *Big Data & Society*, 6(1), 205395171982685. DOI: 10.1177/2053951719826856

Reynolds, M. (2020-21). Called to arms. *American Bar Association Journal. American Bar Association*, 106(6), 62–71.

Richardson, R., Schultz, J., & Crawford, K. (2019) Dirty data, bad predic tions: how civil rights violations impact police data, predictive policing systems, and justice. https://paper s.ssrn.com/sol3/paper s.cfm?abstract_id=3333423. Accessed 24 Aug 2020

Richardson, L. A., Long, C., DeBeck, K., Nguyen, P., Milloy, M. J. S., Wood, E., & Kerr, T. H. (2015). Socio-economic marginalization in the structural production of vulnerability to violence among people who use illicit drugs. *Journal of Epidemiology and Community Health*, 69(7), 686–692. DOI: 10.1136/jech-2014-205079 PMID: 25691275

Rigano, C. (2018). Using Artificial Intelligence to Address Criminal Justice Needs," October 8, 2018, nij.ojp.gov: https://nij.ojp.gov/topics/articles/using-artificial-intelligence-address-criminal-justice needs

Rigano, C. (2018). Using Artificial Intelligence to Address Criminal Justice Needs," October 8, 2018, nij.ojp.gov: https://nij.ojp.gov/topics/articles/using-artificial-intelligence-address-criminal-justice needs.

Rigano, C. (2019). Using Artificial Intelligence to Address Criminal Justice Needs, NIJ Journal 280, January 2019, https:// www.nij.gov/journals/280/Pages/using -artificial intelligence-to-address-criminal-justice-needs.aspx.

Rigano, C. (2019). Using Artificial Intelligence to Address Criminal Justice Needs," NIJ Journal 280, January 2019, https:// www.nij.gov/journals/280/Pages/using -artificial intelligence-to-address-criminal-justice-needs.aspx.

Roberg, R., & Bonn, S. (2004). Higher education and policing: Where are we now? *Policing*, 27(4), 469–486. DOI: 10.1108/13639510410566226

Roberts, D., & Casanova, M. (2012, September) Automated License Plate Recognition (ALPR) Use by Law Enforcement: Policy and Operational Guide, Summary. Retrieved April 3, 2020, from https://www. ncjrs.gov/pdffiles1/nij/grants/239605.pdf

Roberts, H., Cowls, J., Morley, J., Taddeo, M., Wang, V., & Floridi, L. (2019) The Chinese approach to artificial intelligence: an analysis of policy and regulation. *SSRN Electron J*. DOI: 10.2139/ssrn.3469784

Roberts, H., Cowls, J., Morley, J., Taddeo, M., Wang, V., & Floridi, L. (2020). The Chinese approach to artificial intelligence: An analysis of policy, ethics, and regulation. *AI & Society*. Advance online publication. DOI: 10.1007/s00146-020-00992-2

Romei, A., & Ruggieri, S. (2014). A multidisciplinary survey on discrimination analysis. *The Knowledge Engineering Review*, 29(5), 582–638. DOI: 10.1017/S0269888913000039

Rosenberg, M. B. (2015). *Nonviolent Communication, A Language of Life*. (Third Edition). PuddleDancer Press.

Rössler, B. (2015) The value of privacy. https://philpapers.org/rec/ROSTVO-9. Accessed 24 Aug 2020

Rousseau, J.-J. (1984). *A discourse on inequality. New York, NY: Penguin Books. Rousseau, J-J. (2005). The Social Contract*. Barnes & Noble,Inc.

Roy, B. (2009). *41 Shots...and Counting; What Amadou Diallo's Story Teaches us About Policing, Race, and Justice*. Syracuse University Press.

Royal Queens Seeds Blog. (2024). Is Marijuana Stronger Than It Used To Be? Retrieved from www.royalqueenseeds.com

Rubenson, K. (2011). *Adult learning and education*. Academic Press.

Rydberg, J., & Terrill, W. (2010). The effect of higher education on police behavior. *Police Quarterly*, 13(1), 92–120. DOI: 10.1177/1098611109357325

Saferstein, R., & Roy, T. (2021). *Criminalistics, An Introduction to Forensic Science*. Pearson Education Inc.

Sah, S., Shringi, A., Ptucha, R., Burry, A. M., & Loce, R. P. (2017, July 20). Video Redaction: A Survey and Comparison of Enabling Technologies. Retrieved April 1, 2020, from https://www.spiedigitallibrary. org/journals/journal-of-electronic-imaging/volume-26/issue-05/051406/Video-redaction-a-survey-and-comparison-of-enabling-technologies/10.1117/1.JEI.26.5.051406.full?SSO=1

Sandvig, C., Hamilton, K., Karahalios, K., ... (2014) Auditing AI algorithms: Research methods for detecting discrimination on internet platforms. Data and Discrimination: Converting Critical Concerns into Productive Inquiry. Available at: http://social.cs.uiuc.edu/papers/pdfs/ICA2014 Sandvig.pdf (accessed 13 February 2016).

Sartre, J. P. (2011). *Sartre, The Transcendence of the Ego*. Routledge Classics.

Sartre, J.-P. (2004). *The transcendence of the ego*. Routledge. DOI: 10.4324/9780203694367

Savvides, Marios. (2018). A Simultaneous Low Resolution and Off-Pose Angle Face Matching AI algorithm as an Investigative Lead Generative Tool for Law Enforcement" at Carnegie Mellon University, NIJ award number 2013-IJ-CX-K005. DOI: 10.1515/popets-2015-0007

Saxena, N., Huang, K., DeFilippis, E., Radanovic, G., Parkes, D., & Liu, Y. (2019) How do fairness definitions fare? Examining public attitudes towards AI algorithmic definitions of fairness. ArXiv:1811.03654. http://arxiv.org/abs/1811.03654. Accessed 24 Aug 2020

Selbst, A. D., Boyd, D., Friedler, S. A., Venkatasubramanian, S., & Vertesi, J. (2019) Fairness and abstraction in sociotechnical systems. In: Proceedings of the Conference on Fairness, Accountability, and Transparency—FAT* '19, 59–68. Atlanta, GA, USA: ACM Press. DOI: 10.1145/3287560.3287598

Shackelford, S. J., & Raymond, A. H. (2014). Building the virtual courthouse: Ethical considerations for design, implementation, and regulation in the world of Odr. *Wisconsin Law Review*, (3), 615–657.

Shah, H. (2018). AI algorithmic transparency in the news media. *Philos Trans R Soc A: Math Phys Eng Sci*, 376(2128), 20170364. DOI: 10.1098/rsta.2017.0362 PMID: 30082307

Shah, P. V. (2019). A use of deadly force: People with mental health conditions and encounters with law enforcement. *Harvard Human Rights Journal*, 32, 208–221.

Shah, P. V. (2019). The use of deadly force: People with mental health conditions and encounters with law enforcement. *Harvard Human Rights Journal*, 32, 207–221.

Shin, D., & Park, Y. J. (2019). Role of fairness, accountability, and transparency in AI algorithmic affordance. *Computers in Human Behavior*, 98(September), 277–284. DOI: 10.1016/j.chb.2019.04.019

Siegel, L. J., & Worrall, J. L. (2018). *Introduction to Criminal Justice* (16th ed.). Cengage Learning.

Simon, J. (2015). Distributed epistemic responsibility in a hyper-connected era. In L. Floridi (Ed.), The Onlife Manifesto (pp. 145–159). Springer International Publishing., Available at https://link.springer.com/chapter/10.1007/978-3-319-04093-6_17, Retrieved June 17, 2016, from.

Simonite, T. (2019, June 18). How Facial Recognition Is Fighting Child Sex Trafficking. Retrieved April 1, 2020, from https://www.wired.com/story/how-facial-recognition-fighting-child-sex-trafficking

Simonite, T., & Barber, G. (2019, October 17). The Delicate Ethics of Using Facial Recognition in Schools. Retrieved April 1, 2020, from https://www.wired.com/story/delicate-ethics-facial-recognition schools/

Sloan, R. H., & Warner, R. (2018). When is an AI algorithm transparent? predictive analytics, privacy, and public policy. *IEEE Security and Privacy*, 16(3), 18–25. DOI: 10.1109/MSP.2018.2701166

Sowell, T. (2023). *Social Justice Fallacies*. Hachette Book Group.

Spotted Eagle, F. (2000). *Many Paths, Many Spirits*. Spotted Eagle and Associates.

Statt, N. (2020). Amazon Bans Police from Using its Facial Recognition Technology for the Next Year. The Verge. Retrieved from https://www.theverge.com/2020/6/10/21287101/amazon-rekognition facial-recognition-police-ban-one-year-ai-racial-bias

Stringer, H. (2023, June 1). How does marijuana affect the brain? Psychological researchers examine impact on different age groups over time. *Monitor on Psychology*, 54(4). https://www.apa.org/monitor/2023/06/marijuana-effects-brain

Sweeney L (2013) Discrimination in online ad delivery. Queue 11(3): 10:10–10:29.

Sweetman, P. (2003). Twenty-first century disease? Habitual reflexivity or the reflexive habitus. *The Sociological Review*, 51(4), 528–549. DOI: 10.1111/j.1467-954X.2003.00434.x

Taddeo, M., & Floridi, L. (2015). The debate on the moral responsibilities of online service providers. *Science and Engineering Ethics*, •••, 1–29. PMID: 26613596

Taddeo, M., & Floridi, L. (2018a). Regulate artificial intelligence to avert cyber arms race. *Nature*, 556(7701), 296–298. DOI: 10.1038/d41586-018-04602-6 PMID: 29662138

Taddeo, M., & Floridi, L. (2018b). How AI can be a force for good. *Science*, 361(6404), 751–752. DOI: 10.1126/science.aat5991 PMID: 30139858

Taddeo, M., McCutcheon, T., & Floridi, L. (2019). Trusting artificial intelligence in cybersecurity is a double-edged sword. *Nature Machine Intelligence*, 1(12), 557–560. DOI: 10.1038/s42256-019-0109-1

Tarm, M. (2021 – April 5). Explainer: was officer's knee on Floyd's neck authorized? Associated Press. Retrieved from https://apnews.com/hub/death-of-george-floyd

Taylor, L., Floridi, L., & van der Sloot, B. (Eds.). (2017). *Group Privacy: New Challenges of Data Technologies* (1st ed.). Springer. DOI: 10.1007/978-3-319-46608-8

The Editors of Encyclopedia Britannica. (2024). Democratic National Convention of 1968 political event, Chicago, Illinois, United States. Article History. Retrieved from https://www.britannica.com/

The Editors. (2014). Following Ferguson. *America Press Inc.*, 211(6), 5.

The Intelligence Advanced Research Projects Activity. "Janus," Washington, DC: Office of the Director of National Intelligence, https://www.iarpa.gov/index.php/research-programs/janus

Tholen, B. (2022). The virtues of the exemplary moral leader. Lessons from Aristotle's ethics. *Business Ethics, the Environment & Responsibility*, 32(2), 532–543. DOI: 10.1111/beer.12504

Trottier, D. (2015). Open source intelligence, social media and law enforcement: Visions, constraints, and critiques. *European Journal of Cultural Studies*, 18(4-5), 530–547. DOI: 10.1177/1367549415577396

Tufekci, Z. (2015). AI algorithmic harms beyond Facebook and Google: Emergent challenges of computational agency. *Journal on Telecommunications & High Technology Law*, 13, 203.

Tutt, A. (2016) An FDA for AI algorithms. SSRN Scholarly Paper. Rochester, NY: Social Science Research Network. Available at: https://papers.ssrn.com/abstract=2747994 DOI. 10.2139/ssrn.2747994

U.S. Department of Homeland Security. (Feb 2021). Muth vs. Fact: 50 + nights of violence, chaos and anarchy in Portland, Oregon. Retrieved from https://www.dhs.gov

Use of Force Chart. (2024). Retrieved from https://nuqum.com/Our law enforcement officers need new rules of engagement for minor crimes | NuQum.com

Van Otterlo, M. (2013) A machine learning view on profiling. In: Hildebrandt M and de Vries K (eds) Privacy, Due Process and the Computational Turn-Philosophers of Law Meet Philosophers of Technology. Abingdon: Routledge, pp. 41–64.

Van Wel, L., & Royakkers, L. (2004). Ethical issues in web data mining. *Ethics and Information Technology*, 6(2), 129–140. DOI: 10.1023/B:ETIN.0000047476.05912.3d

Veale, M., & Binns, R. (2017). Fairer machine learning in the real world: Mitigating discrimination without collecting sensitive data. *Big Data & Society*, 4(2), 205395171774353. DOI: 10.1177/2053951717743530

Vedder, A., & Naudts, L. (2017). Accountability for the use of AI algorithms in a big data environment. *International Review of Law Computers & Technology*, 31(2), 206–224. DOI: 10.1080/13600869.2017.1298547

Vellido, A., Martín-Guerrero, J. D., & Lisboa, P. J. (2012) Making machine learning models interpretable. In: ESANN 2012 proceedings, Bruges, Belgium, pp. 163–172.

Video Fingerprints Could Help Fight Child Porn. (2014, April 30). Retrieved April 1, 2020, from https://www.nbcnews.com/tech/security/video-fingerprints-could-help-fight-child-porn-n93521

Vollmer, A. (1931). Police education. *The Journal of Criminal Law and Criminology*, 22(1), 7–8.

Vollmer, A., & Schneider, A. (1917). The school for police as planned at Berkeley. *Journal of the American Institute of Criminal Law and Criminology*, 7(6), 877–898. DOI: 10.2307/1133670

Vygotsky, L. S. (1978). *Mind in society. The development of higher psychological processes*. Harvard University Press.

Wang, S., Jiang, X., Singh, S., Marmor, R., Bonomi, L., Fox, D., Dow, M., & Ohno-Machado, L. (2017). Genome privacy: challenges, technical approaches to mitigate risk, and ethical considerations in the united states: genome privacy in biomedical research. *Annals of the New York Academy of Sciences*, 1387(1), 73–83. DOI: 10.1111/nyas.13259 PMID: 27681358

Ward, L. R. (1968). Aristotle on criteria of moral good. *The Review of Politics*, 30(4), 476–498. DOI: 10.1017/S0034670500025195

Webb, H., Patel, M., & Rovatsos, M.. (2019). "It would be pretty immoral to choose a random AI algorithm": Opening up AI algorithmic interpretability and transparency. *J Inform Commun Ethics Soc*, 17(2), 210–228. DOI: 10.1108/JICES-11-2018-0092

Webster's New World College Dictionary, 2016.

Westrope, A. (2019, October 25). New Radio Brings AI Voice Assistant to Law Enforcement. Retrieved April 1, 2020, from https://www.govtech.com/biz/New-Radio-Brings-AI-Voice-Assistant-to-Law Enforcement.html

Whitman, M., Hsiang, C.-y., & Roark, K. (2018) Potential for participatory big data ethics and AI algorithm design: a scoping mapping review. In: Proceedings of the 15th Participatory Design Conference on Short Papers, Situated Actions, Workshops and Tutorial—PDC '18, 1–6. Hasselt and Genk, Belgium: ACM Press. DOI: 10.1145/3210604.3210644

Wiener, N (1950) The human use of human beings.

Wiener, N. (1988). *The Human Use of Human Beings: Cybernetics and Society*. Da Capo Press.

Willis, T., Comartin, E., Victor, G., Kern, L., & Kubiak, S. (2021). Individuals with mental illness who have multiple encounters with law enforcement. *Journal of Offender Rehabilitation*, 60(2), 117–137. DOI: 10.1080/10509674.2020.1863298

Wilson, O. W. (1953). Police science: August Vollmer. *The Journal of Criminal Law, Criminology, and Police Science*, 44(1), 91–103. DOI: 10.2307/1139476

Winner, L. (1980). Do artifacts have politics? *Modern Techn Probl Oppor*, 109(1), 121–136.

Wong, P.-H. (2019). Democratizing AI algorithmic fairness. *Philosophy & Technology*. Advance online publication. DOI: 10.1007/s13347-019-00355-w

Wood, M. A. (2020). Policing's meme strategy: Understanding the rise of police social media engagement work. *Current Issues in Criminal Justice*, 32(1), 40–58. DOI: 10.1080/10345329.2019.1658695

Woods, M. J. (2000, December). Interpersonal communication for police officers: Using needs assessment to prepare for skeptical trainees. *Business Communication Quarterly*, 63(4), 40–48. DOI: 10.1177/108056990006300404

Woska, W. J. (1978). Police officer academic standards. *Public Personnel Management*, 7(5), 312–316.

Xu, D., Yuan, S., Zhang, L., & Wu, X. (2018). *FairGAN: fairness-aware gen erative adversarial networks. In: 2018 IEEE International Confer ence on Big Data (Big Data), 570–75*. IEEE., DOI: 10.1109/BigData.2018.8622525

Yang, G.-Z., Bellingham, J., Dupont, P. E., Fischer, P., Floridi, L., Full, R., Jacobstein, R., Kumar, V., McNutt, M., Merrifield, R., Nelson, B. J., Scassellati, B., Taddeo, M., Taylor, R., Veloso, M., Wang, Z. L., & Wood, R. (2018). The grand challenges of science robotics. *Science Robotics*, 3(14), eaar7650. Advance online publication. DOI: 10.1126/scirobotics.aar7650 PMID: 33141701

Yankah, E. N. (2012). Legal vices and civic virtue: Vice crimes, republicanism and the corruption of lawfulness. *Criminal Law and Philosophy*, 7(1), 61–82. DOI: 10.1007/s11572-012-9161-1

Yu, M., & Du, G. (2019) Why are Chinese courts turning to AI? The Diplomat. 19 January 2019. https://thediplomat.com/2019/01/why-are-chinese-courts-turning-to-ai/. Accessed 24 Aug 2020

Zakaria, F. (2015). *Defense of a Liberal Education*. W.W. Norton & Company, Inc.

Zakaria, F. (2015). *In defense of a liberal education*. W.W. Norton & Company, Inc.

Zarsky, T. (2016). The trouble with AI algorithmic decisions: An analytic road map to examine efficiency and fairness in automated and opaque decision making. *Science, Technology & Human Values*, 41(1), 118–132. DOI: 10.1177/0162243915605575

Zhang, Y., & Bruce, L. M. (2004). *Mississippi Transportation Research Center: Automated Accident Detection at Intersections (Project Number: FHWA/MS-DOT-RD-04-150)*. Mississippi Department of Transportation and U.S. Department of Transportation Federal Highway Administration, March.

Zimabrdo, P. (2007). *The Lucifer Effect: Understanding how good people turn evil*. Random House Inc.

Zimbardo, P. (2007). *The Lucifer effect: understanding how good people turn evil*. Random House Inc.

About the Authors

Reza Gharoie Ahangar is an Assistant Professor of Business Analytics at Lewis University in the Chicago area-Romeoville. Dr. Ahangar has a strong educational background; he earned a B.Sc. in Business Management, an MBA in Finance, an MSc in Finance, an MSc in Business Analytics, and a Ph.D. in Management Science with a minor in Economics. Dr. Ahangar is a proud member of prestigious professional organizations such as the Production and Operations Management Society (POMS), the Institute for Operations Research and the Management Sciences (INFORMS), and the Decision Sciences Institute (DSI). In addition to his academic work, Dr. Ahangar has significantly contributed to his field through publications. He has authored ten books, book chapters, and more than fifty journals and conference publications. His technical publications have received over 750 citations on Google Scholar, a testament to his impact on the business analytics community. Before joining Lewis University in August 2022, Dr. Ahangar was a teaching assistant and instructor at The University of North Texas for seven years. His dedication and expertise have led to many notable accomplishments, including his latest achievement as Editor-in-Chief of the book "Advancement in Business Analytics Tools for Higher Financial Performance," published by IGI Global in August 2023.

Stephen Sherwin is an Assistant Professor of Justice, Law, and Public Safety Studies at Lewis University. Dr. Sherwin is a highly experienced law enforcement professional with a comprehensive educational background. He holds a B.A. in Criminal Justice from Saint Xavier University, a Master of Public Administration (M.P.A.) from Illinois Institute of Technology, and an Ed. D. in Leadership in Adult and Higher Education from Aurora University. With a career spanning over 38 years with the Chicago Police Department (CPD), Dr. Sherwin has been a valuable member of the force as a supervisor for 20 years. Throughout his time with CPD, Dr. Sherwin acquired diverse skills and knowledge, including being trained as a Peer Support Member and serving as a Commanding Officer for CPD recruit training. He is also a trained mediator and a Chicago and National Association of Dispute Resolution (ADR) Chapters member. Dr. Sherwin has utilized his expertise in mediation and conflict resolution to train mediators, develop mediation centers, and provide conflict resolution and mediation training to police departments and civilians. Additionally, he has lent his expertise as an expert witness in court mediations. As a researcher, Dr. Sherwin focuses on subjects such as higher education to improve police/citizen relations, improving policing methods, and the benefits of mediation and conflict resolution. His extensive knowledge and experience in law enforcement and his academic background make him a valuable contributor to the field. Dr. Sherwin is dedicated to promoting police ethics and finding ways to improve relationships between law enforcement and the communities they serve.

Index

M

O

P

R

S

T

V

W

www.ingramcontent.com/pod-product-compliance
Lightning Source LLC
LaVergne TN
LVHW061539290926
849162LV00004B/843